J. REUBEN
CLARK
THE CHURCH YEARS

J. REUBEN
CLARK
THE CHURCH YEARS

Second of the three-volume set on the
life and work of J. Reuben Clark, Jr.

David H. Yarn, Jr., General Editor

Editor's Note: To save often repetition of the full title Church of Jesus Christ of Latter-day Saints, the term Church is used. Additionally, General Authorities of the Church not members of the First Presidency are often referred to as Elder.

J. REUBEN CLARK

THE CHURCH YEARS

D. MICHAEL QUINN

Brigham Young University Press

Library of Congress Cataloging in Publication Data

Quinn, D. Michael, 1944–
    J. Reuben Clark: the church years.

    Includes index.
    1. Clark, J. Reuben (Joshua Reuben), 1871–1961. 2. Mormons–
United States–Biography. I. Title.
BX8695.C287Q56   1983   289.3'3[B]   83-2806
ISBN 0-8425-2137-2

Brigham Young University Press, Provo, Utah 84602
©   1983 by Brigham Young University Press. All rights reserved
Published 1983. Second printing 1983.
Printed in the United States of America
83   64874

CONTENTS

FOREWORD

I have always hoped that those who would write about J. Reuben Clark, Jr. would remember this: To him it mattered little whether he was being praised or criticized; it mattered much, however, whether his course was right and true. Any biographer of President Clark must write the truth about him; to tell more or less than the truth would violate a governing principle of his life. When I first met with those who are writing his biography, I explained that I did not want them to produce a mere collection of uplifting experiences about President Clark (although I knew that numerous such stories could be told), nor did I want a detailed defense of his beliefs. I wanted a biography of the man himself, as he was, written with the same kind of courage, honesty, and frankness that J. Reuben Clark himself would have shown. An account of his life should tell of his decisions and indecisions, sorrows and joys, regrets and aspirations, reverses and accomplishments, and, above all, his constant striving to overcome any and all obstacles.

Marion G. Romney

PREFACE

J. Reuben Clark, Jr. had many secular aspirations—to be U.S. Senator from the State of Utah, to be U.S. Secretary of State, to be a Justice of the U.S. Supreme Court—but he had never aspired for office in the religion of his birth, The Church of Jesus Christ of Latter-day Saints ("Mormon Church"). As a third-generation Latter-day Saint, he felt an identity with the Church and sought to exemplify the Church's moral precepts in his personal and professional life. But as a civil servant in the U.S. State Department, as an ardent member of the Republican party, and as a representative of his government in various diplomatic capacities, he thought of himself as "Mister Clark" or the "Honorable J. Reuben Clark, Jr.," rather than as "Brother Clark."

In fact, prior to 1933, Reuben held such stringent views of the separation of church and state in the United States that he felt high Church leaders ought to be ineligible for civil office, and vice versa. That view necessarily circumscribed his religious activities prior to 1933. Although he had been ordained a seventy, a proselyting office in the Church, he regarded active proselyting as a violation of his position as a civil servant in a secular republic. Therefore, Reuben contented himself with setting an example of Church teachings through living a scrupulously honorable life rather than by fulfilling his priesthood role as perpetual missionary in the non-Mormon society where he lived the greater part of his life prior to 1933.

Reuben's lifelong aspirations were shattered when the President of the Church asked him to become Second Counselor. Nevertheless, he told his governmental associates that he accepted the call from the President of his church just as he would accept a call to duty from the President of his native republic.

The decades of his life as the "Honorable Mr. Clark" determined the manner in which he perceived his mission as a religious leader.

In his call to the highest echelon of Church leadership, Reuben could see in himself no outstanding qualifications aside from his activity as international lawyer and Republican statesman. Therefore, as "President Clark," he fulfilled his new ecclesiastical position in terms of his previous experience. To have attempted otherwise might only have been a futile effort in personality modification and could also have appeared as a repudiation of his prior experiences. Therefore, from 1933 to his death in 1961, J. Reuben Clark, Jr. regarded himself as an elder statesman of international law and of the Republican party who was serving as counselor to the President of the Church.

This view of his life's work after 1932 did not conform to his previous insistence on rigid separation of man's church service from his political and civil functions, but to him there were compelling reasons of personal faith that seemed to demand this modification. First, any other definition of his church service after 1932 would challenge his deeply felt faith that the President had acted by divine inspiration in selecting him for a counselor rather than someone with a more impressive record of Church service. Second, less than a year after the President extended the call, elections in the United States swept into American political power the kind of leadership and philosophies that Reuben viewed as a threat to all that he believed the United States of America represented. This circumstance did not appear as mere coincidence to him, but as confirmation that he had been called by divine inspiration to the highest leadership of the Church so that he could be a spokesman against the new political and social order he regarded as destructive of the nation in which the Church was headquartered.

His view of the priorities of his life's career also shaped his view of what a biography ought to emphasize. When the need for such a work was discussed on 9 November 1960, Marion G. Romney's personal diary records that President Clark referred "to things he had done during his life which might be worthy of note." On this occasion, he specified that a biography of his life should focus on his contributions in the U.S. State Department and other government service, but President Clark made no reference to any Church service or contribution as worthy of emphasis. Less than five months before his death, he again discussed a projected biography, and seriously questioned the suggestion that one man could complete such a study in even three years. "The trouble is," President Clark wrote in his office diary on 15 May 1961, "my brand has been in too many fires. I have been around too many corrals." His misgivings were prophetic, for it has taken several men a number of years to encompass the diversity and complexity of that biography. With the kind of emphasis upon his secular career that President Clark himself preferred, Frank W. Fox wrote the definitive volume, *J. Reuben Clark: The Public Years.*

However, the family and trustees of J. Reuben Clark's papers agreed that despite his modesty about Church experience, a second biography volume should be published concerning his experiences and service in the Church. The present volume therefore only briefly summarizes the secular career that is well presented in Frank W. Fox's biography; this present volume focuses instead upon J. Reuben Clark as a Church leader. Nevertheless, this second volume makes necessary references to the secular world to which President Clark as "elder statesman" in the First Presidency was so closely attuned.

Moreover, the nature of President Clark's Church service requires a departure from the strictly chronological approach of most biographies. He served as a counselor in the First Presidency for more than twenty-eight years, the longest period of such service in the history of The Church of Jesus Christ of Latter-day Saints. Where possible, the full breadth of President Clark's diverse activities is incorporated in the section concerning his service as counselor to three Presidents of the Church from 1933 to 1961. Following this chronological section of the last third of his life are several topical chapters where the author judged that the coherence of his religious life and thought was best understood through separate discussion.

The nature of his Church service also has shaped the presentation of this biography of the latter part of his life. The President of the Church, and not his counselors, has ultimate responsibility for decisions of policy and activity. Although a counselor like J. Reuben Clark oversaw certain areas of general Church responsibility, final decisions always rested with the Church President. Nevertheless, the Church Presidents also expected Reuben to be a vigorous counselor in the decision-making policies approved by the Church President, relieving the President of day to day oversight of matters that could be delegated to a counselor, and defending "the Church" (the administrative vernacular for the office of the First Presidency).

To assess the specific functions and contributions of J. Reuben Clark as a counselor in the First Presidency, it is therefore necessary to document the manner in which he served the decision-making process of the First Presidency from 1933 to 1961. Critically important for such analysis are the Minutes of the First Presidency, which were not available. Therefore, the present biography of President Clark's Church service had to rely on the scattered and incomplete references to his decision-making function found in such documents as his personal papers and those of his associates. Source availability determined the depth and breadth of the biography.

A number of individuals and institutions have provided access to documents that were crucial for this study. The children of President Clark (J. Reuben Clark III, Mrs. Louise Clark Bennion, Mrs. Marianne Clark Sharp, and Mrs. Luacine Clark Fox) generously shared their father with the author. The trustees of the J. Reuben Clark, Jr. Papers authorized the author to research the more than six hundred manuscript boxes of his papers at Brigham Young University, and President Dallin H. Oaks permitted the author to research the full university archives. The First Presidency of The Church of Jesus Christ of Latter-day Saints authorized the writer to research all relevant manuscripts at the Historical Department of the Church. Presidents Spencer W. Kimball and Marion G. Romney of the First Presidency generously granted personal interviews to the author and allowed him to research their own diaries from 1941 to 1961. Family representatives of several close associates of J. Reuben Clark also permitted the author to research diaries that were otherwise unavailable to study at the time.

In addition to the assistance of the Clark family and trustees, the following persons read and made helpful suggestions about the preliminary draft of this biography: Thomas G. Alexander, James B. Allen, Leonard J. Arrington, Frank W. Fox, Marvin S. Hill, Gordon A. Madsen, Robert K. Thomas, and David J. Whittaker. The author appreciates their suggestions, but he alone is responsible for the final product.

Compared to the nearly twenty years the general editor of this series, David H. Yarn, devoted to editing J. Reuben Clark's massive papers, the present author has expended a relatively small portion of his life for this volume. But during five years of his prolonged absences from home to work at the library, one of his children assumed he had been called on a mission, and he must express his gratitude for the patience and love demonstrated by Jan, Mary, Lisa, Adam, and Paul.

Several factors encouraged the biographer to present this eminent Church leader in a manner that is both sympathetic and candid. President Clark himself was consistently his own best critic, and often referred to his personal achievements and limitations in sermons, correspondence, and conversation. Moreover, when he had views that were controversial, he expressed them publicly as well as privately to Mormons and non-Mormons alike. Marion G. Romney, J. Reuben Clark III, and Gordon Burt Affleck, as trustees of the J. Reuben Clark, Jr. Papers, have all expressed the firm conviction that this biography should present him candidly as one of the foremost Church leaders of his generation as well as a man with human limitations and personal challenges.

Specifically, President Clark frequently commented in public and private that he had strong prejudices and views which he expected to be unpopular with many Latter-day Saints. The perspective of history can often see prior controversies in a calmer light, yet this biography may touch on matters that for some readers are still controversial. "J. Reuben Clark was a towering Church leader who held strong views that were often unpopular," Gordon Burt Affleck has told the writer, "but President Romney and I want this biography to present him honestly, even if there are controversies." President Marion G. Romney of the First Presidency of the Church reaffirmed this determination for a candid approach to President Clark's Church service in a published statement.

President Spencer W. Kimball has given the author encouragement for such an approach to the Church service of his own cousin. In his personal interview, President Kimball was very frank in describing certain challenges and difficulties President Clark faced within Church administration. In addition, the recently published biography of Spencer W. Kimball stands as his approved guideline and hallmark for the writing of sympathetic, yet candid, biographies of Church leaders.

Although indebted to the above individuals for their support of historical candor, the author has attempted to achieve a balance in this biography for which he alone is responsible. The author believes that the General Authorities of The Church of Jesus Christ of Latter-day Saints are called to their positions by divine guidance, and he is confident that they seek to carry out their administrative responsibilities by that inspiration. But the author also believes in the important truth expressed by President Clark to religion teachers at Brigham Young University in 1951: "Yet we must not forget that prophets are mortal men, with men's infirmities." This biography of J. Reuben Clark, Jr. seeks to maintain the balanced viewpoint which he recommended.

"THE WASTE PLACES OF ZION ...
THE RIVERS OF BABYLON"

Doctrine and Covenants 101:18; Psalms 137:1

On 1 September 1871, in Grantsville, Utah, Mary Woolley Clark gave birth to her first child, whom she delighted to name after her husband, Joshua Reuben. On that day, seventy-year-old Brigham Young presided over The Church of Jesus Christ of Latter-day Saints ("Mormon") from his stately Beehive House mansion in the bustling Mormon capital of Salt Lake City, only thirty-three miles from Grantsville. The Mormons had settled twenty-four years earlier in what became Utah and had by 1871 broken up its untilled lands and revealed its fertile valleys through irrigation.

Fifty years earlier, neither the Mormons as a people nor the Church as an institution existed except in the solitary visions of an upstate New York farm boy, Joseph Smith, Jr. By 1830 Joseph Smith had published a volume of new scripture, the Book of Mormon, had organized a latter-day restoration of the Church of Jesus Christ, and had proclaimed himself a prophet who communed directly with God and angels, who received prophetic inspiration, and who announced divine revelations.

Despite the First Amendment of the U.S. Constitution, nineteenth-century Americans could more easily tolerate atheists than accept Mormons as neighbors. Enraged by the apparent clannishness, the political bloc voting at election time, the economic solidarity, and the claims of moral and religious superiority of the Latter-day Saints, anti-Mormon mobs in the United States harassed individual Mormons and periodically pillaged entire Mormon communities for more than a decade. Finally, one mob succeeded in killing the Mormon Prophet, Joseph Smith, in 1844 at Carthage, Illinois.

His successor, Brigham Young, vowed to take every Mormon who would follow him away from the populated areas of the United States to the barren Great Basin of the Far West that no one else wanted. For Brigham Young and his tens of thousands of Mormon followers, the well-watered, lush, and verdant America east of the Mississippi River was a latter-day Babylon of spiritual jeopardy and captivity. To these Mormon pioneers who "came to Utah willingly, because we had to," the deserts, mountains, and isolated valleys of the Great Basin were a spiritual haven, the latter-day Zion of God.[1] After securely locating the Latter-day Saints in their refuge, Brigham Young never left the Great Basin, and he wondered why any Mormon would voluntarily leave Utah to reside east of the continental divide, in Babylon.

J. Reuben Clark, Jr.'s parents exemplified this Mormon withdrawal from the outside world. Mary Woolley Clark was born in 1848 as her own parents traveled in a wagon train to Utah. Her father was Edwin D. Woolley, a former Quaker, friend of Joseph Smith, business associate of Brigham Young, and, beginning in 1854, a prominent bishop of a Salt Lake City ward. Joshua R. Clark, son of a minister in the pacifist German Baptist Brethren ("Dunkards"), came to Utah as a freighter in 1867 and converted to Mormonism five weeks after hearing his first sermon on Church beliefs. Joshua hired out as a schoolteacher in Grantsville, where Mary's brother was one of the school trustees. The couple was married in July 1870 and made their permanent home in Grantsville, which had a population of 755 that year.

As Mormon Utah struggled to isolate itself from the Babylon of the rest of America, Grantsville remained effortlessly suspended beyond the mainstream of the social and religious life swirling only thirty-three miles away in Salt Lake City. At the edge of a forbidding alkaline waste, Grantsville eked out such a marginal existence that in 1930, when its native son, J. Reuben Clark, Jr. was at the pinnacle of his national prominence, the town's population was still only 1,240. When he died thirty-one years later, the town stood at barely more than 2,100.

Reuben gravitated to the harsh earthiness of his birthplace and throughout his life liked to escape from the formalities of Salt Lake City to his Grantsville farm where he worked his land and cattle.

Joshua R. Clark Family, 1892. J. Reuben Clark, Jr. is in the center of the back row.

Brigham Young would have understood this. Devotion to the isolated Mormon village was central to President Young's view of the Great Basin as spiritual refuge.

But within J. Reuben Clark, Jr. surged talents and ambitions that propelled him out of Grantsville, out of Salt Lake City, out of Utah, out of the provincial West and into the economic and political capitals of the United States, Latin America, and Europe. There, in Babylon, Reuben sought, achieved, and enjoyed an internationally prominent career.[2] His only comparable predecessors, George Q. Cannon of the U.S. House of Representatives and Reed Smoot of the U.S. Senate, were Mormon apostles who self-consciously served Church interests through public office. The Honorable Mr. Clark, whose Mormon faith surfaced primarily in an impeccable moral life, functioned in high offices of his nation as a secular civil servant. Church leaders and ordinary Mormons in Utah not only praised his achievements but also periodically encouraged him to forego possible Church responsibilities in Utah in order to participate in secular affairs of the outside world, the world Mormons have always regarded with some misgivings. These things Brigham Young might not have understood or imagined possible on the day the Clarks of Grantsville had their first-born son in 1871.

In most respects, his early life in Grantsville showed no promise of any future fame. The often barefoot "Ruby" was the darling of his close-knit Mormon parents, yet they loved him no more than their other nine children. Father Joshua, the patriarch of the family until his death in 1929, recorded in his diary fond descriptions of the activities of his oldest, but gave similar emphasis to the achievements of his brothers and sisters as they followed him through the childhood life cycle of a small Mormon village.

Like a stock actor in a rural drama company, Reuben Clark undertook the prosaic, secular tasks that all Grantsville boys of the 1870s and 1880s experienced.[3] He was milking two cows a morning and irrigating the family garden by the time he was nine years old, and was branding calves and driving cattle from horseback at age eleven. By his mid-teens, he sheared as many as eleven sheep a day, plowed the fields, and sometimes spent days at a time riding the cattle range. The Saturday night bath at the Clark home was his well-earned escape from the grime of the fields. Rabbit hunting, fishing, barnyard pranks, and an occasional party with friends served as Spartan respites from the daily routine of rural sweat and satisfaction.

Yet even for barefoot farmboys in isolated Mormon villages of nineteenth-century Utah, the influence of the Church was pervasive. Beyond the daily family prayers and scripture reading of the Clark home were overlapping Mormon commonwealths. First was Grantsville, despite its village size the "second town of importance in Tooele County."[4] During most of Reuben's childhood and youth, the bishop of the Grantsville Ward was Edward Hunter, mayor of Grantsville and nephew of the Church's Presiding Bishop. Reuben's grandfather, Edwin D. Woolley, had introduced Mormonism to the Hunters in Pennsylvania in the 1840s, and in Utah the prominent Woolleys and Hunters maintained personal and business association.[5] The bishop decided, or was at least consulted about, every community affair from water rights to dancing parties. The president of the Tooele Stake of the Church, which corresponded exactly to the county boundaries of the time, functioned in an identical manner for the Mormon residents of the county. General Authorities in Salt Lake City were similar shepherds for the Utah Territory flock, but rarely saw Mormons outside the Great Basin. So it was that the Clarks in Grantsville had periodic contact with all the existing echelons of Church leadership, at least every three months when Tooele Stake held its two-day quarterly conferences.

When Reuben was only nine, one of these stake conferences brought about a convergence of circumstances and personalities that he may have had some knowledge of, but which foreshadowed unimagined developments in his life. After his father baptized Reuben on 2 September 1879, the young boy was confirmed a member of the Church five days later by Francis M. Lyman, president of the Tooele Stake.[6] In 1877 Brigham Young had asked thirty-seven-year-old Francis M. Lyman to move from Millard County in west-central Utah to live in Tooele City where he was to preside over the Tooele Stake. Although Tooele County residents may have been disappointed that one of their own number was not given this office, Francis M. Lyman was a gregarious leader and able speaker who almost immediately won the admiration and devotion of Mormons in the county.

President Lyman was released in October 1880 to become a member of the Church's Quorum of the Twelve Apostles; and, once again, a replacement was summoned from outside the stake. Twenty-three-year-old Heber J. Grant was sustained as president of the Tooele Stake on 30 October 1880. Not as outgoing as President Lyman, President Grant had difficulty in winning the wholehearted support of members immediately, and his earnest efforts to win acceptance were undoubtedly a topic of conversation in Reuben Clark's family. Heber J. Grant was not only their stake president but since his childhood had been a member of the Salt Lake City Thirteenth Ward, over which grandfather Edwin D. Woolley presided as bishop. Bishop Woolley attended the Tooele Stake conference at which President Grant was sustained, and the good bishop did his best from the pulpit to reassure the Tooele Saints that their new stake president was a fine choice. For his part, Heber J. Grant felt close enough to the Woolleys in the 1880s to attend their family reunions.[7]

This early convergence of the lives of Heber J. Grant and the family of J. Reuben Clark, Jr. took an added turn on 6 October 1881. As Grant stopped in the Salt Lake City store of photographer Charles R. Savage, Savage looked intently at Tooele's shy stake president and solemnly told Heber J. Grant "that within one year [he] would be a member of the Twelve Apostles." A year and four days later the Church President announced a revelation appointing Heber J. Grant as a member of the Quorum of the Twelve Apostles, and seventeen years later the prophetic Charles R. Savage became J. Reuben Clark's father-in-law. Reuben would be six years old before a haunting significance appeared in these seemingly inconsequential intersections of his early life with that of Heber J. Grant.[8]

On summer nights in the 1880s, young Reuben often left the still, oppressive heat of his room to make his bed on a haystack, where he could enjoy the stray breezes and gaze at the Milky Way in the cloudless expanse above him. With the languid wonder of youth, he may have noticed that some stars in that procession only twinkled faintly while others shone brightly. Still others of the brightest magnitude shone from dark places far removed from the multitude clustered along the familiar path of the night sky. As he drifted to sleep with the feel of hay on his back, he may have wondered about his future and potential, as the image of the stars merged with fleeting thoughts of the next morning's farm chores.

His farm boy experiences may have had a universal quality, but his parents noticed a religious intensity in him that was not always characteristic of his peers. When he was nine, his father's diary noted: "The boys sat up late last night and asked a good many questions in relation to the gospel, and what revelation meant. We answered as well as we could do to their understanding."[9] More remarkable than childhood inquiries about doctrine was the fact that between the ages of fifteen and eighteen he often attended morning church services alone.[10] At the very time of life when many young men resist church attendance, Reuben Clark was singularly devoted. At fourteen he gave his first talk at the request of Bishop Hunter in a deacon's quorum meeting, and as a sixteen-year-old, delivered his maiden sermon—a ten-minute "biographical sketch of our Lord and Saviour Jesus Christ" to the joint meeting of the Young Men and Women of Grantsville.[11] His youthful emphasis on Christology in preference to other possible subjects of Church teaching endured throughout his life, especially during those periods when the Honorable J. Reuben Clark, Jr. attended church infrequently. The Grantsville bishop ordained him a priest at the age of seventeen and an elder at eighteen; his father, Joshua, ordained Reuben Clark to the proselyting office of seventy on 30 March 1890. The seventies were intended to be "traveling ministers," and Reuben's ordination to that office coincidentally preceded by only five months his departure from Grantsville.[12]

Father Joshua had tried to provide for his education by encouraging him to read books from the family library, and the young boy was soon reading and rereading *Young Folk's History of Rome, The Child's Natural History,* and Shakespeare's *Complete Works.* He even made several unsuccessful attempts to comprehend Milton's *Paradise Lost.* Joshua included his eldest in a private school he was teaching, but the father soon doubted he was up to teaching his son, and Joshua agreed to let him attend the graded school in the Grantsville City Hall. Even then, Joshua Clark decided that with ten children and little money, "a good common school education" would have to be his son's ultimate goal. The father sorely underestimated eleven-year-old Reuben's thirst for formal education, and the next eight years were a seesaw of frustration for them both.

At the heart of the matter was the fabled Woolley stubbornness which Reuben often acknowledged and described. He said Brigham Young once remarked that if grandfather, Edwin D. Woolley, "is ever drowned, do not look for him down-stream, look up-stream, for he always goes against the current."[13] On another occasion, the adult J. Reuben Clark worked with a non-Mormon whose wife's maiden name was Woolley. The man wondered if she and Reuben were relatives. "Is your wife rather insistent in her opinions?" he asked. "Yes," was the reply. "Does she ever discount her opinions?" "No." "If you have a dispute, is she right and you wrong?" When the man answered in the affirmative, Reuben smiled and said, "Yes, we are related."[14] His youthful quest for education displayed his Woolley nature.

His father's diary noted that "Reuben would rather miss his meals than to miss a day from school" and frequently recorded that his son's determination to attend school caused him to be the only one to leave the house during severe winter storms. Yet the financially strapped father finally had to withdraw his son from the tuition school of Grantsville. Reuben once again had to proceed under his father's admittedly inadequate tutorship. After a few tense days of unrecorded turmoil, Joshua wrote, "I concluded to let Reuben go to school another half term. He started again this morning." During some terms, he could not attend school at all, but after his elementary graduation he doggedly repeated the eighth grade twice more because that was the highest education Grantsville offered, and "there was nothing to do." Joshua confided to his diary little of his son's restiveness and none of his pleas for more education. Without further explanation, Joshua's diary announced resolution of the conflict on 28 August 1890: "Reuben will go with us to the city in the morning. He will stop in there and go to the Latter-day Saints' College."[15]

Grantsville would remain in Reuben Clark's blood, but the city—first Salt Lake, then New York, then Washington—would always be foremost in his mind and dreams after he left Grantsville for an education in 1890. His performance in his first midterm examination at the Latter-day Saints' College more than justified the family gamble on his education: one score of 80 percent, four scores in the 90s, and two 100 percent scores. Out of a class of seventy-five students, many of whom had better educational opportunities, the barefoot boy from Grantsville was the only student to achieve a score of 100 percent.[16] Up until now, his ambitions had been modest but improbable: to obtain more than a common school education despite his family's lack of financial resources, and to distinguish himself in a metropolis despite his provincial background. With a fierce inner drive that even his family could hardly understand, he had pushed himself out of the family nest and into the world of education where individual comparisons were stark and unremitting. Reuben found that he was exceptionally competitive and admirably fit, and for the first time he had an external justification for his self-confidence. Self-congratulation and boasting were alien to him, but the first youthful foray into the big city left him unbloodied and unrivaled among his better-advantaged colleagues. He asked no favors—only the opportunity to prove himself. The more opportunities he seized, the farther Reuben stretched the boundaries of his Grantsville origins.

Ultimately more important than his initial grades at the Latter-day Saints' College was the association he soon developed with the school's guiding light, James E. Talmage. At twenty-nine years, Professor Talmage was president of the college and "a kind of intellectual whirlwind. Now in geology, now in chemistry, now in medicine, now in Biblical scholarship, he swept the horizon before him."[17] With his reputation as a latter-day Renaissance Man of diverse interests and achievement, Talmage had an extraordinary impact on J. Reuben Clark's emerging intellectual aspirations. Equally important, the British-born, Eastern-educated professor was the boy's first significant exposure to urbane gentility. Reuben later remarked that "[I was] a country boy just entering his twenties, as raw as they make them and they can be made pretty raw, [and] I was blessed by being taken under the immediate tutelage of Dr. Talmage."[18]

He led Reuben through Latter-day Saints' College, through the short-lived Church University, and on to the University of Utah.[19] Despite a heavy employment schedule as Talmage's assistant, he distinguished himself at the University of Utah by completing requirements for the Bachelor of Science degree and teaching credentials in four years, by serving as managing editor of the *University Chronicle* during his senior year, and by graduating on 15 June 1898 as class valedictorian.[20] Although the mentor was somewhat austere, their relationship was sufficiently close that Professor Talmage solemnized the marriage ceremony for Reuben and Luacine A. Savage in the Salt Lake Temple on 14 September 1898. This was the first occasion on which Talmage performed a temple sealing for time and eternity.[21]

Beyond providing intellectual expansion and employment opportunities, the professor also had profound influence on the religious attitudes that would govern Reuben's adult life. He created the first religious milestone for the young man in mid-January 1891, and it was well that Reuben had begun the month with a day of fasting and prayer.[22] Shortly after Reuben returned to Latter-day Saints' College in January for the new term, Talmage acknowledged that the First Presidency had appointed him curator of the fledgling Deseret Museum, and that if Reuben would accept the position as assistant curator the Church authorities would accept this service "the same as a mission."[23] All faithful men of the Church, married or unmarried, were expected to fulfill a two-year missionary service

COURTESY HAROLD B. LEE LIBRARY

Reuben as University of Utah valedictorian, 1898.

(often in a foreign land), and Reuben even held the proselyting office of seventy in the Church. Nevertheless, with the blessing of the First Presidency, Talmage offered Reuben the opportunity of secular service for the public relations of the Church in lieu of a religious mission to gather converts. Hesitating only long enough to consult his father, Reuben accepted the position and its concomitant redefinition of what constitutes service to the Church. James E. Talmage thus provided at least part of the rationale for J. Reuben Clark, Jr.'s future life as a secular Latter-day Saint.

Professor Talmage also gave form and organization to Reuben's understanding of Church doctrine. The First Presidency directed Professor Talmage to prepare a series of theological lectures on the Articles of Faith. He meticulously organized, explained, and documented

Church doctrines, submitted his lecture drafts for approval to a reading committee of General Authorities, revised his doctrinal expositions as directed by this committee, and began delivering the lectures and publishing them in full during 1893.[24] By eliminating all conflicting or obscure doctrinal pronouncements and by codifying and regularizing Church doctrines, Talmage (under the direction of the General Authorities) established Mormonism's first systematic theology in his book *The Articles of Faith.* And Reuben Clark was in the middle of this process. "I was with him when he prepared 'The Articles of Faith.' I often jokingly say that I wrote 'The Articles of Faith'—I did—on the typewriter."[25] Reuben typed his mentor's rough drafts, and retyped them with the revisions required by the reading committee or by Talmage himself. From Talmage's perspective, the young man may have been performing merely a mechanical, secretarial function. In reality, J. Reuben Clark, Jr. was Talmage's first convert to the presentation of Church doctrine in a comprehensive, scripturally documented, internally consistent, logically organized, noncontroversial, and easily understood form. Talmage helped define the limits of Latter-day Saint orthodoxy through *The Articles of Faith,* and his disciple imposed that orthodoxy upon Church curriculum when he became a member of the First Presidency.

Reuben Clark often quipped that in his beloved Luacine ("Lute") he had married his social and religious superior. Although his prolific Woolley kindred were at the upper rungs of Utah society, the Clarks of Grantsville had no illusions about their social or economic standing, especially in the "big city" of Salt Lake where Luacine's famous photographer-father, Charles R. Savage, had provided his family with a comfortable living and social acceptance. As regards religious devotion, Reuben held a lifelong belief: "Almost always there is less of the earthly and more of the spiritual in woman than in man."[26] He sought out and married a young woman who fulfilled that expectation, and for five years he struggled to provide Lute with financial security and at least the beginnings of social prestige in the mountains and valleys of Zion.

With the help of his father-in-law, Reuben secured his first teaching position in September 1898, and took his new bride with him to Heber City where he launched "one of the first steps toward a public high school" in Wasatch County.[27] His wife missed the familiar life of Salt Lake City but thoroughly enjoyed this alpine setting where, as an emigré from Salt Lake City society, she was the center of Heber's social life. "Well, we danced until ten o'clock, and there being such a small crowd present the party was suddenly dismissed. But we didn't care, as Anna had a sumptuous repast ready for us." Lute also commented on the first significant Church assignment of her husband's life, as well as her own unaccustomed absence from church service: "Reuben's Sunday School class is quite interesting. They are studying the 'Life of Christ.' I am going to try and go: it is quite a change not to teach a class."[28] Reuben, however, found life in Heber City unfulfilling.[29] His teaching was hardly a failure, though, since three school principals and a physician eventually emerged from his class of thirteen students.[30]

Back in Salt Lake City, Reuben started the 1899–1900 school year teaching Latin, Shakespeare, grammar, rhetoric, and civil government at Latter-day Saints' College, but he joined the principal, Joseph Nelson, and four other faculty members in a mass resignation due to a salary dispute with the Church Board of Education. They resigned on Friday, and pluckily signed contracts to begin teaching the following Monday at the Salt Lake Business School. After his frustrating 1900–1901 school year as acting principal of the Southern Branch of the State Normal School in Cedar City, during which his conservative budget request for the following year and his reappointment were both declined by the state, he returned to teach at Joseph Nelson's Salt Lake Business School. Beginning to see himself as a vagabond schoolteacher, Reuben was as miserably frustrated in his desires for further education now as he had been as a teenager in Grantsville. He made halfhearted attempts to prepare himself for the bar examination by studying law books at home, but his restive eyes looked beyond the mountain cloister of the Wasatch Range.[31]

According to the expectations of his family and culture, Reuben Clark had obtained his ultimate education and had begun a respectable teaching career. Few of his peers wanted more than this. But he concluded that he could achieve his ambitions only outside the Great Basin, and outside Mormon culture. When he expressed that conviction to his wife, her averted eyes told him that she could accept social isolation in a Mormon village more easily than religious isolation in a gentile metropolis. He tried to find personal fulfillment in all the approved avenues of Zion, including his Sunday School teaching in every community where he had a secular teaching position, but it all left him as desolate as the alkaline deserts from which his people had carved out tree-lined oases. Ancient Babylon brought remorse to the captive children of Israel, but Reuben felt captive in his own land and yearned for the lush opportunities of America's modern-day Babylon on the eastern seaboard.

When, at last, he decided to test the waters of Babylon, Reuben tried to calm his wife's fears and his own guilt by securing the protective sponsorship of Church leaders. In November 1902, with the written endorsement of Church President Joseph F. Smith, Reuben applied for the position of private secretary to senator-elect and Apostle Reed Smoot, who would be in Washington, D.C.—where Reuben could attend George Washington Law School. He never forgot the coolness with which Smoot ignored this Church-endorsed application. Ultimately, Reuben's friend and associate in the 1900 conflict with the Church Board of Education made his eastward hopes a reality. Joseph Nelson provided an interest-free loan that financed the exodus of Reuben's little family and enabled him to attend prestigious Columbia Law School in New York City.[32] Before he left in August 1903, he sought a parting benediction from the Church President, who set J. Reuben Clark, Jr. apart on a "general" mission to be an exemplary Latter-day Saint among the gentiles of the world.[33] It was not the usual mission calling, nor was Reuben's sojourn in Babylon typical. Its effect upon his personal development was so profound that he later remarked, "I was reared among the heathen Gentiles."[34]

When Reuben Clark arrived in New York City he was thirty-two years old, he was married and the father of two daughters, and he was a Mormon from the American West. The only thing he had in common with the younger, Eastern Establishment students he met the first day at Columbia University Law School was the determination to become a lawyer. His aspirations had mildly estranged him from his people in Utah, but for the next thirty years his Mormon identity created "an intangible but real barrier" between him and those upon whom he depended for the fulfillment of those aspirations.[35] The Psalmist had asked, "How shall we sing the Lord's song in a strange land?" It was an uncomfortable question for one

Reuben enters Columbia University Law School, 1903.

who was among religious strangers voluntarily, and Reuben was never entirely satisfied with his own answer.

One approach that seemed at least to simplify his encounter with the Eastern Establishment was Reuben's lifetime habit of working long hours, often in the studious retreat of a library. Not content with the traditional isolation of the law school's carrels, he slowly built a personal law library in which he could find academic seclusion even after the school library closed for the night. "The Clarks have always been noted as late-to-get-up and late-to-go-to-bed," he once remarked,[36] and it was common for him to study in his home library long after midnight.

Reuben's drive and monastic study habits purposely limited his awkward social contacts with non-Mormons and also brought him distinction at Columbia, as they would everywhere else. As one of the top-ranked students in his class, he joined the editorial staff of the *Columbia Law Review* at the beginning of his junior year. In his senior year he was "Recent Decisions" editor, which provided added opportunity for his intense, almost awesome, practice of reading everything he could find about a topic as preparation for analytical memoranda. His reputation as a brilliant and driving student led to his employment in the spring of 1905 as a summer research assistant for one of Columbia's law professors, James Brown Scott. After Scott became Solicitor of the U.S. State Department, he appointed J. Reuben Clark as Assistant Solicitor in 1906, following graduation from Columbia Law School.[37]

During the six-and-one-half years Clark served in the Solicitor's office of the U.S. State Department, he advanced to full Solicitor and also became virtual Secretary of State in crisis situations when a vacuum of leadership forced him to make policy decisions for the government. He struggled for a time as the unappreciated ghost-writer for Solicitor Scott's memoranda, which were highly praised within the Roosevelt and Taft administrations. Scott's eccentricities as Solicitor taught Clark to scrutinize everyone, regardless of status, and to accept, realistically, the necessity to help ease Scott from his position. By the time Clark became Solicitor in 1910, he had learned indelible lessons about the responsibilities of office and the realities of bureaucratic infighting.

Although Solicitor Clark functioned in the foreign relations of the United States with many countries, he gained some of his most significant experience in arbitration, diplomacy, and crisis negotiation in dealings with Latin America. In particular, the torturous experience of the Mexican Revolution involved the Solicitor's office in so many ways that he began shaping much of U.S. policy toward Mexico from 1910 to 1913. When the Secretary of State and the Acting Secretary of State were absent from Washington, he sometimes found himself in the difficult position of having to act on his own authority or make recommendations directly to the President when crises demanded immediate action. Although much of Reuben's work was behind the scenes, the crowning public achievement of his career as Solicitor was his published memorandum, *Right to Protect Citizens in Foreign Countries by Landing Forces.*[38]

After leaving the State Department in 1913, due to the election of Woodrow Wilson as President, Clark conducted a decade-long private legal practice, with his principal offices in Washington, D.C., and New York City, and a smaller law partnership in Utah. Nevertheless, he never lost interest in the affairs of his government, and his government (particularly its Republican administrations) did not lose sight of the valuable former Solicitor. From 1913 to 1914 he served as General Counsel for the American-British Claims Commission. In 1916 the Judge Advocate General of the U.S. Army asked him to accept a special commission as major in the Officer's Reserve Corps so that he could assist in the formulation of a "selective service" program. He accepted the position, but in 1917 the Justice Department obtained his reassignment to become "Special Assistant" to the Attorney General. In 1918 he became executive officer and second-in-command to the Judge Advocate General. Although Reuben declared with embarrassment that he had not merited it, he was awarded the Distinguished Service Medal for his services in World War I. In his last major government service of this period, he was Special Counsel for the U.S. State Department in the difficult negotiations of the Washington Arms Conference of 1921–1922. During this decade he also served as ghostwriter for Judge Advocate General Enoch Crowder, Attorney General Thomas W. Gregory, Senator William E. Borah, and especially for former Secretary of State and current Senator Philander Knox in a campaign against United States participation in the League of Nations. Although Clark had maintained a law partnership in Salt Lake City since 1915, he was preoccupied with his New York firm where he was legal counsel for "America's first multinational conglomerate," the American International Corporation.[39]

The Jews languished seventy years among religious strangers in their Babylonian exile, and the earlier Israelites wandered forty years in the Sinai wilderness until they were sufficiently purged of alien ways to enter the Promised Land. For nearly thirty years J. Reuben Clark discovered how intoxicating his opportunities and successes among the "heathen gentiles" could be for this self-imposed exile from the Latter-day Zion of the Great Basin.

Although he maintained significant personal, family, professional, economic, and religious ties to what one geographer called the "Mormon Culture Region" that centers in Salt Lake City,

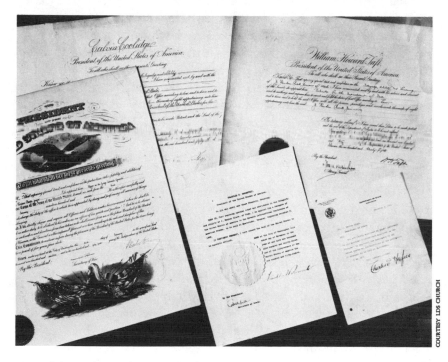

Some of the certificates of appointment from three decades of J. Reuben Clark's service in the U.S. government.

17

Reuben discovered that his sojourn in modern Babylon exacted a price in his personal life. In particular, the years from 1903 to 1923 not only witnessed his extraordinary successes in America's Eastern Establishment, but also reflected some uncomfortable changes in Reuben's family and religious life. Later, as a member of the First Presidency, J. Reuben Clark told a conference of young men, many of whom would also seek their fortunes in the world outside the Mormon culture region: "A great portion of my mature life has been spent away from association with members of the Church, and I have had to live more or less my own spiritual life."[40]

His professional aspirations and activities from 1903 to 1923 required many personal adjustments that made Clark's family life unusual even by the standards of the Babylon of the American East. After she endured the academic widowhood of law school, Luacine Clark hoped their life would resume the normalcy they had known in Utah. Instead, Reuben worked more than six years in the Solicitor's office, and Luacine found the heat of Washington so insufferable that she routinely returned to Utah with the children to spend the spring and summer. She wanted Reuben to move to Utah permanently, but each of his professional triumphs diminished her hopes. When he failed to reach Utah in time for the birth of their third child in 1908, he absented himslf from the State Department for six weeks to remain with Luacine and his family. Luacine endured a few more months of separation, and announced her intention to join him in Washington, despite her preference for Utah.[41]

Luacine undoubtedly rejoiced when the Democratic victory in 1912 required Reuben's resignation from the State Department. She hoped he would be satisfied with the laurels of public service he had already won and would take up permanent residence in Utah. Instead, he opened law offices in Washington and New York, which demanded even more separations, in addition to the annual pilgrimages of Luacine and the children to Utah from spring to fall for her health and their religious education. Reuben stayed in New York weekdays during the fall and winter and visited Luacine and the children in Washington only on weekends.[42] He rarely visited his Salt Lake City office during this time. This uncomfortable arrangement ended when he moved the family to New York early in 1920.

But this reunion of his family residence with his New York work ended in June 1920, when Reuben moved the entire family back to Salt Lake City for "political reasons"—to establish a Utah residence from which he could fulfill his aspirations to become U.S. senator.[43] With Luacine and the children located permanently in Utah (aside from a five-month Washington residence in 1921), he still spent much of the time in New York City from 1921 to 1923. Although he and Luacine communed through daily correspondence and weekly long-distance phone calls, the strains of such a life echoed in J. Reuben Clark's remarks to the women of the Church nearly thirty years later: "We of the Priesthood are out in the world. We meet all kinds of conditions. We are engaged in something of a battle from day to day, trying to secure those things which maintain life. We do not have much time with you, nor with the children, and so we must look to you, and do look to you, and we are not disappointed, to build the home and to make it a home. . . ."[44]

When Reuben was with his wife and children during the twenty years following his enrollment at Columbia, their home was a combination of excited animation, peaceful languor, and individual study. The Clark children often met important government officials and heard discussions of their father's equally important work. At the family dinner table he listened with interest to his daughters' talk of boyfriends and school activities, but when their social life seemed to be uppermost in priority, he counseled them to obtain a serious education, preferably at Bryn Mawr.[45] After dinner the children listened to the gramophone and played at their father's feet as he took a short nap, and "if a comment or correction was in order, Reuben would duly pronounce it, his eyes still closed, his face immobile."[46] Following the after-dinner relaxation, he quietly went to the study. "My father always said, 'Every night should be family home evening,'" reminisced Marianne, who was a teenager during much of the Clark family's residence in the East. "That was the way our family was. We were always at home. We would have our dinner and then my father would go upstairs and study or work every night of his life. I always remember him working. You just took it for granted. But we could always go up and visit him."[47] Perhaps Reuben's studious isolation during his evenings at home intensified his children's adoration of their father, who they knew had the respect of the world's leaders. Even though he was absorbed in his study, his wife and children cherished having him at home and they knew that a knock at his open study door would get them his complete and affectionate attention.

If the intense church activity the family experienced in Utah was not always possible in the East during those years, Mormon influence was still pervasive. "We didn't have much formal study of the Church," Marianne remembered, "But it was just in the very air we breathed that we didn't do some things that other people did and that our roots were here in the West. It was just an understood thing."[48] Isolated from the Mormon culture region in an era before

Reuben captioned this 1917 photograph of his family: "Life's fruition—a healthy and intelligent family."

Church-wide emphasis on family scripture study and family prayers, each of Reuben's children (as he did) lived "more or less my own spiritual life." Without coercion, he encouraged his children to become knowledgeable about the gospel, but several of them did not finish reading the Book of Mormon until they were in college. Reuben prayed with his family at the dinner table, but it was grandfather Joshua who introduced the Clark children to the practice of holding formal family prayer in Grantsville. Formal church services were also limited in Washington, D.C. During the family's residence in the capital only evening sacrament meetings were held—no priesthood meetings for the men, Relief Society for the women, Mutual for the youth, Primary for the children, nor Sunday School for families. As a result, the Latter-day Saints in Washington had to fend for themselves, and the Clark children occasionally attended Sunday morning services at local Protestant churches. The spare formalities of the Church in the East so little resembled the abundance of Zion in Utah that it is little wonder that Reuben and Luacine postponed the children's baptisms until their annual summer stays in Utah, where they could participate in the reality of the church they were entering. The incomplete religious experiences of the children in the East were symptomatic of the spiritual cost that preoccupation with secular matters was exacting from J. Reuben Clark.[49]

He felt obliged to spend his Sundays attending to his staggering workload, a habit that prompted Luacine to admonish him to "above all, quit working on Sundays."[50] Part of the problem was that Reuben was trying to define how he could function as a Mormon in government service at the same time the Senate was trying to expel Reed Smoot because he was a Mormon Apostle. The national press and official Senate minutes quoted Smoot's own defense that he had never been "a very active" Mormon and that as a senator he was aloof from the Church. Moreover, Smoot took pains to become known as an effective seven-day-a-week senator, and for that reason provided only Sunday evening services, which incidentally were held in the Smoot home, for the Mormons of Washington.[51] Reuben, not forgetting what he was convinced was an intended insult when Smoot ignored his application to come to be Smoot's secretary four years earlier, felt that Smoot was at best patronizing in their Washington relationship. He simply avoided the senator when he could, and this in large measure kept him from the consistent church meeting attendance that was typical of him when in Utah.[52]

Aside from his personal coolness toward Reed Smoot, Smoot's continued presence in the Senate was the catalyst for Reuben's strong opposition to Church influence in politics. On 2 March 1907, shortly after three years of embarrassing testimony and ecclesiastical bloodletting for Mormons ended with the narrow defeat of the effort to unseat Smoot, Reuben wrote a "Why Not?" memorandum: "No Apostle–Presidency of Church, etc. including Presidents of Stakes—shall while holding such office be eligible for election to a political office."[53] Shortly afterward he wrote his father that the Church involvement in politics was "un-American," had always caused trouble for the Mormons, and was unnecessary to protect the Church or its members.[54] When he discussed "Church (Mormon) interference in politics" with Mathonihah Thomas in 1914, Reuben expressed grudging support for Reed Smoot's continued presence in the Senate, but added "that a religious leader might also possess the qualifications of learning, wisdom and experience necessary to make him a great civil leader, and therefore entitle him to be listened to in civil matters; but that it was the latter qualifications and not his religious position or [religious] qualifications which gave to him this position, power and right."[55]

However, as he spent more Sundays in New York City and Salt Lake City from 1913 to 1922, he could attend church without Smoot's inescapable presence, and Reuben's resistance to consistent church activitiy softened. In 1914 he spoke at church meetings on "Present Day Tendencies," and "Causes of the European War," and in 1915 and 1916 he even spoke at sacrament meetings in Senator Smoot's home on such religious topics as "Relation Between Material and Spiritual" and "Feed My Sheep."[56] But Reed Smoot's Washington was Reuben's Washington, and their resolution of the Latter-day Saint sojourn in modern Babylon was similar: the young lawyer developed the habit of sandwiching in church meetings between long hours of legal work;[57] and he allowed his inability to participate in temple worship in the East to affect his participation in temple work even when in Utah.[58] Moreover, crushed under the burden of school debts, unprofitable investments, and maintenance of multiple residences, Reuben found payment of tithing to be a real struggle.[59]

He also interpreted his two secular mission calls by the First Presidency as indicating that promising young men could serve the Church by excelling in their professional development, and Reuben felt that his brother Frank should continue his engineer's profession without the interruption of a proselyting mission.[60]

Although Reuben Clark chafed at some of the external manifestations of Mormonism, he unflinchingly identified himself as a Mormon when the very name was a national epithet. The pressures for him to conceal his Mormon identity were strong enough at Columbia, where his religion was academically unfashionable, but the situation was worse when he entered the State Department in 1906. Since the beginning of 1904, newspapers throughout the nation had been filled with sensational headlines and denunciatory editorials about "the Mormon question" due to the Senate's investigation of Reed Smoot and the practices of the Church. With all the detachment of a circus sideshow, Mormon leaders were subjected to relentless cross-examination in the Senate committee's chambers, Mormon doctrines and practices were ridiculed by senators and caricatured in the press, and—most serious for Reuben's career—Mormon loyalty to the government was seriously questioned.[61] Aside from voluntarily proclaiming one's self a Latter-day Saint, the surest means of Mormon identity was strict observance of the Word of Wisdom: total abstinence from alcohol, tobacco, tea, and coffee. Although he knew that such observance made him a social pariah in Washington, and even though he deeply worried that his Mormon identity would result in his dismissal from government service, Reuben studied alone during coffee breaks in the State Department, declined the obligatory cigars in meetings with diplomats and governmental superiors, and served lemonade to startled dinner guests.[62] There were limits to the accommodations a Latter-day Israelite could make in Babylon, and Reuben would neither deny his heritage nor violate its ethical imperatives.

Moreover, he doggedly maintained the simple faith of his youth even when he rigorously questioned certain aspects of Mormonism that he regarded as irritating tangents from the central gospel. On the very occasion in 1914 when he criticized political actions by Church leaders, Reuben affirmed: "In other words, I took the position that religion is divine, and therefore not subject generally to human questions, alterations, or interferences, and further that the words of those authorized to speak for divinity, must be implicitly accepted, when speaking pursuant to their agency i.e. speaking on religious matters."[63] In his mid-forties, Reuben Clark was expressing the verities of his father and of his Utah mentor, James E. Talmage.

By 1917, however, Reuben was asking himself some religious questions that took him years to resolve. In one personal memo he began, "If we have truth, [it] cannot be harmed by investigation. If we have not truth, it ought to be harmed." From that premise he added the observation that scientists and lawyers (like himself) were not blindly believing and that they must refuse to be deceived by others or by their own wishful thinking. "A lawyer must get at facts, he must consider motives—he must tear off the mask and lay bare the countenance, however hideous. The frightful skeleton of truth must always be exposed . . . [the lawyer] must make every conclusion pass the fiery ordeal of pitiless reason. If their conclusions cannot stand this test, they are false."[64] During the same year the increasingly introspective lawyer asked himself the questions: Are we not only entitled, but expected to think for ourselves? Otherwise where does our free agency come in? His answer was a resounding: "If we are blindly to follow some one else we are not free agents. . . . That we may as a Church determine for ourselves our course of action, is shown by the Manifesto [abandoning the practice of polygamy]. We may not probably take an affirmative stand, i.e., adopt something new but we may dispense with something."[65] Perhaps he had never before questioned the assumptions that lay behind some of the simple faith of his youth, but at midlife J. Reuben Clark, Jr. proclaimed that there must be no forbidden questions in Mormonism.

The directions to which his philosophy of religious inquiry led him were indicated in his musings about two essentials of Mormonism: the revelations of Joseph Smith, Jr. and Church belief in progression toward godhood. As he examined the revelations in the Doctrine and Covenants concerning the structure of Church government, Reuben Clark wondered to what extent Joseph Smith's reading or experience, "his own consciousness," had contributed to what he set down, and when Reuben pondered the Mormon belief in the potential of individuals to attain the godly stature of their Father in Heaven, his logical mind boggled a bit. "Is Space or occupied portions of it divided among various deities—have they great 'spheres of influence'? War of Gods—think of wreck of matter involved—if matter used—or would it be a war of forces?"[66] In his mid-forties, he regarded these as legitimate doctrinal inquiries but soon realized that each question concerning doctrine led to other questions, each of which was further removed from rational verification. Reuben soon came to the conclusion he described in later years to the non-Mormon president of George Washington University: "For my own part I early came to recognize that for me personally I must either quit rationalizing . . . or I must follow the line of my own thinking which would lead me I know not where."[67]

But J. Reuben Clark soon recognized where an uncompromising commitment to rational theology *would* lead him, and he shrank from the abyss. "I came early to appreciate that I could not rationalize a religion for myself, and that to attempt to do so would destroy my faith in God," he later wrote to his non-Mormon friend. "I have always rather worshipped *facts*," he continued, "and while I thought and read for a while, many of the incidents of life, experiences and circumstances led, unaided by the spirit of faith, to the position of the atheist, yet the faith of my fathers led me to abandon all that and to refrain from following it. . . . For me there seemed to be no alternative. I could only build up a doubt.—If I were to attempt to rationalize about my life here, and the life to come, I would be drowned in a sea of doubt."[68]

All the confidence of J. Reuben Clark's commitment to rational inquiry in religious matters evaporated. He had once believed that in intellectual faith "we may not probably take an affirmative stand, i.e., adopt something new but we may dispense with something," but Reuben found that such an attempt could only lead to dispensing with everything. As he cast about for some way of explaining his position to others, he discovered an anecdote about Abraham Lincoln, who justified reading the Bible despite his reputed agnosticism with the comment: "I have learned to read the Bible. I believe all I can and take the rest on faith." To a friend, Reuben related the Lincoln story and added, "Substituting in substance the words 'our Mormon Scriptures,' you will have about my situation."[69] He later commended that anecdote to a general conference of the Church.[70] Convinced that no religious faith could withstand uncompromising intellectual inquiry, Reuben concluded that in Babylon as well as in Zion, the refusal to rationalize one's religious beliefs was the highest manifestation of faith.

As he was resolving his crisis of faith in the solitude of his New York City study, Luacine was struggling to resolve her crisis of identity in Salt Lake City. She was in the third year of intermittent separation from her husband's career nearly three thousand miles away. He had returned from the Washington Arms Conference to give a majesterial nod of acquiescence to the efforts of his friends to get him elected U.S. Senator from Utah. He wanted the office without stooping to campaign for it, and he was strangely miffed when the Republican Convention in July 1922 steamrolled over his lackluster "availability," and gave the party's banner to his well-organized Jewish opponent.[71] It was now 1923. Reuben was in New York, as usual, and Luacine was abjectly alone in Salt Lake City. This year became a watershed in their personal lives and in his own religious development.

Reuben Clark's life was changed by loving reproof from the deserts of Zion and by the ruthless currents of Babylon. On 6 January 1923 Luacine reported that their last child, her namesake, was baptized, like the rest of their children, in her father's absence.[72] His daily letters poured forth his anticipations that his legal work for the American International Corporation (AIC) would finally bring them the financial bonanza to make all their sacrifices worthwhile. Lute had heard this for twenty years, and no longer believed in the dream. On 14 January she reported that their teenage son, Reuben III, was refusing to attend his church meetings, and she concluded: "While it can't be helped, it seems a pity that our only boy should have to be away from his father when he is going through the most trying period of his life. I hope your work and ambitions are worth the sacrifice."[73]

In the next few months, Lute peppered her daily letters with her anxieties and frustrations about their situation. She recounted how she "nearly went to pieces trying to adjust herself" to their prolonged separations but had finally resigned herself to living that way indefinitely, even though it embarrassed her to have neighborhood servants assume that she was a widow. She asked him "to frame up a nice speech for me to make when I am asked when you are coming home," and she feared he would miss their silver wedding anniversary.[74] She reminded him that "everyone loves to hear you talk" in church meetings, and urged Reuben to seek out those opportunities.[75] But he seemed so close to making all his dreams and sacrifices as a secular Mormon worthwhile that he continued his seven-day work weeks for the AIC.[76] But internal problems at the AIC were forcing him either to cooperate in unethical transactions or to risk losing his job. For Reuben the outcome was inevitable.[77]

His letter of 12 July 1923 "flabbergasted" Lute with the announcement that he was leaving his position at the AIC and returning home for good. Twenty years in Babylon were at an end for him. Although he would return in unexpected ways to the world he was now leaving, Reuben would never again feel the same detachment from his desert Zion. "I have longed for this news and of course was thrilled," Lute wrote, "but when I think of your schemes and what this means to you, I feel I should not rejoice so exceedingly." She added later: "I know your future can't look very rosy to you, but I am sure we won't starve, we can live on love for a while."[78]

J. Reuben Clark's first talk after his return to Salt Lake City in 1923 was unabashedly religious: "The Purpose of Sabbath Meetings." He continued to speak in church on such secular topics as "America's Contribution to World Peace" and "Memorial Day," but during the next six years he gave more than thirty sermons in Salt Lake City, Washington, and New York on "Christmas," "Easter," "We Stand for an Individual Testimony of the Divinity of Jesus Christ," "Divine Authority and the Latter-day Saints," "Divinity of Jesus Christ," "the Testimony of John," "Faith," "Genealogy," "Joseph Smith," "Obedience," "Salvation for the Dead," "The Personality of God," "The Book of Mormon," "The Material Age," "The Mission of Motherhood," "Testimony," "The Free Agency of Man," "Administering to the Sick," and "The Crucifixion."[79] For the first time since he went to Columbia University in 1903, Reuben was completely active in the Church.[80] On 7 June 1925 he was named to the general board of the Young Men's Mutual Improvement Association,[81] and during 1925 and 1926 he lectured to departing missionaries, talked to tourists at the Sunday morning service at the Salt Lake Tabernacle, and gave a series of sermons on Church-owned KSL radio.[82] To a close friend in the State Department he wrote: "I thoroughly enjoy living out here in the desert wilderness and while I miss the fleshpots of Egypt and sometimes I am in sad need of a helping from them, I am still quite willing to forego the mere lucre for the sake of the real life which I am able to live."[83]

In April 1926 a telegram from the State Department summoned J. Reuben Clark back to Washington for the first of a series of government appointments that would thrust him into the international limelight. During the first decade of his career he voluntarily left his Mormon home to seek fulfillment of his aspirations for civil service and wealth. When he chose to leave those aspirations in 1923 and return to his Utah home, Reuben assumed that the price of his renewed devotion to the interests of his family and his religion was the loss of a future career in his government's service. As it turned out, a divine providence decreed that no longer would J. Reuben Clark, Jr. need to seek opportunities for position, power, and prestige in the world, because these would be thrust upon him throughout the balance of his life. He had been willing to surrender his secular dreams to return to his people, church, and family; and his rewards would be greater and more varied than he could have imagined in 1923.

The next seven years were delayed ripples from his plunge into the morass of the 1910–13 Mexican Revolution. The revolution jolted Mexican society with such force that American interests were involved, often disastrously, from the start. Decades later the shock waves of this first social revolution of the twentieth century continued to jolt the diplomacy of Mexico and its overbearing colossus to the North, the United States. From 1926 to 1927, Reuben Clark was first Agent and then General Counsel of the American Agency of the United States-Mexico Mixed Claims Commission, which was charged with settling nearly one billion dollars of claims by U.S. citizens against Mexico for losses suffered during the revolution. He found the bureaucratic maze within the American commission as convoluted as the claims themselves, and was less than satisfied with his accomplishments.[84] But Reuben was dealing with the "possible" rather than the "desirable," and officials in Washington and Mexico City were impressed with his encyclopedic understanding of the issues, particularly the claims of oil companies against the Mexican government. As a result, from 1927 to 1928 he found himself scurrying between Washington and Mexico as special adviser to the U.S. Ambassador to Mexico, Dwight W. Morrow.[85]

When he was asked to become Under Secretary of State, Reuben was actually irritated at his government's interruption of what he thought would be the conclusion of his work in Mexico. He managed to transcend his administrative routine as under secretary by including an incisive analysis as a preface to what was intended by the Secretary of State as a routine compilation of statements concerning the Monroe Doctrine. The result was J. Reuben Clark, Jr.'s crowning publication, the *Clark Memorandum on the Monroe Doctrine,* which defined the limits and abuses of the historic document that had intimidated Latin America more than Europe.[86]

The Clarks returned to Mexico in 1929 for Reuben to continue his advisory position with Ambassador Morrow, and on 3 October 1930, upon Dwight Morrow's resignation to fill the unexpired term of New Jersey Senator Walter E. Edge, J. Reuben Clark, Jr. was appointed U.S. Ambassador to Mexico. From that date to February 1933 he represented the crucial interests of his government in the Latin land he had grown to love.[87]

Ambassador Clark faced a number of diplomatic and personal challenges in Mexico. On the strictly diplomatic side, he had to cope not only with problems common to any embassy, but also with special ones deriving from the Mexican Revolution. His judicious work with the Mixed Claims Commission, his association with the highly popular Dwight Morrow, and his scathing *Memorandum on the Monroe Doctrine* all helped smooth his ambassadorial relations with Mexican officials. On the personal side, Reuben's modest means had been a topic of newspaper discussion as well as government debate as to whether he could afford to be ambassador, since ambassadors traditionally spent thousands of dollars of their own money to conduct the obligatory social diplomacy that exceeded government stipends to embassies. He solved that by spending virtually his entire personal savings on a stringently reduced embassy expenditures budget. The last challenges involved, typically, Reuben's Mormonism.

The first issue was the Latter-day Saint Word of Wisdom, and it received the greatest publicity. Long before the ratification of the Eighteenth Amendment in 1920, the Clarks served lemonade rather than alcohol to prestigious government guests in Washington. Their

Under Secretary of State, 1928.

choice was awkward, but U.S. officials indulged them. It would have been another matter, however, for Ambassador Clark to require alcoholic abstention of diplomatic guests due to his religious beliefs. The existence of Prohibition as the law of the land was the way out. All embassies technically were territories of their respective nations, and Reuben announced that since Prohibition was the law of the land in the United States, it would be strictly observed within the Mexican Embassy. Because he was apparently the only ambassador to apply such legalism, he received his share of newspaper criticism. Nevertheless, from 1930 to 1933 the embassy in Mexico City served punch, grape juice, and lemonade rather than port, claret, and scotch.[88]

COURTESY HAROLD B. LEE LIBRARY

Ambassador Clark presenting his credentials to President Ortiz Rubio of Mexico, 1930.

There were limits, however, to the extent to which he could insist on strict observance of the Word of Wisdom. Ambassador Clark could prohibit alcohol in the embassy on legal grounds, and he could politely decline to accept the obligatory cigars in diplomatic exchanges, but he could hardly refuse to allow diplomats and other visitors to use tobacco in the embassy.[89] Still more difficult was Ambassador Clark's necessary attendance at almost nightly socials as the honored guest of other foreign diplomats and of Mexican officials who provided alcoholic beverages to him as part of the art of diplomacy. He described his response to this situation:

As to the cocktails: When we were in Mexico I usually quietly waived the cocktail aside. However, when so to waive it was too conspicuous I took it, raised it to my lips, held it, and set it down at the first opportunity. . . .

31

When you are at dinners where coffee is served, or liquors, you can more or less ostentatiously and actor-like turn the coffee cup upside down and ditto with the liquor glasses, accompanied by some loud remark about you being a tee-totaller. This is of course void of all tact and may get you in trouble.[90]

J. Reuben Clark, Jr. was not the first Mormon to develop social contacts with government officials in the United States, but he was a pioneer in living the Word of Wisdom in diplomatic situations where social offense could affect the relations between nations.

Another difficulty for the Clarks in Mexico was the matter of participation in Church services, an issue of delicate diplomatic consequence at the time. Mexico had a long tradition of anticlericalism and conflicts with the Roman Catholic Church, and the revolutionary Constitution of 1917 embodied draconian restrictions on church prerogatives. Although directed at Roman Catholicism, these constitutional measures applied to all religious bodies in Mexico. Among the supplementary decrees by the presidents of Mexico was one in 1927 which prohibited foreigners from participating in religious propaganda in any church or other public place.[91]

The Clarks came to Mexico as regular attenders of church services but faced the language barrier and the question of the emotional, sometimes violent, church-state conflict in Mexico. Might there be diplomatic repercussions from the regular attendance of the U.S. Ambassador at services of a religious organization originally based on proselyting by foreign missionaries? On the other hand, native Mexican Saints knew that he was a Latter-day Saint from the world headquarters of their church and that he had spoken at a Church general conference just prior to assuming his ambassadorial duties. If Ambassador Clark declined to participate or speak in any Church services to avoid even the suspicion of violating Mexican law, would he offend the testimonies of the Mexican Saints who might think that their "representative" from Church headquarters was shunning them? Rather than choose either alternative exclusively, he decided on a careful middle course.

Ambassador Clark navigated between the diplomatic and religious hazards by attending and speaking at Church services in Mexico in a limited way. Reuben went with his family to the little Mexican branch on the average of once a month while he was ambassador.[92] To a Latter-day Saint in Utah he wrote, "You ask whether we have any L.D.S. meetings here, in reply to which I wish to say that we have some Indian members who have meetings near here and that occasionally Sister Clark and I go to them, but since they are conducted in Spanish, we do not get much of what is going on."[93] When he did attend the Mexican branch, it was usually to speak, and on several occasions he spoke "a few words in Spanish."[94] His wife also tried to speak to the Saints in their native tongue, and their daughter Luacine delighted everyone with her fluency in Spanish at branch meetings.[95]

Coping with the Spanish language and the church-state restrictions were burdensome to Reuben. After attending a meeting of the Saints across the border in El Paso, Texas, he wrote Luacine, "It did seem good however to understand the whole service, to be able to speak at the *service* instead of at a social."[96] Still, next to the president of the Mexican Mission, Ambassador Clark was the most important representative of the Church there: the First Presidency corresponded with him about Mexican Church affairs; he and the Mexican branch president together selected the site for a future chapel, and when the Mexican branch honored Reuben at his final departure from Mexico, "Pres. Juarez arose to speak [and] he was so overcome he could scarcely talk. When he finished he really wept."[97]

Under the circumstances, the Clark family spent most of their Sundays as a respite from the hectic days and nights of the rest of the diplomatic week. After sleeping late, and a quiet lunch, they sometimes attended concerts, or toured the pyramids with Utah visitors.[98] Social activity was infrequent and low-keyed. "Slept late. Ione and Harold Kidder came to have dinner with Luacine. Spent the day here, went to Kidders in the evening. At four thirty we went to a Tea in San Angel to the McGregor Mills. Spent some time in the garden. After supper we entertained 15 guests listening to Movie Actors talking over the Radio—served refreshments."[99]

Reuben's life in Mexico was generally less hectic than the previous twenty-five years of his life. Aside from the unprecedented experience of his taking time in Mexico to be a tourist, he renewed his youthful expertise in horseback riding. He became so serious an equestrian in Mexico that he obtained a leather riding suit for his regular horseback rides. Moreover, it was in Mexico that Reuben discovered the world of grand opera.[100]

As was his custom, Reuben spent many hours in his study, but his thought and energies were increasingly upon the things of the spirit. To his missionary son he wrote: "May the Lord bless you spiritually with a rich outpouring of the gift of the Holy Ghost that there may come to you such spiritual gifts as will aid you in reaching the honest in heart, may he give you faith, humility, wisdom, and cleanliness of spirit; may he bless you mentally that you may have cleanliness of mind, that your understanding may be quickened, your memory strengthened, your mental processes intensified and enlarged that you may comprehend more and more of the Gospel and be able to impart it to others to bring them to a knowledge of the truth. . . ."[101] Ambassador Clark himself was trying to understand "more and more of the Gospel" for the purpose of writing a *magnum opus* on the Mission of Christ. He asked his son-in-law to send to him scholarly studies of the New Testament,[102] and when free of other obligations the ambassador studied these books in relation to the standard works of the Church.

Reuben described the scope of his project in a letter to John A. Widtsoe, his son's supervising missionary president and a member of the Quorum of the Twelve Apostles. He wanted to begin with an analysis of "the philosophy which lies behind John's great Hymn to the Messiah. . . . Then I am trying to make rather full discussion of Priesthood . . . I am treating the subject by dispensations, tracing the Priesthood line, showing as far as possible the functions and duties of the Priesthood as disclosed by the record of each dispensation. The Mosaic Dispensation is a very large order by itself. There will be more pages and a more elaborate discussion of details than I have seen brought together in one place. . . . Other subjects besides the Priesthood will be the Godhead, faith, baptism, resurrection, work for the dead, etc."[103] He would never have sufficient time to complete such a massive study, and a decade later John A. Widtsoe would publish (under the direction of the Quorum of the Twelve Apostles) a study of priesthood along the lines the ambassador envisioned. But Elder Widtsoe and other General Authorities of the Church were increasingly impressed with J. Reuben Clark, who had been heralded as early as 1914 in Church publications as a "Utah Boy . . . who, entirely upon his own merits and in a surprisingly short time, has arisen to a position of international prominence and honor."[104]

The most important of his watchful admirers in the Church was Heber J. Grant, who became Church President in November 1918. Three months earlier, President Grant said he had heard that, for his age, Reuben "was the greatest international lawyer in the U.S."[105] A year later President Grant was advocating U.S. participation in the League of Nations, and found that the talents of this able international lawyer were undermining those efforts. Reuben used his eloquent and masterful analysis in anti-League talks to overflow crowds of ten thousand in the Salt Lake Tabernacle and elsewhere in Utah. President Grant continued to support the League of Nations, but respected Clark's views.[106] In June 1920 President Grant, in New York City on business for the Utah-Idaho Sugar Company, stopped in at Reuben's law offices and asked him for "general friendly advice" about the contract which had already been approved by Church lawyers.[107]

Although Heber J. Grant and J. Reuben Clark did not have a close association prior to the 1930s, the Church President expressed enough confidence in the younger man that Reuben had the courage to give unsolicited advice on Church matters during the 1920s. When the First Presidency announced in 1922 that the new mission president in New York City would be B. H. Roberts, who had been excluded from the U.S. House of Representatives in 1900 for having plural wives, Reuben dashed off an immediate letter of concern.[108] President Grant's reply thanked Reuben for his letter, agreed that Roberts's presence might stir up controversy, but drily noted that "I can not help but feel that in your enthusiastic interest for the welfare of the Church in that splendid mission you are perhaps a little over exercised about the matter."[109]

Undaunted by the mild rebuff and encouraged by President Grant's sympathetic reception of advice, Reuben even prepared drafts of official proclamations he thought should be presented to general conferences of the Church. In September 1923 Reuben drafted a resolution for the October conference that he thought would permanently resolve the question of Church interference in politics:

First: That from and after this date no member of the First Presidency or the Quorum of the Twelve shall participate in any political discussions or activities of any nature whatsoever, nor seek to exercise either directly or indirectly or publicly or privately any influence or control in any political matters whatsoever ... [excluding] matters of morals or temperance ... but in such discussions there shall be no discussion of parties, or their principles, or candidates.

Second: That from and after this date no members of the Quorum of the Twelve shall accept any office or employment of profit or trust under the State or the Federal Government, or under any county, city, or municipality of the state, nor any nomination or appointment for such office.

Third: Any member failing to obey either or both of the two foregoing rules shall by that act forfeit his membership in the Quorum of the First Presidency or in the Quorum of the Twelve respectively and he shall not be again eligible for membership in such Quorums.[110]

Reuben may have been disappointed that the First Presidency did not issue such a sweeping proclamation in October 1923, but he remained a Republican loyalist despite his implacable opposition to political activity by General Authorities. He even gave the nominating speech on 9 May 1924 for Reed Smoot to be Utah's delegate to the Republican National Convention.[111]

During the next seven years he continued to attract the attention of President Grant. He researched the legal background and consulted with other General Authorities about President Grant's cherished, but unrealized, plan for providing life insurance for priesthood bearers of the Church.[112] He displayed extraordinary skills as an orator in ward sacrament meetings, and Heber J. Grant told the April 1926 general conference that Reuben's recent radio talk was "one of the finest sermons on Priesthood that I have listened to."[113] Reuben's unsuccessful 1928 campaign to secure the Republican nomination for the U.S. Senate and his appointments as Under Secretary of State and U.S. Ambassador to Mexico brought much attention by national leaders and newspapers to Utah and the Church—so much that Heber J. Grant concluded that J. Reuben Clark, Jr. was a rank-and-file Latter-day Saint without peer. He invited Reuben to speak for the first time at a general conference of the Church in October 1930, and introduced the newly appointed ambassador with the words, "All Utahns are proud of the honor that has come to one of our citizens."[114]

In view of his unparalleled prominence among Utah Mormons it is not surprising that traditional speculations about new appointments to the apostleship included the ambassador. On 19 May 1931 one of his Salt Lake City friends reported the gossip that he was to fill a vacancy in the Quorum of the Twelve Apostles. With typical bluntness, Reuben answered, "I think there is no more danger of my being named [an Apostle] than there is of my flying to the moon. I have never sought or craved church office."[115] However, there was more substance to the gossip than he dreamed possible.

On the day after the report of this popular speculation, President Grant's journal records that there was serious discussion of the ambassador as a possible choice to fill the current vacancy.[116] President Grant himself wrote, "Unless I get the impression otherwise, I am unqualifiedly in favor of Brother Clark." Nevertheless, the First Presidency prayerfully contemplated the choice for five months, and President Grant felt impressed to call another man.[117]

On 11 December 1931 another vacancy occurred with the death of Charles W. Nibley, Second Counselor in the First Presidency. President Grant's first choice as counselor might have been Senator Reed Smoot, but he had decided not to call Smoot as a counselor in 1925 because "it would not do for [Reed Smoot] to leave the Senate as [he] could do more good there for our people than in any other position."[118] In 1931 President Grant still believed Elder Smoot's most important service was in the U.S. Senate, and therefore he thought more deeply about his choice for a new counselor. It had been more than half a century since a man had been advanced to the First Presidency without already being a General Authority, and then Brigham Young had chosen his own son for the position. Farther back than that, he remembered that President Young had chosen President Grant's father-in-law, Daniel H. Wells, as a counselor in 1857. Although President Wells had had no significant ecclesiastical experience, he had been prominent in civil office in Nauvoo and Utah. Suddenly, as Presidents Grant and Ivins renewed one of their many discussions about a replacement for Charles W. Nibley, Heber J. Grant exclaimed, "I know who we can get. This man Clark, the Ambassador to Mexico." "You can't get him, Heber," Ivins replied, "because he is a $100,000 a year man." President Grant gave a characteristic chuckle and said, "We can ask him."[119]

It was just before Christmas 1931, in Mexico City. Louise and Marianne were visiting their parents in the embassy. As Louise sorted through the day's mail, she found a letter from the First Presidency to her father. "It's for you from President Grant," Louise said with merriment, "he is probably asking you to be his counselor." Louise joined in the laughter this seemed to produce in the entire family but then noticed the ashen appearance of her father's face as she handed him the letter. Reuben turned the letter over in his hands, examined the return address, and slowly put it into his coat pocket without opening it. When conversation seemed to lag, he excused himself, went to his study, and locked the door.[120]

J. Reuben Clark felt he already knew the meaning of the letter as he slowly opened the envelope, but he refused to believe his feelings, because it was not rational to have such thoughts or fears. His eyes

The Clark family on the steps of the embassy at Mexico City, December 1931, at the time Reuben received the letter calling him to the First Presidency.

quickly skimmed through the usual greetings, the reminder of President Nibley's death, and then froze on the words, "After prayerful consideration our minds definitely revert to you as the man whom the Lord desires to fill this vacancy."[121] The rest of the letter became a blur as the ambassador absently brushed his hand across moist cheeks. "Gone were the dreams of a lifetime in law, vanished the ambitions of his life!"[122] His brother's death, his sisters' deaths, his father's death, his humiliating political defeats—nothing so overwhelmed Reuben as this letter from the President of the Church. For a while he sat at his desk as if in a daze, then slowly Reuben read the letter again and again. As he did, his mind was bombarded with discordant thoughts, "give up my life's work ... thrust aside financial opportunities that promise very large returns ... about to the time when I might begin to garner a real harvest. . . ."[123]

After what seemed a lifetime of contemplation in his study, he thought he knew how to respond. His reply took him hours to complete. First, Reuben wrote a long "MEMORANDUM OF EXPLANATION" concerning the nature of his assignment by U.S. President Hoover and Secretary of State Stimson in Mexico, the fact that the negotiations were still in progress, and closing with his fear that President Hoover would consider him a "deserter" if he resigned as ambassador to become a member of the First Presidency. Then Reuben wrote a cover letter for this memorandum, and absentmindedly dated it 19 December 1931, the date of the Presidency's letter to him rather than the date of his reply:

> On the other hand, you Brethren must have an enormous amount of work and be in need of help, so much so that you will not care to postpone filling the vacancy for an indefinite time.
> In this latter event, I can conceive that, if you think it best not to give opportunity for irritation [to President Hoover and Secretary Stimson] through my leaving before they desire it, you may wish—instead of waiting for me—to fill the vacancy by appointing some one else. If you take this view, I hope you will feel entirely free to act.[124]

It was a supreme example of J. Reuben Clark's diplomacy: he had not actually declined the invitation to become a counselor in the First Presidency, in fact he had even expressed gratitude for their confidence in him, but he had presented the situation in terms that would probably lead President Grant to choose another man as counselor rather than wait for Ambassador Clark to complete his work in Mexico.

Reuben felt emotionally drained as he finished his last rereading of the memorandum and letter. Instead of folding the pages, addressing an envelope to the Presidency, and putting the letter with next day's outgoing embassy mail, he put the Presidency's letter, his memorandum, and his letter in a locked drawer without folding them. He felt exhausted and frustrated—too disconcerted to tell even his wife about the First Presidency's letter and his reply. He tried to go through the motions of enjoying Christmas Eve and Christmas Day, but his unexplained dejection infected the whole family. It was the worst Christmas the Clarks ever experienced, yet no one asked Reuben what the problem was because they knew the impenetrable silences of "The Great Sphinx" of the family too well. Finally, Reuben told Lute of the First Presidency's letter to him. His own feelings had been so somber that he had no anticipation of her joyful reaction to the news. He did not tell her of his memorandum and reply.[125]

Reuben took the sheets of paper from the locked drawer on 28 December, reread them, and laid them to one side of the desk top. He then wrote a different letter to the First Presidency.

I have never aspired to Church office—its honor and dignity I appreciated, but its responsibilities seemed too grave. I do not now so aspire. If I felt that my personal preferences should now control me, I would ask to be allowed to continue working in the ranks.

But when, as now, a call comes from my superior officers, charged with the responsibility of presiding over the Church and acting under the inspiration of the Lord, then I, responsive to my training and my faith, must answer to the call, not only as a clear duty but as a great privilege.

It is for the Lord to say how and where I shall serve. I trust Him to help me meet the responsibilities of my task.

I know, at least in part, my own shortcomings and unworthiness. I appreciate the honor the call brings to me.

This letter was from his heart and his love for his heritage. The other letter and memorandum were from his head and the lifelong strivings to succeed in a world that could not comprehend him. He placed this letter of acceptance on top of his letter of demurring and the memorandum, folded them together, and mailed the fat envelope to the First Presidency. Now it was out of his hands; it was their decision.[126]

When Reuben's letter arrived at the First Presidency's office on 2 January 1932, President Grant was in California, and Anthony W. Ivins opened the envelope. As soon as he read the reply of 28 December, President Ivins telegraphed Heber J. Grant, "Party agreeable to our recommendations. Beautiful letter."[127] If President Ivins looked at the long memorandum and other cover letter, he did little more than skim them, and probably never realized that Reuben had expected the First Presidency to make a conscious choice between his brief letter of acceptance and his detailed suggestion that they choose someone else as Second Counselor. To President Ivins the other pages in the envelope probably seemed only to be the background for a beautiful letter of acceptance, and Reuben would have agreed.

The next year was a very difficult one for Ambassador Clark. He tried to wrap up negotiations in Mexico, and contemplate how and when he would submit his resignation to the U.S. President. At the same time he had to give whatever comfort he could to an over-worked and incomplete First Presidency who wanted him to assume Church work as soon as possible. Still another problem involved rumors and second-guessing about his Church office and public office.

On 9 January 1932 Reuben wrote Heber J. Grant to express his concern about the timing of his resignation as ambassador. But these were not his worst fears:

> I have gathered from your letters that you wish to announce my appointment at the April Conference, even though I might still be here. I am afraid that the Mexican Government, in its present temper, would not wish to have a high Church official of any Church stationed here as American Ambassador. If they took this attitude, they might ask for my recall, which would be a grave reflection not only upon myself (which might be disregarded) but also upon the United States and upon the Church.[128]

On 3 March 1932, after his return from a trip to Washington and New York, President Grant informed the Quorum of the Twelve that he had chosen Reuben as his Second Counselor, but that the appointment could not be announced until he was free of his ambassadorial responsibilities. The next day President Grant wrote that

Reuben should leave Mexico with full approval of the U.S. President and the Secretary of State and that nothing should be done to bring the "calamity" of his recall as Ambassador to Mexico. This letter relieved Reuben's anxieties and also reassured him of the acceptance by the Quorum of the Twelve of his appointment. Elder Melvin J. Ballard was visiting in Mexico when President Grant announced the appointment to the Quorum.[129] Since Reuben was telling no one about it, Elder Ballard came to the next meeting of the Quorum of the Twelve in complete ignorance of developments. At first Brother Ballard could not understand why he caused such amusement when "he remarked that he had met a young man in Mexico City who because of his integrity, testimony, power and ability could some day be used in the higher councils."[130]

In his letters to President Grant of 11 March and 20 June 1932, Reuben enclosed correspondence he had exchanged with Utahns who were urging him to allow Republican leaders to nominate him for candidacy as governor or as senator. "I do not suppose there is the slightest chance of the Republican Convention nominating me for governor when I am not a candidate for the nomination," he wrote on 20 June, "but if the idea should show signs of life, I hope you can find a way to kill it."[131] Since his unsuccessful efforts to get his party's nomination in 1928, he had achieved such distinction in government service that not even the divided Republican party of Utah could have denied him the nomination had he sought it. But his acceptance letter to the Presidency of 28 December 1931 had changed everything, even though he could not explain that to his bewildered political supporters in Utah. On 28 August 1932 he wrote President Ivins, requesting that he be excused from attending October conference lest he be dragged into the election campaign, and added: "Ever since I received the first letter from you Brethren, I have been under constant strain and, at times, much anxiety lest the course I was following was not the course I should follow. I have constantly prayed about the matter and have had no answer other than a constant feeling that I should finish here fully to guard against my being swayed by personal considerations. . . . I am constantly trying to learn what the Lord wants and to do it. Whatever help you Brethren shall give me will be most thankfully received."[132]

The Democratic landslide in the November election of 1932 simplified the timing and circumstances of Reuben's resignation as ambassador. As a Republican officeholder he gracefully departed his diplomatic post just prior to his party's departure from the White House.[133]

He was hard put to be equally adroit in responding to rumors and queries that began as soon as President Grant informed the Quorum of the Twelve of his call. When a member of the Church in New York City congratulated him on his call to the Presidency on 19 April 1932, Reuben replied:

> I am obliged to inform you that I have not been so appointed. During the past few months I have been made, by rumor in Utah, Governor of the State, United States Senator from the State, a member of the Quorum of the Twelve, and a Councillor to President Grant. . . .
>
> As I recently wrote a friend of mine, I suppose I shall have to wait until I return to the State of Utah in order to work out which, if any, of these various honors may be mine.[134]

As time went by without public announcement of a new counselor, Utah gossip concluded that President Grant was delaying because he wanted Reed Smoot as counselor and hoped that Smoot would be defeated in the November election. In the process of protecting Senator Smoot from the political consequences of that rumor, President Grant nearly tipped his hand regarding Reuben. In a statement of 29 October 1932 the First Presidency said that Reed Smoot was not in line for the position of counselor because "selection was made months ago and accepted," and on 3 November President Grant added that the man "who has accepted is hampered by business from accepting at this time."[135]

By early 1933 all the rumors pointed to J. Reuben Clark as the new counselor, but he could not acknowledge their truth as long as he was ambassador and as long as the First Presidency had not made an official announcement.[136] When reporters in Austin, Texas, asked the Clarks on 16 February why they were returning to Salt Lake City, Lute laughed, "To get back to work and make a little money," and when asked the question again upon their arrival in Salt Lake City, Reuben replied, "I'm a candidate for the law business."[137]

J. Reuben Clark

On 20 March 1933 J. Reuben Clark's mind swirled with thoughts and images. He had been baptized shortly before Heber J. Grant became his stake president, and now they were to meet for the first time since he agreed to join the Presidency of the Church. As Reuben ascended the granite stairs, he thought of his steps from Grantsville, to Salt Lake City, to Columbia University, to the State Department, to the Embassy in Mexico. He looked up at the inscription above the doors he was about to enter, "Administration Building of The Church of Jesus Christ of Latter-day Saints." He was now sixty-one years old, and he thought fleetingly of the steps he had hoped to take—to Park Avenue, to the Utah Governor's Mansion, to the U.S. Senate, to the Cabinet, perhaps to the U.S. Supreme Court. Then Reuben remembered a passage from Dante: "Abandon hope, ye who enter here," smiled to himself, and crossed the portals.[138]

"THE DIFFERENCES OF ADMINISTRATION"

Doctrine and Covenants 46:15

Through the publicity of his governmental achievements for more than twenty-five years, J. Reuben Clark was no stranger to Church administrators, but he was a stranger to Church administration when he entered the First Presidency in 1933. Whereas nearly all his predecessors had years of service as local presiding officers and General Authorities prior to their appointment as counselors in the First Presidency, Reuben remarked, "The bulk of the work which I did in the Church until I was called to my present position was as a teacher in the Sunday Schools."[1] He had learned his administrative skills in law and government and seemed to introduce a different style to Church administration.

A major difference was his lifelong practice of doing intensive personal research on a question and then preparing a detailed analysis of the matter in a memorandum. Few, if any, of his predecessors did their own research concerning the subjects about which they had to make decisions but instead delegated the research to a clerk or secretary, who summarized it for them. President Clark's departure from that practice awed his associates. Marion G. Romney observed, "Brother Clark was a student. He never said anything or did anything that he couldn't back up with the authorities. And nobody could ever find a loophole in his presentation"—a view echoed by Spencer W. Kimball.[2] Another admirer of his administrative style wrote:

> For a long time I have watched the way you have decided matters, always carefully dissecting them from every angle and taking a firm stand according to your decision regardless of circumstances or other people's opinions. For this reason, I have come to regard your views as impartial and always built up from solid rock.[3]

Even when he did not do academic research into a matter, President Clark approached every decision with probing verbal questions, a process of administrative interrogation. This was a product of his law school training and government service. Although several General Authorities had obtained their doctorates from universities, he was the first member of the First Presidency who had ever earned a graduate degree and was almost alone in having completed college. All these factors lent tremendous stature to J. Reuben Clark as a Church administrator.

Because he arrived at decisions slowly, after much research and analysis, Reuben tended to maintain his views rather inflexibly once he came to a conclusion. At times this tendency exasperated his wife, Lute, who once reported a business assessment by Reuben's brother with the comment, "I feel you won't consider this at all, feeling your way is best. I only tell you this hoping you may get some one's viewpoint besides your own."[4] He was the last person to deny the inflexibility of his opinions and conclusions and once made an ironic observation about this trait in a letter to his brother: "We Clarks are a good deal like the Harvard man,—you can tell a Harvard man wherever you see him—but you can't tell him much. Even so with us."[5]

Unwillingness to reconsider his decisions had possible disadvantages, but it was the product of intensive reflection rather than quick judgment. In fact, President Clark did his best to avoid prejudicial judgment, as he once wrote:

> The directing of the affairs of the Church is an over-powering responsibility and undertaking. No man can properly approach it except in the deepest humility, with something of an adequate realization of his own limitations, his prejudices, predilections, and human judgment. But every man with Church responsibility must try to cope with and bring under control these elements so far as it is possible for him to do.[6]

With that kind of caution, he arrived at decisions slowly but firmly. In fact, it was the stability of his well-considered views that caused so many of his associates to use images like "solid rock" in describing J. Reuben Clark.

Through his experience in private law practice and in government service, Reuben had also developed the trait of expressing himself emphatically. To some extent in correspondence, but especially in verbal communication where there was no written record, he often repeated his essential points as many as four times.[7] This was especially his practice in declining a request: "when you tell people no, you better tell it in emphatic terms; if you say it in a nice way they think you indicate yes."[8] To those in the Church who were unaccustomed to such firmness of expression, President Clark's practice of "rarely pulling punches" seemed harsh at times, especially when combined with his habit of using a gruff tone when engaged in good-natured banter.[9] These were simply administrative approaches that had worked well for him during many years of government service and which he almost unconsciously continued in Church administration.

Although he might attribute it to his Woolley ancestry, J. Reuben Clark's blunt statement of the facts as he perceived them was equally a product of government service. He had too often seen petty bureaucrats attempt to ingratiate themselves with their superiors by providing selective information. As a member of the First Presidency, he refused to engage in such practice: "I admonished President Grant that people were prone to say to him what people thought he wanted to hear."[10] Nevertheless, President Clark carefully avoided the pitfall of trying to convert the President to a particular point of view:

> I have always felt that as a second man it was my duty fully to explain any views that I had on any problem and to make sure they were understood by my Chief, but that there my responsibility ended. It was for the Chief to make up his mind what he wanted to do. It was not my business to try to over-persuade him to do as I thought he should do. I am not sure this is the right attitude, but I am sure it has kept me out of trouble sometimes. At any rate, it has eased off situations that might have led to real difficulties if I had been too insistent.[11]

He was too honest and strong willed to be a yes man or to cater to anyone's prejudices, but in counseling the President of the Church he also felt a special obligation to avoid even the hint of usurping the prerogative of a latter-day prophet. No matter what the circumstances, J. Reuben Clark, Jr. was a strong counselor but never the "power behind the throne."

In the decision-making process of the First Presidency, there was not always agreement (as President Clark often told members of the Church), but there was absolute loyalty to the final decision of the President. To one member of the Church he stated that there was often a free discussion of differing views in the Presidency "before a decision is reached, but everybody supports the decision, whatever his previous views were."[12] To his brother he wrote that the process of decision making by the Church President was not governed by majority rule, and he related an illustrative anecdote about Abraham Lincoln. When Lincoln once called for a vote on a matter, every member of his Cabinet voted for it, only he voted against it, and Lincoln declared that the balloting showed the negative voters won. In like manner, Reuben continued, "The President of the Council therefore declares the decision of the Council."[13] Members of the Presidency themselves were sometimes amused at the turnabouts this policy could produce. When the Apostle who had opposed the creation of a new stake in a particular place was the one who later helped organize the stake, a member of the First Presidency quipped, "Funny church, isn't it?"[14]

A corollary of that policy was President Clark's consistent practice of dissociating his views from the First Presidency when his statements pertained to matters upon which the President of the Church had not ruled. He understandably made such a distinction when he expressed partisan political views, but he also did it as a part of routine Church administration. For example, when he held a three-hour meeting with individuals "about general conditions and problems at B.Y.U. I made it clear I was not speaking for the Church nor the First Presidency."[15] President Clark realized that it was all too easy for members of the Church to assume that any expression of a member of the First Presidency was "Church policy" or had the specific approval of the Church President, and to guard against inaccurate assumptions of this nature, he carefully distinguished between his independent views and the statements he made by the authority of the Presidency.[16]

Loyal to the authority of his superiors in the First Presidency, he also respected the prerogatives of his subordinates in Church administration. For example, when two men traveled from Logan, Utah, to ask President Clark about a particular matter, "I told them that the matter was not one that was immediately under my charge, that it was in the hands of the Executive Committee of the Board of Education, and I would speak to Brother Joseph Fielding Smith about it."[17] Reuben had learned during his first years in the State Department how frustrating it was for a subordinate to have his responsibilities expropriated by a superior, and therefore he always sought to preserve and respect the principle of delegation in the Church.

President Clark was absolutely loyal to the prophets, seers, and revelators with whom he counseled, but he wanted also to help Church members avoid extremist views about the decisions of the First Presidency. Because he had direct experience with the give-and-take of decision making, the sometimes necessary reliance on incomplete information, and the human element that exists even within prophets, he tried to help the Latter-day Saints avoid the pitfall of assuming that decisions of the First Presidency were infallible. "We are not infallible in our judgment, and we err," he told the April 1940 conference, "but our constant prayer is that the Lord will guide us in our decisions, and we are trying so to live that our minds will be open to His inspiration."[18] He was even more blunt about his own limitations. To one critic he wrote, "I hoped I might escape a charge of insincerity, though I might not hope to escape the charge of ignorance or of inexperience. I have always tried to be honest however much I might be mistaken."[19] A man of intense views, he was also disarmingly unpretentious and candid. He knew the prophets as few know them; he saw how they struggled in faith and prayer to be the mouthpieces of God to His children on earth, and he joined with the rest of the First Presidency in seeking God's inspiration in all things. J. Reuben Clark gave his full loyalty and devotion to the President of the Church and expected the same of the Saints, but he wanted that loyalty to be untainted by the myth of infallibility.

Still another characteristic of his administrative style was an insistence on expeditious meetings. In government offices and in diplomacy, he had learned that lengthy meetings were usually counterproductive. Marion G. Romney observed that President Clark conducted administrative meetings "with great dispatch and efficiency."[20] Ernest L. Wilkinson simply observed that President Clark "always wanted brief meetings."[21]

A very important aspect of J. Reuben Clark's administrative approach was that he tried to think of all possible negative consequences of any proposal under discussion. Taking a "worst-case" approach to problem solving minimized unpleasant surprises but also tended toward a pessimism his secretary in the Presidency's office described as follows: "In his own life he has felt it wisest to approach problems from the point of view that things may get worse than better, for so approaching you are then prepared for the worst, if the worst comes."[22] This somber strategy went hand-in-hand with his intensive prior research, and the combination resulted in extraordinarily cautious decision making and implementation. If Reuben felt pressed for a conclusion, he acted swiftly with what information he possessed; but if the urgency was felt only by others, he wanted time to think through all the implications. This conservative approach may have spared him unwise decisions; its essential pessimism resulted in many fulfilled prophecies of doom, but it also limited innovation and made President Clark resistant to decisions based on optimistic projections from current circumstances.

One dimension of his personality that softened the impact of his occasional abruptness and forbidding manner was a keen sense of humor. A master of self-deprecation and irony, President Clark often delighted congregations with his dry humor. Church administrators who worked closely with him discovered still another side to his humor that was virtually unknown to other members of the Church. President Clark often relieved the tension or boredom of administrative meetings by indulging in slapstick mimicry of a specific individual known to the persons he entertained.[23]

One remaining personality trait affected how he could be approached as an administrator. Reuben had seen too much shallowness in the world to be influenced by flattery, and he had achieved too much success to need praise. "If you do not quit saying so many nice things," he wrote to Elder Richard R. Lyman, "you will have me believing them one of these days, and that would be a real tragedy."[24] Resistant to flattery himself, he had long been appalled at the susceptibility of the Latter-day Saints. In 1931 he wrote the president of Brigham Young University, "We repeat complimentary things said of us with so much gusto and smacking of our lips."[25] Once in the First Presidency, J. Reuben Clark plainly told his fellow Latter-day Saints that they were gullible to flattery:

> I wish that we could get over being flattered into almost anything. If any stranger comes among us and tells us how wonderful we are, he pretty nearly owns us. . . . You would not think of letting one of our own people suddenly blow into town, boost you a bit, and then carry him around on cushions. These approaches are crude and frequently disingenuous.[26]

Although most of his criticism focused on Mormon susceptibility to non-Mormon praise, he knew enough of human nature to realize that Church members of various ranks consciously or unconsciously used flattery to ingratiate themselves with Church leaders. Since President Clark was near the pinnacle of Church authority, where the possibilities of such approaches were greatest and most dangerous, he refused to accept any praise without a disclaimer.

J. Reuben Clark lacked previous experience in Church administration but often awed his associates in the councils of the Church. Every Church leader has his own strengths of personality and procedure, but Reuben brought to the Presidency an administrative style that was the distillation of twenty-five years of association, service, and negotiation with the highest leaders of business, national government, and international diplomacy. He had distinguished himself as a notable civil servant and would become known as an extraordinary Church leader.

"THREE PRESIDING HIGH PRIESTS"

Doctrine and Covenants 107:22

HEBER J. GRANT, 1933–1945

President Grant knew he was choosing a counselor who had little experience in Church administration, but he accurately concluded that the Church would obtain unparalleled recognition through the service of J. Reuben Clark, Jr., who had received various government appointments during the administrations of six U.S. Presidents. Reuben felt far more awkward about his lack of Church experience than President Grant did. After the general conference sustained him as Second Counselor on 9 April 1933, he said:

> Should any of you have hopes about my work in this high office to which I am called, I trust I shall not too much disappoint you. If any of you have misgivings, I can only say that your misgivings can hardly be greater than my own. I am keenly conscious of my own deficiencies. I come late in life to a new work.[1]

As Heber J. Grant's new Second Counselor, J. Reuben Clark launched his 1933 Church service in a whirlwind of public activity. He spoke at the graduation exercises of the LDS Hospital School of Nursing on 18 May, the McCune School of Music and Art on 22 May, the Utah State Agricultural College on 28 May, the University of Idaho at Pocatello on 4 June, and Earlham College in Indiana on 12 June. He also gave talks to the Salt Lake County Bar Association, the Provo Chamber of Commerce, and the Los Angeles Chamber of Commerce. President Clark's position in the First Presidency required his close attention to the many business activities of the Church, and within a matter of weeks he joined the boards of directors of ZCMI, Zion's Securities Corporation, U & I Sugar Company,

53

Beneficial Life Insurance Company, Zion's Savings Bank, Utah State National Bank, Hotel Temple Square, Hotel Utah, Heber J. Grant & Company, and Utah Home Fire Insurance Company. It was a dizzying pace even for one accustomed to intensive activity.[2]

President Clark's 1933 agenda of Church work began with equal intensity. From the end of April to early May, he was working on prepublication editing of General Authorities' talks at the April conference. On his own initiative he drafted a statement against unauthorized plural marriage, which he presented to the rest of the Presidency on 24 May and which they issued as an official statement on 17 June. On 20 July he presented a twenty-nine-page recommendation for Church relief work to the First Presidency. On 28 August he "discussed very briefly with President Grant the subject of Church divorce. I expressed the view we should tighten a bit," and three days later he volunteered to read every Church instructional manual prior to publication. Reuben told the April 1933 conference that he came to a new work late in life, but he came at full speed.[3]

At the same time President Clark was launching forward vigorously as a new member of the First Presidency in Salt Lake City, he was being pulled contrary to his own expectations and desires in other directions. He had been willing to forsake his dreams of flourishing in Babylon as a sacrifice for service in Zion, but Babylon was unwilling to forget J. Reuben Clark. This required President Clark to balance priorities of Church service and secular responsibilities, and at times he was no more comfortable with the tension between the two than he had been during the twenty years he had devoted himself primarily to secular achievement.

The effort at striking a balance would not have been necessary had Heber J. Grant asked his new counselor to devote himself exclusively to religious administration; but he wanted Reuben to maintain the esteem of the world's leaders, to be a spokesman for the Church on the civil matters in which Reuben had already gained the respect of non-Mormons, and to represent the First Presidency in secular contacts that would be possible only because of Reuben's pre-1933 government service. "I think that J. Reuben Clark Jr. is one of the great statesmen of America," President Grant wrote of his counselor, and then added: "He is the man of all men who could best

COURTESY THE IMPROVEMENT ERA

First Presidency, 9 April 1933.
Anthony W. Ivins, Heber J. Grant, J. Reuben Clark.

occupy the presidential chair in this present crisis in which we are situated."[4]

President Grant made it clear that he expected Reuben to serve the broad interests of the Church by means of his government service and associations. The Church President had sought to expand the esteem and influence of the Church through his own extensive business contacts, and he expected no less of the former ambassador to Mexico. President Clark described his own view in a letter to a newspaper editor:

> I never had much use for hermits who ran away from the problems of the world out into the desert and merely prayed. That has never seemed to me quite the highest type of human activity. So I must be allowed just a word of defense to say that while I am out in the desert and while I do pray, I am, nevertheless, trying to do a very great deal more.[5]

He described himself as one of his nation's "elder statesmen" and was likewise so designated in Church publications.[6]

He did not need to seek the role of elder statesman, for representatives of business, government, politics, and media throughout the United States repeatedly imposed it upon him. Even though he was out of government service and in the First Presidency, President Clark testified before the U.S. Senate Foreign Relations Committee, and his advice and opinions were solicited by men like former U.S. President Hoover and future Secretary of State John Foster Dulles.[7] He was the invited speaker at national meetings of the American Bar Association, Boy Scouts of America, Sons of the American Revolution, National Association of County Officials, and many others. The national reputation of J. Reuben Clark as an elder statesman in the First Presidency was best expressed when the editor of a New York City newspaper solicited a lengthy comment from him about national policy: "Your opinion on this subject should have weight with the People of the Nation."[8]

The first secular distraction from his new Church call occurred barely a week after he was sustained Second Counselor in the First Presidency. At 10:30 A.M. on 17 April 1933, a phone call from New York City invited him to join the board of directors of one of America's largest life insurance companies, The Equitable Life Assurance Society of the United States. President Clark accepted his mounting business directorships in Utah as an unavoidable burden of his new Church office, but this was a thunderbolt from the East. Aside from its compliment to him personally, he could see little to commend his acceptance of a directorship in a New York City company in which the Church had no financial interest and which might appear to Latter-day Saints as a competitor to the Church-owned Beneficial Life Insurance Company. Reuben's own misgivings about the benefits of the offer were not shared by President Grant, who had been active in the insurance business his entire adult life and saw this as a compliment of national proportions to the First Presidency. Despite President Grant's endorsement of the proposition, Reuben mulled over all the ramifications in his characteristic fashion and did not telephone his acceptance for six hours.[9] He remained a director of The Equitable Life Assurance Society for twenty-five years; and the Presidents of The Equitable regarded his presence on the board as being so valuable that they kept him ten years beyond the age of retirement for directors, ignored his repeated offers to resign, and appointed as President Clark's successor his close friend and protégé, Harold B. Lee.[10]

At New York City five months later, the U.S. government again extended a call for his services. On Friday evening, 22 September 1933, a secretary to the U.S. Secretary of State telephoned him at his daughter Marianne's home, with the request that Reuben meet with President Franklin Delano Roosevelt in the next few days. Recognizing that such a request was really a command, the former ambassador met alone with President Roosevelt three days later. FDR asked him to be a delegate to the upcoming Pan-American Conference at Montevideo because of his expertise in Latin American affairs. President Clark explained that he preferred to be in Salt Lake City at that time because of the Church's efforts to organize a relief program for the unemployed and needy: "I said, however, that it had always been my practice that when any National Administration really felt that I could be of service and asked me to help with the belief that I could be of help, rather than with the thought of paying me a compliment, I had always accepted the service." He emphasized his Church responsibility and concluded "that my own situation was such that I would leave the matter this way: That if he really wished me to go to the Conference, I would go though I preferred not to go."[11] They had known each other at Columbia Law School but were political antagonists, and Reuben found no difficulty in giving Franklin D. Roosevelt ample opportunity to reconsider the invitation. Nevertheless, FDR was an astute judge of Reuben's talents and loyalty to government calls, and the President reaffirmed his desire that he go to Montevideo.

As he left the White House, President Clark felt the strain of divided loyalties. The Equitable Life offer had presented no difficult choice: the prestige in financial circles meant nothing to him personally, and he could have easily rejected the opportunity except for President Grant's encouragement that he accept. At most, it involved only occasional attendance at directors' meetings in New York City. But now the President of the United States had asked him to accept an assignment that involved a four-month absence from Church headquarters at the very time the First Presidency hoped to set up the organization of a Church-wide relief program for thousands of out-of-work Latter-day Saints. How things had changed since the previous March when Reuben remembered the lines from Dante! What he thought he had given up was now seeking him out. He was no longer free even to reject these offers out of hand but felt that he must present all their pros and cons to his "Chief," the President of the Church. President Grant listened to the proposition and all its ramifications, conferred with his First Counselor Anthony W. Ivins, and together they proudly encouraged Reuben to accept the assignment in Montevideo. To give the Church an added boost from his acceptance of this assignment, Reuben arranged a meeting with FDR in the White House for all members of the First Presidency and Elders Reed Smoot and Stephen L Richards.[12]

President Clark returned to Salt Lake City from his White House meeting in time to attend the general conference of the Church in October, but those meetings were barely over when the U.S. government jolted him with still another requisition upon his services. On 13 October 1933, Secretary of State Cordell Hull invited him to come to Washington to help with an organization that was to seek recovery of more than a billion dollars in defaulted foreign bonds owned by U.S. citizens. No one in the Presidency welcomed this new government assignment that was sure to involve protracted absences of the Second Counselor from Salt Lake City, but response to the offer was inevitable. Reuben felt duty-bound to accept any assignment from his government (unless the Church President required strict adherence to his prior Church obligation), and President Grant had committed himself to the proposition that President Clark was as valuable to the interests of the First Presidency in answering such unsought calls to service as he was in Church administration.[13]

Reuben was unable to attend the initial meeting in Washington, but he sent a letter of acceptance with a lengthy outline of the benefits of such a proposed organization. The White House included the full text of his letter in its announcement on 20 October 1933 of the formation of the Foreign Bondholders' Protective Council, and the *New York Times* also printed his letter in full.[14] He served the FBPC as general counsel from October 1933 to February 1934, as president from 1934 to 1938, as chairman of the executive committee from 1938 to 1945, as director to 1953, and as emeritus thereafter. A subsequent president of Foreign Bondholders' Protective Council said that J. Reuben Clark, Jr. "was chiefly responsible for laying down the procedures and principles which have ever since governed the Council's work."[15]

President Clark concluded his 1933 service in the First Presidency by joining with the rest of the Presidency in meeting Franklin D. Roosevelt on 4 November and dedicating the Washington Chapel on 6 November, after which he started for the Seventh Pan-American Conference at Montevideo.[16] As an accredited diplomat of his country, he did not seek to break Church-state disassociation by imposing religious discussions on others, but in Rio de Janeiro "I was rather flabbergasted at the dinner by having Mrs. Rihl say she wanted me to explain Mormonism to her—this coming out of a clear sky."[17] On Sundays, and during the week when he finished his work for the Pan-American conference, President Clark studied the New Testament, read scholarly studies of the Gospels, started work on his own parallel version of the Gospel accounts of the life of Christ (later published as *Our Lord of the Gospels*), and made several unsuccessful attempts to think through his remarks for the April 1934 general conference.[18] After completing his intensive diplomatic work with the Secretary of State at the Montevideo conference, he wrote, "I may have made some friends that will stand me in good stead hereafter.—One can never tell."[19]

When Reuben's ship docked at New York harbor on 13 February 1934, he found that President Grant had been waiting there for him for a month but was confined to bed with a cold. The next day, John Foster Dulles asked him to accept the presidency of Foreign Bondholders': "I told them I did not know anything about the subject and that in Brazil I had been a veritable Little Red Riding Hood. They insisted. I then asked if they knew of my Church job: they said Yes. I explained that when we took such a job we undertook not to take on anything else except with the consent of our associates and that therefore I must consult President Grant." Despite his freely acknowledged ignorance of high finance, Reuben's skills as a disarming diplomat and tough administrator had caught up with him and his Church assignment again. When he presented this additional request to divert his full attentions from Church work, Heber J. Grant immediately "said he was for it, though he saw the

J. Reuben Clark as chief counsel for U.S. Secretary of State Cordell Hull at the Seventh Pan American Conference at Montevideo, December 1933–February 1934.

possibility that the Church might feel I was going on as before and not caring much about the Church."[20]

President Grant was accurate in his prediction that Church members would criticize J. Reuben Clark's frequent absences from Salt Lake City for non-Church activities, even though he had not sought the assignments and fulfilled them only with the repeated encouragement of the Church President. "I do hope you can be here more," Lute wrote. "There is quite an undercurrent about your being away."[21] The extent of the problem was precisely tabulated in a First Presidency office daily record of Reuben's non-Church activities from April 1933 to April 1945, which showed that he had been away from Utah for non-Church activities a total of four years, two months, and three weeks during that twelve-year period.[22] He was doing what President Grant wanted him to do in bringing prestige to the Church but felt extremely awkward about his absences from Church headquarters. When a member of the First Council of Seventy, whose primary responsibility was proselyting, expressed gratitude for the great work of public relations and missionary work that

President Clark was accomplishing by being president of Foreign Bondholders' in New York City, he glumly replied: "I may say that I am here only because the Brethren expressed themselves as you have expressed yourself. I sometimes personally question whether it is worth my absence from my home and from my family, as well as from the work there. But, for the present at any rate, following the wishes of the Brethren, I shall continue in this work."[23]

A far more difficult situation was being created by the efforts of Utah Republicans to get him to be the Republican candidate for the U.S. Senate. When someone tried to get a commitment about his political views and future in July 1933, he replied that he "was out of politics—politically dead." But momentum continued to build in support of his nomination for the 1934 senatorial contest and, after talking with Ernest L. Wilkinson about the matter on 21 February 1934, Reuben mused, "I suppose I may be forced to make a decision on this. [As it] looks to me now I can make no effort to get the nomination, but if it comes, they [Presidents Grant and Ivins] may wish me to accept it." On 4 March, he learned that Utah Democrat Hugh B. Brown confided to Washington Mormons "that if I did run, the jig was up with the Demos."[24] Although the U.S. Senate had been his life's ambition,[25] he had quashed the 1932 effort to nominate him because he felt his unannounced acceptance of the position in the First Presidency ended any future government service. After his first year in the Presidency, however, Reuben had discovered repeatedly that Heber J. Grant was willing for him to accept unsought government appointments.

President Grant, however, had serious misgivings about the prospects of his Second Counselor becoming the Republican candidate in the 1934 Senate race. First, Reuben would not simply be shuttling back and forth between Utah and the East Coast every few weeks or months, but the U.S. Senate would require his full-time presence in Washington, D.C. at least eight months out of the year. When he raised the question on 5 March 1934, President Grant "said he felt more or less clear that he needed a counselor, to which I replied that the decision was for him to make."[26] Second was the matter of how he could be First Presidency counselor and U.S. senator at the same time. President Grant told one of the Mormon advocates of a Clark candidacy "that if Brother Clark were to resign as one of the

Presidency they would not care to have him nominated, and certainly it would be counted as Church influence if one of the Presidency were to be running for the Senate." Immediately after this 3 April conversation, President Grant met with his two counselors, and President Clark thrilled him by saying "he crossed that bridge when he accepted the position as one of the Presidency" and had always been opposed to the idea of a member of the First Presidency or Quorum of the Twelve as U.S. senator.[27] Third, President Grant feared that all the prestige Reuben gave to the First Presidency would be devastated if Utah Mormons (who had overwhelmingly elected all Democratic candidates in 1932) were to defeat Republican candidate Clark in 1934: "It would be one of the most humiliating things to me that could happen to have one of my counselors nominated for the Senate of the United States and then left at home."[28] The matter seemed closed to President Grant, and he told one man on 5 May 1934, "We can't spare him now. There is no likelihood of my changing my mind on this matter."[29]

But as the clamor mounted for the 1934 Republican state convention to draft him as candidate for the U.S. Senate, President Clark himself found it impossible to categorically deny the possibility. His pronouncements appeared to vary from indifference to cryptic encouragement to outward disinclination. On 7 March he told the *Deseret News* that talk of his being named Republican senatorial candidate "is all news to me. I am not thinking about and am not discussing politics," and on 4 April he told the *Salt Lake Tribune* that rumors of his being drafted by the Republican convention should not be taken seriously.[30] Nevertheless, after one of his supporters reported President Grant's emphatic refusal to consider letting him be the senatorial candidate, Reuben replied on 21 May, "Perhaps no one can yet tell what the actual outcome will be."[31] By early June such non-Mormons and non-Utahns as the president and general manager of the *Los Angeles Times* and the chairman of the board of Bankers Trust Company of New York City were urging President Grant to allow his counselor to become the Republican candidate for the Senate, and President Clark decided to be in New York during the Republican state convention.[32] On the eve of his departure, Reuben refused to comment about the efforts to secure his nomination, and the pro-Clark *Salt Lake Telegram* surmised that "his continued silence regarding his position, is believed to presage acceptance of his nomination if delegates declare for him by acclamation."[33] In response to that report, President Clark sent a telegram from New York City on 17 June 1934 to Byron D. Anderson, chairman of the Republican State Committee, reaffirming that he was not a candidate for the office of U.S. senator and asking his friends to stop their efforts to draft him.[34]

His "Anderson Letter" was actually a skillfully devised document that revealed the extent to which President Clark was keeping his own counsel. In reviewing his statement, the *Deseret News* proclaimed "PRES. CLARK REFUSES TO BE CANDIDATE," the *New York Times* headlined, "Clark Refuses to Run in Utah," and President Grant concluded "that he does not care to be a candidate for the Senate, over which I rejoice."[35] All these interpretations were in error, as President Clark stated in a later memorandum. He had worked over the Anderson statement until nearly 2 A.M. on the morning he sent the telegram, and its meaning turned on the implications of the possibly too-careful wording. "Careless and hasty reading of my Anderson statement left some with an impression, and with others a conviction, that I had by it definitely withdrawn from the race or definitely indicated I would not accept the nomination. The fact that the statement had no such effect or meaning is beside the point; they thought or believed otherwise." He indicated that the crucial passages of the statement were: "Being now *actively engaged* in the duties of a high Church office, I do not consider myself available for high office during the existence of *such activity*," and unraveled that cryptic wording by saying that he hoped to "set a precedent" by being relieved of his "active Church work in high Church office to take on high civil service." His close friend and former law partner Albert E. Bowen complained that "Democrats have chosen to interpret your published telegram as duplicitous, implying that you want the nomination and intend to get it, and have chosen this means of securing it. Of course we all know that is not so." That letter set Reuben's teeth on edge, as he ruefully wrote in the memorandum, "When Democrats pointed out the real meaning, Republican friends holding the opposite view further committed themselves."[36]

Few of his friends understood President Clark's underlying meaning about his active Church service, but his staunch advocates doggedly "pointed out that the telegram still left the way open for the Republican state convention on July 18 to draft Mr. Clark for the nomination of United States senator."[37] That was probably what he hoped for but could not acknowledge to any of his supporters. He continued to protest weakly against their efforts and their suggestions that he resign from the First Presidency, but "I agree with you that it might bring trouble on the Party to have myself or anyone else nominated and then have the nomination declined."[38]

President Clark chose Independence Day as the time to reveal to Heber J. Grant his full strategy in the 1934 senatorial drama. After expressing "no wish to become the candidate," Reuben said all indications pointed out that the Republican convention was going to draft him as candidate anyway. He said that he had stopped short of "saying that I would not take the nomination even if it were given to me by the Convention" for four reasons: (1) It would repudiate his lifelong public affirmation that "civil service when called was the highest civic duty of every patriotic American citizen"; (2) it would "merely play into the hands" of persons wishing to charge him or the Church with Church influence in politics; (3) his refusal to accept the Republican convention's draft nomination would be blamed as a partisan act of the nominally Democratic Heber J. Grant and the ardently Democratic Anthony W. Ivins in the Presidency; and (4) it would portray the Church in the eyes of the nation as defying "the expressed will of one of the great parties" and the principles of party government under the U.S. Constitution. President Clark expressed regret that "I must either be released or furloughed from my present position" if he were drafted and accepted the nomination for the reasons stated, and then provided President Grant with the drafts of three proposed telegrams: (1) his acceptance of the nomination; (2) his telegram asking President Grant to "release me from my duties as your counselor," and (3) President Grant's telegram to President Clark "to release you from your active duties as my counselor for the period of your civic service. This release will take effect this day."[39]

Heber J. Grant took this extraordinary letter in stride, conferred with Anthony W. Ivins, and agreed to all of President Clark's proposals, including the texts of the three telegrams. President Grant concluded his letter of 9 July 1934 with the statement, "In view of all the circumstances, if you should be nominated by the convention I shall feel that it is providential and will eventually work out for the best interests of the Church as well as yourself," and he reported the correspondence and his decision to the Quorum of the Twelve Apostles the following day.[40]

When Reuben opened President Grant's letter in his New York offices on 13 July 1934, it seemed that lifelong aspirations and dreams were at the threshold of achievement. He had wholeheartedly forsaken his ambitions for future government service to accept the call of the Church in December 1931, and now in a fulfillment of Matthew 10:39 he had received everything he thought he had given up for service to the Church. Reuben's impractical belief that the party should seek him rather than his scrambling for the nomination had humiliated him in 1922 and 1928, but in 1934 there was no force within the Republican party of Utah that could deny him the nomination for U.S. senator. With deep gratitude, he wrote on 13 July that President Grant's agreement to his proposals "clears the atmosphere and enables me in a measure to see through what has been for myself personally, the most difficult position I have ever faced in my life."[41] In addition to President Grant's reluctant agreement to release him if drafted by the convention, five members of the Quorum of the Twelve Apostles privately urged Republican leaders to draft him as senator.[42] Only five days remained until the Republican convention that everyone expected to stampede to a first-ballot nomination of Reuben as U.S. Senate nominee. Within a week, J. Reuben Clark would be released from the First Presidency at least long enough for the three-and-a-half-month campaign and possibly for the six-year term in the U.S. Senate to which he aspired. All he had to do was wait.

The wait proved too long for President Clark, and within three days he decided to abandon the apparently assured realization of his life's ambitions. First, he brooded about his "duty to my Church, which many would rank paramount to everything else," but he affirmed, "I have never failed to meet any call made upon me. I am therefore not in need of penance service. . . ." Although he regarded service to "Party and Country" very highly, he worried about the popular assessment of his service to President Grant: the published statement that he had delayed starting his service in the First Presidency for more than a year while he completed more important work, and the fact that in the fifteen months he had been President Grant's counselor, "I have been absent from Church offices on public or semi-public service about 9 months," which had caused many Latter-day Saints to feel and express criticism. "To have retired from Church work, (by leave of absence, or release, or whatnot)," Reuben wrote, "would inevitably have raised the question, among Church members, as to whether I thought more of personal political ambitions or of my service to my Church. The distinction between service to the Church and service to the Country would be drawn by some Republicans (Churchmen) and no Democrats."[43]

To a man accustomed to anticipating all the worst possibilities of any decision, President Clark's euphoria of 13 July 1934 evaporated as he thought through the disasters that could follow his acceptance of the Republican nomination. Despite President Grant's acquiescence, he might not be able to work out a temporary release from the Presidency, in light of President Ivins's probable opposition to such a course.[44] Then he would be left to the uncertain political mercies of Utah's electorate. No one of his pessimistic viewpoint could mount the unbridled optimism required of election candidates. Accepting his dark visions of potential disaster as probable reality, Reuben concluded that "my reputation would have inevitably been seriously injured if I had taken the nomination—to the hurt of myself, my family, and the Church, more hurt than any of us could unnecessarily take on."[45]

On 16 July 1934 his letter of enthusiastic preparation for the outcome of the Republican convention arrived in the First Presidency's office. At four o'clock P.M., Utah time, he telephoned President Grant long distance, offering to write a second telegram to Byron D. Anderson "to the effect that moreover I could not take the nomination if it were tendered to me." To close the door a second time on his life's ambition was excruciatingly hard, and he seemed to hope that President Grant would try to talk him out of it. Apparently, however, he underestimated the President's desire to retain him in the First Presidency; his "Chief" was quite willing to have him send an unambiguous telegram of refusal to Republican headquarters.[46]

Even so, it was after midnight the next morning before Reuben could bring himself to send the following telegram: "In the event my name comes before the Republican convention for nomination as United States Senator I ask you immediately to inform convention that as set out in my telegram of June 17 to Chairman Anderson I am not a candidate for the nomination and I am not available for the nomination. Moreover I should not be able to accept the nomination if it were tendered to me."[47] Despite some last-minute efforts of his supporters to draft him anyway, the Republican convention of 18 July 1934 accepted the refusal. With ironic comfort, the previously anti-Mormon *Salt Lake Tribune* (which had vociferously opposed the election of Elder Reed Smoot to the U.S. Senate in previous decades) editorialized at the conclusion of the Republican convention: "The ticket selected, considering the circumstances which prevented the unanimous nomination of J. Reuben Clark, Jr. for the United States Senate, is a good one."[48]

In a letter of consolation, Elder John A. Widtsoe expressed relief that President Clark would not be subject to the humiliation of being defeated by Mormon voters "benefiting by the stream of easy money [who] might vote for existing conditions [of the Democratic New Deal] rather than to take a chance on stopping the flow from the open tap in the treasury." Elder Widtsoe expressed grief that the elderly Heber J. Grant and Anthony W. Ivins of the Presidency were not "as vigorous as in the days gone by, and the problems of this day are the most difficult known to me in my association with the Church." The national situation, Utah's condition, and the Mormon situation added up to one conclusion for J. Reuben Clark's admirers in Salt Lake City: "We need you here."[49] For Republicans and anti–New Deal Democrats, the problem was not the Great Depression that caused 25 percent national unemployment, a 54 percent drop in Utah's farm income, and a farm mortgage delinquency of 49 percent.[50] The horrifying problem was Franklin D. Roosevelt's New Deal response to the depression, and the welcoming embrace by at least half the Latter-day Saints of a Democratic program that violated conservative political dogmas about laissez-faire economics and the limited role of federal government.[51] "It is one of the most serious conditions that has confronted me since I became President of the Church," wrote Heber J. Grant.[52]

President Grant, a nominal Democrat at best after World War I, "left the Democratic party" and became a Republican when the Democrats supported the repeal of Prohibition in 1932.[53] Although he instinctively recoiled from the economic and bureaucratic innovations of the New Deal, his cousin-counselor Anthony W. Ivins brought a strongly sympathetic view of the New Deal into First Presidency deliberations. The staunchly Democratic views of First Counselor Ivins caused inevitable conflicts with the staunchly Republican Second Counselor. When Reed Smoot and President Clark complained to Presidents Grant and Ivins on 1 September 1933 about the pro–New Deal attitude of the *Deseret News*, Reuben wrote that "a rather sharp difference of opinion developed between President Ivins and myself."[54] When President Ivins in a First Presidency meeting on 12 September 1933 urged that the general conference endorse Roosevelt's National Recovery Administration, President Clark refused to reply to him, as he also declined to do the next day, when President Ivins argued that since they all loved the American form of government, "that we must therefore support the [Franklin D. Roosevelt] Administration." After the Presidency meeting, when he was alone with President Grant, Reuben complained that he "was too old to be made a Democrat by Bro. Ivins."[55]

Nevertheless, Anthony W. Ivins temporarily succeeded in pouring oil on the conservative waters of Heber J. Grant's political soul. J. Reuben Clark may have winced when President Ivins urged the Latter-day Saints at the October 1933 general conference "to get in harmony with the civil officers of the country," or when Apostle (and Democrat) Stephen L Richards at the same meeting advocated support of the NRA and urged that even critics of the New Deal support the Roosevelt administration as "in an emergency an army follows its commander."[56] But by the time Reuben declined the opportunity in 1934 to cross swords with the New Dealers as a U.S. senator, a new day was dawning in the First Presidency as he responded to the anti–New Deal plea of John A. Widtsoe, "We need you."

Despite Anthony W. Ivins's persistent efforts to reconcile Heber J. Grant to Franklin D. Roosevelt and the Democratic New Deal, President Grant's objections to the New Deal were bubbling to the surface by mid-1934. "I am hoping and praying," he wrote on 2 June

1934, "that President Franklin D. Roosevelt and his cabinet are sincere in their efforts to benefit the country by their vast expenditure of money, but I am harassed with doubts."[57] After President Ivins died in September 1934 there was no one who could impede President Grant's deepening conviction that New Deal philosophy and policy were tragically wrong.[58] By the 1940s Heber J. Grant could not even talk about FDR without raising his blood pressure.[59] The only thing that bothered President Grant more than Franklin D. Roosevelt was the horrified conclusion that "about half the Latter-day Saints almost worship him."[60]

After the death of Anthony W. Ivins, President Grant on 4 October 1934 advanced President Clark to the position of First Counselor and ordained him a member of the Quorum of the Twelve Apostles "so that he would be entitled, if he should outlive the rest of the brethren, to be promoted to the Presidency of the Church."[61] Ardent Mormon Democrats concluded that as soon as he became First Counselor, Reuben launched an all-out campaign against the New Deal.[62] In reality, he only provided eloquent reinforcement to President Grant's already entrenched prejudices against it.

A few hypersensitive Church members also regarded as anti-Roosevelt remarks the warning of President Clark to the conferences of October 1934 and April 1935 "that in some states of this Union the issue now seems to be between an ordered, law-governed society and a despotism" and that "there is no room in America for a dictatorship." But these remarks could easily have been understood as referring to the elective dictatorships of Mississippi's Governor Theodore G. Bilbo and Louisiana's Governor Huey Long, the Italian Fascists of New York City, the millions of political followers of Father Charles E. Coughlin's radio broadcasts, the American Nazi clubs, and the 1934 testimony of Major General Smedley D. Butler about an alleged American Legion plot to establish a military dictatorship in the United States.[63]

Even though the First Presidency was now free of its Democratic advocate, and even though President Clark was now the second presiding officer of the Church, he refused to make the frontal assault on the New Deal that many anticipated and almost demanded. When he answered a newspaper reporter's query about the New Deal with the simple statement that he was still an advocate of

COURTESY HAROLD B. LEE LIBRARY

President Clark at his desk in the Church Office Building, 1935.

"constitutional government," the *Salt Lake Tribune* in June 1935 claimed that Reuben was finally "breaking a long silence on government affairs."[64]

During the years immediately following his surrender of the Senate nomination, President Clark had quite enough to distract him from any campaign to convert some Latter-day Saints from their New Deal apostasy. Aside from his many weeks in the New York offices of the Foreign Bondholders' Protective Council, he received an invitation in 1935 from one of the senior partners of J. P. Morgan & Company for him to return to Mexico in the interests of the Eagle Company (an affiliate of the Dutch Shell Oil Company). When he wrote the First Presidency about this offer, he pointed out "the advantage it would be to the Church to have me make such contacts and acquaintances as I have indicated" and then asked "if it appears I can render real service justifying to my own conscience the employment by this company, you would think I ought to accept it." President Grant and the new Second Counselor, David O. McKay, replied, "Unhesitatingly we recommend that you accept the offer made by the shareholders of the Mexican Eagle Oil Co." Aside from intangible public relations benefits to the Church, President Clark's employment with the Mexican Eagle Company brought him the kind of financial windfall he gave up hoping for when he accepted the position in the First Presidency. In addition, he was elected on 8 April 1936 to serve on the Commission of Experts on the Codification of International Law of the Pan-American Union and was elected on 1 May 1937 to the board of editors of the *American Journal of International Law*.[65]

With his employment in the Mexican Eagle Oil Company and in the Foreign Bondholders' Protective Council, President Clark spent much of his time scurrying between Salt Lake City, New York City, London, and Mexico City. Church members were generally unaware of President Grant's enthusiastic encouragement for him to take on these added secular responsibilities, and therefore the "undercurrent of comment" about his absences continued. This did not bother President Clark, who knew his secular activities had the wholehearted blessing of the President of the Church, but Luacine fretted about the situation at home. "I saw Pres. Grant on the street. He didn't mention you. In fact people have quit asking when you are coming."[66] Even Heber J. Grant was criticized by those who preferred the Presidency to be more sedentary. "Sister Grant was telling us that Golden Kimball said in some ward, I think, that the Lord can't give revelations to Pres. Grant," Lute wrote, "because he does not stay in one place long enough—he travels so much."[67] Heber J. Grant and J. Reuben Clark shared an expansive view of the role of the First Presidency that would take others a generation to adopt.

Presidents Grant and Clark occasionally participated in joint activities during this period of frequent travel outside Utah. In September 1934, for instance, they were with the Tabernacle Choir at the Chicago World's Fair, and in June 1935 they traveled to the Hawaiian Islands to organize the Oahu Stake.[68]

As President Clark returned from Hawaii, he engaged by telegram in the playful banter that characterized the warm relationship he had with his children. On 11 July 1935 Louise and Reuben III

71

COURTESY HAROLD B. LEE LIBRARY

President and Mrs. Clark with President and Mrs. Grant in Hawaii, June 1935.

telephoned him about some sudden medical problems at home. That same day they telegraphed him at Los Angeles: "Do not shorten beautiful and delightful pleasure trip just because [of] our paltry sufferings. Would suggest you return home via [Panama] Canal and Europe."[69] President Clark was no slouch at repartee and wired back: "Many thanks for your wonderful suggestion, inspired as it was by the utmost unselfishness, high spartan courage, and indomitable fortitude. Sailing soon on Good Ship Life Long Indifference and Gross Parental Neglect."[70] President Clark's keen sense of humor enlivened his family life, both in necessary separation and in joyful homecoming.

Not long after their return to Salt Lake City from Hawaii, he began to encourage President Grant to delegate unessential office responsibilities. For most of his life, including the first eighteen years as Church President, Heber J. Grant had personally dictated all of his correspondence, both official and personal. Although his nervous insomnia gave President Grant opportunity to record several cylinders of letters on a dictaphone in the predawn hours of each morning, it still often took him months to answer correspondence. Heber J. Grant was ecstatic over the results.

> Saturday [18 April] Was a happier man tonight than I have been for years. Brother Clark started in Thursday answering letters for me without my telling how I wanted him to do it, and I believe in the last two days he has written more than fifty letters, and for the first time in years the drawers in my desk in the President's office, also the papers on my table to the left of my desk have all been disposed of by Brother Clark.
> ... [On 17 April] I found a piece of paper in his handwriting: "Brother Grant, this is your desk, J.R.C." Certainly, I did not recognize it, and it made me very happy to be so nearly caught up with my personal mail.[71]

Henceforth, Heber J. Grant routinely had him answer the mail, observing that "I am going to try to think more, work less, and have other people do a good share of the work that I have done myself."[72] President Clark learned administrative delegation by executive officers during thirty years of government service, and he brought those practices to the First Presidency's office.

Another administrative reform introduced by J. Reuben Clark in the First Presidency's office was limiting access to the President of the Church. Prior to the 1930s almost anyone could walk into the office and see the President if he was not already in a meeting, and on some occasions Heber J. Grant spent as long as two hours in conversation with members of the Church who came to his office without an appointment.[73] "That was changed when President Clark came upon the scene," observed one Latter-day Saint, "and the public was fenced out."[74] This critical appraisal obviously expressed preference for the earlier days of informality, and resistance to the screening of walk-ins by Presidency secretaries was shared by other Mormons. But just as the growth of Church membership made it impossible for the Church President to personally read and answer all his correspondence, it also made it impossible to maintain the administrative informality of earlier decades.

The year 1936 also marked the beginning of J. Reuben Clark's overt assault on the Democratic New Deal, after three years of virtual silence about national politics. Undoubtedly, he had experienced an inward debate between his thirty-year insistence that General

Authorities ought not to speak on political matters and his recognition that Heber J. Grant expected him to be the spokesman of the First Presidency against the New Deal, whose political and economic philosophies were offensive to both men. Again, it was an unsought call to civic duty that moved Reuben in 1936 to represent the anti–New Deal sentiment of Utah.

On 5 March 1936 he met in New York with an emissary of Alfred Landon, Governor of Kansas and aspirant for the Republican nomination to challenge Franklin D. Roosevelt as U.S. President. Governor Landon was "very anxious" for Reuben to attend the Republican national convention on June 9th as delegate-at-large from Utah so that he could assist in the drafting of the 1936 Republican platform. In a letter to the Second Counselor in the Presidency, David O. McKay, President Clark asked his two associates in the Presidency to decide whether he should accept the offer and observed:

> The possible developments and implications of my participating in the Convention and in the nomination, if he be nominated, might be that I would be asked to take an active part in the campaign itself, possibly not alone as an advisor, but as a speaker and in the event of the election of the Governor, I might possibly be asked to take some responsible position in the Administration.[75]

Reuben was being modest, for Alfred Landon offered to appoint him as U.S. Secretary of State in the event that Roosevelt was defeated in 1936.[76] Heber J. Grant may have shuddered at the renewed prospect of having to release J. Reuben Clark as counselor in order to serve in public office, but in the two years since the 1934 Senate problem, President Grant's opposition to the New Deal had stiffened sufficiently for him to encourage Reuben to join Alfred Landon's forces. Reuben helped draft the Republican platform; witnessed the nomination of Landon in June 1936; and conferred with him in Topeka in July, after which visit President Clark announced to reporters in the First Presidency's office: "Governor Alf M. Landon of Kansas will make a great president."[77]

More than half of the Latter-day Saints, however, disagreed with that political assessment, and it upset Lute to hear her husband criticized for his political stance.[78] President Clark continued to work for Landon's campaign outside Utah, but a letter from his brother Ted in Grantsville underscored the tense political and religious situation in Utah: "I am fully convinced that if you go on the stump here among the Saints that much of that respect and good feeling towards you will change, as it has to all the other leaders who have done it. If I have any influence at all with you, I want to say don't do it. You can't afford to. Many of your own side will lose confidence if you do."[79] His brother's words were echoes of Reuben's own pre-1933 convictions, and six days later he declined the request of the Republican National Committee that he give twelve speeches for Landon's campaign in Utah because "I would harden this situation and solidify opposition rather than gain votes."[80] He gave speeches in the 1936 campaign for Landon in Idaho, California, Arizona, Texas, and Colorado, but not in Utah.[81]

Heber J. Grant, however, was becoming increasingly impatient with Church members who supported New Deal policies and was becoming convinced that the First Presidency would have to take a very strong stand. The result was an unsigned editorial on the front page of the *Deseret News* on 31 October 1936 entitled "The Constitution."[82] Without naming Franklin D. Roosevelt, this editorial, the work of President Clark, accused Roosevelt of knowingly promoting unconstitutional laws and of advocating communism, whereas the "other candidate has declared he stands for the Constitution and for the American system of government which it sets up."[83]

On the eve of the 1936 presidential election, this editorial had a sensational effect on the Mormon electorate.[84] Of the letters sent to the First Presidency about the "Constitution" editorial, 71 percent criticized it, assuming that the First Presidency was responsible for its publication and that President Clark had written it. Although the minority in favor of the editorial described it as courageous and inspired, many saw it differently and a few were vehement in their disagreement.[85] More than 1,200 Latter-day Saints cancelled their subscriptions to the *Deseret News* on account of the editorial, and a few days after its publication, 69.3 percent of Utah's votes went to Franklin D. Roosevelt and the New Deal.[86] Landon's landslide defeat as presidential candidate in 1936 not only ended Reuben's hopes of becoming U.S. Secretary of State, but his sister also feared that the pervasive criticism of him in the wake of the election might result in his being released from the First Presidency.[87]

Such criticism might have given pause to a man of lesser mettle than J. Reuben Clark. "Speaking personally," he told the next general priesthood conference, "I am more or less accustomed to criticism. Not a little of my life has been spent in public office ... and practically without exception, I have found this criticism to come from men whose selfishness was not being served by the way in which I was attempting to carry out and perform the duties of my office." Then he concluded by observing, "Criticism seems to be an inescapable accompaniment of the doing of righteousness, strange as that may seem."[88] Six months later he told another general priesthood meeting that he was unaffected by any criticism as long as he knew he was doing what President Grant wanted and as long as he was "doing my best in the Lord's work."[89]

He directed these pointed remarks to priesthood conferences of the Church because through correspondence and personal contact he knew that some of his most vocal nay-sayers considered themselves devout Latter-day Saints.[90] But Reuben privately nicknamed them "Sons of Belial" and observed that "I am not forgetting them, even though I forgive them."[91] When people criticized the programs he was promoting, he classified them in various categories of opprobrium in letters to Herbert Hoover and in talks published in the *Church News.*[92] Although he told a general conference that he usually tossed anonymous letters into the wastebasket without reading them and likewise disposed of "signed scurrilous letters,"[93] Reuben's personal papers indicate that he read and kept most, if not all, anonymous and signed letters of criticism. "One cannot harbor the spirit which you have put into your anonymous and other letters, and that you have expressed to me personally," he wrote to one critic, "without suffering grave injury. I say this in all kindliness and without any personal rancor whatever."[94]

The extent to which he was affected by criticism from members of the Church may be indicated by his increasing tendency to begin his sermons with an anticipation of rejection. "What I shall have to say tonight," he told one general priesthood meeting, "will probably be not too popular. I shall try to say it in as sweet a way as I can...."[95] Yet President Clark was obviously more upset to think that some Mormons were openly and equally critical of President Grant. "The word constantly comes back to us," he told the General

Welfare Committee, "that some of our general boards and members are not loyal to President Grant.... I am tired of the way people speak about him. I don't believe you would ever have gotten along if you hadn't been loyal to the Presidency of the Church."[96] He strongly felt that all Latter-day Saints owed their Prophet complete loyalty.

Throughout his service in the First Presidency, President Clark dismissed criticism by other Mormons as disloyal, self-serving, and unworthy of reflective examination, but on occasion he was disarmed by the soul-searching reservations of a genuine admirer. "I am sorry," he wrote to a mission president, "that on a few occasions I have given you some difficulty in following along with me, and all I can say is that maybe you are right and I am wrong."[97] Aside from that rare hypothetical reflection, Reuben gave no ground to his critics.

After their failure to dissuade the Latter-day Saints from voting for the New Deal in 1936, the First Presidency was preoccupied with promoting the Church's new relief program at home and abroad. Although President Clark had authored the first comprehensive statement of the relief program's philosophy and organization in 1933, his responsibilities with Foreign Bondholders' in New York City prevented his close supervision of the Church Security Program (later renamed Welfare Program) until the 1940s.[98] Nevertheless, while in New York City he was able to have direct influence on the national publicity given to the Church relief program by the media. *Time* not only covered the announcement and initial steps of the Welfare Program but also included the Church's effort in a motion picture news digest called the "March of Time." While in New York City, he was able to correct misconceptions in the scripting and filming of the "March of Time" newsreel: "I have impressed upon them that President Grant was a business man of large experience, and was not the clerical type at all," he wrote to the rest of the Presidency. "The scenario as I first saw it had one 'shot' of him retiring to a room for communion and reflection. The script stated something of the sort. I told them that was not President Grant; that we did not do our Church work in that style."[99] With the refinements that he was able to persuade Time, Inc., to bring to their production on the Church and its relief program, the First Presidency was quite pleased when this particular "March of Time" was screened in motion picture theaters throughout America early in 1937. President Clark's own family was ecstatic about the production. "I saw the March of Time, and Popsy, old dear, you stole the show," his daughter Luacine wote. "I clapped loudly and vociferously, for weren't you my Pa? . . . The voice sounds exactly like yours, so if a solitary tear accompanied by a soulful sniff and a choked sob was wrung forth from your beauteous, plump and slightly nutty daughter, who was to blame?"[100]

If President Clark concentrated on the Welfare Program, Heber J. Grant continued to be preoccupied with challenging the New Deal.[101] President Grant's counselors shared his deep reservations about the New Deal but acted as restraints upon his hopes to ask the members of the Church to choose between the charisma of Franklin D. Roosevelt and the authority of the First Presidency. After the April 1937 conference, President Grant reported to David O. McKay that a member of the Church in Las Vegas wondered if it was not time for the Lord to have the First Presidency openly reject the New Deal, and Heber J. Grant commented to his counselor, "I have sometimes thought the same thing, but we don't seem to be a unit, and until we are I guess it is wise to let things alone."[102] Although J. Reuben Clark became a member of the Republican National Committee in December 1937, he joined President McKay in restraining President Grant's inclination for an official denunciation of the New Deal, and he confided to the governor of Utah that he "had tried studiously to avoid doing anything that was really political."[103] If Reuben was the most qualified of the First Presidency to criticize the political philosophy and programs of the New Deal, when he did speak out it was at the prodding of Heber J. Grant.

In more than sixty-one years of his life as a General Authority, Heber J. Grant's closest associates were Joseph F. Smith and Anthony W. Ivins; but J. Reuben Clark, Jr. was probably next in his affections and esteem. Not only did the Church President stand in awe of President Clark's international reputation, his administrative skills, and his eloquence of speech and writing, but President Grant was also overwhelmed by his absolute loyalty and eagerness to promote the President while remaining in the background himself. Reuben helped prepare a major address for Heber J. Grant to deliver. President Grant responded in June 1937: "Your memorial speech was one of the finest I think that has ever been delivered," and then he added, "Once during the reading the tears came into my eyes, and it was a little awkward for me to read. I have never received more compliments for an address than for that which you prepared." President Grant changed the wording of the text from the first person to the third person in order to give greater credit to the man who was satisfied to remain unacknowledged to others, and he wrote: "I will just say that I thank the Lord for J. Reuben Clark, Jr. as one of my counselors and for the wonderful address that I was able to read."[104]

As he began reducing his commitments with the Foreign Bond-holders' Protective Council in 1938, Reuben spent more time at Church headquarters in council with the First Presidency and other Church leaders. On 12 August 1938, he became president of the Church-owned radio station KSL, and he also began exercising more direct oversight of the Church Welfare Program. By 1940 he met with the General Welfare Committee as often as did President McKay, and by 1943 President Clark continued as the only member of the First Presidency at most of the General Welfare Committee meetings.[105]

With Reuben's more frequent presence in Salt Lake City, President Grant increased the regular meetings of the full Presidency to three times a week in December 1938.[106] Among the myriad of administrative problems they discussed was the frequent change of bishops. President Clark concluded that the rate of change was unnecessary and so informed a special meeting of priesthood leaders. "Last year we installed approximately two hundred bishops in the Church, which is twenty percent, roughly, of the Church bishoprics. . . . At that rate we would change bishops every five years and that is too often. A bishop can hardly get his feet under him in five years." Then he urged the stake presidents not to request a change of bishop just to get rid of a disagreeable personality because "you will have to live with your bishops as others may have to live with you."[107]

The smiles and chuckles that attended that remark were indicative of his use of humor to ease the impact of corrective counsel. Aside from reinforcing the intended instruction, such humorous comments made his criticisms delightfully memorable. During remarks about the importance of performing vicarious temple work,

President Clark told the bishops, "I feel quite sure that the person who goes into the temple session and sleeps through the ceremony is not gaining very much himself," and then he convulsed the meeting by adding, "It is almost like work for the dead being done by the dead."[108]

There were world developments, however, that were beyond the amelioration of humor. The stability of Europe (where the Church had hundreds of American-born missionaries and tens of thousands of native-born members) had deteriorated steadily since the rise of Adolf Hitler's National Socialist Party had brought Germany out of more than a decade of postwar chaos. The price of Nazi revitalization of Germany, however, was the creation of Hitler's bellicose empire—through the 1935 rearmament in repudiation of the Treaty of Versailles, the 1936 remilitarization of the Rhineland, the 1938 military occupation of Austria and negotiated seizure of the Sudetenland portion of Czechoslovakia, and the March 1939 military seizure of the rest of Czechoslovakia followed in April by the invasion of Albania by Nazi Germany's ally, Fascist Italy. Hitler's often-stated next conquest was Poland; and when Germany signed a nonaggression pact on 24 August 1939 with its archenemy, Soviet Russia, in which the two imperialist powers divided up continental Europe into German and Russian spheres of influence, Europe was poised on the brink of war. All that was necessary to ignite the powder keg was a German attack on Poland that would surely bring Great Britain and France to its aid.[109]

The entire First Presidency viewed these events with concern, but President Grant deferred to Reuben's judgment as to the best policy to pursue concerning the American missionaries in continental Europe. When Europe seemed on the verge of warfare in September 1938, due to Hitler's demands to annex the Sudetenland of Czechoslovakia, the First Presidency sent word through the U.S. ambassador for all American missionaries in Germany to evacuate immediately to the Netherlands and Denmark. When the Munich Pact at the end of September seemed to resolve the crisis, the missionaries gradually returned to Germany.[110] President Clark continued to monitor European developments through the news media and his personal contacts in the U.S. State Department, and by 21 July 1939 he felt the situation demanded preparations for closing the German mission. In a meeting of the First Presidency, "I raised the question as to whether or not we wished to continue to send missionaries to Germany, pointing out that in case of war it might be a question of getting our missionaries out of Germany and having them thrown into concentration camps, with all the horrors that that entails." Presidents Grant and McKay agreed with his assessment, and they decided to stop sending new missionaries to Germany.[111] As representatives of Hitler and Stalin signed the nonaggression pact, he concluded that the lives of American missionaries would be forfeited by any delay in evacuation, and he flew into action. "President Clark has practically given his whole day to this matter," Heber J. Grant wrote, and the First Presidency on 24 August 1939 arranged with the U.S. State Department for visas and cabled the mission presidents in Germany to evacuate all missionaries immediately to Holland or Denmark.[112]

J. Reuben Clark had not faced such a life-and-death decision since his days at the State Department when the Mexican Revolution erupted, and his timing of the evacuation orders for the 150 missionaries in Germany could not have been more precise. Elder Joseph Fielding Smith and his wife were touring Europe at the time, and when they reached the West German Mission headquarters in Frankfurt on 25 August, "things were surely popping. Phone calls, telegrams and cablegrams, and everyone busy packing."[113] The mission president had arrived by air from Hanover on the plane's last civilian flight before it was diverted to military activity on the Polish front, and Elder Smith and his wife crossed the border from Germany into Holland on 26 August. Barely an hour after the Smiths entered Holland, the Dutch closed the border, stranding the mission president, his family, and most of the missionaries in Germany. The telegraph and telephone service was discontinued, and the German government announced that passage on railroads was not guaranteed after 27 August. Amid the chaos of war mobilization and the efforts of foreigners and native Germans to flee Nazi Germany, dozens of missionaries could neither be reached nor accounted for by the mission president before he left Germany for Denmark. Nevertheless, by the evening of 28 August 1939, the mission presidents of East and West Germany, their families, and all the missionaries were out of Germany and Poland and were preparing for passage to the United

States. Reuben had timed the escape and provided the diplomatic avenues. On 1 September, Hitler's forces invaded Poland and World War II began.[114]

During the same time period, the national press remained unconcerned with Reuben's contributions to the Church but eagerly reported any of his talks at general conferences or at annual meetings of business groups where his remarks concerned national economic and political conditions.[115] Much to President Clark's chagrin, his public visibility as a national figure caused many of his friends in Utah and throughout the nation to try to resurrect his long-dead political aspirations. When he was informed in May 1938 that Republican leaders in Congress hoped he would become a candidate for U.S. senator, President Clark replied that he preferred to live in Utah, had no desire to go to the Senate, and had no intention of becoming a candidate; but "I then said I wished to make this reservation (merely because I could not definitely see into the future), that if the circumstances changed and it did seem really to be more or less imperative that I run—a situation which I felt very confident would not arise as a practical matter, that as a theoretical matter it was a possible situation—that then I might change my determination, but that I had no present intention whatever of becoming a candidate."[116] He was again leaving the door to public office slightly open, but the contingency never materialized that made it "imperative."

Nevertheless, a local political leader tried to encourage him to run for U.S. senator in 1940, whereupon President Clark said, "Nothing doing," and made it clear that he wanted no talk of a draft.[117] People were still urging him to seek the U.S. Senate in the mid-1940s, and he replied with resigned finality: "As I look at Washington now and see how almost eveything that is done is at variance with all of the convictions that I have, I am sure that if I were there I should become nothing but an unheeded nuisance," to which he added wryly, "I cannot imagine any worse punishment than to have to live in Washington. It would be worse than having to live in New York."[118] Just as he could no longer take seriously any talk of his becoming U.S. senator in the 1940s, he had never taken seriously the suggestions made since the mid-1930s by such men as Harry Chandler, owner of the *Los Angeles Times,* that he become a candidate for the U.S. Presidency.[119] But the persistence of these appeals and suggestions is one measure of the esteem in which J. Reuben Clark was held by America's leaders.

By 1940 the physical disability of the Church President made it difficult for President Clark to consider prolonged absences from Salt Lake City anyway. He had tried to husband Heber J. Grant's aging vitality by getting him to delegate many of his activities in 1937, and in April 1938 he gave confidential instructions to a closed meeting of General Authorities, welfare workers, stake presidents, and bishops to avoid taxing the energies of President Grant.[120] In November 1939 President Grant was confined to his bed for more than ten days, but he refused to relax his pace of work. Then, during a visit to Los Angeles in February 1940, eighty-three-year-old Heber J. Grant suffered a stroke that paralyzed the left side of his body, disfigured the left side of his face, and severely impaired his speech.[121]

In the dark days of these initial symptoms, Reuben asked what instructions the President had for the authorities of the Church in Salt Lake City. Heber J. Grant gamely replied that "he would live as long as the Lord wanted him to live and lead the church" and that he was sure that he would outlive the two Apostles next in line for the Presidency, Rudger Clawson and Reed Smoot.[122] He was prophetic, for he outlived Elder Clawson by nearly two and Elder Smoot by more than four years. Although President Grant's fierce determination enabled him within several months to overcome the worst of the initial stroke symptoms, the residual effects remained for five years; and although his mind continued alert until a few days before his death, he was the first President in Church history to be physically incapacitated for an extended period of time.[123]

President Grant's physical debility was compounded by the absences from the Presidency's office of the Second Counselor, David O. McKay. At the very time President Grant was stricken, President McKay was seriously ill with a lung ailment that kept him at home for several weeks, and he had periodic health problems thereafter.[124] In addition, President McKay loved to visit with the members of the Church in stake conferences and other meetings, and he was often absent from Salt Lake City on that account.[125] "President Grant has been threatened by a cold," President Clark wrote to explain why he would not be able to visit his daughter in New York City, "although he is down again this morning, and President McKay is

First Presidency, 1940.
J. Reuben Clark, Heber J. Grant, David O. McKay.

away until Monday and I do not like to leave the place here alone even for a day."[126] From 1940 to 1945 he found himelf forced to assume increasingly heavy administrative responsibilities. By August 1942, one of the other General Authorities observed: "President Clark probably has as great a load to carry as any man in the Church ever had."[127]

President Clark's observations on the gravity of this challenge and his attitudes toward it deserve full attention. On 15 February 1940, he wrote the absent Presidents Grant and McKay:

No matter how crowded a house may be with people nor how busy one may be with the affairs of the day, one is always lonesome when the head of the house and a helpmeet is away. So, I must confess to a good deal of loneliness as I jostle around in these big shoes where I so often feel the need of the wisdom which you brethren could bring.

However, the most of my life has been spent not in command but as an assistant, more or less far down the scale, to those who were in command, and during

84

that rather long experience I have learned how to postpone action on matters of real importance, and hope I have some skill also out of this experience in determining what is important and what is not. I am aiming in my work here to make no determination on matters of major policy or importance. I hope this will give you a measure of restful sense of security that I shall at least try not to do anything that you could not approve of.

. . . .

I hope you are not worrying about me. During many years of rather intensive work I have learned reasonably how to take my rest under strain and stress, and am doing the best I can to be careful now so that I can continue to be around. I am feeling very well indeed. I am sensible, I think, of the responsibility which rests upon me, but at the same time I am always remembering Rule 6, the nubbin of which was, you will remember, "Don't take yourself so d--- seriously."

. . . From the little I know of the situation of each of you, this is not a matter of days and perhaps not of weeks. I ask you to take the full time necessary; a relapse for either one of you might be a very serious thing.

In the meantime I shall try to carry on as best I know how. I shall try to make as few major decisions as possible and reduce my mistakes to a minimum, though mistakes I shall of course make because we, most of us, make mistakes.[120]

This administrative philosophy became a way of life for him from 1940 to 1945, when Heber J. Grant was confined at home or while David O. McKay was also absent from the Presidency's office. With an iron loyalty to the President of the Church and a healthy awareness of the potential of this situation for self-aggrandizement, J. Reuben Clark consistently worked to keep himself subordinate to the absent President and coordinate with the absent Second Counselor.

President Clark used several administrative stratagems to avoid any unnecessary accretion of power to himself in the 1940s. When someone tried to get him to make a decision for the First Presidency upon his own authority, he "said First Presidency must decide, that [he] could not."[129] He visited President Grant at home several times a week to inform him of matters discussed in administrative meetings at Church offices and to present matters to the President for approval prior to action being taken.[130] If he conducted any major business without advance approval by President Grant, he quickly announced the fact to the President. "I apologized for not consulting him before K.S.L. stockholders meeting—told him about putting Ivor Sharp on Board of Directors; told him of condition of company."[131]

He was also scrupulous in his efforts to include the Second Counselor in the decision making of the Presidency in the 1940s, when President Clark himself was most often the initial contact for all decisions. When President McKay was ill, President Clark telephoned him for consultation prior to decisions.[132] When people tried to get him to make decisions about matters within the delegated responsibilities of the absent Second Counselor, he told them to make arrangements to see President McKay.[133] He often conferred with President McKay prior to presenting a matter for Heber J. Grant's approval;[134] but if Reuben had conferred first with the President, then he reported at the next opportunity to the Second Counselor.[135] Even after he had presented to Heber J. Grant the consensus of the Twelve on important matters discussed at the weekly temple meeting, they "decided to await return of President McKay."[136] At the very time circumstances in Church leadership might have allowed J. Reuben Clark to become "the power behind the throne," he consistently subordinated his administrative prerogatives.

Although Heber J. Grant was ailing physically, President Clark found it necessary as late as the 1940s to exercise a restraining influence on President Grant's vehement anti-Roosevelt feelings. Franklin D. Roosevelt was seeking an unprecedented third term as President, and Heber J. Grant toyed with the idea of a formal statement signed by all the General Authorities against such a possibility.[137] At this point J. Reuben Clark decided that he needed to defuse this potentially explosive situation in Church-state relations of Utah. On 13 October 1940 he worked on a political statement "so as to have something ready if matters became imperative, due to President Grant's feelings." He presented this to Heber J. Grant as an unsigned editorial for the *Deseret News* against Roosevelt's third term, with the information that he had consulted with political leaders who thought the intended statement by all the General Authorities would cause great problems without much hope of changing votes. Heber J. Grant reluctantly deferred to that assessment.[138] President Clark undoubtedly would have preferred that the *Deseret News* not publish any election-eve document that could be construed as attempted Church influence upon voters; but in his often-stated desire not "to try to over-persuade" the Church President, he regarded the publication of an unsigned political editorial by the *Deseret News* as preferable to issuing a partisan edict signed by all the General Authorities.

On 31 October 1940, the *Deseret News* published the unsigned "Church and State," which argued that Church leaders had the civil right to speak out on political issues; and on 1 November the *Deseret News* printed Reuben's unsigned editorial, "The Third Term Principle," which argued the constitutional danger of electing a U.S. President to more than two terms. Latter-day Saint voters were apparently unimpressed by the logic of either editorial, and 62.3 percent of Utah's votes helped elect Franklin D. Roosevelt to his third term.[139]

At the same time President Clark was navigating these troubled political waters in Utah, he conducted preliminary services in Idaho for one of the most important spiritual endeavors of the Church. On 19 October 1940 he conducted and presided at the cornerstone-laying ceremony for the Idaho Falls Temple. President Grant was too ill to attend the services, and the two counselors officiated in his absence. Before President McKay laid the cornerstone, Reuben gave the principal address. "Our whole philosophy as a Church and a people is bound up in the building of temples," he said. "We are the greatest people of temple builders, taking our interpretation of the word temple, that has ever walked on the face of the earth." After this talk about the history of temples, President McKay laid the southeast cornerstone and offered the prayer.[140]

As J. Reuben Clark began the second year of trying to coordinate the First Presidency's decisions with an often bedridden Church President, he reflected upon a similar situation in the Quorum of the Twelve Apostles, where the younger Apostles had to carry the added burdens of travel and administrations impossible for their very elderly colleagues. On 19 February 1941, President Clark discussed with the Second Counselor the possibility of appointing assistants to the Quorum of the Twelve Apostles.[141] After his counselors discussed this proposal with Heber J. Grant, he approved it and submitted his recommendation to the Twelve on 13 March 1941. The Apostles approved this innovation, with the suggestion that those selected be high priests who would be given the authority needed to function as needed but not given a special ordination.[142] As a result, on 6 April 1941 the general conference sustained Harold B. Lee to

COURTESY HAROLD B. LEE LIBRARY

Presidents McKay and Clark at the laying of the cornerstone for the Idaho Falls Temple, 19 October 1940.

fill a vacancy in the Quorum of the Twelve Apostles and five high priests as Assistants to the Twelve.[143] Elder Lee and one of these new assistants, Marion G. Romney, would soon become among the closest associates of J. Reuben Clark among the authorities of the Church.

As President Clark contemplated the growth of the Church membership geographically, he suggested another innovation in March 1941. He "pointed out that increasingly few—proportionately—of our people came to Conference; that few saw one Conference pamphlet; that few sermons were printed in our ordinary magazines; that few took the *Deseret News;* that the old time method of Presidents of Stakes and bishops returning and giving accounts was largely in discard and so few people really know what went on at Conference." To correct that situation in a growing Church population, he suggested to President Grant that the stake presidents in the Los Angeles, southern Idaho, southern Utah, and northern

Arizona areas rent auditoriums large enough to accommodate expected attendance and that a closed-circuit radio broadcast then transmit all the general conference sessions to these areas where the reception of the Church radio station, KSL, was not adequate. Moreover, in the rural areas of KSL radio coverage, President Clark suggested that a radio be placed in the chapels so that those who did not have home radios could listen to the general conference broadcasts in the chapels. President Grant enthusiastically accepted this recommendation, and the April 1941 conference began this use of media for Latter-day Saints outside the Great Basin of the American West.[144] Moreover, as a personal consideration for the bedridden Church President, President Clark arranged to have KSL radio provide a private line to the Grant residence so that he could listen to all the proceedings of the June 1941 MIA conference.[145]

The year 1941 might have merged in memory with other years for J. Reuben Clark and his family, except that the placid Sunday of 7 December was shattered by the news of a surprise bombing attack on the U.S. naval fleet anchored at Pearl Harbor, Hawaii. More than a year earlier, he had written his brother, "I am not fearing Japan, although they may lick our navy in the first conflict," and then added, "Whether Japan will attack us or we attack Japan I do not know."[146] When news of the Japanese attack first interrupted all radio broadcasts in Salt Lake City about 1 P.M. on 7 December, President Clark felt a cold terror: his beloved son-in-law Mervyn Bennion, Louise's husband, was stationed at Pearl Harbor as captain of the battleship *West Virginia*. When unconfirmed reports flashed across the radio that the *West Virginia* was sunk in the air raid, he immediately sent a telegram to his cousin Ralph Woolley, president of the Hawaiian Mission, asking about the safety of the missionaries and Hawaiian Saints and about the status of the *West Virginia*. For three days the Clarks lived in a limbo of hope and despair until they received official word that Mervyn died on the bridge of his ship.[147] President Clark "showed deep emotion as he spoke of the death of his son-in-law," for he loved Mervyn Bennion as a son.[148] Like December 1931, he would always remember December 1941 with special poignancy.

In 1942 President Clark continued to demonstrate his insistence that attention should be given to the Church President or to the First Presidency as a unit rather than to one of the counselors who out of necessity was performing yeoman's service. On 6 April 1942, "President Clark read a long Address of the First Presidency," wrote Heber J. Grant. "We approved and signed it, but he wrote it, and it was a very fine address. I was perfectly willing that he should take the credit of preparing it, but he insisted that it was the Address of all three of us, and that it would not be right for him to sign his name to it." President Clark also wrote nearly all of the document presented as the First Presidency's message on 3 October 1942, but again he declined President Grant's offer that the message show President Clark as author.[149]

In 1943 he initiated still more suggestions for President Grant's consideration. On 6 February 1943, "President Clark asked me what I would think of holding regional priesthood meetings in our temples, the priesthood meetings to be held by the First Presidency and the Council of the Twelve with the attendance of the priesthood of the region." President Grant readily agreed to holding such solemn assemblies in the temples, the first such meetings held for decades.[150] After several years of his personal study, J. Reuben Clark presented to the rest of the First Presidency a comprehensive reorganization of Church financial operations, which plan was ratified by the Quorum of the Twelve Apostles in April 1943.[151]

Despite all President Clark's efforts to minimize the pressures on the Church President, by mid-1943 Heber J. Grant's determination to continue working had sapped his energies and eroded his temporary recovery from the 1940 stroke. President Grant was too weak to speak to a general conference of the Church after April 1942, and a year later he was unable to attend the important weekly meetings of the Presidency and Quorum of the Twelve in the temple. "President Heber J. Grant has not met with the brethren in a meeting on Thursday for many weeks," wrote Joseph Fielding Smith on 3 June 1943. "He is confined to his home most of the time, but is keen on many matters, especially everything financial."[152] On 1 July President Grant's diary stated, "There is nothing of any great moment," and commented that his counselors were opening and answering all the mail and that his secretary, Joseph Anderson, gave a brief verbal summary of letters before President Grant signed them. For the period 1 July to 31 December 1943, Joseph Anderson wrote the following as secretary to the President of the Church: "President Grant did not dictate his journal for this period. He was still convalescing from an illness of nearly four years ago. He comes to the office nearly every day for a short time and signs the mail that had been prepared by his counselors for the First Presidency, also missionary calls and letters pertaining to missionary work." A later secretary in the First Presidency's office commented that, during the 1940s, "J. Reuben Clark was the *de facto* President of the Church, and President Grant not only knew it but allowed it."[153] Nevertheless, President Grant's weakened condition was not critical, nor did it demand the ever-present attention of the First Counselor; and during this same period Reuben visited "a dozen stakes and missions of the Church in Canada, and the Pacific Northwest and Idaho" and spoke at a national insurance convention in Chicago.[154]

President Clark himself continued his busy schedule, and 1944 was a particularly trying year for him. In January he suggested the structure of a "reading committee to read all stuff put out by us—whether by Twelve or by Dept. of Education, or for use by our Priesthood quorums or auxiliaries"; in February he gave an important address on public policy to the Los Angeles Bar Association; in March he attended the organization of a stake in his native Grantsville; and from March to May he helped resolve a problem with the draft boards concerning deferments for members of ward bishoprics.[155] Although continuing his varied responsibilities of Church oversight, he was grieved with his wife's terminal illness that began manifesting itself in the spring of 1944. When he asked Harold B. Lee and Marion G. Romney to administer to Lute on the morning of 5 July 1944, "He seemed very broke and was filled with emotions as he tried to talk about her." Although Lute continued to "waste away," President Clark bore testimony that her pain (which had previously required drugs) stopped on the morning Elders Lee and Romney administered to her. By the end of July he was resigned to the passing of his beloved Lute. When she died on the morning of 2 August 1944, Harold B. Lee visited J. Reuben Clark at home and commented, "It is a wonderful experience to stand in the presence of a great man bowed in sorrow."[156]

The depth of Reuben's love for his wife of forty-six years—and the magnitude of his loss in her passing—were kept from open display. His public image was of an immensely controlled man responding skillfully to the unyielding demands of Church and community service. On 10 August 1944 the president of the Western Pacific Railroad, headquartered in San Francisco, asked him to become a director of the company, and President Grant urged him to accept the offer, even though President Clark wondered whether the interests of the Church really demanded such added responsibility.[157] In the fall of that year he also oversaw the redefining of presiding quorum responsibilities, a matter which had needed consideration with the appointment of Assistants to the Twelve.[158]

President Clark was unceasingly productive, but the strain of trying to compensate for President Grant's absence from the Presidency's office as well as shouldering the grief of Lute's last illness and death seemed to drain him physically. In an unusual departure from his robust health, he suffered digestive disorders in January 1944 that kept him at home for three days; he was sick for four days with a cold in March; and from 27 September to 1 October he was down with the flu. In November 1944 he openly indicated his physical weariness when George Albert Smith, the President of the Quorum of the Twelve, suggested that all the General Authorities participate in a special proxy endowment session on Heber J. Grant's birthday and President Clark replied, "I counseled against asking the Brethren to go to the Temple on Pres. Grant's birthday. I have said so far as I was concerned, I must for the present time at least, husband my strength."[159]

He was very skillful in husbanding his strength despite the enormous demands of the First Presidency's office, but he was increasingly concerned about Heber J. Grant. On 1 February 1945 he "expressed some anxiety" about the President's weakening condition, but he continued to meet with him weekly to present matters for approval and to administer to him.[160]

April 1945 conference brought increased pressures due to the illness of the President, but it also confronted Reuben with a delicate situation of propriety. The presidency of the Church Women's Relief Society was being reorganized, and Presidents Clark and McKay notified Belle S. Spafford on 4 April that she was to be advanced from second counselor to president of this international women's organization of the Church. The next day, Sister Spafford met with President Clark to present her choice of counselors. The interview began humorously when Sister Spafford said that she understood from a conversation with the retiring president that the call as Relief Society general president was for a five-year period. President Clark looked at her over the rims of his glasses and quipped: "Sister, you may not last that long!" But he greeted with momentary silence her choice of his own daughter, Marianne, as one of her counselors. "Now Sister Spafford," he intoned with emphasis, "you'd better think again about that. She's my daughter, and you'd better think again about that." He was determined to avoid any suggestion that he gave preferential advancement in Church service to his own children. He was taken back, however, by Sister Spafford's protest that Marianne should not be discriminated against simply because of her relationship to the First Counselor in the First Presidency of the Church. Torn between his parental pride for a daughter's achievements and his sense of administrative properiety, he told Sister Spafford, "Well, you think about it."[161]

Belle Spafford thought it over and remained firm in her recommendation in a meeting several hours later. Therefore, Marianne Clark Sharp was sustained as first counselor in the Relief Society at general conference on 6 April 1945. Nevertheless, to preserve his rigid sense of propriety, any official correspondence between the father in the First Presidency and the daughter in the Relief Society presidency was very formal: Marianne addressed him as "Dear President Clark" and signed her full name, and he addressed his letters to "Dear Sister Sharp" and signed his full name.[162]

On 12 April 1945, the death of Franklin D. Roosevelt heralded the end of Heber J. Grant's deep concern about this most controversial of Presidents, and the surrender of Nazi Germany on 8 May brought to a close what he regarded as one of the greatest tragedies of the last twelve years of his presidency, the commencement of the Second World War. As if the apparent resolution of these two great issues relieved his pressing burdens, his physical condition rapidly deteriorated until his death six days later on 14 May 1945.

As the death of President Grant seemed imminent, Reuben prepared for the orderly transition of authority to the President of the Quorum of the Twelve Apostles, George Albert Smith, who was visiting the eastern states. On 14 May 1945 President Clark informed the next senior Apostle, George F. Richards, of the precarious condition of President Grant and said that if Elder Smith was still out of town when President Grant died Elder Richards "would have to take over."[163] President Grant died that day, and when the Apostles met in the temple the next day, Reuben entered the meeting with no thought of clinging to his previous twelve years of presiding. "Pres. Clark took his place next to Brother Callis [in order of apostolic seniority], but was invited to sit with Pres. McKay at the head of the table. . . . Bro. Richards made a brief talk by way of introduction, then requested that Pres. Clark take over and direct the discussion."[164]

By the time of President Grant's funeral on 18 May, George Albert Smith had returned to the city. He began the funeral services by announcing that Reuben, no longer a member of the now discontinued First Presidency, would conduct the services. Spencer W. Kimball, then a junior member of the Quorum of the Twelve, described his reaction to the former First Counselor's demeanor in this first public meeting as a General Authority in a subordinate position to eight Apostles:

> Then when Pres. Clark announced the speakers he said " 'President' George Albert Smith will now address us" etc. then "ELDER DAVID O. MCKAY OF THE COUNCIL OF THE TWELVE APOSTLES will address you" then "ELDER J. REUBEN CLARK JR. OF THE COUNCIL OF THE TWELVE APOSTLES will address you." Such humility!!! Such power!!! Such honor!!! (Most anywhere else in the world that I know of, there would have been evidence of ambition, envy, jealousy, ill feeling.) It is the work of the Lord. These are truly great and inspired and "called" men of God who have been leading the Church through the declining days and months and years of Pres. Grant's presidency.[165]

J. Reuben Clark had been in the world; he had experienced its honors, its opportunities, and its strifes. The man who had called him away from that world to serve as an elder statesman in the First Presidency was now dead. It now remained to his presidential successors to steer the course of Church leadership and to decide in what capacity President Clark would continue to serve.

"THREE PRESIDING HIGH PRIESTS"

Doctrine and Covenants 107:22

GEORGE ALBERT SMITH, 1945–1951

When George Albert Smith was thirteen years old, a local patriarch gave him a blessing prophesying that the young man would become an Apostle (which he did at age thirty-three), that his Church service would excel that of any of the members of his family (his grandfather had served as First Counselor to Brigham Young and his father served as Second Counselor to Joseph F. Smith), and that he would become a "prophet in the midst of the sons of Zion."[1] That prophetic blessing was fulfilled on 21 May 1945, when the Quorum of the Twelve Apostles and the Patriarch of the Church assembled in an upper room of the Salt Lake Temple. On motion of George F. Richards, the second-ranking Apostle in seniority, a unanimous vote sustained seventy-five-year-old George Albert Smith as the eighth President of the Church. On that occasion President Smith chose J. Reuben Clark as his First Counselor and David O. McKay as his Second Counselor, preserving their respective positions in the former First Presidency.[2]

Some people expected President Clark to be disappointed that he was no longer carrying the major load of the First Presidency's office.[3] Actually Reuben felt profoundly relieved. To his close friend, Elder Harold B. Lee, President Clark "expressed himself as being at ease now with a third man to make decisions and to be responsible for them," and to one of his non-Mormon associates he frankly stated on 15 June 1945 that "I have less responsibility because the new President, George Albert Smith, is reasonably well and therefore able to take the responsibility."[4]

95

COURTESY HAROLD B. LEE LIBRARY

The First Presidency, 21 May 1945.
J. Reuben Clark, George Albert Smith, David O. McKay.

In less than two weeks, however, he had cause for concern about the health of the new Church President. On 27 June 1945 President Smith was too weary due to overwork to join the rest of the General Authorities in a temple session commemorating the martyrdom of Joseph and Hyrum Smith.[5] Fatigue in a septugenarian was not unusual, but President Smith's obvious work strain and his occasional comments about "tired nerves" were disturbing echoes of his earlier health problems. In fact, President Clark's greatest challenge from 1945 to 1951 was his effort to shield George Albert Smith from the administrative pressures that could cause the Church President to relapse into an earlier health breakdown.

The severity of previous health problems required President Clark to give first priority to preserving President Smith's medical stability. Assistant Church historian Preston Nibley wrote that as a young Apostle, George Albert Smith "had exhausted his supply of nervous energy."[6] Due to overwork and a frail physical condition, Elder Smith had suffered from January 1909 to mid-1913 with what was described in his diary as a "general collapse," by a physician friend as "nervous prostration," and by a recent biographer as "nervous collapse."[7]

By whatever name one classifies the health difficulties of George Albert Smith, the symptoms seemed to emanate from the pressures of his Church service. After attributing the onset of his symptoms in 1909 to overwork in the previous year, his condition deteriorated to the point that he perspired, trembled, had "a nervous chill," and had to sit down after speaking to a general conference of the Church for only three minutes. Elder Smith made several unsuccessful attempts to continue his Church activities, but his withdrawal from public life was so intense that beginning in November 1909, "I remained in bed until about the 1st of May [1910] when I had my clothes brought to me and dressed for the first time in over five months." With much recuperation and relative seclusion in Ocean Park, California, he was finally able to resume active service as an Apostle in mid-1913.[8]

He seemed to be able to cope with the physical and nervous strain of Church service from 1913 until 1930, when Church President Heber J. Grant feared that the Apostle was heading for another breakdown, because he "is getting very nervous."[9] For the next three years he seemed to be teetering on the ragged edge of a collapse, as indicated in his self-descriptions: "a condition of nervousness that was most distressing," "my nerves were run down," "My nerves very much unstrung," "Why am I so nervous?," "My nerves are nearly gone but am holding on the best I know how," and "I was appointed to Alpine Stake Conference but my nerves are trembling so I have been excused."[10] Twelve years later, George Albert Smith received the office of ultimate responsibility (and therefore greatest pressures) in the Church. In view of his breakdown of 1909–1913 and his near relapse of the 1930s, nothing was more important for the Church in 1945 than the preservation of the new president's emotional and physical health. His First Counselor was therefore determined that he would spare President Smith from as many of those pressures and intense activities as possible.

Although Reuben regarded it as his primary responsibility to relieve the President from the strains of the office, he was not as successful in this effort as he wished. "I was trying to do all I could to help him," he explained to George Albert Smith's daughter Emily, "but that in some respects he was difficult to help." He then gave as examples the fact that President Smith disliked being away from the office on any day, including holidays, and that he insisted on reading all incoming and outgoing correspondence of the First Presidency's office, a practice that President Clark had persuaded Heber J. Grant to abandon in 1937. "I observed that if her father could get confidence in us [Presidents Clark and McKay], it would save him a good deal of labor." In an earlier conversation with Emily he agreed that her father loved meeting with people, but that such activities exhausted him. President Clark had succeeded in instituting careful screening by secretaries of walk-ins to the Presidency's office during the Grant administration, but George Albert Smith wanted an open-door policy that sapped his energies and diverted his time from administrative concerns in a growing Church population. President Clark confided these observations to Emily because she had more influence with her father than anyone else did, and "I thought maybe she might get something over to him."[11]

In fact, it was the influence that Emily Smith Stewart had with her father that constituted an especially sensitive challenge for President Clark. Following his wife's death in 1937, George Albert Smith remained a widower and lived with Emily's family. He apparently welcomed her "strong willed" nature as needed support, but President Smith's recent biographer observes that as early as the 1930s her influence had brought him into conflict with other General Authorities.[12] Spencer W. Kimball, who became Church President many years later, recalled that there was a general awareness of those circumstances.[13] Reuben himself once recorded that President Smith telephoned from his home to give instructions on a matter, and "as the conversation progressed he said Emily was sitting by him and I could hear her prompt him."[14] Reuben could understand President Smith's emotional ties to his daughter following the death of Sister Smith, for Reuben himself was a widower who felt mutual dependence and support with his own widowed daughter, Louise, who now shared the Clark residence at 80 D Street. The similarities of their bereavements and familial residence patterns made it far easier for the First Counselor to cope with the administrative dimensions of President Smith's love for his daughter.

Because George Albert Smith had different views of the secular role of the First Presidency than did his predecessor, the new Church President eventually asked President Clark to provide an accounting for the counselor's varied secular activities from 1933 to 1945. From 10:00 to 11:45 A.M. on 3 August 1945, Reuben "made a very comprehensive, though relatively brief explanation" in which he related the circumstances of his delayed entry into the First Presidency, the encouragement by President Grant for him to take on such secular activities as the Foreign Bondholders' Protective Council, and also "the KSL situation at the time I took over, explaining the infelicities of that situation and telling him of the growth of the institution." President Clark also had his secretary, Rowena Miller, summarize his Church activities from 1933 to 1945. President Smith was apparently somewhat perturbed by the fact that President Clark had spent more than a third of his service to President Grant away from Utah in non-Church activities, and he requested his counselor to curtail still further his already diminished non-Church activities.[15] As a result, Reuben resigned from the executive committee of Foreign Bondholders' in 1945, and limited his previous commitments to occasional attendance at directors' meetings of FBPC and Equitable Life Assurance Society in New York City and of Western Pacific Railroad Company in San Francisco.[16]

Nevertheless, like his predecessor, George Albert Smith was impressed by the extent to which non-Mormons outside Utah continued to seek the secular wisdom of his seventy-four-year-old First Counselor. Therefore, President Smith also allowed President Clark to function as one of America's national resources. Reuben served as a member of the Commission of Experts on Codification of International Law of Phi Delta Phi from 1945 to 1950, as the invited speaker in November 1945 at the annual meeting of the National Industrial Conference Board in New York City and at the Chicago meeting of the Insurance Agency Management Association in November 1947, as a trustee of the Foundation for Economic Education of Irvington-on-Hudson, New York, from 1948 onward, and as a trustee for the Theodore Roosevelt Memorial Association of New York City from 1950.[17] Still, President Clark did not hesitate to decline secular appointments: he suggested a subordinate General Authority to fill his own invited place on a state cancer organization in

COURTESY HAROLD B. LEE LIBRARY

J. Reuben Clark with U.S. Secretary of State George C. Marshall, 14 July 1947.

1946 because "the moment we got on one we have to get on others, or by refusing make them mad," and he declined the 1949 invitation of the U.S. Secretary of State to attend the signing of the North Atlantic Treaty, to which Reuben was unalterably opposed.[18] George Albert Smith was a different personality and President from Heber J. Grant, but both men recognized the unique contributions that J. Reuben Clark gave to the Church as an elder statesman.

Less than two months after Presidents Smith and Clark discussed his secular activities, President Clark participated for the first time in the dedication services for a completed temple. He had given the address at the cornerstone ceremony for the Idaho Falls Temple in 1940, and now he gave the first major address at the first session of the temple dedication on 23 September 1945. "He said that he believed that with the people that morning in this House of the Lord were those who have gone on before. He said he believed that Joseph Smith, the prophet of the Lord, was rejoicing with us and he said also that he was sure President Heber J. Grant was there also."[19] After President Smith gave the dedicatory prayer in the first session, President Clark also read the dedicatory prayer at subsequent sessions of the dedicatory service on 24 and 25 September 1945, and the three members of the First Presidency alternated in giving keynote addresses and readings of the dedicatory prayer for each session thereafter.[20]

Although President Smith resisted delegating his heavy responsibilities, his health seemed to be holding up, much to President Clark's relief. President Smith presided at all the sessions of the October 1945 general conference, and also traveled with his two counselors to attend the Long Beach (California) Stake conference in February 1946. He was also able to attend all the general sessions of April 1946 general conference but did decide to rest at home rather than attend the bishops' evening meeting during this conference. That fact became the occasion for some of Reuben's self-deprecating humor. "I am what Elder Lee (I think it was) last night referred to as a 'destitute,' " President Clark said as he began his remarks to the bishops. "President Smith was to talk to you tonight but he is unable to be here, and this is the result."[21]

He also took occasion in the bishops' meeting of April 1946 to make a public statement about a new development in general conferences: reading conference talks from prepared texts. Although Reuben usually gave secular talks from prepared texts, he almost never prepared the text in advance for a Church talk but spoke instead by referring to handwritten notes on small scraps of paper.[22] As early as 1943 he warned his protégé Harold B. Lee that prepared conference talks tended to be "abrupt and out of harmony," and urged the junior Apostle to join with him in using "our influence to get others to desist from the practice of reading their talks."[23] Because general conferences were now being broadcast widely, prepared texts were becoming increasingly common, yet President Clark was adamant in his opposition to them. To the bishops on 5 April 1946, J. Reuben Clark complimented a speaker and then made a statement that was really directed to all the General Authorities in attendance at the bishops' meeting: "I hope he will never read another speech. You read well ... but you are a great speaker. That is the way with many others who read what they could better speak."[24] The tide of media packaging of general conferences was against President Clark in this respect, but he was accustomed to swimming upstream.

Another area in which he resisted the dominant trend was in the youth programs of the Church. When President Clark learned that the general leaders of the Young Men's and Young Women's Mutual Improvement Associations thought he was opposed to their programs, he replied that he supported them, but "that they were in a rut; that the young people wanted religion; that we overemphasized amusement, making it an end in itself rather than a means to an end."[25] Nevertheless, the MIA continued to conduct extensive athletic, camping, speech, drama, dance, singing, and other recreational and cultural activities that seemed to President Clark to subordinate the religious instruction that was technically part of the MIA youth program. On the other hand, George Albert Smith had enthusiastically promoted this activity approach for Church youth as general superintendent of the YMMIA from 1921 to 1934 and as a member of the National Executive Council of the Boy Scouts of America since 1932. When President Smith urged a meeting of the Expenditures Committee in November 1946 to allocate more funds for the youth programs of the Church, "Pres. Clark said he thought it was time we were teaching our young people to work rather than to play."[26] Neither President George Albert Smith nor President David O. McKay shared his view of the youth programs of the Church, and it was not until President Clark's protégé Harold B. Lee entered the First Presidency as a counselor in 1970, and as President in 1972, that the annual all-Church athletic and dance competitions were relegated to local, diminished status and the almost autonomous MIA organizations were reconstituted and put directly under priesthood administration.[27]

Another area in which J. Reuben Clark maintained a strong position was in his effort to curtail all expenses of the Church and to eliminate any expenditure he regarded as incompatible with the sacrifices of Latter-day Saints who paid tithing to the Church. President Clark demonstrated this in a comic-opera situation that occurred during the Smith administration. He walked into the First Presidency's office area and found delivery men from ZCMI with a large oriental rug for immediate installation. Upon inquiry he learned that Emily Smith Stewart had prevailed upon her father to consider replacing the drab coverings in several prominent areas with expensive handwoven oriental rugs, and she had, in fact, ordered several to be delivered to 47 East South Temple. President Clark discussed this awkward situation with President Smith, and resolved the problem without emphasizing Emily's role. The influence of daughter upon father may have been a fact, but Reuben did not allow it to become an obstruction.[28]

At the October 1947 conference he gave an address that was possibly his most moving, most personal, and most artistic sermon to that date. In his "Tribute to Pioneers" (later published as *To Them of the Last Wagon*) in the centennial year of the arrival of the Mormon pioneers in Utah, Reuben intended to challenge two popular practices that were especially obvious in 1947: the incessant adulation of prominent pioneer leaders of Mormonism rather than the common folk of pioneering, and the tendency of present Latter-day Saints to bask in the reflected glory of their ancestors. On the first, he began by expressing reverence and tribute to "those souls in name unknown, unremembered, unhonored in the pages of history"; and on the latter practice he concluded: "We may claim no honor, no reward, no respect, nor special position or recognition, no credit because of what our fathers were or what they wrought. We stand upon our own feet in our own shoes. There is no aristocracy in this Church."[29] In this respect he was again swimming against the main current of the pioneer centennial, but his sermon was more than a statement against elitism among Utah Mormons.

At another level, his October 1947 sermon was a prime example of J. Reuben Clark's eloquent use of the English language in spoken discourse.

So through the dust and dirt, dirt and dust, during the long hours, the longer days—that grew into weeks and then into months, they crept along till, passing down through its portals, the valley welcomed them to rest and home. The cattle dropped to their sides, wearied almost to death; nor moved they without goading, for they too sensed they had come to the journey's end.

That evening was the last of the great trek, the mightiest trek that history records since Israel's flight from Egypt, and as the sun sank below the mountain peaks of the west and the eastern crags were bathed in an amethyst glow that was a living light, while the western mountainsides were clothed in shadows of the rich blue of the deep sea, they of the last wagon, and of the wagon before them, and of the one before that, and so to the very front wagon of the train, these all sank to their knees in the joy of their souls, thanking God that at last they were in Zion.[30]

One of the reasons that many Mormons compared J. Reuben Clark, Jr. with Winston Churchill was the perceived similarity of the two men in masterful use of the English language, as well as in their keen perceptions of government.[31] His friend Henry D. Moyle commented that when President Clark gave a talk, "not another man in the Church could have duplicated it," and President George Albert Smith once wrote, "It is a beautiful talk and beautifully delivered, as only President Clark can do it."[32] In the judgment of many he was the most eloquent speaker in the Church from 1933 to 1961.

His October 1947 conference talk also had a more personal dimension. He had long recognized the unpopularity of many of his views among fellow Saints, particularly when he felt it necessary to chastise them. He had publicly expressed indifference to his critics, but he knew that many of the Church members regarded him as aloof even though he had their interests at heart. President Clark used the tribute to the average Mormon pioneer as a means of communicating to the present Latter-day Saints an awareness that he understood their occasional estrangement from "the Brethren who sometimes seemed so far away ... [from] the last wagon, [where] not always could they see the Brethren way out in front, and the blue heaven was often shut out from their sight by heavy, dense clouds of the earth." And using the pioneer exodus as a symbol for his own exhortations to the present members of the Church, he observed, "So corrective counsel, sometimes strong reproof, was the rule, because the wagon must not delay the whole train. But yet in that last wagon there was devotion and loyalty and integrity, and above and beyond everything else, faith in the Brethren and in God's power and goodness."[33] He appreciated the underlying bedrock of faith even in those members of the Church he chastised, and his 1947 conference address was a quiet expression of hope that they understood his compassion for them.

In January 1948 he began a series of KSL radio lectures on Sunday evenings. His announced theme was "On the Way to Immortality and Eternal Life," and his intention was to give a detailed outline of Church doctrine. These lectures were published a year later as half of President Clark's first book of religious writings. Most of the lectures (and later the book) emphasized scriptural justification of Mormon doctrines, with frequent citation to scriptural and scholarly sources; but as he outlined Church beliefs in the separate identity of God the Father and His Son Jesus Christ, President Clark's prose became emotionally expressive and lyrical, transcending the style of the rest of the book.

Then, on the cross, when the lees of life were ebbing away, and mortal strength had almost gone, he cried out in the words pre-voiced by the inspired Psalmist a full millennium before, "My God, my God, why has thou forsaken me?" So questioned the Son of the Father as the darkness of mortal death blinded his eyes.

All these are not the outcries in prayer of a mighty soul in divine agony to an immense, formless, impersonal, spiritual essence, without body, without parts, without passions. These are the heart outpourings of a loving Son, weighted with the sins of men, to a divine Father, who knew, who suffered when the Son suffered, who loved his Only Begotten as only God can love; a Father who had mercy; a Father in whose image and likeness the Son was; a Father who could speak and answer back, who could give aid and succor to a Son in distress as he had done time and time again during the Son's mission on earth.[34]

Since his childhood, Reuben had been most eloquent when speaking of the Savior, and this passage stands in stark contrast to the didactic, proof-text style of the rest of the lectures in this series.

In fact, he prefaced his presentation with the warning that "the book is not light reading. Perhaps much of it will be tedious and dull." But he commended it to all Christians because he sought to demonstrate through scripture and historical scholarship the errors of traditional Christianity and the correctness of the Latter-day Restoration.[35] The fact that the Roman Catholic Bishop of Salt Lake City was at the same time giving Sunday radio talks over Church-owned KSL tended to turn both series of lectures in 1948 into a continuing debate. The exchange occasionally became pointed, and the published version of *On the Way to Immortality and Eternal Life* contained a 220-page appendix about Roman Catholic beliefs and practices. Some felt he was being much too direct, while others cheered his forthright expressions.[36] A review of the book in the Unitarian press observed, "While sharply critical of the practices of the Roman Catholic Church, he is singularly free of carping and bigoted criticism," and the review concluded that the "book is worthy of careful study by Unitarians, because it reveals the personality and the faith of one of the outstanding religious leaders in America today."[37] Because KSL was owned by the Church and the station's president was J. Reuben Clark himself, the continued presence of Monsignor Hunt's broadcasts is a measure of the tolerance that existed between contending religious groups in Utah.

President Clark did not limit his penetrating gaze to the structure and evolution of Roman Catholicism; he also saw disturbing implications in the accelerating growth and complexity of his own church. On 12 June 1948, when he was spending a Saturday in the Presidency's office, he jotted in his office diary two of his nagging fears about the directions in which he saw the Church moving.

1. Appraising Church activities by business asset-liability procedures. [Can spiritual development and achievement be measured statistically, or will the use of statistical measures of success and failure in Church activities actually undermine spirituality by glorifying external piety? Yet should Church funds continue to be spent to support statistically unproductive proselyting areas or administrative programs, for which there are only isolated claims for rich spiritual development? Could efficiency become the end rather than spirituality?]

2. Church activities widening so much in scope and variety in fields where Church leaders have little training and experience, so that non-leaders are able to suggest better means and methods than leaders, all of which breaks down influence of Church leadership.[38]

He had personally experienced the dramatic increase of bureaucracy in the U.S. State Department from 1906 to 1929, and was now witnessing the rise of a bureaucracy at Church headquarters. He saw that the increased influence of Church bureaucrats and technocrats was inevitable in a Church of geometric growth, but what were the implications of the growing dependence of prophets, seers, and revelators upon "non-leaders" in decision making? Could presiding quorums inadvertantly surrender their autonomy to bureaucrats? Would the situation be remedied by calling technocrats to be General Authorities? He saw the problems in embryo, but he saw no easy solutions. President Clark instinctively resisted the administrative developments he so briefly described, and he knew those disturbing tendencies would increase with greater Church population. He decided on a watch-and-warn policy that would characterize his private administrative counsel during the last decade of his service in the Presidency.

Yet, in 1948 he was trying to cope with a more immediate problem that centered in the work-driven disposition of President George Albert Smith. The only success President Clark had achieved in getting him to delegate his heavy burdens and reduce his pressures was that the President retained the services of D. Arthur Haycock as a private secretary. But the President still drove himself mercilessly. Moreover, he could not accept any hint of relaxation by the other hard-pressed General Authorities. At the last temple meeting of the Presidency and Quorum of the Twelve in July 1948 prior to their designated vacation period, President Clark urged the Brethren to take "a real rest" and to decline speaking requests; but George Albert Smith immediately responded by instructing "the brethren that they ought to be constantly available throughout the vacation period and not to expect to make it a full vacation."[39] The counselor maintained a respectful silence, but feared that President Smith would drive himself into the kind of problems he experienced in 1909.

By the fall of 1948 President Smith's condition came frighteningly close to repeating his earlier breakdown. On 6 October 1948 his diary read, "My nerves are giving me some discomfort as a result of exhaustion," and his condition gradually worsened until he recorded in January 1949 that he remained at home in bed "with tired nerves." President Clark dreaded a return of George Albert Smith's 1909–1913 incapacity, or of the conditions in the First Presidency from 1940–1945, and grimly remained at his post in the First Presidency's office as the President's condition worsened. President Smith was admitted to a Los Angeles hospital on 20 January, from which he was discharged on 8 February so that he could recuperate at Laguna Beach until early March 1949. Despite the rest, he was not able to attend all the sessions of general conference in April.[40]

President Clark had previously reassured President Smith's brother that he and President McKay would relieve the President as much as they could from the burdens of the President's office, but in April President McKay went to California to assist his wife in her recovery from an illness. On 3 May 1949 Reuben wrote to one of his associates in Foreign Bondholders':

> I cannot tell when I can get East again. The situation here gets a little more difficult and confining all the time. Just when I can take time away from the office I do not know. I do not mean by this that I am "*the* indispensable man," but so long as one has a job one has to do one's best to do it, which is my situation at the moment. President Smith is able to spend only two or three hours a day at the office, and that leaves a situation where I have to be here more than I otherwise would.[41]

Two days later President Smith's physician informed him that there was "nothing organically wrong with me"; yet the President remained in bed instead of attending the temple meeting of the Presidency and the Twelve.[42]

It seemed like the beginning of 1940 all over again for President Clark, but he was now nearly seventy-eight years old and was uncertain that he could indefinitely shoulder the burdens of the Presidency's office as he had during the last years of Heber J. Grant's presidency. If he did not husband his own strength and that of President McKay, they might soon join President Smith in nervous exhaustion. On 15 July 1949 he acted with a sudden resolve that typically sprang from long contemplation. As recorded by David O. McKay, "While I was dictating to Clare, President Clark came in. Said that he wanted to talk to me about *vacations*; that he felt [we] should both go on a vacation, and that it should be settled here and now." Reuben gave President McKay first choice of time period, and they decided upon a vacation of 8–22 August for President McKay and of 22 August–5 September 1949 for President Clark.[43] It was the first vacation Reuben had taken since he became a member of the First Presidency in 1933, and it was "one of the fewer than half dozen I think I have had since I went into the State Department in 1906."[44]

Unlike Presidents Smith and McKay, he had always had an iron constitution that justified his own work-centered ways, but if he were to persuade them to preserve their strength in between emergencies, then he would have to take vacations from the Presidency's office as well. Besides, it was not a bad idea for a seventy-eight-year-old man.

Although President Smith resisted some of President Clark's solicitous attempts to ease his burdens, he felt both admiration and affection for his First Counselor. When the Church President learned that the Grantsville First Ward was to be dedicated on 9 October 1949, he insisted on joining in honoring the place of President Clark's birth and ranching operations. On Sunday President Smith and his daughters, Emily and Edith, left the Stewart home, picked up his secretary, D. Arthur Haycock, and drove to President Clark's ranch house in Grantsville. There they met with the stake presidency and ward bishopric and ate a lunch prepared by President Clark's daughter Louise. President Smith then took a nap at the Clark ranch and attended the dedication services of the Grantsville First Ward.[45]

Although by now President Smith was trying to reduce the tensions he was under and to rest a little more, the strains of the Presidency caused further deterioration of his health. Ten days after President Smith's pleasant visit at the Clark ranch in Grantsville, his younger daughter Edith Elliott telephoned President Clark at the Church offices to report that her father would not be in the office due to "a dose of nerves."[46] For months President Smith had tried to ease his administrative burdens in the Presidency's office by consulting alone with President Clark on many matters prior to meetings of the full First Presidency so that the formal meetings of all three members of the Presidency could conclude in half an hour.[47] But by December 1949 President Smith was having difficulty being in the Presidency's office even to do this. "At 5:00 President Clark came in to say that he was holding two or three important matters which he wished to go over with me for my opinion."[48] President Clark had adopted again the strategems designed to insure the administrative preeminence of an ailing President of the Church. From 12 January to 27 February 1950 George Albert Smith was at Laguna Beach, California; he returned there for ten days in March and from 30 July to 29 August President Smith was absent on a trip to Hawaii, a trip taken primarily for recuperative purposes.[49] Added to these absences from Utah were the days when President Smith rested at home or was able to be in the First Presidency's office only a few hours.

J. Reuben Clark shouldered the added burdens of the First Presidency's office without complaint, but a newsy letter he wrote to some non-Mormon friends indicates the kind of adjustments necessary in his life:

The fact is, I am usually at work by eight o'clock in the morning and I normally am constantly at the office until 5:30 and sometimes nearly six, and am here every Saturday. In the night time I usually rest until perhaps nine and then do some work at home. Even then I have great difficulty in keeping anywhere near up on my day to day tasks. I have almost entirely given up any social life beyond the great blessing which is mine in having my children clustered about me [in homes on the "Avenues" of Salt Lake City], all but Reuben [at Brigham Young University, in Provo], and they come in and visit me practically every evening for a few minutes. I cannot conceive of any greater blessing than this that could come to me.[50]

He wanted to do even more to help George Albert Smith, but the President read and dictated correspondence even during his recuperative absences. President Clark knew that this only worsened the situation, but he continued to be supportive of the President and did not nag him about self-preservation. He eagerly made whatever adjustments necessary in his own activities and office routine to accommodate President Smith's failing health, frequent absences, and diminishing attention span. Under these circumstances it exasperated President Clark beyond words when he stepped into a hole on the way home from the Twentieth Ward on 18 September 1950, injured his head, ankle, and knee in the fall, and had to remain at home four days.[51]

He returned as soon as he could to full activity in the Presidency office because he did not want to fail to be there whenever President Smith needed him. He realized that insistence on monitoring even trivial activities in the Presidency's office was not only a reflection of President Smith's lifelong hypertension, but also was a manifestation of his unexpressed fear of surrendering the unsurrenderable responsibility of being President of the high priesthood of God on earth. Yet Reuben also realized that the President's condition was such that the presence of the counselors was essential for operation of the First Presidency's office.

The growth of the Church by 1950 was already demanding careful attention to new approaches and reexamination of former policies. In a letter to a member of the Church on 26 September 1950 he suggested an innovation that soon became a new policy in the Church: saving enormous amounts of expenditures for new chapels by building chapels "so as to house *wards* instead of *a ward* in such buildings."[52] In this case J. Reuben Clark's famous parsimony blended well with the needs of a growing Church population.

After President George Albert Smith attended all sessions of the October 1950 general conference his health began to falter so much that he had to delegate more of his office responsibilities. On 24 October 1950 he consented to having Presidents Clark and McKay alone sign routine Presidency letters, and to reserve "only the more important and policy matters for the signature of three, thus husbanding my strength," and in the next few months President Clark needed to consult with President Smith more frequently at his home or at the hospital, where he went on 3 February.[53] They expressed their deepest feelings to each other about the situation facing the First Presidency on 14 February 1951:

> [President Smith] ... It has been suggested to me that I go to some other part of the country and try to get better. I have felt that the headquarters of the work of the Lord was here. Most of the financial interests of the Church are controlled from here, and I have thought we ought to have men in charge so that in the event of the sickness of the President they could carry on. If the President is sick, things would go forward anyhow. ...
>
> President Clark: I have done all I can and will do all I can to carry on. I have a real affection for you. I have no desire except to help you and help carry on the Lord's work.

Following these words, President Smith requested that President Clark administer to him with the assistance of D. Arthur Haycock and President Smith's relatives.[54] Everyone realized that the state of his health was nearing a critical point.

At his request, George Albert Smith left the hospital on 24 February 1951 and began constant medical care at his home. President Clark visited him at least every other day, but on 13 March his private physician "ordered that nothing be brought to him for decision." The President had suffered a stroke, had recovered partially, and then had had a relapse. The end seemed only a matter of days away.[55] On 2 April 1951 President McKay, the second-ranking Apostle in the Church and the successor to George Albert Smith, visited the president. "He did not seem to recognize me—the first time since his sickness," wrote President McKay. "I realized that possibly the end was not far off. It came as quite a shock to my nervous system, for I fully sensed then what his passing means."[56] President Clark continued his daily visits, and stayed at his bedside from 1:30 to 4:30 P.M. on 4 April 1951. President Smith died three hours later, and Presidents Clark and McKay rushed back to the Smith home to see their departed President and to comfort his loved ones.[57] A gentle, loving spirit had finally found rest from the cares of the Church to which he had too rigorously devoted the energies of his life. George Albert Smith was dead, and as senior living Apostle, David O. McKay was President of the Church even prior to the formal sustaining vote and organization of a new First Presidency.

In the preparations and conduct of the funeral, President Clark displayed the same refusal to assert his prior authority in the now discontinued First Presidency as he had at the death of Heber J. Grant. When the Quorum of the Twelve met in the temple on 6 April 1951 to prepare for both the funeral and April general conference, which was only hours away, he immediately took his place in seniority as the sixth Apostle. When President McKay asked for his assistance in planning the funeral, the former First Counselor replied to the former Second Counselor: "You don't need to feel you need to honor me, Brethren. I know my place and I am happy." When the General Authorities entered the tabernacle an hour later for the first session of conference, President Clark immediately took his place with the Apostles, without presuming to have any special function in the conference. President McKay called him from his seat with the Apostles to join in presiding at the first session and to conduct the second session. President Clark "made it beautifully clear that he conducted it by delegation, not by right when he said: 'I conduct this Conference by courtesy,' and never before did that word COURTESY mean so much," wrote Spencer W. Kimball, then of the Quorum of the Twelve Apostles. Elder Kimball added: "Brother Clark is magnificent!!"[58]

"THREE PRESIDING HIGH PRIESTS"

Doctrine and Covenants 107:22

DAVID O. McKAY, 1951–1961

While he was at the University of Utah in the 1890s, Reuben became acquainted with David O. McKay, whose future wife, Emma Ray Riggs, graduated with Reuben in 1898. Ten years later, after Reuben had served two years in the State Department during the same time that his college friend was a newly appointed member of the Quorum of the Twelve, Lute wrote, "I also met Apostle McKay who said many nice things about you, and wished to be remembered to you."[1]

When J. Reuben Clark entered the First Presidency as a high priest in 1933, Elder McKay was the seventh Apostle in seniority (including Presidents Grant and Ivins). Following the Ivins funeral on 27 September 1934, President Grant said that he wanted to select David O. McKay as counselor, to which President Clark replied, "I am very glad; he is the man that I had thought of and would like."[2] After the general conference of October 1934 sustained President Clark as First Counselor and President McKay as Second Counselor in the First Presidency, the latter remarked: "I have known President Clark since my school days in the University of Utah. I admired him then. I considered him one of the choicest young men I had ever seen or had ever known. . . . I love him as a friend, and to be associated with him now in this high quorum, the highest in the Church, makes me feel very happy and thankful, but also very humble."[3] The association of these two men was one of the most extraordinary in Church history.

David O. McKay and J. Reuben Clark served together in the First Presidency for twenty-seven years, from October 1934 to October 1961. Theirs was the longest presidential association in Church history. The nearest competitors in time were the twenty-one years of Brigham Young and Heber C. Kimball, the twenty years of Brigham Young and Daniel H. Wells, the twenty years of Anthon H. Lund and Charles W. Penrose, and the cumulative total of nearly nineteen years of joint service in the First Presidency by George Q. Cannon and Joseph F. Smith. Aside from its longevity, the Clark-McKay presidential experience was also the first example of someone serving as a co-counselor with a man and then later serving as counselor to the same man as President of the Church.[4] Therefore, the service of Presidents McKay and Clark was possibly the most significant presidential association in Church history and certainly was the most important association in the First Presidency's office for Reuben.

There were several similarities between the two men. A week after Reuben's second birthday, David O. McKay was born in Huntsville, Utah, a town with a population only three hundred persons greater than Grantsville. Both boys grew up with a love of farm life that they perpetuated throughout their lives by continuing to operate farms in their respective birthplaces. Both men became General Authorities as "outsiders" from the mainstream of the business, economic, social, and ecclesiastical life of Utah's cities, and neither Elder McKay nor Reuben had enough presiding experience in the Church to be ordained a high priest prior to his call as a General Authority.[5] Moreover, the two men were among the few General Authorities in Utah who were not closely related by kinship or marriage to other General Authorities at the time of their own Church calls.[6] Both were called as General Authorities at times of great stress for the Church: Elder McKay during the difficult days of the U.S. Senate's investigation of Reed Smoot, and Reuben during the Great Depression.

Despite these similarities, they were vastly different in personality and administrative style. A later counselor in the First Presidency, Marion G. Romney, once observed that Presidents Clark and McKay were men "of an entirely different type . . . a balanced pair of counselors."[7] The differences in these two men are crucial for understanding twenty-seven years of Reuben's Church service, because David O. McKay and J. Reuben Clark were members of the First Presidency in counterpoise. President Romney characterized the administrative differences between these two members of the First Presidency by observing that President McKay was a gentle poet-philosopher whereas President Clark was a determined administrator-legalist.[8]

During the years Reuben was teaching business school, studying law, and developing awesome administrative skills in the practice of law, government, and diplomacy, David O. McKay was a liberal arts teacher before his 1906 apostolic call and thereafter developed his own administrative style in the congenial atmosphere of Sunday School administration. Where he quoted secular writers in sermons, President Clark usually cited legal and political science authorities and only occasionally cited literary sources. On the other hand, President McKay often quoted his own poetry, as well as the writings of Robert Burns, Lord Byron, Thomas Carlyle, Charles Dickens, John Dryden, Ralph Waldo Emerson, Johann Goethe, Oliver Goldsmith, Thomas Gray, Heinrich Heine, William James, Henry Wadsworth Longfellow, James Russell Lowell, Joaquin Miller, John Milton, Alexander Pope, Jean-Jacques Rousseau, John Ruskin, Sir Walter Scott, William Shakespeare, Herbert Spencer, Alfred Lord Tennyson, Leo Tolstoy, William Makepeace Thackeray, John Greenleaf Whittier, and William Wordsworth.[9] Everyone acknowledged Reuben's administrative skills; but another tough administrator, Ernest L. Wilkinson, observed with special emphasis that "President McKay is a great spiritual leader."[10]

Although both men valued spirituality, David O. McKay tended to give it preeminence in Church administration, whereas Reuben tended to ally spirituality with rational examination. He urged Latter-day Saints to "listen to the still, small voice," in their decisions, yet for him the process was one of rational experimentation: "Spiritual knowledge may be gained through reading, observation, and conduct of experiments,—experiments in right living, right thinking, and a complete and whole-hearted search for truth, spiritual truth."[11] His testimony had passed through a fiery ordeal more than a decade before he entered the First Presidency, and he kept his faith simple. Although he believed implicitly in divine inspiration—

particularly to the President of the Church—President Clark tended to be cautious in ascribing divinity to his own moments of inspiration.

> Occasionally I have the experience of seeming to have a ray of light strike through my mind that, like a lightning flash, illumines for the fraction of a second, some infinite truth, but it is gone so quickly that it leaves only an impression, like a lightning flash of a landscape that I would like to study. But I try not to let these things mislead me in my thinking. I try to hang to hard facts.[12]

David O. McKay's acceptance of personal impressions and J. Reuben Clark's preference for studious examination led to a major administrative difference between the two members of the First Presidency with respect to decision making. President Clark's demand for thorough research prior to a decision and President McKay's willingness to make immediate decisions based upon his own personal impressions continued to separate their administrative approaches throughout a twenty-seven-year association in the First Presidency.[13]

The ways in which they arrived at administrative decisions also affected the permanence of their decisions. Because President Clark arrived at his administrative decisions methodically, he almost never changed his mind. On the other hand, President McKay was willing to reassess decisions as often as he felt new circumstances required.[14]

Their decision making widened even further with respect to being influenced by others. J. Reuben Clark had been involved in administrative battlefields of the State Department, law, and international diplomacy for nearly thirty years before he entered the First Presidency, and he was insulated against questioning his decisions or modifying them because of the criticism or the attempted flattery of others. President Clark once noted that "I have learned to accept criticism, opprobrium, and even hate without too much disturbance," and one of his admirers praised him for making Church decisions despite the attempts by persons to influence him in their favor.[15] On the other hand, David O. McKay loved intimate association with crowds and individuals, treasured close fellowship with the Latter-day Saints, shrank from criticism, and was therefore more vulnerable to those seeking to influence his administrative decisions in the First Presidency.[16]

Their personalities also had profound administrative significance. President Clark at heart was an unreconstructed pessimist who "felt it wisest to approach problems from the point of view that things may be worse than better" and whose view of humanity was summed up by his comment: "So far behind us as we can reach with history, tradition, or myth, there are in man the same selfishness, envy, avarice, cruelty, ambition, domination, love, and hate, that exists in him today, no other or different."[17] By contrast, President McKay was an unshakable optimist who assumed that the worst of conditions would improve, that favorable conditions would become even better, and that man's nature was basically good.[18] Their views regarding the idea of progress and human nature affected how they planned for the Church: J. Reuben Clark favored slow growth and cautious, even parsimonious, expenditure of funds, whereas David O. McKay favored expansive growth and a more liberal expenditure of funds.

As Church administrators they also had differing conceptions of the national and international character of Mormonism. Thirty years of training and experience before 1933 predisposed Reuben to see everything in terms of U.S. nationalism, and even his conceptions of secular and religious neutrality in time of war were reflections of his idealistic views of the mission of America and of Americans (including the Latter-day Saints). Moreover, all his activities and sermons as elder statesman in the First Presidency were based upon the assumption that the most important issues of Mormonism lay within the United States. In contrast to Reuben's lifelong tendency toward religious nationalism, President McKay was a lifelong internationalist in his view of the Church. Whereas J. Reuben Clark never studied or visited a foreign country except in the interests of the United States of America, David O. McKay's patriarchal blessing, received when he was a thirteen-year-old boy, promised that he would "assist in gathering scattered Israel." He served a proselyting mission among the people of Great Britain from 1897 to 1899; he toured the missions and prospective missions of the Church in the South Pacific, Asia, the Near East, and Europe from 1920 to 1921; he served as president of the European Mission from 1922 to 1924, in which capacity he revisited the Near East in 1924; he visited the far-flung membership of the Church outside the Intermountain West as often as he could and stated in general conference in April 1927, "Most earnestly do I hope that we shall never lose the great conviction that the world is our field of activity."[19] This difference of emphasis on the national and international character of Mormonism, as well as their respectively conservative and expansive views of the activities of the Church, caused the two leaders to approach administrative decisions in divergent ways.

Their administrative and philosophical counterpoise as counselors in the First Presidency for nearly seventeen years was an observed fact for both Mormons and non-Mormons. As early as 1934 David O. McKay expressed concern "with the highly conservative attitude of J. Reuben Clark" during a two-hour interview with a member of the Church.[20] In 1942, *Time* reported a "disagreement in the First Presidency itself" when President McKay made a strong appeal concerning the wartime objectives of the Allies that seemed to contradict a statement drafted and read by Reuben at October conference the previous day.[21] And, after interviewing twenty-one influential Utahns, John Gunther wrote in 1947, "A counterweight to Clark to some extent is the benign old second counselor, David O. McKay, a middle roader."[22]

Moreover, for various personal, philosophical, and administrative reasons, most Church administrators in Salt Lake City tended to align themselves either with J. Reuben Clark or David O. McKay. During the 1930s, when President McKay manned the office while President Clark was in New York City, some Church members and administrators preferred to await Reuben's return rather than consult the Second Counselor.[23] President Spencer W. Kimball observed that the popular division of the General Authorities and other administrators into "Clark men" and "McKay men" could easily be exaggerated, but he verified that there was a gravitation of men either toward President Clark's leadership and philosophy or toward President McKay's leadership and philosophy. President Kimball further observed, "There was no serious division, but President Clark supported President McKay despite his non-agreement with President McKay's policies."[24]

In spite of personal and administrative differences, there was always a cordial relationship between them. As counselors they addressed and signed their letters to each other in the familiar "David" and "Reuben," although President McKay often addressed the First Counselor in the more formal "President Clark." President McKay, who was more of an enthusiast for entertainment and cultural events, often sent complimentary tickets for these activities to President Clark and his family.[25] Moreover, Reuben continually fretted about David O. McKay's health and his tendency to abbreviate recuperation from his frequent surgeries and illnesses. "I hope you will take care of yourself and that your strength will rapidly return," he wrote after President McKay had been periodically ill in 1938. "Among the many bits of wisdom I have dropped at your feet, mostly to be trodden upon, do not forget this one: You cannot do a full day's work at the office and then a full day's work on the farm in the same twenty-four hours."[26] On other occasions (such as April and May 1938, March 1940, July 1945, November 1946, and April 1950), President Clark felt that the Second Counselor was too ill to resume regular activities, and he virtually ordered him to stay away from the Presidency's office for recuperation. President McKay's typical reaction at these times was: "I'll have to admit that I am weaker than I thought I would be. . . ."[27]

President Clark's being in the office while President McKay was absent was actually a reversal of the situation that existed during the first few years after David O. McKay entered the Presidency. At that time Reuben was most often in New York City on business for Foreign Bondholders'. When President Grant started a three-week California vacation in January 1935, Lute wrote Reuben at his FBPC office in New York City: "Poor Bro. McKay—I suppose you are hard at work at your office."[28] Because Reuben thrived on office routine (whether in Washington, New York, or Salt Lake City), he probably needed Lute's comments to help him realize the extent to which office isolation burdened the Second Counselor. When the two counselors unitedly faced the challenges in the Presidency's office during the prolonged illness of President Grant, they made necessary adjustments in their responses and approaches, as Reuben noted in 1944: "Had conference with D.O.M. we ironed out some differences."[29]

One circumstance that they could not themselves alter was the fact that the man with nearly thirty years' seniority as an Apostle was Second Counselor. This troubled both Presidents McKay and Clark; but neither had created the circumstances of their respective callings, and they accepted the decisions of Presidents Grant and Smith in this matter.[30]

The issue might have seemed resolved when George Albert Smith died on 4 April 1951 and David O. McKay became senior Apostle and automatic President of the Church. But President McKay prayerfully considered the reorganization of the First Presidency and his choice of counselors. It was generally expected that he would advance his closest friend among the General Authorities, Stephen L Richards, to be a member of the First Presidency; but many expected Elder Richards to be made Second Counselor.[31] President McKay knew that was the expectation of others but was troubled at the thought of putting his closest friend in the same situation he himself had been in for sixteen and one-half years. Stephen L Richards had more than seventeen years' seniority over President Clark as an Apostle in the Quorum of the Twelve. Moreover, Elder Richards shared President McKay's administrative expansiveness, optimism, and other views foreign to President Clark.[32]

President McKay waited as long as he could to confide his decision about the change of counselors. For the first time since 1906 (when he himself had been sustained an Apostle), a general conference of the Church had convened on the Church's anniversary date of 6 April without presenting the General Authorities for a sustaining vote. The morning session of 8 April passed without the presentation of officers, and only one day of conference remained in which to reorganize the First Presidency. To delay longer would cause comment, but David O. McKay first had to inform Reuben of the change and to present it to the Quorum of the Twelve Apostles for their sustaining vote. By noon on 8 April, President McKay knew he could postpone the action no longer.

As she always did, Louise had brought some sandwiches to her father's office to eat alone with him during the recess between conference sessions. They had just begun eating at 12:30 when President McKay knocked at the door and asked President Clark to come to his office. A few minutes later, Reuben reentered his office, and, avoiding his daughter's puzzled look, said he wanted to eat alone and take a nap. She knew better than to ask what the matter was, but her father's cheerfulness had turned into an inwardness that filled her with gloom.[33]

For a few minutes after Louise quietly shut the door behind her, Reuben stared thoughtfully at the door and mentally pictured the nearby office of the man who was now President of the Church. They had served together in the Presidency's office for nearly seventeen years, during which time they had loyally counseled two presidents and had supported each other. Reuben's own words to the priesthood meeting the night before returned to him: "And so I come back to my theme song in all of these meetings: We must have unity. We must work together. We must submerge our individual likes and dislikes."[34] President McKay had said something to him about seniority of apostleship as the reason for the change in counselor position, but it seemed a difficult decision to bear.

Reuben had never aspired for Church office, but he had to admit pride in feeling that he had faithfully and vigorously fulfilled the office of First Counselor in the Presidency since 1934. No matter what public explanation was given, would not Church members regard his being made Second Counselor after so many years as something of a demotion? His thoughts drifted back, and he seemed to see his beloved Lute and the strain in her face of all their separations and sacrifices for a public career he eventually surrendered for the Church service that had now come to this. He suddenly remembered a letter he had written Lute in 1929 about a retiring diplomat. "The poor old 'dodo' (with respect) weeps whenever he thinks of leaving the service. He is one of the nicest old ladies I have ever met," he had written caustically, and then he added the reflection, "But as we get older we all get more tearful—so I suppose it is something to be looked forward to."[35] Reuben thanked God silently that Lute had not lived to see this general conference of the Church, and then he gave vent to unaccustomed emotion in the solitude of his office. He was nearly eighty, and the next decade would be difficult.

President McKay asked all the members of the Quorum of the Twelve Apostles to meet in the temple following the afternoon session of general conference on 8 April 1951. As everyone anticipated, he began the business of the special 4:30 meeting by explaining the need for reorganizing the First Presidency in view of the death of George Albert Smith. Joseph Fielding Smith, the second Apostle in seniority, immediately moved that David O. McKay be sustained formally as the President of the Church. The motion was seconded by Stephen L Richards, third Apostle in seniority, and unanimously voted in the affirmative by the assembled members of the Quorum of the Twelve. Spencer W. Kimball described the reaction of the apostles when President McKay announced his choice of counselors.

I was stunned when he explained that he had chosen Elder Richards first, Pres. Clark having served as first counselor for long years to President Grant and Pres. Smith. I looked around and found the other brethren stunned. It was hard to understand. I knew Elder Richards had been a close and lifelong friend but I was not prepared for this.... All the others of the Twelve seemed to be alike stunned. We had been wholly unprepared for this shock. Pres. Clark had stood and accepted this call and in this order like a god. What a man! What fortitude! What courage and self control! What self mastery! How could any mortal take a blow like that and stand? But he did.

After the assembled men unanimously voted to sustain President McKay's choice and ordering of counselors, Elder Kimball recorded that the rest of the Apostles left their room in the temple in unaccustomed silence and "walked back to the office building numb. The other brethren from Bro. Lee down came together at the corner of the building and commiserated together.... Our hearts were breaking for that elder stalwart who for two regimes had carried the major load."[36]

Reuben began the morning of 9 April 1951 with an earnest prayer that the Lord would sustain him through one of the most difficult experiences of his life. Not even his own children knew that he would be made Second Counselor at the solemn assembly which would sustain the new First Presidency. Added to that change in his life and his fears of the effect it might have on his own children, he had to bear one further burden: David O. McKay asked him to present the names of the new First Presidency and other officers of the Church for the sustaining vote. Thousands of people in the Salt Lake Tabernacle and tens of thousands of television and radio listeners would be able to detect the slightest trace of emotion in his voice as he announced his altered position in the First Presidency. All these circumstances added up to one of the most electrifying moments in the history of the Church's general conferences. His daughter Marianne later wrote:

Your calm, judicious manner with no hesitancy, no tremor, and without rancor, greatly increased the spirit of solemnity. I guess most everyone believed that you had made a mistake as you read the second name, but no one who did not

President Clark presenting the authorities of the Church for sustaining vote, on this occasion in October 1958, seven years after he presented President David O. McKay, First Counselor Stephen L. Richards and Second Counselor J. Reuben Clark for sustaining vote on 9 April 1951.

know, could have imagined that there was the slightest personal connection between you and what you were saying. . . .[37]

President McKay then explained that apostolic seniority rather than "any rift" was the reason for the change in President Clark's status, which the President insisted was not a demotion.[38] Then he called on the newly sustained Second Counselor to speak before the newly sustained First Counselor.

J. Reuben Clark's words at this moment have often been quoted in later years without an understanding of the truly dramatic circumstances of their utterance: "In the service of the Lord, it is not where you serve but how. In the Church of Jesus Christ of Latter-day Saints, one takes the place to which one is duly called, which place one neither seeks nor declines."[39] Spencer W. Kimball recorded in

123

his journal that "the congregation was breathless ... [and] there were many tears throughout the great congregation.... No one could tell if Pres. Clark carried any scars or injuries.... No complaint, no self-pity neither in act nor attitude. He accepted it. He proclaimed the majesty of the Church." And Elder Kimball added that this "did more in his perfect reactions perhaps to establish in the minds of this people the true spirit of subjection of the individual to the good of the work, more than could be done in thousands of sermons."[40] Joseph Anderson, secretary to the First Presidency, wrote that on this occasion President Clark spoke "with a courage that has seldom been equalled, I am sure, in Church administration."[41] On 9 April 1951 he maintained his rock-like stability and strength and also characteristically tried to moderate the adulation of his admirers. After the conference session Elder Kimball took the hand of his first cousin and expressed heartfelt admiration for what he described as the greatest demonstration of self-mastery he had ever witnessed, to which President Clark simply said: "It wasn't easy."[42]

Beyond the General Authorities of the Church, reaction to the reorganization of the First Presidency was mixed, tending to reflect the divergent attitudes among Latter-day Saints and non-Mormons about J. Reuben Clark's political influence and statements. Newspaper columnist Drew Pearson wrote that President Clark was "a reactionary of the worst sort, [who] has finally been demoted by the new President of the Church, David O. McKay."[43] Most who applauded or decried the 1951 change were looking at the matter in terms of political influence or ecclesiastical status—the tokens of power. There were others, however, who felt only the personal dimension of this event.

President Clark had worried about the effects his new role might have on his family, but he underestimated the strength he had given them. Marianne Clark Sharp expressed the feelings of all President Reuben Clark's children in a letter she wrote him on 19 April 1951:

> Of course I felt stunned and heartsick and kept questioning in my mind as to how such a thing could come to you following your years of devoted service to the Lord. As I thought of it during that day these words kept coming to me and comforting me, "For whom the Lord loveth he chasteneth."

Never before that day, with all my love and appreciation for your great and noble soul and of your achievements, have I felt so proud to have you for my father.

. . . .

To me this experience through which we are passing is the greatest lesson which you have taught us, an example which should encourage and sustain us always and bind us closer together in the eternal family unit, coming on top of your wonderful teachings.

I believe your spirit grew to a new height that day—perhaps one to which you might never have attained without this experience.[44]

As for Reuben himself, he masked his inner feelings about the situation whenever friends expressed their unconcealed resentment about the change, but on one occasion his own emotions nearly overtook him at the very moment he was defending President McKay. Two days after the solemn assembly he answered one person's criticism by relating the occasion as a new counselor in the Presidency when he complained to Anthony W. Ivins about someone's faults, to which President Ivins had responded that he would accept all of the person's failings if he could have the person's virtues. After recording this defense, he added a note in the office diary: "I was happy that I got through without any blubbering. The Lord blessed me."[45]

Initially, President Clark told even his non-Mormon friends that he was unsure whether or not his responsibilities would diminish now that he was Second Counselor in the Presidency.[46] A major question in the minds of many was whether President McKay would relieve him of supervising the Welfare Program of the Church, and there was an unusually large attendance at the regular Friday meeting of the Welfare Committee on 13 April. Marion G. Romney observed, "The brethren and sisters evidently came to see what would happen under the new administration. President Clark took charge as usual," and Elder Romney learned later in the day that the President had asked Reuben "to proceed as usual in the welfare work."[47] Moreover, although the Presidents of the Church had served as chairmen of Utah's "This Is the Place" Monument Commission since 1937, President McKay recommended that the governor ask President Clark to accept the appointment.[48]

Although Reuben was pleased with these decisions of the new Church President, the former First Counselor refused to allow the new First Counselor to defer to him. To begin with, he had a long-standing friendship with Stephen L Richards, who was "among the very oldest acquaintances and friends that I have in Salt Lake City," and he had written in 1949 that of his close friends "none is more staunch" than Stephen L Richards.[49] President Richards had no responsibility for the subordination of the former First Counselor, but he demonstrated obvious awkwardness about the situation in the first few months of the new Presidency as he tried to honor his friend's previous position.

When President McKay was unable to attend the weekly temple meeting of the Presidency and Quorum of the Twelve on 3 May 1951, Stephen L Richards seemed willing to have President Clark conduct the council meeting due to his years of experience in that capacity; but Reuben insisted that as Second Counselor he should take the lead only when the other members of the Presidency were absent from the temple meeting.[50] A month later he publicly stated

First Presidency, 9 April 1951.
Stephen L Richards, David O. McKay, J. Reuben Clark.

that principle at the June conference of the Mutual Improvement Associations. President McKay was unable to attend the opening sessions of the conference, and at this first public meeting where the newly sustained counselors presided in the absence of the Church President, President Richards again deferred to the Second Counselor. President Clark immediately corrected any impression this incident might cause to those who witnessed it:

> I think with his [Stephen L Richards's] permission I ought to say a word. In his well-known kindness and consideration and courtesy, he said to me before he began, did I wish him to go forward, and I said "Yes," but I do not want you young people to get any erroneous idea from that. He is the presiding officer of this conference in the absence of President McKay. He does not need to consult me, though he graciously did so.[51]

As deeply as he might have felt about his subordination in 1951, J. Reuben Clark refused to allow the slightest hint that any of the prerogatives of the First Counselor's position remained with him. His demonstration of that principle at the June conference of 1951 so deeply impressed one of the local MIA leaders in attendance that twenty-three years later the man described it as "the most beautiful example I've ever seen in Church procedure. . . ."[52] Unflinching loyalty to the order of the Church was more important to President Clark than any personal consideration.

Nevertheless, he firmly believed that integrity to one's personal beliefs was synonymous with loyalty to a superior, and he continued to state his views frankly to the President of the Church. Although Presidents McKay and Richards were enthusiastic supporters of the youth activity programs of the Church, in a temple meeting with the Apostles on 7 June 1951 President Clark restated his uneasiness about the Church efforts "to continually further recreational activities."[53] Moreover, when he soon found himself equally uneasy with the united position of Presidents McKay and Richards about the expenditure of Church funds, President Clark told the First Counselor on 30 August 1951, "If you two brethren feel that way, of course I will go along with you. I am not going to stand out. If you feel that way, I will go along."[54]

Perhaps to a greater degree than David O. McKay had anticipated, it was obvious that he and Stephen L Richards were usually of one mind, whereas Reuben often saw things differently. The fundamental differences between Presidents McKay and Clark after April 1951 were consistently resolved in the same manner: Reuben would state his reservations to the views and decisions of President McKay, but the counselor would then loyally sustain the authority and decision of the Church President. As President Clark informed the secretaries to the First Presidency on one occasion, "I know who the President of the Church is, I know what his authority is, I know what he wants and that is what he shall have, even if I don't like it."[55] He was implacable both in bluntness and in loyalty.

President Clark had resigned himself to his diminished status in the First Presidency and he could dismiss with cavalier disdain public comment about tensions within the David O. McKay Presidency,[56] but he worried from 1951 to 1961 about potential or actual reversals by David O. McKay of President Clark's most treasured achievements in Church administration. Suddenly unsure of the permanence of his contributions to the Church, Reuben became increasingly concerned about his protégés and programs and wary of any innovations.[57]

His concern for the possible diminution of his protégés was intensified by a situation that existed in the office of President David O. McKay. Clare Middlemiss had been his private secretary since 1935, and in 1949 she stated, "I have devoted my whole life to President McKay—I want nothing more."[58] What a recent biographer of President McKay has called "the watchful diligence" of Clare Middlemiss became a factor in the ease with which people were granted access to the President. Personal access to President McKay was administratively crucial because he often made on-the-spot decisions, and it is understandable that Reuben was worried about the fact that it was the "McKay men" to whom Clare tended to give immediate access and "Clark men" whom she tended to postpone.[59]

If some were made to wait, President Clark had no difficulty in seeing his "Chief." But President McKay was so reluctant to receive counsel that was contrary to his own judgment that he often made decisions without consulting his Second Counselor.[60] To some extent this was David O. McKay's unique administrative style during his entire service as President, and it indicated as well the degree to which he tried to avoid opposition from those closest to him.

Presidents McKay, Richards, and Clark meet with President Dwight D. Eisenhower.

From 1951 to 1959, however, it was difficult to simply exclude Reuben's contrary advice from First Presidency deliberations. During most of these years he was usually at his desk in the Presidency's office while President McKay was touring missions for weeks at a time, and the *Deseret News* aptly noted in July 1952 that "President Stephen L Richards and President J. Reuben Clark Jr., who have carried on the heavy burdens of the office of the Presidency, were glad to see their President back."[61] More important, because of repeated illnesses and hospitalizations of David O. McKay and Stephen L Richards from 1951 to 1959, President Clark was "by all means the most vigorous of the three and the most productive" until 1959.[62]

Yet when the three counseled together, Reuben sometimes found himself in the unfamiliar position as a conservative voice in a

129

more liberal First Presidency. Ever the elder statesman, he drafted a Presidency Christmas message for 1953 that proposed to lecture the peoples of the world on their responsibilities, and Presidents McKay and Richards decided not to use it because "some outside of the Church might look on it as arrogance."[63] President Richards was also not opposed to accepting federal grants to Brigham Young University on at least a limited basis—a course which Reuben condemned as "socialistic"; but the President was willing to go along with the First Counselor.[64] In the public eye, President Clark continued to be a vigorous leader and eloquent spokesman as Second Counselor from 1951 to 1959, but administratively he was often in checkmate.[65]

Although some people might expect these tensions to have poisoned the feelings of the First Presidency toward one another, quite the opposite was true. Church administrator Gordon Burt Affleck knew of the administrative conflicts between Presidents Richards and Clark and assumed that they heartily disliked each other, but he discovered that they shared a deep respect and affection that they expressed publicly and privately.[66] Marion G. Romney observed, "I don't remember seeing a time when Brother Clark and Brother Richards seemed so friendly. It was a delight to be in their presence."[67] The three strong-willed members of the First Presidency often shared moments of hilarity as well, one of which was captured in a *Salt Lake Tribune* photograph of their laying the cornerstone of the Relief Society headquarters in Salt Lake City on 1 October 1954. Reuben presented a copy of this photograph with the following explanation: "With embarrassing apologies for so much levity on a solemn occasion. The masons were sort of removing the excess mortar we three had spread on too thick; Pres. Richards observed: 'The fault of all amateurs is to spread it on too thick.' "[68] And a loving brother could not have been more solicitous than he was when Presidents McKay and Richards were ill.

Moreover, despite President Clark's personal hope for administrative consistency, he loyally defended the President's agonizing changes of heart during the so-called Ricks College controversy, which David O. McKay defined in 1960 as "the most important matter that he had had to decide as President."[69] On the surface, the issue was simple: whether to keep the Church-supported Ricks College in the town of Rexburg, Idaho (where the school was founded

Presidents McKay, Richards, and Clark at laying of the cornerstone for Relief Society Building, Salt Lake City, 1 October 1954.

at the turn of the century), or to move the college to the city of Idaho Falls (where the Church had larger membership and a temple). Complicating the question was the understandable personal, historical, financial, and religious commitment of the Latter-day Saints of Rexburg for keeping the college in their town, despite whatever merits might exist for moving the institution elsewhere. When Rexburg citizens expressed concern about rumors that Church authorities were considering such a move, David O. McKay impulsively replied on 17 March 1954, "Rest assured there will be no change in Ricks College." Unfortunately, President McKay sent this

131

message before the First Presidency and the Church Board of Education had begun their intended investigation of the merits of a possible move of Ricks College to Idaho Falls.[70] Decisions to move Ricks College were made, modified, and reversed in 1957, then reversed again in 1958. This all provided grist for years of controversy that peppered Church councils and erupted into the public press.[71]

Throughout the increasingly bitter controversy about whether or not to move Ricks College, J. Reuben Clark adamantly defended President McKay. In a meeting of the full Presidency with Ricks College administrators on 15 November 1958, one man insisted that the fervent prayers of the Rexburg people had been answered by the Lord contrary to the statements of the First Presidency in support of moving Ricks College. President Clark interrupted the man by saying, "You know, we prayed about it too, and after all ours were the prayers that counted in this situation and not his individual prayers. . . ."[72]

By February 1959 the controversy had escalated into a fever pitch of public and private animosity. "President McKay felt that he needed to be sustained in some way" and had persuaded Ernest Wilkinson to publish the argumentative pamphlet, *Rick's College: A Statement,* despite the conviction of Wilkinson and the other Church authorities that such a publication would widen the controversy.[73] Sure enough, the citizens of Rexburg replied with the vitriolic *Dr. Wilkinson's Role in the Proposal to Move Ricks College.*[74] In a two-hour meeting of the First Presidency with local leaders on 10 February 1959, President Clark unleashed the full power of his lifelong loyalty to the Presidency of the Church:

President Clark made this statement, "May I ask a question? This of course we will agree with is a Church matter, but this Committee of 1000 has appealed to the people of the United States. Am I right about that?"
[B****** T*****]: "That is right."
President Clark: "That is wholly contrary to the discipline of the Church."
. . . .
President Clark: "May I put one question to you? When you go on your knees to pray, do you pray that the Lord will guide and direct the Prophet, Seer, and Revelator to change his mind, is that your prayer? . . . I do not see how you can talk to the point that you go on your knees to pray to the Lord to instruct the prophet of the Lord."
. . . .

President Clark: "May I say this, I have wondered as I have known of your position, I have wondered what I would say if I got down on my knees to change a decision of the First Presidency."

[B****** T*****]: "We have never asked the Lord for that."

President Clark: "But you have treated it as if no decision had been made."[75]

Four days after this meeting the First Presidency published in the *Deseret News* a condemnation of the Rexburg publication and a reaffirmation of the decision to move Ricks College to Idaho Falls.[76] But the Rexburg people would not relent their pressure privately and publicly upon President McKay to give reconsideration to the matter.[77]

When Wilkinson asked President Clark if David O. McKay would agree to meet with these Church lobbyists again and reopen the deliberations, he replied, "I don't know. The President is failing fast."[78] Despite the strength of his loyalty to the Church President's decision, he knew how much David O. McKay needed to feel everyone's love and how deeply the criticisms of Rexburg Latter-day Saints tormented him. President McKay's life would continue another decade, but his ability to resist the pressures of the Rexburg people lasted only another year, at which point he reversed himself for the last time. Ricks College remained at Rexburg, Ernest Wilkinson remained chancellor of the Church schools, and J. Reuben Clark remained unshaken in his rock-like loyalty to David O. McKay, whom he respected too much to try to manipulate or "overpersuade."

If President Clark regarded himself as administratively diminished in being called as Second Counselor in 1951, relatively good health enabled him to continue his varied activities. He remained a director of Church-affiliated corporations, as well as of Equitable Life Assurance Society and of Western Pacific Railroad. He received an honorary doctor of laws degree from Brigham Young University in 1952 and shortly afterward published his decades of New Testament research in two volumes (*Our Lord of the Gospels* in 1954 and *Why the King James Version?* in 1956). His talks to university commencements and general conferences of the Church continued to appear in pamphlet form, and he also gave major addresses before such diverse groups as the American Society of Beet Technologists, the Utah Farm Bureau Federation, and the Utah Cattlemen's Association.[79]

COURTESY HAROLD B. LEE LIBRARY

President Clark upon receiving an Honorary Doctor of Laws degree from Brigham Young University, 1952.

As an octogenarian, he continued energetic contributions to the progress of the Church from 1951 to 1959. Aside from dedicating seven chapels and two welfare buildings himself, he also participated in the groundbreaking, cornerstone laying, and dedication of the Los Angeles Temple. In 1933 President Clark had suggested an idea—later elaborated upon—of establishing Church regions comprising several stakes for the purpose of administering the new Church Welfare Program, and in 1953 he proposed that the increasing growth of the Church justified the creation of a regional priesthood council of total Church administration between the stake presidents and the General Authorities.[80] He was also a dynamic influence in several Church councils and general boards. In November 1958 Reuben wrote the closest associate from his days in the U.S. State Department fifty years earlier:

I feel fortunately for myself, and I hope reasonably so for some others, that my whole life was changed almost a quarter of a century ago since which time my thought and my writing have turned primarily to matters religious. It has been a great thing for me, Fred, to have the course of my thought change. I think it has kept me from falling into some of the incidents of normal old age.[81]

J. Reuben Clark had been a dynamic member of the First Presidency as long as many members of the Church could remember during the late 1950s, and he continued to awe his associates in Church administration by the vigor of his mind and body.

Nevertheless, events within the circle of his dearest friends and loved ones had caused Reuben to think increasingly of the ravages of mortality and the impermanence of life. In February 1952 he wrote a melancholy letter to a friend describing the events of the previous month: the death of the mother of one of his dearest friends, Preston Richards, followed a few days later by the deaths of Preston himself, of President Clark's sister-in-law, of his daughter-in-law's mother, of his former bishop, of his unborn great-grandchild through miscarriage, and of his "very dear friend" Joseph F. Merrill of the Quorum of the Twelve. Six months later another granddaughter was partially paralyzed by polio.[82] Moreover, as President Clark reached each birthday in his eighties, he noticed that public demonstrations became more dramatic as if in anticipation of limited opportunity for added celebration. This was particularly true on his 84th birthday in 1955, when he was feted by a special equestrian show at the Salt Lake County Fairgrounds and given this eulogistic tribute by Elder Harold B. Lee as the inscription of an oil portrait:

> In him are superbly blended a quality of faith which transcends reason, an indomitable courage of decision no matter the odds, a high sense of honor and devotion to duty, a keenness of perception which approaches spiritual seership, an intellect to challenge the converse of the mightiest, and yet a tenderness in his nature which prompts a genuine consideration and sorrow for the unfortunate as though their afflictions were his own.[83]

His closest associates and family members would one day express disappointment that he had completely given himself over to the conclusion he expressed in 1953—"I am, unfortunately, reaching the place where all of my future is behind me"[84]—but they had inadvertently contributed to such a conclusion by their fervently expressed living eulogies and appreciations that he was still alive. But with

President Clark's 1955 birthday party hosted by the Ute Rangers, Salt Lake County Fairgrounds.

typically sardonic humor, President Clark told his friends, "Give me a little more taffy while I am with you, and a little less epitaphy when I am gone."[85]

The melancholy undercurrent in J. Reuben Clark's last decade of life was partly the result of his situation in the First Presidency after April 1951. Without mentioning his feelings about his lessened situation, he told a secretary in the First Presidency's office in 1957 that he enjoyed the personal associations in the Presidency's office but that his position there was one of "the accidents of life" and that "I think there are few duties which will count for much in the Hereafter."[86] President Clark undoubtedly expected to die as Second Counselor to David O. McKay, but the year 1959 brought unexpected changes to the First Presidency.

Stephen L Richards had been periodically ill with coronary ailments, and his sudden death in May 1959 created a vacancy in the First Presidency. His death nearly devastated David O. McKay, with whom he had shared a David-and-Jonathan love.[87] Aside from its personal dimension, the passing of Stephen L Richards also had an important effect on President McKay's administration. Ernest L. Wilkinson stated in his diary that

President Richards has been a great strength in the Presidency of the Church and will be missed sorely by President McKay who relied completely on him. He undoubtedly had more influence under President McKay's administration than any other man save President McKay himself and he was responsible for many of the decisions of President McKay.[88]

As President McKay surveyed the Quorum of the Twelve Apostles for a possible replacement for his First Counselor, he faced the reality that the six senior members of the Twelve were either protégés of President Clark or were closer to his philosophy than they were to President McKay's. In addition, he had justified making Reuben Second Counselor in 1951 by calling into the First Presidency one who had greater seniority in the Quorum of the Twelve. But for that seniority argument to work in 1959, President McKay would have had to call upon Joseph Fielding Smith, with whom the Church President had almost as many personal and philosophical differences as he had with President Clark.

On 12 June 1959 President McKay responded to the need for filling the vacancy in the First Presidency by calling Reuben as his First Counselor and Henry D. Moyle as his Second Counselor. Harold B. Lee thought it was "almost too good to be true" for President Clark to be elevated to his former position and for one of his acknowledged protégés to be made Second Counselor.[89] There were, on the other hand, elements in the situation that presaged future difficulties: Henry D. Moyle (a Democrat and fiscal liberal) had increasingly manifested support for expansive Church expenditures advocated by President McKay and opposed by President Clark.[90] Nevertheless, Reuben and his close associates rejoiced in the developments of June 1959.

Whereas he had muted his feelings at being chosen Second Counselor in 1951, he made no effort to conceal his happiness now that the situation was reversed. President Clark frequently told others that his reappointment as First Counselor in 1959 was a "promotion," and he told the MIA conference of June 1959, "President McKay has appointed me again as a First Counselor in the Presidency of the Church. I am grateful beyond expression for the confidence that implies, grateful for the respect, also, and for the affection which I am sure lay behind it."[91]

Although President Clark had lived long enough to resume the office of First Counselor in 1959, that same year marked the steady deterioration of his health. Throughout the early 1950s he had been troubled with more frequent colds and flu, and from January to March 1959 he was at home with illness.[92] For six weeks in July–August 1959 he was again nearly incapacitated at home with

First Presidency, 12 June 1959.
David O. McKay, J. Reuben Clark, Henry D. Moyle.

what his physician allowed him to believe was "a nervous breakdown and fatigue"; but his physician confided to others "that most
of his heart had gone and he gave him only another year."[93] He had
another relapse in November 1959, which was caused by thrombosis,
and four months later he had a brief case of Bell's palsy on the left
side of his face.[94] His physician, family, and friends concealed from
him their fear that he could die at any time, and this approach succeeded in uplifting his evaluation of his general health.

The ailment that no one could conceal from him and which ultimately eroded President Clark's will to live was the increasing inability of his legs to support his large frame and body weight. Although he maintained an enjoyment of such delicacies as pecans,
Gorgonzola cheese, and lobster Newburg, Reuben had struggled
since the age of thirty to avoid obesity by eating moderately and
skipping breakfast altogether (and sometimes lunch as well), only to

find himself gaining more weight.[95] The combination of his great weight, arthritis, and other weaknesses incident to old age created such difficulty in walking that he installed a small elevator in his home in 1957. He could not walk up steps without assistance by June 1959 and could "hardly stand" at all in November 1959.[96] By July 1960 the weakness had extended to other extremities as well, and he reported, "My fingers are becoming all thumbs so I have difficulty sometimes dressing myself in the morning."[97]

President Clark missed the opening sessions of October 1960 conference because of his walking difficulty, but "the people were breathless" when he attended the morning session of 9 October 1960.[98] He took faltering steps to the pulpit with the aid of President McKay and then gave what would be his last public sermon. Sandwiched between humorous comments about his physical decline, President Clark declared: "I renew to you this morning the testimony I have given to you for over a quarter of a century, I believe every conference, a testimony that God lives, that Jesus is his son and is the Christ, a testimony that the Father and the Son appeared to the Prophet."[99] From this time forward he attended no public meetings and fewer and fewer of the regular meetings of the First Presidency or of the temple meetings with the Quorum of the Twelve. He became dependent upon his daughter Louise, his friend Gordon Burt Affleck, or the Presidency secretary A. Hamer Reiser to push his wheelchair when he left home.

For a man accustomed to good health and to bearing others' burdens, this physical incapacity caused him to become morose about himself. As early as February 1960 his traditionally good-natured, humorous comments about himself had become bitingly gloomy: "Today I called the telephone company ... I was curious what the fellow on the other end looked like and whether he was as ugly as I am."[100] Due to his inability to attend the early conference sessions of October 1960, Reuben wept openly for the first time in the presence of David O. McKay and again in meeting with Marion G. Romney, who observed: "He feels like he's unwanted and useless."[101] By November 1960 Harold B. Lee was commenting that President Clark "has become obsessed with the idea that a man in his ninetieth year is through and ought not to hope to get well"; when Elders Lee, Moyle, and Romney visited the Clark home to discuss Welfare

President McKay assists President Clark as he gives his last address to a general conference of the Church, 9 October 1960.

Program matters, they found he was interested only in arranging for his funeral, death bequests, and biography.[102] President Clark told the temple meeting of the Presidency and Council of the Twelve in April 1961, "Brethren, I am still able to crawl around. . . . It is hard to have led the life I have led in activity in various positions, and then to have to give all that up," and in June that "he had nothing special to report. He said he was sitting around considerably," then added, "Idleness is not happiness."[103] His physical misery and wounded pride even spilled over into personal relationships, and Marion G. Romney observed that President Clark was increasingly "testy," "sharp and firm" with his closest associates.[104]

President Clark's gloom about his own condition began to be mirrored in an increased pessimism about the condition of the Church. In meetings of the Church Board of Education, he accused BYU President Wilkinson of asking for too much money.[105] President Clark was likewise uneasy with the expanding Church financial expenditures and the explosive growth of the Church building program.[106] He also had little confidence in the accelerated baptism program that his close friend and associate Henry D. Moyle was promoting from 1959 onward and warned that "we should not become too engrossed in the number of baptisms to the expense of actual conversions."[107] Occasionally, Reuben was the lone dissenting vote in Church administrative board meetings.[108] Reuben often said that he was grateful he had not become U.S. senator during the New Deal years as he had once hoped, because "his views would have been so out of date with the prevailing philosophy that he would have been known as a common scold" and would have become "an unheeded nuisance."[109] Sadly, this is how he regarded his last years as a member of the First Presidency.

President McKay had always had difficulty coping with Reuben's contrary views, and President Clark's frequent absences from First Presidency meetings after 1959 allowed the Church President greater ability to act without consulting the reinstated First Counselor. By November 1960 Harold B. Lee observed that President Clark was brooding "over matters about which he is not kept too well informed," and other Church administrators made similar observations within a few months.[110] In retrospect, Hugh B. Brown observed:

Well he [J. Reuben Clark] was being severely tried by the fact that the President was making a number of decisions without referring to him in any way, and that hurt him. He felt that his advice, his counsel should have been sought. Not always followed but at least considered.[111]

Reuben was so unhappy about his physical condition and his virtual impotence as a counselor that he exerted himself to attend the First Presidency meeting of 14 June 1961 for the express purpose of urging that a counselor be called to provide the help to the Presidency that he was unable to. President McKay reassured him:

Let me tell you, you are not going to be relieved of your position. We are going to call in another man to do work that we need done, but we are not going to release you of any position. You are the first counselor in the First Presidency, and you will remain that, so you need not be worried. We shall call in the necessary help. The Lord bless you! The work will go on, and you come whenever you can. There is no embarrassment to us.

Undeterred by these supportive words, Reuben replied, "You do whatever you think best, and if that means relieving me, it will be all right." A week later, Reuben burst into tears when President McKay again reassured him that he wanted Reuben to remain as First Counselor.[112]

The man President McKay chose to take up the slack in the First Presidency was Hugh B. Brown, a member of the Twelve who was philosophically close to President McKay. After President McKay announced to the temple meeting with the Apostles that Elder Brown was being called as a special counselor to the First Presidency, Elders Lee and Brown immediately went to the Clark home, where Reuben "wept like the dickens" but reassured President Brown that this appointment was in accordance with his own counsel.[113]

For J. Reuben Clark, the remaining three months of his life were a burdensome wait for the release of death. Early in July, Marion G. Romney visited him and observed, "It is a sad thing to see him and talk to him—a man of mighty power intellectually and spiritually, gradually breaking down."[114] Harold B. Lee, Marion G. Romney, Henry D. Moyle, Joseph Fielding Smith, Mark E. Petersen, Gordon Burt Affleck, and other close associates visited President Clark at home and periodically blessed him. His family, friends, and associates (including President McKay) celebrated with him a quiet ninetieth birthday.[115]

President Clark with his family on his ninetieth birthday, 1 September 1961.

His life was in its ebbtide at the very time the Church was moving forward to its general conference. One of the last visits by a Church authority to President Clark was that of David O. McKay on 23 September to discuss upcoming business connected with the October general conference.

His devoted daughter, Louise (Mrs. Mervyn Bennion) answered the door and took me to President Clark who was in his wheelchair with a shawl around his shoulders. With tears in his eyes he listened to the matters that I presented to him, and gave his approval of the proposals made. I could see that it would be impossible for him to be with us at our Conference meetings. This was my last conference with him in this mortal life. He did not pay much attention to the details. He said, "Whatever you Brethren have decided, I approve."

We went back to our schooldays. We remembered that he and Sister McKay graduated together from the University of Utah. . . .

President Clark was very emotional as he recalled the schooldays, and particularly the 27 years that we have stood shoulder to shoulder in the First Presidency. We caressed and bade each other goodbye. I left the house with a heavy heart.[116]

143

It was a conclusion of quiet drama for an unparalleled personal and administrative association in Church history. The elder statesman and gentle philosopher of the First Presidency had come to final terms. Three days later President Clark was incapacitated by a stroke from which he never recovered and which prevented his receiving those other visitors who wished to share farewells.

J. Reuben Clark's name was presented for his last sustaining vote of the Church members at the conference, and he died peacefully in the early afternoon of 6 October 1961. It came as he had expressed in the poem, "When I Would Pass."

> When the light on the eastern cliffs
> Sweeps upward to be lost in dusk
> And the rich glow of living amethyst
> Fades into the steel grey
> Of twilight, and then darkness, the realm
> Where day dies and fecund dawn is born,
> The herald of the sun-lit day to come,—
> > Then I would pass,
> > > Silently, in peace.[117]

Whether by youth or recent conversion, more than half of the 1.6 million Latter-day Saints throughout the world in 1961 had no recollection of a First Presidency without J. Reuben Clark. In one way or another, his influence touched every Church leader living in 1961. Among the immediate reactions of those who learned of President Clark's death, perhaps the most appropriate was that of Marion G. Romney: "For him it is a relief and a release from frustration. He has been a mighty man, a great 'Prophet Statesman.' Surely he has gone to a great reward."[118]

COURTESY HAROLD B. LEE LIBRARY

Presidents McKay and Moyle pay their last respects to President Clark.

"MINISTERING TO THE SAINTS"

2 Corinthians 8:4

Most of J. Reuben Clark's Church service involved public speaking and high-level administration, and he tended to be somewhat detached from the intensive personal ministry of local Church officers. As a member of the First Presidency, "I felt myself that the problems of the Church were sufficient to absorb our energies, and that the individual problems ought to be left for others. . . ."[1] This was a logical and prudent use of his time and energies, and he also felt a responsibility "to work for others, to give to others, to relieve human suffering, to keep people as reasonably happy as we can."[2] Although President Clark tried to fulfill that service primarily as an exponent and administrator, he also extended himself in a personal ministry.

Reuben Clark had been ordained to the proselyting office of seventy when he was eighteen years old, but he never regarded himself as a very successful missionary. As a civil servant, he avoided imposing religious discussions on the non-Mormons among whom he lived and worked and was content to allow his Mormon identity and ethical living accomplish a work of passive proselyting. He seldom brought up the question of religion, but neither did he hesitate to answer any inquires from his non-Mormon friends about Latter-day Saint beliefs. When orchestra maestro Leopold Stokowski visited Mexico City in 1931, he asked Ambassador Clark to explain the basis of Mormonism, and Stokowski later remarked, "I am not a religious man, I am a musician, yet the religious ideas expressed to me by Mr. Clark appealed to me as being eminently good, beautiful and true."[3]

Although he was never a forceful missionary, J. Reuben Clark more actively promoted Church teachings among his non-Mormon friends after he became a member of the First Presidency. On

5 September 1936, while at Buenos Aires, he performed his "first baptism" for a "brother-in-law of Richard Evans," and fifteen years later the man was an active member of the Church in Chicago.[4] Still, President Clark did not consider his first baptism in 1936 as a conversion story, because he had merely performed the ordinance without having taught the gospel to the individual.

Although President Clark's efforts at proselyting individuals were infrequent, they were impressive. To an Episcopalian who was vice-president of Chase Manhattan National Bank and director of fourteen other major corporations, he wrote in 1941:

> I notice that you have no thought of joining the Church. On my part I have no thought that I am converting you. I thank you for the compliment to me personally regarding my mode of life.
>
> I am not sure that I agree with you that "it is scarcely worth while for two busy men to enter into a discussion of theology." I am not sure that if theology be given the field and importance it claims, there is very much else in the world worth a real discussion between two honest men, however busy they may be.

And despite his disclaimer of a proselyting motive, President Clark went on to outline in detail the position of the Church regarding the gospel of Jesus Christ and his own convictions about it.[5] After entering the First Presidency, J. Reuben Clark sent unsolicited copies of the Book of Mormon and other religious publications to his associates in the State Department and the business world, and during the last decade of his life he maintained a regular religious dialogue by mail with the president of George Washington University in Washington, D.C.[6]

Nevertheless, President Clark was as suspicious of overly enthusiastic missionary work as he was of any other enthusiasm. When someone told him in 1943 that nonmembers of the Church had been included in the canning operations of Welfare Square as a missionary activity to make non-Mormons "feel good toward us," President Clark replied, "We are not here to make people feel good. We are here to do our work and preach the gospel."[7] He also opposed superficial conversions. A non-Mormon friend in Salt Lake City wrote that his member children wanted him to join the Church and that he had attended many Church services with his children, had grown very fond of the ward bishop, had met several times with the missionaries, had read "a good deal" of the Book of Mormon, but had not decided whether he should join the Church. President Clark's reply was immediate:

Do not join our Church merely to please your son. Do not join unless you have what we call a testimony, which is a burning realization that Joseph Smith was a prophet, that through him the Lord restored the Gospel and His Priesthood, and that this work was divinely set up and is divinely led. If you were to join on any other basis than this, unhappiness would be your lot, and things probably would arise which would result in your separation from the Church, which would be unsatisfactory for you and for us.[8]

To others, this might have seemed a "golden opportunity" to urge the man to follow his inclinations toward joining the Church, but J. Reuben Clark's lifelong disdain for emotionalism and quick decisions could not be quenched even at the prospect of a ready convert.

Until he was seventy-six years old, J. Reuben Clark was convinced that his missionary efforts had utterly failed. During October conference in 1947, a young married woman from California surprised him by explaining that she had converted to the Church after reading some of his published explanations of the gospel, to which he replied that "she was his first and only convert, then." But a few years later he "was utterly amazed" to learn that a married couple had joined the Church after hearing him explain the gospel to a gathering of newspapermen. J. Reuben Clark's missionary efforts had been passive most of his life, but he would tell a missionary meeting in 1956, "In spite of that kind of missionary labor (President McKay, I might as well unburden the whole thing here)—I have at least three converts to my credit, who came in and told me so."[9]

Although Reuben would never claim he had the gift of healing, he frequently demonstrated his faith in the ability of God to heal through priesthood administrations. In the mid-1920s a young couple moved into the Salt Lake Twentieth Ward, where he was the gospel doctrine instructor. The husband became ill, and his wife asked Reuben to administer to him. After he did so, he took the woman aside "and told her to get a doctor as soon as she could, that her husband had a bad case of appendicitis." Even though the attending physician had no clear diagnosis of the man's difficulty, the couple went to the hospital for tests, where it was determined that the man did have appendicitis. The doctor who performed the emergency surgery "said he ought to be dead, but he recovered."[10] On another occasion, he administered to a young woman who had Hodgkin's disease and was pregnant with her first child even though her physicians had told her she could not survive childbirth. He later commented, "The Lord listened to our prayer on that occasion when I administered to her, and she has not only had a child but several others, her family now numbers nine. Again I say, the Lord can do wonders."[11] Moreover, Elder Spencer W. Kimball described it as "*A MIRACLE*" when President Clark administered to him in 1950 for his loss of speech, which was restored to him immediately after the blessing.[12]

As he spoke with people about his priesthood administrations for healing, J. Reuben Clark absolutely refused to let them think the healing occurred because he was the one performing the ceremony. "I want you to understand this," he told the wife of a General Authority as he was about to administer to her, "that in and of myself I have no power to heal you, but I have faith that the Lord can do it and we will ask the Lord to bless you."[13] When a woman came to him for a healing blessing because he was a member of the First Presidency, even though she had already received administration from Elder LeGrand Richards of the Quorum of the Twelve Apostles, President Clark quietly observed that "there was no more spiritual man than Brother Richards."[14] His frequent counsel to accept the will of the Lord in physical difficulties was severely tested during the polio epidemic of 1952 when a member of his own family was stricken with that disease, but to the priesthood session of October conference that year he stated:

When physicians tell you that little can be done, that they know nothing about the disease, I tell you, you fall back awfully fast on the Lord, in humility, having lived reasonably righteously, the Lord will hear us . . . and then, it being his will and in his wisdom, he gives us the blessings we ask for, for ourselves and for our loved ones.

Then in a spontaneous expression of compassion, he told the priesthood conference that he had learned that the son of tabernacle organist Roy Darley had been stricken with polio, and President Clark prayed, "May the Lord bless and heal his little one." He later learned that the child had a high fever up until the time of the priesthood meeting, after which the boy's temperature returned permanently to normal.[15]

President Clark felt special compassion for the Latter-day Saints when death came to their loved ones despite priesthood administrations, despite promises of patriarchal blessings for long life, and despite the youth and potential of the deceased. He once wrote a two-page, single-spaced, typed letter to a grieving widow who could not understand the precipitous deaths of her husband and his brother.

> Personally, I am not sure that the time of our going, certainly if our lives are righteous, is of any particular importance in the Great Plan, or to the individual, nor is the manner of our going of any importance; it may be by disease, long and lingering, by tragic suffering to the one passing and to his loved one; it may be by sudden failure of the heart, or a blood clot in the brain, or it may be by accident. The method makes little difference. . . .
>
> . . . .
>
> It is my prayer that the Lord will bless you and give you a surcease to worrying and pondering about matters concerning which the Lord has given us no distinct revelation, and that you may be able to travel forward in faith, relying on the Lord's kindness, mercy, and justice.[16]

He was not simply stating platitudes—a practice alien to his very nature—but he was expressing the deep convictions of one who had suffered through the deaths—both lingering and precipitous—of his parents, his wife, his son in law, and many other loved ones. "Why is a good man taken and an evil one left? This is an inscrutable problem," President Clark wrote, but he found comfort in the gospel of Jesus Christ that "makes things bearable."[17]

Knowing the grief of death in his own life, he could not take lightly the grief of others. When Elder George F. Richards grew faint the day after his wife's funeral in 1946, Reuben embraced him. When a young man was killed in a freak accident at the Hotel Utah in 1949, President Clark looked up the young man's Church membership record so that he could ask the ward bishop to comfort the fellow's parents. When some young girls were killed by lightning during an outing in Idaho in 1951, he suggested that the general presidency of the young women's organization of the Church send flowers and a personal letter of condolence to each of the parents. In

June 1952 an automobile struck a little girl in front of the Salt Lake Twentieth Ward chapel where President Clark was attending an evening meeting. Dressed in a white summer suit, Reuben rushed to the scene of the accident and took "that little, bleeding child into his arms" until medical assistance arrived.[18]

Reuben was accustomed to giving religious counsel about sickness and death when he entered the First Presidency in 1933, but his limited experience in Church administration left him unprepared for other realities of ministering to the saints. His first exposure to "religious cranks" came in July 1933, when a man wrote the "word of the Lord" in which Reuben was condemned for being "a man of the world, and not of the Holy Priesthood" and then was "disfellowshipped" from the Church for not resigning from the First Presidency.[19] The pathetic instability of such persons was indicated in a letter from another Latter-day Saint who wrote, "You wouldn't want to see me in an insane asylum, would you?" and then asked President Clark to tell two men to go to hell, and concluded with a request for $12,000.[20]

Even members of the Church who were mentally stable could make bizarre demands upon President Clark's time. One woman wrote him with a request that he help her complete her income tax forms, and another woman came to see him in the Presidency's office in order to learn how to patent and market something she had invented.[21] He grew to resent such demands and strongly urged other General Authorities to give less emphasis to counseling.[22] Nevertheless, J. Reuben Clark did not want to turn away any Latter-day Saint who came to him for counsel, nor would he indicate to the person an impatience with the time consumed by the interview. It was not uncommon for him to spend forty-five minutes or longer with Latter-day Saints who sought his listening ear.[23]

Although President Clark tended to be a legalist in many areas, he took a different approach in counseling with the Latter-day Saints. His attitude is best indicated in the blessing he gave when he ordained his brother a bishop in 1941:

We bless you, dear brother, with the spirit of fatherhood, that you may be able to be a father to all the members of your Ward. We bless you that you may be able to put out from your heart every feeling but one of affection and kindness to every man, woman, and child in your Ward.[24]

J. Reuben Clark could deliver blistering condemnations to his opponents and be unnervingly blunt with his closest associates in Church administration, but in personal counseling with the Latter-day Saints, he spoke with the restraint, compassion, and openness of a loving father. To priesthood leaders in 1937, he said:

We always like to try to make a rule and then to fit everything into the rule, and having made one ruling under a given set of circumstances we try to make the same sort of ruling under every other like set of circumstances. Now, brethren, I don't believe you can do that where you are dealing with the spiritual side and that is the most important side in all that we are trying to do.[25]

Throughout his varied experiences in the secular world, he found both complexity and diversity in people's motives, actions, attitudes, abilities, weaknesses, and vulnerabilities. As one of the highest leaders of the Church, he felt that one could not righteously ignore such diversity among those who struggled to be Saints. "I fear that some of us are going to be greatly surprised," President Clark once wrote, "to see in the Celestial Kingdom a number of people that we would have assigned to a far lesser Kingdom."[26]

President Clark was particularly concerned about the Mormon tendency to categorize certain people as "inactive" or "apostate." Although he used these terms himself, he tried to encourage the Latter-day Saints to recognize that the words described a particular response to the Church that might not be permanent. "Do not go to them and approach them on the basis that they are lost or on the basis that they are criminals," he warned the bishops of the Church in 1948.[27] He later told the bishops, "Occasionally you will find in the Church the greatest good coming from putting in [ward positions] men even before they have reformed."[28] He also wrote letters of encouragement, pleaded for spiritual renewal, and spoke of "more sorrow than I can express to you" to members of the Church who had discarded their religious testimonies.[29] Even for apostates who came to his office with "blasphemous" words and arrogant attitudes, "I tried to talk calmly and kindly but straight-forwardly."[30] Those who saw J. Reuben Clark, Jr. only as the elder statesman, only as the

Republican loyalist, only as the vigorous administrator, only as the self-sufficient scholar, only as the legalist and constitutionalist, failed to understand that he was capable of compassion.

Because most "inactives" did not practice total abstinence from coffee, tea, alcohol, and tobacco as required in the Church's "Word of Wisdom," he also urged the "active" Latter-day Saints to keep observance of outward commandments in perspective. "I hope I will not be misunderstood," he told the bishops, "for I am a thorough believer in the Word of Wisdom, but I should like to say that the use of tea and coffee and tobacco is not the worst offense in the world."[31] Moreover, with reference to the location of the Word of Wisdom in the 89th Section of the Doctrine and Covenants, J. Reuben Clark criticized "the 89ers—Word of Wisdomers" who made tea, coffee, tobacco, and alcohol more significant than lying, stealing, cheating, hating, backbiting, character assassination, and gossip.[32]

By contrast, J. Reuben Clark could be very explicit in his public instructions concerning sexual conduct and morality. He told the young ladies of the Church that in matters of sexuality, he did not trust his own daughters, himself, or anyone else.[33] He criticized the men of the Church for walking around nude in gymnasiums, and said it "is not healthy" for a young man and woman to dance together all evening.[34] He publicly warned the men and women of the Church against specific immoralities.[35] He also told the youth that they should guard chastity with their very lives.[36]

President Clark spoke harshly against sexual immorality to prevent the chaste from succumbing to temptation, but he also realized that his words might crush the hearts of youths and adults in the Church who had already committed sexual transgression. In his own copy of Edward Gibbon's *Decline and Fall of the Roman Empire,* he penned the following marginal note: "Because in our weakness we cannot live the lofty moral and spiritual life of the gospel is no argument that such a life is not desirable or that it is not the life prescribed by the Master."[37] He felt the obligation to condemn sexual sin in the strongest possible terms but also sought to preach the gospel's entreaty: "All you repentant transgressors come, partake of God's all-wise divine justice and of his boundless, infinite mercy and love. To transgressors, yet unrepentant, the Lord calls. . . ."[38] Members of the Church responded to President Clark's condemnations as well as his entreaties: a woman who had committed adultery twenty-seven years before and who had since that time "done nothing but sorrow and repent for her misdeeds"; an applicant for Church employment who had committed sexual transgression as a youth; a teacher at a Church school who had engaged in homosexual intimacy for several years ("He enquired about whether he should be handled churchwise. I said thus far we had done no more than drop them from positions they held"); a woman who had committed adultery twenty years before but who had lived "a good, clean life" since that time, to whom President Clark said, "Where transgression has been in secret, the essential thing is repentance."[39]

J. Reuben Clark publicly raised a warning voice against sin of all kinds, but he spoke healing words to the transgressors who sought his counsel. To a former Apostle, Richard R. Lyman, who had been publicly excommunicated from the Church for violating Church rules of moral conduct, he wrote:

> With reference to the other matter to which you refer, it is a consolation to know that however much we who are here may err in our judgment and decisions, nevertheless the Lord knows all and in the Hereafter He will see that all wrongs are righted and all proper restorations accomplished.
>
> My own formula with reference to these matters I have often expressed as follows: I believe that the Lord will bestow upon us all the rewards that it is possible for Him to bestow, having in mind in connection with His infinite mercy and love and charity, the absolute demands of justice. On the other hand, I think that He would impose the least penalty for our errors and misdoings that it is possible to impose, having in mind His love, charity, and forgiveness, that the demands of justice absolutely require.[40]

In matters of legal justice, President Clark could also urge the broadest leniency: he once petitioned the chief of the Los Angeles probation department to grant probation to a Latter-day Saint convicted of perjury because even though the man had taken "no active part in church work, he has always been a man of profound religious convictions" and had been a devoted husband and father.[41] Moreover, concerning the suicide of an elder of the Church, he said "that the idea was to be as comforting to the family as possible, [because] in cases of suicide [the family] had double grief"; and President Clark authorized the Church funeral and burial in temple clothes of the suicide victim "on the theory that no person in his right mind would commit suicide and as he was not in his right mind there was no crime involved."[42] Reuben always remembered the legal dimensions of justice, but reminded himself and others not to lose sight of the human dimensions of compassion.

President Clark also took frequent opportunity to give counsel about marriage. When a woman Church member asked if she would be sinning by marrying a non-Mormon, he replied, "There is no sin in honorable marriage." He reminded her that the basis of a happy marriage should be mutual love, but he added that converting her intended husband to the Church would also contribute to their happiness.[43] To the anxious mother of a young girl who wanted to marry a non-Mormon, he reminisced about his own worries that his daughters might marry non-Mormons, then he remarked:

Quite obviously, measures of force are out of the question, even if they were wise, and they usually are not. If you could get her to put off her marriage for a period, then get her back into active Church work, it might make your problem easier.[44]

When a young couple came to his home in Grantsville to ask that he perform their marriage ceremony, the young girl looked through the home, verbally admired its construction and conveniences, and told her fiancé how nice it would be for them to have such a home. After listening to her tell the young man how she expected things to be, President Clark turned to her with the words, "Sister, I have been seventy-five years building this home. Don't you expect this young man of yours to build it for you next year."[45]

He also stressed the necessity for consideration and equality within a marriage. He expressed his views humorously to an audience of young men and women when he praised the women of the Church by saying: "When we are by ourselves, we men admit that we are no good without them. (laughter) We do not dare admit that before them because they know it already."[46] But to a relative he expressed the earnestness of his convictions about the relations between husband and wife:

In the first place, there will not be happiness in any household, true happiness, if there be not love, true love, accompanied by trust and consideration and courtesy. . . .

In the next place, there cannot be true happiness nor peace nor the Spirit that should be in a home where either the man or the woman assumes or tries to assume a dominant spirit to the point that what the dominant party wants is always right, no matter what it is, which, of course, means that the dominant party assumes what I will call the entire household wisdom resides in the dominant party. That is almost never true.[47]

Beyond his private counsel, he publicly advised the men of the Church to respect the dignity and rights of their wives.[48]

Nevertheless, President Clark had little enthusiasm for those who bemoaned the second-class status of women, and who urged measures to give greater "equality" to women. When a young unmarried man expressed dissatisfaction about the inequality of women's position in the home and in the world generally, "Pres. Clark rather smiled and said he would find out after he was married more about this 'inequality.' "[49] When a new bride described her employment, civic activities, and career plans, he wrote an immediate reply of "deep anxiety," in which he said, "I, of course, come from a very old vintage, where the thought was that it was the woman's place to make the home and the husband's place to earn the living. There were, of course, always exceptions to this rule, but there should be some reason for it wholly acceptable to both."[50] Although Reuben resisted any effort to alter in theory or practice the traditional position of women as housewives and mothers (in which he perceived no inequality), he was well aware that his own Republican party national platforms since 1940 had called for an amendment to the U.S. Constitution "providing for equal rights for men and women."[51] J. Reuben Clark regarded such a proposed amendment as unnecessary at best and dangerously innovative at worst, but he also expressed a calm reassurance to the general conference of April 1944 that the purpose of the U.S. Constitution was to protect minorities, and whenever "that inspired document" is amended as prescribed by the Constitution itself, "it will be an amendment that the Lord will approve. . . ."[52] Reuben rested secure in his faith that the Lord would safeguard both the divinely established institution of marriage as well as the divinely inspired U.S. Constitution.[53]

He publicly proclaimed that "Motherhood is the highest type of service of which we mortals know,"[54] and expressed disapproval of efforts to restrict the birth process. Nevertheless, President Clark recognized that special circumstances also needed to govern the general recommendation. To a woman who favored government programs encouraging birth control,

I told her that so far as I knew the Church had never officially taken a position upon the question of birth control though all of our teachings were against it. . . .

. . . .

I stated that we had a belief in the free agency of man and that that belief forbade us to attempt to coerce people. I stated that in this view the question of birth control was left for determination to each individual man and wife, who would, however, if the matter came up, be reminded of the principles of the Church that govern such matters.[55]

Aside from the question of free agency, he also recognized that the medical welfare of the mother governed the matter of birth control. When a mother of five children asked if she should be sterilized as two physicians had recommended because of her physical condition, President Clark said that he would advise her as "if she were my own wife or my own daughter." He recommended that the opinion of two of the best physicians available to the woman should be consulted, and then if the physicians recommended sterilization and if the woman herself felt that this was the best course of action, then "I thought I would tell the wife or the daughter that she do as the doctors advised. . . ."[56]

Even though J. Reuben Clark and other members of the First Presidency shared a general abhorrence of abortion,[57] he recognized that there were circumstances where a medically approved abortion might be necessary due to the emotional-physical health of the pregnant woman or the medical condition of the unborn fetus. When a Latter-day Saint woman sought his counsel—on behalf of herself and several other pregnant women who had contracted German measles—whether she should have an abortion:

I told her she should seek the advice of her physicians, getting such advice and counsel as she can, and also seek the Lord in prayer. She said that in such cases the hearing of the child may be affected, or the child may even be Mongoloid. I suggested that she might wish to get the advice of two or three doctors in the matter.[58]

These questions of birth control and abortion were fundamental to society and to the gospel. But despite his own preference for unrestricted birth in marriage, President Clark counseled that special circumstances might allow departures from the preferred rule of "multiply and replenish the earth," after consultation with competent medical authorities, earnest prayer, and mutual agreement between husband and wife.

Reuben rejoiced so greatly in his own children and their devotion to the Church that he felt immediate concerns for the righteous upbringing of all Latter-day Saint children. Although he firmly believed that both husband and wife must be parents to their children, he reminded the men of the Church that practical circumstances focused the parenting function:

> Now, brethren, at best we are somewhat clumsy at leading and directing our children. We are away from home, of necessity, a great part of the time, our thoughts are along other lines, we have to battle for our existence, for the livelihood of our families. . . . And so to the sisters of the Church . . . we must primarily look for the rearing of our children.[59]

In speaking to women's groups, he invariably praised their efforts, burdens, and accomplishments in childrearing. Yet occasionally, he believed that a father also deserved special praise:

> I doubt if there be anybody in the Church who has a better record, or even an equivalent one,—to rear a family of fourteen, all of whom marry in the Temple, all of whom have college degrees, and all of whom are living as good members of the Church.[60]

Nevertheless, even such righteous parents as Adam, Noah, Jacob, Lehi, and modern apostles and prophets had wayward children. To counter the criticism of some people that the children of leaders in the Church strayed from the gospel because of the church service of their parents, President Clark repeated an anecdote of J. Golden Kimball:

> Brother Kimball said well, he spent a good deal of time preaching the Gospel, doing the Lord's work, and if his family went astray he was sorry, but he said, "I get some consolation out of the fact that when I go around and see the people, I think the Lord has not done too good a job, Himself."

After the laughter died down from this story, Reuben stated with utmost seriousness to the bishops of the Church, "Do what you can to save the young people in your own homes."[61]

Indeed, despite his preoccupation with Church administration, J. Reuben Clark was deeply concerned about the spiritual welfare and present happiness of the Latter-day Saints. Even his attention to procedures and programs was a manifestation of interest in the children, youth, husbands, wives, widows, poor, infirm, and elderly of Zion. He conducted his personal ministry to them in his own way and according to his own talents, and this service was a product of his lifelong sense of identity with the Latter-day Saints and his feeling of responsibility to them.

"BY STUDY AND ALSO BY FAITH"

Doctrine and Covenants 88:118

Throughout his life, J. Reuben Clark had ambivalent feelings toward the interplay between the life of mind and the life of faith. He treasured the world of "facts" but recognized their insufficiency as a way of life. He was an avid reader and researcher but was convinced that a total commitment to intellectual inquiry led inevitably to atheism. He urged the primacy of faith but was uncomfortable with the "overly-spiritual" person. He expected people to consider his pleas that they abandon their inadequate secular and religious positions, but he rarely read anything that was contrary to his own views. He was appalled by the confidence of the ignorant and suspicious of the smugness of the intellectual. He was a living exemplar of higher education but preferred limited education in Church colleges. He defended freedom of thought but frequently decided that censorship was necessary. He relied upon the scriptures for doctrine but resisted doctrinal dogmatism. He urged an unquestioning obedience to the decisions of the Latter-day prophet but reminded everyone that the prophet could be mistaken. As a private person and as a member of the First Presidency, he sought a conservative balance between the imperatives of reason and revelation.

People often referred to Reuben's brilliant intellect, but he felt uncomfortable with the description. As a freshman member of the State Department in 1906, he wondered if such praise was really a form of mockery. His wife Lute replied, "I believe you get a wrong idea of the things people say about you. I sincerely think they are all meant," and then she added, "Never mind, Honey, you cant help being bright; only dont get the big head."[1] After Reuben became a member of the First Presidency, many Latter-day Saints expressed awe at his knowledge, but others leveled anti-intellectual criticism at him. His sister reported in 1940 that a young man told a ward Sunday School class that "Pres. Clark knows too much for one person," to which she responded, "I guess he thinks there should be a more even distribution of brains."[2]

Part of Reuben's discomfort with the popular view of him as a gigantic intellect was his recognition that he was not a Renaissance man of learning. He tried to make his personal library a self-contained collection of "the greatest minds of all history that have left records, both in the religious and the secular worlds," but his library and his personal research focused primarily in international law, constitutionalism, biblical studies, and Latter-day Saint scripture.[3]

He readily admitted that he did not have an insatiable thirst for knowledge even in those areas in which he was vitally interested. One of his "fundamental rules" was "that I never read anything that I know is going to make me mad, unless I have to read it. To this rule I have added another, which is applicable here: I read only as time permits materials which merely support my own views."[4] Even when he published a book that distilled years of research into the higher criticism of the Bible and the importance of the King James translation, he admitted that ignorance of Biblical languages and lack of rigorous training in the field left him still very much a novice. When Church publishing friends chided him for being overly modest in this disclaimer of scholarship, President Clark sent his secretary to his private library "for copies of the books to show what scholarship was."[5]

In shunning the designation "intellectual," he was not simply being modest but was acknowledging a fundamental limitation. He was a master of research and categorizing mountains of facts and concrete data, but Reuben was impatient with abstract ideas. "I can hardly get through a couple of verses of Paul and not get lost," he once wrote. "I know this is my fault, because Paul's logic and reasoning are all too subtle and refined for me. I can do a little better with Peter."[6] He gave up his effort to understand the writings of Mary Baker Eddy because they were "entirely beyond the powers of my mind and my reasoning powers"; and likewise he shunned discussion of Oriental religions because "they involved an understanding of abstractions that he, personally, did not understand."[7]

COURTESY HAROLD B. LEE LIBRARY

President Clark preparing the publication of his book Our Lord of the Gospels, *1954.*

When the president of Equitable Life Assurance Society sent to his friend a copy of a speech, Reuben replied that he nearly drowned trying to understand it, "but I sort of held my breath and struggled to the top." He then concluded, "I accept your conclusions whether or not I fully understand the reasons, and I congratulate you on another fine speech."[8] Despite the brilliance of his mind and speech, Reuben shrank from the complex and abstract, felt a lifelong estrangement from those he referred to as "so-called intellectuals," and would probably have agreed immediately with a subsequent Pulitzer Prize winning book that there is an essential difference between a "mental technician" and an "intellectual."[9] J. Reuben Clark was a mental technician and would have understood why 92 percent of surveyed Mormons who held Ph.D. degrees did not list him among "the five most eminent intellectuals in Mormon history."[10]

In fact, distrust of Mormon intellectuals was a direct by-product of his own spiritual-intellectual crisis in earlier life. In the attempt to rationalize and intellectualize the latter-day gospel, he found himself heading toward skepticism and atheism, which he avoided only by refusing to question faith in the fundamental principles of the gospel.[11] Assuming that his own experience had universal application, he told a general conference of the Church, "I have come to feel that there is none who can safely rationalize."[12] He also expressed to the Latter-day Saints his gratitude that he had the sixth sense "that enables him to believe in Mormonism."[13] When a man asked which Church leader after Joseph Smith contributed most to the intellectual life of the Church, he typically replied: "I am not sure that I can see in what way the answer to the question would materially help us in solving the problems of daily life, which, after all, is the prime consideration in any study of the Gospel."[14] As he often told members of the Church, President Clark kept his faith simple.

J. Reuben Clark adopted a double-edged educational philosophy as a member of the First Presidency. First, he regarded all highly educated people, particularly intellectuals, as potential atheists. Second, he insisted that to justify their existence, all Church educational institutions, but especially Brigham Young University, must provide their secular training within a religious atmosphere that gave priority to faith. Even prior to his call to the First Presidency, Reuben voiced this concern to BYU's president, Franklin S. Harris, in response to a talk Harris gave lauding the higher educational backgrounds of Church leaders.[15] In 1938 President Clark stated this explicitly to Church educators in his Aspen Grove talk, which has been quoted and referred to in succeeding decades.

> You do not have to sneak up behind this spiritually experienced youth and whisper religion in his ears; you can come right out, face to face, and talk with him. You do not need to disguise religious truths with a cloak of worldly things; you can bring these truths to him openly, in their natural guise.[16]

As an outgrowth of his emphasis, President Clark became the prime mover in 1944 to establish at BYU what he called a "School of Theology," a "post-graduate school in gospel," or a "divinity school."[17] As envisioned in a First Presidency letter he formulated, this post-graduate program at BYU was "only for the purpose of developing and demonstrating the truth of the Restored Gospel and the falsity of the other religions of the world, and thereby upbuild the faith and knowledge of post-graduate scholars."[18] When this program evolved in the 1950s into a traditional graduate school at BYU with graduate degrees being offered in secular fields, he voiced his dissatisfaction to the university president:

> I assume that I am an apostate, that I am no friend of higher learning, that I am just a low-down ignoramous, but in that ignorance I want to say to you that I am not at all concerned with the relative fewness of our attendance at the Y who are graduate students. In this ignorance of mine, I have a feeling that the mission of the Brigham Young University is not to make Ph.Ds or M.A.s, but to distribute among as wide a number as possible the ordinary collegiate work leading to Bachelor Degrees and to instill into the students a knowledge of the Gospel and a testimony of its truthfulness.[19]

J. Reuben Clark was never reconciled to the enlarged enrollments and educational programs at Brigham Young University, and he consistently opposed the physical, academic, and financial expansion of the university that occurred during the last decade of his life.[20]

Nevertheless, he also chafed against what he perceived as mental laziness and conformity among the Latter-day Saints. "Too many of our people have quit thinking,—Politically,—Socially,—Spiritually," he wrote in 1947.[21] For example, he believed that the intelligent thinking of a community is both expressed and encouraged by its newspapers, and he said in 1936, "I am most anxious to make our paper [the *Deseret News*] do for our Church what *The Christian Science Monitor* has done for the Christian Science Church."[22]

Even though he warned against intellectualizing the Gospel and delving into its mysteries, he regarded each of those activities as legitimate, even if they were dangerous. When he wrote his response to a philosophical treatise by N. L. Nelson in 1941, President Clark observed at the outset: "You have thought deeply and it seems to me, in the main, logically, about many fundamental matters, most of which I assume would be classified as 'mysteries,' which you have thought the little we are told through to a conclusion"; and he concluded his six-page, single-spaced typed analysis of Nelson's manuscript with the words: "Praying that the Lord will bless you in your labors of strong, vigorous, creative thinking."[23] When someone asked for permission to excommunicate persons he suspected of having disloyal and apostate attitudes, "Pres. Clark cautioned that they ought to be careful about the insubordination or disloyalty question, because they ought to be permitted to think, you can't throw a man off for thinking."[24] At its most extreme, the insistence upon spiritual and mental conformity in the Church resulted in Mormons whom President Clark classified as "The Celestial Kingdomers," who accepted "Only those who believe and act as they do: They have narrow rules; narrow principles. The Prescriptions of the Talmud are of their kind of thinking. They cut off men who do not follow them."[25] This antipathy for religious narrowness led him to a position of tolerance for the doctrinal views of others with whom he might disagree.

A few years before his own call to the First Presidency, Reuben had advised his missionary son that "The philosophy of the Gospel is so deep and many sided, its truths are so far reaching it is never safe to dogmatize, even about the most elemental principles, such as faith."[26] Because he disliked religious dogmatism, President Clark was able to be remarkably noncommittal when asked about deeper aspects of doctrine. To one inquirer he wrote that "it does not make any difference to your service nor to mine, whether God is progressing or whether He has come to a stand-still."[27] To one man who inquired about the Adam-God theory he wrote, "I understand that in the days of President Young, this controversy raged with considerable fury, but I believe with no casualties and with no one winning a decision." Then he concluded, "I am equally sure that none of us can understand it because we are dealing with matters of infinity and we are only finite. The Lord has not revealed these mysteries to us."[28] When a member of the Church asked about the fate of the sons of perdition, he merely observed that he was "trying never to become one."[29] With good humor and an emphasis upon the importance of simple faith, J. Reuben Clark sidestepped many doctrinal speculations.

Even in religious disputes about which J. Reuben Clark had pronounced views, he avoided setting himself up as the arbiter of what was possible for God. For example, he had deep reservations about Roman Catholicism and publicly condemned the adoration of the Virgin Mary,[30] but he was unwilling to denounce reported visions of Mary as false or devilish. In one of the most famous of these reported experiences, a fifty-year-old Mexican Indian named Juan Diego saw a vision of Mary on 9 December 1531, and the result was the cult of Our Lady of Guadalupe.[31] President Clark wrote his reaction to this story in a letter to the president of one of the Church missions in Mexico.

I have always had a natural interest in the story of Juan Diego and the "visitation" to him of the Virgin Mary. I have always been a little more tolerant toward the concept of some sort of vision on the part of Juan Diego, or somebody else, because, though the Spaniards were trying to set up a Christian concept and practice that we know to have been false, nevertheless that concept, whatever it was, was far ahead of the cannibalistic worship of sacrifice which the Aztecs held. I have always felt that perhaps the Lord permitted something in order to add an appeal to the Mexican mind that was not embraced in the concepts which the Spaniards were trying to give of Christianity. However, this is my own idea.[32]

When members of the Church tried to get him to make authoritative and inflexible pronouncements about doctrines he considered debatable, he declined to do so.[33] President Clark followed his own counsel to young missionaries who might be tempted to give authoritative answers to obscure or unimportant doctrinal questions: simply answer, "I do not know."[34]

President Clark demonstrated this attitude most clearly in a letter he wrote concerning the theory of organic evolution. Even though Reuben himself had questioned the consistency of scientific theory in a 1915 sermon "Evolution,"[35] he indicated an unwillingness to reject the theories of modern science on the basis of brief scriptural references to creation. In a long letter in 1946, President Clark observed that "Much of your argument loses significance when we cease to give highly technical meanings to general terms." Then he continued:

You seem to think I reject the scriptures, or some of them. I do not intend to do so, but obviously I am no more bound by your interpretation of them than you are by mine.

. . . .

You observe, "Reason teaches us that the Lord worked during the creation *on his own time.*" The point has no significance to my subject, but reason does not teach me that. Reason teaches me that in the infinite, finite time of any measure has little if any importance or value. Indeed, from our mortal point of view, there probably is no *time* as we know it, in eternity, either simple or in multiple.

The periods of temporal creation are of no importance to my subject.

You quote from Section 77 of the Doctrine and Covenants. I do not get from that section the meaning you give it.

Apparently the basic difference between us is this: you do not accept the scriptural record as given in historical sequence; I do. . . .

Now, as to what the earlier brethren have said,—where they have declared themselves as speaking under inspiration and by the authority of the Lord, I bow to what they say. But where they express views based on their own understanding and interpretation, then none of us are foreclosed from exercising our own reasoning powers, inadequate though they may be; but the earlier views do not foreclose us from thinking. This is particularly true, where we come to interpreting their interpretations.[36]

Because of this difficulty in interpreting the interpretations of General Authorities on speculative matters, President Clark warned Church members against feasting upon the speculations of prominent leaders because "some matters have come to my attention where the Brethren not only differ among themselves, but where they differ with the First Presidency."[37]

President Clark stated this principle most clearly in a talk to Church educators in 1954. He referred to "expeditions of the brethren into these highly speculative principles and doctrines" where honest differences of scriptural interpretation were possible. He commented that sometimes General Authorities and other prominent priesthood leaders had spoken about matters in which the revelations of the Lord were not conclusive and in which the President of the Church had not declared the official doctrine of the Church, and yet these individuals still declared their doctrinal views "with an assured certainty that might deceive the uninformed and unwary." President Clark's talk, "When Are Church Leader's [*sic*] Words Entitled to Claim of Scripture?" was published in the widely circulated *Deseret News Church Section* in 1954, republished in pamphlet form by the Church Department of Seminaries and Institutes in 1966, included in the Church's lesson manual for Melchizedek Priesthood quorums in 1969, and reprinted elsewhere.[38]

On occasion, President Clark was willing to employ censorship because he wanted to avoid the spiritual equivalent of shouting "Fire!" in a crowded theater. To counter what he regarded as the longstanding infusion of liberal theology into Church lesson manuals, he urged the establishment of a "Literature Censorship Committee" in 1940, and he formulated the purposes of the subsequently designated Committee on Publications in a letter of the First Presidency in 1944:

> The function of this Committee is to pass upon and approve all materials, other than those that are purely secular, to be used by our Church Priesthood, Educational, Auxiliary, and Missionary organizations in their work of instructing members of the Church in the principles of the Gospel and in leading others to a knowledge of the Truth. . . .
>
> To meet such required standards for use by Church organizations, such materials must:
>
> 1. Clearly set forth or be fully consistent with the principles of the restored Gospel.
>
> 2. Be wholly free from any taint of sectarianism and also of all theories and conclusions destructive of faith in the simple truths of the Restored Gospel, and especially be free from the teachings of the so-called "higher criticism." Worldly knowledge and speculation have their place; but they must yield to revealed truth.
>
> 3. Be so framed and written as affirmatively to breed faith and not raise doubts. "Rationalizing" may be most destructive of faith. That the Finite cannot fully explain the Infinite casts no doubt upon the Infinite. Truth, not error, must be stressed.
>
> 4. Be so built in form and substance as to lead to definite conclusions that accord with the principles of the Restored Gospel which conclusions must be expressed and not left to possible deduction by the students. When truth is involved there is no place for student preference or choice. Youth must be taught that truth cannot be blinked or put aside, it must be accepted.
>
> 5. Be filled with a spirit of deepest reverence. They should give no place for the slightest levity. They should be so written that those who teach from and by them will so understand.
>
> 6. Be so organized and written that the matter may be effectively taught by men and women untrained in teaching and without the background equipment given by such fields of learning as psychology, pedagogy, philosophy and ethics. The great bulk of our teachers are in the untrained group.[39]

These directives were a distillation of J. Reuben Clark's often expressed views about Church instructional materials, and the philosophy he used in drafting this Presidency letter became the charter of what was later known as Church correlation.

Although he wanted everything in Church instructional manuals to "breed faith and not raise doubts," his preferences for the public image of Mormonism varied considerably. Aside from his well-known frankness in talking to the Saints about himself and many things in Church administration, he could also be disarmingly candid with non-Mormons about the Church's problems. When a representative of *Look* magazine asked him about Church divorces in 1942, he replied, "Our divorces are piling up, we are influenced by the same waves of emotion and sociological elements as affect the whole country. We are just all mixed up, but I think that still our divorce rate is lower than the average."[40] On the other hand, President Clark urged the Guggenheim Foundation in 1949 to drop its support of Dale L. Morgan's projected multivolume history of Mormonism, and also successfully interceded with representatives of the motion picture industry in 1951 to cancel Warner Brothers' intended production of Juanita Brooks's *The Mountain Meadows Massacre.*[41]

In other cases where the free agency of individual Latter-day Saints conflicted with his sense of propriety, he declined to use his powers to impose censorship while at the same time leaving no uncertainty concerning his own recommendations. The best example of this occurred in 1957, when he learned that his nephew, Professor James R. Clark of Brigham Young University, was planning to publish a study on the defunct and little-understood Council of Fifty in Church history. He tried to dissuade his nephew by saying that the fact of their family relationship would make it appear to members of the Church that the study had President Clark's approval, that "You are telling a lot of things you don't know anything about," that "I don't think any good Churchman should do it," and that "I think it is unwise." Yet when his nephew asked if he was specifically asking him to discontinue the project, President Clark declined to insist upon the censorship that his Church position and family relationship allowed him to exert: "I think you should not touch it, but you can if you want. I am not going to tell you not to do it, but I think you will make a mistake if you do it. . . ." James R. Clark published the article on the Council of Fifty in 1958, and, with the cooperation of the First Presidency he subsequently edited a multivolume publication of First Presidency messages given during the years 1833 to 1951.[42] The principle of personal freedom was too important an issue to J. Reuben Clark for him to use his administrative powers against ordinary members of the Church who chose to write and publish things he preferred be left alone.

Nevertheless, he did not hesitate to urge the suppression of publications by General Authorities who he felt were inadvertently creating problems for the Church. When a committee under the direction of Elder John A. Widtsoe published a *Year Book of Facts and Statistics* in 1949, President Clark suggested to President George Albert Smith that "this booklet contained some information that would be better not circulated," and President Smith asked Elder Widtsoe to withdraw it from circulation.[43] When President Stephen L Richards and Elder Mark E. Petersen recommended against a 1955 republication of an article published about the temple ordinances in 1921, President Clark agreed that it should not be reprinted, but disagreed with the proposal to publish the article in altered form. "I did not think we were justified in re-writing articles that had been prepared by men who were dead."[44] For J. Reuben Clark, publications by General Authorities required not only prior permission of the Church President but also disclaimers of official endorsement. Therefore, even after President Clark obtained the permission of President McKay to publish *Why the King James Version?* the book's first words were: "For this book I alone am responsible. It is not a Church publication."[45]

In all of President Clark's attitudes toward the relationship of intellect, scripture, doctrine, and faith were three fundamentals: his unwavering testimony, his insistence on the freedom of intellect, and his loyalty to the President of the Church as prophet of God. To the general conference of April 1949, President Clark said, "I bear my testimony that I know that God lives, that Jesus is the Christ and the first fruits of the resurrection. I know that the gospel and the Priesthood were restored through the Prophet Joseph."[46] To him, all other considerations were secondary to that testimony. With reference to the role of intellect, despite his own misgivings about intellectuals, President Clark told that same general conference: "The priesthood never compels. God himself does not compel the intellect, nor does he attempt to overthrow it."[47] Concerning the role of the President of the Church, President Clark affirmed that only the President of the Church "has the right to rationalize," that only he "has any right to change or modify or extend any revelation of the Lord," and that the Latter-day Saints can always follow the Prophet, who will never lead them astray because "The Lord has never permitted it and he never will, because that would be an act of deceit of which He is incapable."[48] Nevertheless, President Clark also reminded the general conference of 1940 that the First Presidency "is not infallible in our judgment, and we err," he told the general conference of April 1949 that the President of the Church "was a prophet only when he spoke with the spirit of prophecy," and he instructed Church educators in 1954 that "even the President of the Church has not always spoken under the direction of the Holy Ghost." President Clark told the general conference and Church educators that it was only through diligent study, earnest prayer, and faithful listening to the promptings of the Holy Ghost to the individual whereby a person would know when the First Presidency was acting correctly and when the President of the Church or any other General Authority was speaking the will of God.[49]

"A WATCHMAN UNTO THE
HOUSE OF ISRAEL"

Ezekiel 3:17

J. Reuben Clark's perception of his obligations to warn the Latter-day Saints and monitor their responses to his warnings was strikingly similar to the prophetic calling of Ezekiel. President Clark felt that he could not remain silent lest he contribute to the spiritual destruction of the people he served, and thus he tirelessly devoted himself to safeguarding the Saints concerning dangers he perceived and enemies he recognized. He directed much of his effort to matters concerning religious heterodoxy and apostasy but also gave great attention to constitutionalism, communism, and local political activism.

Although he expressed a certain amount of toleration for Church members who had "disloyal thoughts," and who probed doctrinal mysteries he thought should be left alone,[1] President Clark was an unrelenting critic and administrative opponent of those who violated the priesthood order of the Church or who taught things that undermined what he perceived as the simple, orthodox gospel of Christ. He did not see himself as a witch hunter or grand inquisitor, and he publicly condemned the historical policy of Roman Catholicism to "attack and follow up all heretics."[2] Nevertheless, J. Reuben Clark firmly believed that he could not discharge his responsibility to the Church without raising a warning voice to the Saints and to fellow Church administrators about those Latter-day Saints who advocated what he perceived as heterodoxy.

Fundamental to his campaign against Mormon heterodoxy was a conviction that the Latter-day Saint Church was vulnerable to the same kind of apostasy that occurred in the early Christian church President Clark voiced this concern publicly in the October 1944 general conference:

173

I want to say to you brethren, and I am not professing any spirit of seership or prophecy, I am only going on the lessons which history has taught me, but I tell you we are beginning to follow along the course of the early Christian church. So long as that church was persecuted from without, it prospered, but when it began to be polluted from within, the church began to wither.[3]

A year later he warned those attending the general conference of the Church to beware of two elements of the apostasy of early Christianity—the introduction of specified dress in church administration and the accretion of pageantry in church ceremonies.[4] In 1950 he reminded the bishops of the Church that one of the first signs of apostasy among the early Christians was their desire for the praise and acceptance of nonbelievers, and then Reuben asked darkly, "Do any of you brethren know anything about such a tendency as that?"[5] In 1952 he informed the general priesthood meeting of April conference, "There is a startling parallel between the course that is coming in to us today and the course that was in the early Church, so startling that one becomes fearful," this in reference to the little groups of dissenters within Mormonism which were presently of inconsequential size but which might one day overwhelm the Church as they previously did the early Christian church.[6] Because he anticipated parallels between early Christian apostasy and latter-day apostasy, J. Reuben Clark focused his attention on three groups: devoted and well-meaning Church members who incorporated secular scholarship with the gospel; all teachers in the Church educational system (particularly at the Church's only university, Brigham Young University); and those who constituted what he regarded as the only significant schismatic movement of his Church experience—the men and women who continued to advocate and practice plural marriage (polygamy) contrary to twentieth-century Church policy.

Convinced that efforts to reconcile Greek philosophy with Christ's teachings had corrupted the early Christian church, Reuben found a latter-day parallel in efforts to reconcile the gospel with the "higher criticism" of the Bible by secular scholars. With antecedents in the sixteenth century, higher criticism developed in the nineteenth century as a self-conscious scholarly analysis of the Bible, with emphasis upon the reliability of various ancient texts of the Bible, the literary style and historical context of the Bible, and the original transmission and construction of the Biblical narratives.[7] Although many higher critics were believing Jews and Christians, the atheists among the higher critics and the inevitable revisions of traditional assumptions about the scriptures caused all Biblical literalists and many religious leaders of various persuasions to brand higher criticism as an atheistic attack on Judeo-Christian religion.[8] Although not all General Authorities shared his feelings, President Clark was adamant in rejecting the higher critics and their scholarly analysis of the Bible.

Before entering the First Presidency, he had already begun a decades-long discussion with Elder John A. Widtsoe about Biblical analysis. In his 1930 book, *In Search of Truth,* Elder Widtsoe wrote, "Higher criticism is not feared by Latter-day Saints" and added, "To Latter-day Saints there can be no objection to the careful and critical study of the scriptures, ancient or modern, provided only that it be an honest study—a search for truth."[9] Elder Widtsoe was one of Reuben's respected friends, but Ambassador Clark wrote a letter to him in 1930 that was not very subtle in its implied criticism of the way the Apostle had approached higher criticism:

> However, I come to deplore the fact that some of our "literatti" as I call them, do not spend more time on the philosophy of the gospel as revealed in ancient and modern times, and less on the pagan philosophy of ancient times and the near-pagan philosophy of modern times.[10]

Four years later, after entering the First Presidency, he read one of the books by Charles A. Briggs, a Protestant whose higher criticism had resulted in a sensational heresy trial, and Reuben dismissed him as "impudently cocksure, and yet so shallow and so unscientific so far as his consideration of evidence goes" and concluded, "If all higher criticism is of this sort, it surely is worth little."[11] In contrast, Elder Widtsoe published an article in 1940 describing higher critics as "lovers of the Bible" whose "avowed objective is not to discredit the Bible, but to discover truth." However, Elder Widtsoe tempered his praise with the caution, "The purpose of Higher Criticism may be acceptable; but its limitations must ever be kept in mind ... theories are forever changing."[12] Reuben could not accept even such a qualified endorsement, and he was uneasy to find that a member of the Quorum of the Twelve Apostles was giving even limited encouragement to Church religion teachers who were incorporating higher criticism in their instruction.

By the time John A. Widtsoe republished his endorsement of higher criticism in a 1943 book,[13] President Clark was preparing an administrative counterattack directed at all Church instruction. On 19 April 1943 he informed the superintendent of all Church Sunday School instruction:

> Furthermore, the tenets of the "higher critics" do not agree with the fundamental doctrines and teachings of the Church; their doctrines are, in practically every case, calculated to destroy the simple faith of our people; the theories of the "higher criticism" cannot be taught with sufficient thoroughness to youth, or even grownups, to enable those to whom they are taught either to judge of their falsity or, if convinced of their falsity, to explain the same to others. I therefore venture to suggest that all such teachings as this should be completely eliminated from our Church institutions.
>
> . . . .
>
> ... There is abundant evidence that those who are preparing the lessons for our Church institutions have something of a knowledge of sectarian scholarship, which they seem rather fond, if not proud, to display; but there is almost nothing to indicate that they have ever really delved into our own Church history or doctrines.[14]

A year later President Clark achieved the final consolidaton of his position on Biblical higher criticism when he drafted a letter, signed by the First Presidency, which instructed the Church Committee on Publications (of which John A. Widtsoe was a member) that "paganistic theories and tenets of the so-called 'higher criticism' have not been without their influence [in LDS publications]; none of these have a place in our Church. They should be wholly eliminated from our literature."[15]

Although he had maintained public silence about higher criticism as long as Elder Widtsoe's endorsements continued without ecclesiastical challenge, after the 1944 First Presidency letter J. Reuben Clark took frequent opportunity to become the primary spokesman of the Church against modern Biblical scholarship. In June 1945 he used a college baccalaureate as the vehicle for a massive assault upon higher criticism, which he aligned with Nazism, Bolshevism, and Fascism as enemies of Christianity, and which he described as a "sinister school of thought," as "pettifogging scholarship," as an "attack upon God and Christianity," and as atheistic in all its manifestation.[16] President Clark regarded most scholarly analysis of the

Biblical text as an effort to deny divine origin of the scripture, and he refused to take even one step down a path he was convinced would lead ultimately to rejection of scriptural inspiration. In 1953 he advised the youth of the Church not to use the word "love" in rendering I Corinthians 13, "as the modernists would have us," and President Clark devoted his main address at April 1954 general conference to attacking higher criticism and the Revised Standard Version of the Bible.[17] This was all preliminary to his final statement on the matter, the 473-page *Why the King James Version?*, which he had painstakingly researched for twenty-five years and published in 1956. To Reuben, the King James version was not simply a Biblical translation, but it was *the* Bible, and he used scholarly sources to defend that supremacy.[18]

During the years of this public campaign against Biblical scholarship, he was pleased at the general support of most of the members of the Quorum of the Twelve, but he was disappointed that President David O. McKay did not share the ardor of his repudiation of higher criticism. President McKay had acquiesced to his request to address the 1954 conference of the Church on higher critics and the Bible, but when Reuben asked the Church President for authorization to publish *Why the King James Version?*, President McKay replied "that he thought we ought to be a little bit careful about criticizing the Revised Version." When President McKay observed that the revised text was more accurate than the authorized text in some instances and eliminated the use of confusing or antiquated English terms, President Clark countered with the observation that President McKay would probably not wish to rewrite the plays of Shakespeare for the same purpose. The Church President agreed with that point, and assented to Reuben's publishing the book.[19]

J. Reuben Clark felt understandable elation in being able to publish his magnum opus in 1956, but he expressed to the president of George Washington University his disappointment that few of his fellow Church members and associates shared the intensity of his views about Biblical scholarship.

Contrary to your kindly prediction, I have not had many comments on the book. My own fellow communicants who are of the scholarly class, concluded (I am sure with one or two exceptions) that I knew nothing of what I was talking about and so paid little attention to the book.[20]

The first copy of Why the King James Version? *is inspected by President Clark. From left to right: Louis Jacobson, Deseret News Press general manager; President Clark; Elder Thomas S. Monson, Deseret News Press sales manager; Rowena Miller, President Clark's personal secretary; Alva Parry, Deseret Book Company manager; and Elder Mark E. Petersen,* Deseret News *general manager.*

It was a bitter-sweet conclusion to his scholarly effort to defend the purity of the gospel against the inroads of latter-day paganism, but he was always more interested in bearing witness than in counting converts.

In fact, because he was convinced that he could not persuade all teachers to abandon the enticement of higher criticism and comparable scholarship in teaching the gospel, he exerted continuing administrative pressure against these "modernists" within the Church educational system. President Clark began in a 1934 letter to Presidents Heber J. Grant and Anthony W. Ivins by recommending that every prospective high school seminary teacher and BYU professor be "carefully examined as to his beliefs."[21] Four years later he announced this publicly in his Aspen Grove talk:

> For any Latter-day Saint psychologist, chemist, physicist, geologist, archaeologist, or any other scientist, to explain away, or misinterpret, or evade or elude,

or most of all, to repudiate or to deny, the great fundamental doctrines of the Church in which he professes to believe, is to give the lie to his intellect, to lose his self-respect, to bring sorrow to his friends, to break the hearts and bring shame to his parents, to besmirch the Church and its members, and to forfeit the respect and honor of those whom he has sought, by his course, to win as friends and helpers.[22]

He continued to question the faith of Church educators throughout the Presidency of Heber J. Grant and in 1946 informed President George Albert Smith that "we had a number of teachers that were so imbued with modern trends and higher criticism that it was not possible for them to teach the Gospel as we understand it."[23]

To some extent, Reuben simply assumed that any church educator with a Ph.D. degree was suspect, and he commended one man by saying, "I am most grateful for yourself and for a few others who, having their Ph.D.'s, still are able to hold the Gospel in its simplicity."[24] His assumptions about the perilous condition of Church education were reinforced by his finding evidences of secular scholarship in Church manuals written by Ph.D.'s and by descriptions of the secularism and alleged lack of faith in BYU professors as reported to him.[25] Therefore, President Clark felt completely justified in expressing anxiety to his protégé Marion G. Romney in 1959 about "the so-called liberals at Brigham Young University" and in telling the president of BYU, "You have got some members of the faculty who are destroying the faith of our students. You ought to get rid of them."[26] Many intellectuals and Ph.D.'s in the Church educational system, at Brigham Young University, and throughout the Church, felt that their faith and devotion to the Church were unjustly questioned, and many within the new majority of college-educated Mormons chafed against what they perceived as anti-intellectualism in Church leaders.[27] Nevertheless, the fact remained that in the eyes of J. Reuben Clark and his like-minded associates, it was faith, not intellectuality, that was on the defensive.

Long before Reuben became interested in higher criticism and Church education, he had begun a lifelong battle against those who entered into new plural marriages after the Church's "Manifesto" of 1890. Polygamy had been common in the Woolley family before the Manifesto, but his father had remained a monogamist for twenty years before Wilford Woodruff officially announced in 1890, "I now publicly declare that my advice to the Latter-day Saints is to refrain from contracting any marriage forbidden by the laws of the land."[28] On the basis of the 1890 Manifesto and subsequent assurances of the First Presidency, the government campaign against the polygamous Mormon Church ended, Utah was finally granted statehood in 1896, and Latter-day Saints began their occasionally rocky path toward full acceptance and general admiration by the American public.[29]

The greatest single obstacle to that transition into acceptance was the reemergence of Mormon polygamy as a national issue between 1898 and 1910. The Senate investigation of Reed Smoot from 1904 to 1907 created newspaper headlines nationally and four volumes of official testimony which indicated that for several years prominent members of the Church had entered into and performed plural marriages after 1890. If the sensational newspaper reports did not convince Reuben, family members soon verified the published Senate evidence that his first cousin's husband, Elder John W. Taylor, had married two plural wives in Utah during 1901, that another of Reuben's first cousins had become the plural wife of a patriarch in a ceremony performed in Salt Lake City in 1900, and that his aunt became the plural wife of a stake president in another polygamous ceremony of U.S. origin. Moreover, Senate testimony also indicated that the bishop of Reuben's Grantsville ward married a plural wife at Salt Lake City in 1900 and lived with her in Utah.[30] These were obvious violations of the 1890 Manifesto and of Utah's laws, but even the disclosures of post-1890 plural marriages in Mexico gave no amelioration to the situation, because Mexican law also specifically prohibited polygamy or polygamous cohabitation with plural wives married in other countries.[31] These disclosures of post-1890 polygamy humiliated Mormons like J. Reuben Clark who had assumed that the 1890 Manifesto was an inflexible document that had ended the "Mormon polygamy question" for all time.

Reuben's religious demand for administrative and doctrinal consistency recoiled at the spectre of new polygamy coexisting with repeated public denials by the First Presidency that there had ever been authorized plural marriages after the 1890 Manifesto. As a totally innocent bystander to the controversies swirling around the Senate investigation of Reed Smoot, Reuben was in a particularly agonizing situation once he became Assistant Solicitor of the State Department in 1906. As one of the nation's highest legal advisors, he could not look upon polygamy after the 1890 Manifesto with the least degree of allowance, because it not only offended his religious principles, it also violated state and international laws. He welcomed President Joseph F. Smith's official pronouncement of April 1904 that future plural marriages would be subject to excommunication and greeted with grim satisfaction the April 1906 announcement of the forced resignations of John W. Taylor and Matthias F. Cowley from the Quorum of the Twelve Apostles for entering into post-1890 plural marriages. But even this was not enough to salve his personal humiliation as a "modern" Mormon or redeem the Church's honor, and on 2 March 1907 Reuben wrote himself a memorandum urging the excommunication of all persons "who have married [polygamously] since Manifesto."[32]

But Reuben and the General Authorities had to face a far more difficult challenge than the generally benign resolution of the authorization of plural marriages after the Manifesto. Certain Mormons would not stop performing and entering into new plural marriages despite the concerted opposition of the First Presidency and Quorum of the Twelve Apostles after 1906. When the First Presidency learned in 1910 that a patriarch had assumed the authority to perform plural marriages after the 1904 declaration, the First Presidency issued instructions at October conference for all stake presidents and bishops to excommunicate any person "who advises, counsels or entices any person to contract a plural marriage . . . as well as those who solemnize such marriages, or those who enter into such unlawful unions."[33] But polygamy among the Mormons would not down, and Reuben was stunned to learn in 1914 that his eighty-two-year-old uncle, John W. Woolley (a temple worker and patriarch), had been performing plural marriages, for which he was excommunicated from the Church.[34]

Reuben was proud of his Woolley ancestry and relations, and he was saddened that the Woolley name should be so prominently associated with the defiant practice of polygamy. Rarely in Utah himself, he did not know much about the arguments advanced by those advocating the continuance of polygamous marriages. The many statements against continued solemnization of plural marriages did not address that issue,[35] and as a rank-and-file member of the Church,

Reuben drafted a statement that he hoped the First Presidency would adopt at the October 1923 general conference:

> Resolved that the Church of Jesus Christ of Latter-day Saints, in solemn conference assembled, hereby reaffirms the rule and order of the Church as it has always heretofore existed and as it does now exist, namely that all delegated keys, powers, and/or authorities cease and determine, and become of no force, value, or efficacy whatsoever, upon the death of the person making the delegation thereof, and that all ordinances, sealings, bindings, promises, or other acts whatsoever made, done or performed under and persuant to such delegated keys, powers, and/or authorities and made, done, or performed after the death of the person who made the delegation, as null, void, and of no efficacy or effect whatsoever. . . .[36]

His proposed statement sidestepped the historical issue of whether or not any Presidents of the Church prior to Heber J. Grant had authorized the performance of plural marriages after 1890 and instead argued that any such delegated authority ended with the death of the Church President involved. President Heber J. Grant was too outraged with the people who continued to perform and contract plural marriages for him to give much notice to a lawyer's unsolicited legalisms, and he was particularly furious that Reuben's cousin Lorin C. Woolley was circulating numerous stories about polygamy that seemed to have no basis in fact. Instead of issuing Reuben's proposed declaration in October 1923, President Grant dismissed Lorin C. Woolley as a pathological liar—which led to Woolley's excommunication in January 1924 for "pernicious falsehood."[37]

When J. Reuben Clark was sustained a member of the First Presidency in April 1933, Lorin Woolley (ever active to give his claims legitimacy) spent the last year of his life telling his polygamist group that President Clark had been associated in various ways with the activities and claims of John W. Woolley and Lorin C. Woolley. When one of their excommunicated followers asked for verification of these stories, Reuben set the record straight. He did not recall whether Lorin C. Woolley claimed to have "the fullness of the apostolic authority" and had never heard John W. Woolley make such a claim, and Reuben himself had never accepted such a claim. He denied that Lorin Woolley had ever counseled him to be a civil servant, or to accept President Grant's call as a counselor. Reuben also pointedly denied Lorin Woolley's claim that Reuben had ever been sympathetic to post-Manifesto plural marriages.[38] Because of the wild stories Lorin C. Woolley circulated about Reuben and about other matters, President Clark concluded "whether he knew he was falsifying I did not know, but he did not tell the truth."[39] Of far greater worry to Church authorities than the personality of Lorin C. Woolley were the periodic discoveries of new plural marriages among the Mormons.

Heber J. Grant had been denouncing renegade polygamists for years, and the Church President encouraged Reuben to bring his many talents to that battle almost as soon as he entered the First Presidency. President Grant gave the first orientation for this assignment on 25 April 1933.[40] Within a month, President Clark upon his own initiative drafted the longest denunciation (fourteen printed pages) the Church has ever officially published against post-1890 polygamy.

As approved and issued by the First Presidency on 17 June 1933, the "Official Statement" went far beyond previous Church statements that had simply denied post-1890 plural marriage as a matter of Church policy. The 1933 statement drafted by J. Reuben Clark combined for the first time historical, legal, ecclesiastical, and doctrinal denials of the legitimacy of plural marriage after 1890. The statement summarized U.S. legal actions against Mormon polygamy, gave a doctrinal justification for the 1890 Manifesto, referred to the 1891 petition for federal amnesty signed by the First Presidency and Quorum of the Twelve, reminded readers that the federal government granted Utah statehood upon the provision of perpetual abandonment of plural marriage, and that the Utah constitution incorporated that provision. The statement relegated the performance of plural marriages from 1890 to 1904 as actions of "a few misguided members of the Church, some of whom had been signers of the petition praying for amnesty." Adopting the legalistic argument of Reuben's unused 1923 statement, the First Presidency pronouncement of 1933 described the revelation of September 1886 (which affirmed the practice of plural marriage and had been attributed to Church President John Taylor) as a "pretended revelation" of which the Church archives had no record or corroboration, dismissed the alleged setting apart of men to continue plural marriage as "illegal and void," and condemned "the corrupt, adulterous practices of the members of this secret, and (by reputation) oathbound organization" of Mormon Fundamentalists as a modern-day version of the satanic Gadianton Robbers of Book of Mormon history.[41] To a non-Mormon, President Clark explained that the First Presidency issued the 1933 statement against polygamy "because some carnally-minded old birds are saying the Church is not in earnest about the matter, and were winking at the situation."[42]

To the First Presidency and to many Mormons who had always opposed post-1890 plural marriages, the 1933 statement seemed exactly what the Church had long needed. As crafted by President Clark, the denunciation of post-1890 polygamy was comprehensive, legalistic, and uncompromising, and it directly denied the priesthood claims of Lorin C. Woolley and his followers. Unfortunately, just as State Department Solicitor Clark had inadvertantly transformed the civil unrest of Mexico "from a sandlot revolt into a full-blown rebellion" by issuing a bellicose statement in 1912,[43] he had drafted a First Presidency statement in 1933 that he later realized had transformed a rag-tag collection of polygamist sympathizers who valued their Church affiliation into a cohesive movement of true schismatics (known popularly as "Fundamentalists") who rejected the Church and its leaders, militantly proselytized, and for the first time in the twentieth century became an actual threat to the Church. With his typical candor, President Clark said in 1945 that "one of the reasons why the so-called 'Fundamentalists' had made such inroads among our young people was because we had failed to teach them the truth."[44]

President Grant gave J. Reuben Clark a mandate to suppress the present practice of polygamy, and President Clark went at it with a vengeance. Although he did not originate the idea of requiring persons suspected of polygamist sympathies to sign a loyalty oath, Reuben's experience in overseeing Justice Department activities against suspected subversives during World War I predisposed him to favor a Church-wide requirement in the mid-1930s for suspected Fundamentalists to "solemnly declare and affirm that I, without any mental reservation whatever, support the Presidency and Apostles of the Church; that I repudiate any intimation that any one of the Presidency or Apostles of the Church is living a double life ... that I denounce the practice and advocacy of plural marriage ... and that I myself am not living in such alleged marriage relationship."[45] In 1938 he began commissioning loyal priesthood leaders to identify "the adulteryites" by conducting surveillance on all persons attending meetings at residences of known Fundamentalists.[46] In 1939 he encouraged the Salt Lake City public librarian to exclude Fundamentalist polygamy literature from library holdings, and in February 1940 asked the Salt Lake City postmaster to prohibit the mailing of Fundamentalist publications.[47] At a meeting with stake presidents of Salt Lake County a month later, one stake president suggested that the district attorney "was a good Latter-day Saint and would persecute [*sic*] the 'new polyg's' criminally if it were deemed wise," to which President Clark responded that criminal prosecution should begin as soon as possible.[48]

President Clark's overseeing of this quiet campaign to ferret out polygamists was at times frustrating and dismaying. The Fundamentalists discovered the surveillance almost immediately in 1938, and in August 1939 Joseph W. Musser published an open letter which identified J. Reuben Clark as the General Authority responsible for "clearing the community of polygamous teachings and living. . . ."[49] Although President Clark was also receiving separate lists of Fundamentalists from the Salt Lake City Police Department in 1940, that source of information was cut off when a new police chief assigned the police investigators to other work in 1941.[50] Although Reuben hoped that a decline in polygamist growth would result from the combination of Presidency statements, Church court actions, and the activities he was directing, the coordinator of the Salt Lake City surveillance program reported to him that the Fundamentalist "group is growing by leaps and bounds and the attendance of young people is astonishing."[51]

Despite such setbacks and administrative frustrations, Reuben pressed on with his efforts to oppose Mormon polygamists. In 1944 a lawyer representing men on trial for polygamy telephoned him at home with an offer to withhold testimony embarrassing to the Church if the First Presidency would stop supporting civil prosecutions of polygamists. President Clark rebuffed the offer on the basis of the legal distinction between *Malum in se* (intrinsically bad) and *malum in prohibitum* (bad only because it is prohibited, not because it is intrinsically bad).

As he talked he tried to draw some distinction between malum prohibitum and malum in se. I said: "Well, in the eyes of the law and disregarding entirely religious considerations, the pre-Manifesto people were guilty of adultery and so are these people guilty of adultery." I asked him whether adultery was malum in se or malum prohibitum, to which he replied "I won't answer," to which I replied, "You have answered."

As the conversation progressed I said, "Well, there is nothing the Church can do about it under any circumstances. We cannot go down and ask that this indictment be quashed."[52]

On this occasion and subsequently, President Clark denied that he had instigated any legal actions against the Fundamentalists, and in 1951 he even declined to furnish evidence against the polygamists to a detective agency representing the Arizona Attorney General. But he encouraged Latter-day Saints to report what they knew about current polygamists to the civil authorities, he monitered the progress of criminal court cases involving polygamists, and he classified as "Ultra Confidential" the ten days' advanced notice Arizona's governor gave him of the world-famous police raid against the polygamists of Short Creek, Arizona, in 1953 (which *Time* said had "the ponderous secrecy of an elephant sneaking across a skating rink"). Because of a national backlash of sympathy for the Fundamentalists after the 1953 Short Creek raid, President Clark took care during the last years of his life to arrange for local news blackouts of stories that could give favorable publicity to the Fundamentalists.[53]

Since World War I, J. Reuben Clark had believed that social and political upheavals were the result of conspiracies by small groups of dedicated revolutionaries,[54] and as a Church leader he was constantly watchful for evidence of religious subversion and treachery among the Latter-day Saints. The polygamist revolt was by far the longest standing preoccupation of his scrutiny, because he felt that it was almost impossible for a Church member to be loyal to the Church once the person had become entangled in the theological, psychosexual, and familial web of renegade polygamy. Of later origin but equal intensity was his assault on higher criticism of the Bible in particular and upon higher education in general. As one who had abandoned intellectualism to preserve his own religious faith, President Clark regarded complex religious inquiry as an addiction that usually led to overdoses of intellectualism and death of faith, and he was an unrelenting critic of teachers and writers who did not share that view. Superimposed upon his other concerns was his conviction that the Church was subject to the same centrifugal pressures and corrupting influences as early Christianity.

J. Reuben Clark was a watchman on the tower whose sight and weaponry were directed within the fortress, rather than without. That also applied to his statements and activities about matters some might regard as outside the sphere of religion: the U.S. Constitution, communism, and local political activism.

As a young man in the State Department, Reuben had regarded the constitutional restraints of the U.S. Senate on foreign affairs as an irritating handicap,[55] but as he matured, his reverence for the U.S. Constitution grew. He frequently told general conferences of the Church, "to me the Constitution is a part of my religion. In its place it is just as much a part of my religion as any other part." The foundation for his constitutional views were revelations in which God expressed approval of this crucial document of 1787, but he did not regard the divinely instituted U.S. Constitution as static.[56]

It provided for its own amendments, and Reuben reassured one conference that God would approve any amendment adopted the way the Constitution prescribed.[57] Although he cherished free enterprise, he believed employers and corporations were "rapacious" in their exploitation of workers. Therefore, he not only supported the idea of unions but also foresaw a revision of the Constitution.

The Constitution was framed to provide for a government over what was essentially a non-industrial world. The great bulk of the people were engaged in agricultural pursuits. . . .

. . . .

. . . Inevitably this new world calls for some new rules and regulations if men are to be protected against one another, employer against the employee, and the employee against the employer. . . .

. . . .

Human liberty against the political despot, tyrant, or what-not, was gained but slowly over the centuries, without any predetermined pattern or plan. It may be that the new relationships that arise, indeed that are part of our new industrial world, will have to be worked out in the same way, yet if the problem was envisaged and studied it might be that an easier, quicker and less costly solution could be found.[58]

He also personally favored amendments to provide a 25 percent limit to taxation and a six-year limit to the service of the U. S. President.[59]

Nevertheless, he made a clear distinction between those who revered the Constitution and sought to amend it to meet necessary conditions and those "defamers" who actually wished to discard the Constitution and the government it provided in order to establish a new social and political order he decried as "despotism."[60] He warned the Saints in the 1930s and 1940s that the national government seemed to be moving dangerously beyond the Constitution, and observed:

You and I have heard all our lives that the time may come when the Constitution may hang by a thread. I do not know whether it is a thread or a small rope by which it now hangs, but I do know that whether it shall live or die is now in the balance.[61]

He saw little, if any, improvement in the constitutional situation during the last twenty years of his life but did not "grow despondent" because of his faith that the Lord would not allow the Constitution "to be thrown down, but that on the contrary, that He would cause it to be preserved."[62] Although he believed the gospel and the Church of Jesus Christ would always support the Constitution and its principles, he was wary of those Latter-day Saints who suggested that the elders of Israel would one day save the Constitution by military intervention: "President Clark wishes me to acknowledge your letter and to say that he has never felt that the Church would save the Constitution by armed force."[63]

Reuben's reverence for constitutional principles and his abhorrence of violence and social upheaval were the foundation of his forty-two-year campaign against Marxism and communism. True to his policy of avoiding disagreeable reading, he never devoted much time to studying Marxism as a political philosophy or communism as a social system and wrote Ernest Wilkinson in 1949: "I am sorry to say that you have an exaggerated notion about what I have done in the matter of studying Communism, because I have done practically nothing at it except for a most casual reading, so I cannot supply you with any bibliography."[64] But Reuben foresaw the dangers V. I. Lenin and the Bolsheviks represented to world order, and he was privately expressing conern about the influence of the Bolsheviks two years before the Russian Revolution of 1917.[65] The successful Bolshevik revolution of October 1917, the slaughter of the Czarist family and of anti-Bolsheviks during the ensuing civil war in Russia, the radical transformation of property and power in the USSR, the ruthless suppression of all dissent and diversity, and the crusading zeal of the communists horrified Reuben.[66] Only one thing caused him greater alarm: among both intellectuals and industrial workers in Europe and the United States there was evidence of sympathy for the Russian Revolution and support for the Marxist ideology underpinning it. Therefore, as early as 1919, Reuben, as a private citizen, "began my crusade against Communism."[67]

When he entered the First Presidency in 1933, he intensified this campaign. Although the First Presidency had not officially commented upon communism up to this time, President Clark believed that it was essential to make an official statement because he was convinced that Latter-day Saints were affiliating with communism in one way or another. Therefore, he drafted the message which the First Presidency issued on 3 July 1936.

> With great regret we learn from credible sources, governmental and otherwise, that a few Church members are joining, directly or indirectly, the Communists and are taking part in their activities.
>
> Since Communism, established, would destroy our American Constitutional government, to support Communism is treasonable to our free institutions, and no patriotic American citizen may become either a Communist or supporter of Communism.
>
> Communism being thus hostile to loyal American citizenship and incompatible with true Church membership, of necessity no loyal American citizen and no faithful Church member can be a Communist.[68]

This was the first time the Presidency officially attacked a legal political party in the United States: the Communist party had appeared on the Utah ballot since 1928 and had achieved more than 900 votes in the 1932 election.[69] Unsatisfied with simply issuing a declaration, two weeks later President Clark opposed the request of Communist party candidate Earl Browder to speak at the Salt Lake Tabernacle and recommended that the American Legion in uniform attend the communist rally at Salt Lake City's Liberty Park to help preserve order.[70] From July 1936 until April 1940, the chief of Salt Lake City's detectives was also sending to the Presidency reports of surveillance and infiltration of Communist party meetings in Salt Lake City, and David O. McKay indicated the degree to which he shared Reuben's viewpoint upon receipt of one of these reports: "Communist rats are working here in the United States and are gnawing at the very vitals of our government, and I wish every one of them could be sent to Russia where he belongs."[71]

President Clark also made repeated statements against sympathy for communism because of the Church's practice of the United Order. The 1936 Presidency statement affirmed:

To our Church members we say: Communism is not the United Order, and bears only the most superficial resemblance thereto; Communism is based upon intolerance and force, the United Order upon love and freedom of conscience and action; Communism involves forceful despoilation and confiscation, the United Order voluntary consecration and sacrifice.[72]

This unequivocal statement apparently did not resolve the difficulty, and at October 1942 general conference President Clark decried the idea of "communism being merely the forerunner, so to speak, of a reestablishment of the United Order. I am informed that ex-bishops, and indeed, bishops, who belong to communistic organizations, are preaching this doctrine," and at the conference a year later he reaffirmed: "Communism is Satan's counterfeit for the United Order, that is all there is to it."[73]

Despite the popular alliance of the United States and Russia against Nazi Germany, Reuben wrote in 1944: "But it is not Fascism that I am fearing. The world has dealt with Fascism since the beginning of time. It is Communism that is the real danger, except that a lot of these fellows have not the courage to denounce Communism because of Russia."[74] He later amplified his position by stating:

There is this difference between Nazism and Communism—the first leaves private property and individualism, however much appropriated and curtailed to meet the immediate crisis; the second destroys both private property and individualism, making the state all-pervading, all-absorbing, a god of human mind.[75]

Reuben was never reconciled to the wartime alliance of the United States and the Soviet Union because it seemed to imply a grudging acceptance of the communist system.

He was especially anxious that no Latter-day Saint be identified in any degree with communist terminology, become too knowledgeable about communist philosophy, or be sympathetic to the Soviet Union. "I have harped on the general tenor of communism until people think I am 'screwy' on the subject," he wrote in 1943, "but I have never been more earnest, and I think, never more right, than in my position on this matter."[76] After World War II he opposed the use of the term "Youth Conference" in the MIA, "Because of the connotation given to the name through the communists."[77] He opposed publishing much about what the communists actually believed, because "you do not build virtue in the home by picturing the allurements of a house of prostitution," and for the same reason he did not want Latter-day Saint youth or young adults to travel to the Soviet Union.[78]

Despite his own campaign against communism, President Clark had mixed views about anticommunist crusades. On one hand, he tended to blur, if not eliminate, any distinctions between Marxists, communists, socialists, revolutionaries, and New Dealers. He said that scientist Albert Einstein was "at heart a socialist, if not a communist,"[79] and he accused Drew Pearson and other news columnists of being proto-communists because "the things for which Pearson stood were things that inevitably led to communism, if followed through."[80] Like the respected conservative columnist William F. Buckley, President Clark also praised the intent of Senator Joseph McCarthy's anticommunist campaign.[81] On the other hand, Reuben acknowledged that fervent anticommunists were sometimes guilty of character assassination: he himself was classed as a fellow traveler with communists because he opposed NATO, and he comforted a U.S. senator who had been similarly accused by saying, "I have always understood that you lay over on the right side of the communist line, which is the farthest away you can get from the communist party."[82] President Clark was especially leery of those he regarded as extremists within the anticommunist movement: he declined to assist one man in forming an anticommunist organization in 1946; he declined to help the first Mormon anticommunist pamphleteer distribute his literature and warned J. Reuben Clark III in 1948 to "be awfully careful in using his stuff"; and when a California stake president sent him a stridently anticommunist national publication in 1954,

President Clark responded, "I am always troubled to know how much reliance can be placed in this kind of literature."[83]

But President Clark agreed with Elder Ezra Taft Benson, who was U.S. Secretary of Agriculture from 1953 to 1961, that the communist menace in America was real, and that anticommunists who were stable and wise should be supported.[84] With the permission of President Smith in 1948, Reuben became a trustee of the New York-based Foundation for Economic Education, which published pamphlets like *Where Karl Marx Went Wrong,* as well as its monthly *The Freeman* with articles, "UN Versus US," "The Collectivist Menace," and "Not Victories for Communism." President Clark persuaded Church-affiliated businesses to contribute to the Foundation for Economic Education, with which he continued to affiliate until his death. He also gave encouragement to what he perceived as wise anticommunist speeches and books.[85] Following Reuben's October 1959 conference address against Marxism, the secretary to the First Presidency reported President Clark's earnest concerns about the Latter-day Saints:

> President Clark wishes me to say that he did not expect Marxian sympathizers, whatever their particular Marxist cult might be, to approve of what he said; but he hopes that Latter-day Saint Marxist cultists will give sober, prayerful thought to the whole problem before abandoning truth for error.[86]

Because he regarded the Democratic New Deal as anti-constitutional and pro-communist,[87] Reuben became even more ardently a Republican when he entered the First Presidency. In a draft of one talk he wrote: "The Republican Party was born to save the Union; it has lived that it might save our Constitution with its free institutions."[88] By 1940 even local Republican leaders regarded him as the virtual head of the party in Utah, despite his disclaimer "that I had no such place, in fact nor in thought. . . ."[89] Without his solicitation, county and state Republican leaders, candidates, and officeholders met with President Clark in the Church Office Building seeking political counsel and support for more than a decade.[90] Despite repeated attempts by prospective candidates to obtain his official endorsement, Reuben sought to remain noncommittal and explained "that the Church could not undertake to pick candidates, but after the candidates were picked, our interest in the general

welfare would lead us to try to exercise such persuasion as we properly might to get the best men elected."[91]

When elected officials, both Republicans and anti-New Deal
Democrats, asked Reuben about the course they ought to pursue in
specific matters, Reuben stated the position in 1939 that governed
his approach to this situation for the rest of his service in the First
Presidency:

> We were in a position where we could not keep our mouths closed and then
> condemn them for what they did or did not do. I observed that of course we were
> in a position to indicate, for example, that we thought they ought to do all they
> could to lower taxes; to decrease State employees instead of to increase them; to
> avoid radical labor legislation; to avoid all Communistic legislation. . . .[92]

By the late 1940s President Clark adopted the policy of referring
nearly all political inquirers and matters to three trusted associates:
questions of financing Republican candidates and causes to Orval
Adams, President of Zion's First National Bank; Republicans to
Harold B. Lee, member of the Quorum of the Twelve since 1941;
and Democrats to Henry D. Moyle, member of the Quorum of the
Twelve since 1948.[93] President Clark explained the nature of this delegation to one inquirer: "I suggested that he see Brothers Lee or
Moyle, or both of them; that while they were not undertaking to
guide the Church in politics, nevertheless we had determined that
they should interview people so that we would only get one expression or explanation."[94] Because he was conscientiously seeking to
avoid using his Church position to influence local politics, President
Clark wrote a bristling reply to Drew Pearson's nationally syndicated
column in November 1950 which described Reuben as Utah's Republican boss who had unseated a New Deal senator.

> In view of this background I think probably you would be glad to know that
> you are almost completely misinformed regarding my work and position here in
> Utah. For years I have taken no part whatever in politics, and while I have let my
> personal views be known about various matters political, I have no reason to be-
> lieve that they have had any particular influence. I believe I know who some of
> the persons are who have talked with you to the building up of a bogie-Clark who
> has no existence except in their imaginations. I took no part in the recent cam-
> paign. I believe if I had taken part there might have been more "lame ducks" than
> there were. Senator Thomas was defeated because people were tired of him and of
> the things for which he stood. I did not defeat him.[95]

Despite his ardent Republicanism, President Clark also opposed one-party rule even by the GOP, and he expressed the view that "a Democratic Congress, as a brake on a Republican administration, during these critical times, was not a bad arrangement. . . . It will be irritating to the President at times, but it will also be safe."[96] Ever the Republican, Reuben was ever more the constitutionalist with an abiding suspicion of the evils of popular election mandates for the Chief Executive and one-party rule.

In only one respect did President Clark maintain a close political consultation with an elected official in Utah, and this was his well-known association with Governor J. Bracken Lee.[97] The governor was a non-Mormon and an independent anti-New Dealer who frankly expressed to other political leaders his own view of Utah politics.

> Gov. Lee: I said to them you are never going to have any success in Utah unless you let the leaders of the Church give you some advice. You better make it a point to talk with the Church officials to find out if they are going along with it or not.[98]

Nearly every contact between the two men was at Governor Lee's initiative,[99] and when Reuben did initiate a meeting with Governor Lee, he began by saying: "I told him that I appreciated that it was almost impossible for a man to divest himself of his position in a matter about which he talks, but so far as it was possible to do so, I was divesting myself of my position, and was coming to him merely as an American citizen."[100] Oftentimes, President Clark declined to contact the governor, even when other Church officials urged him to do so.[101]

One time that President Clark felt duty bound to contact Bracken Lee was when it was rumored that the governor was going to veto the Utah legislature's Sunday closing law. When the governor argued that Seventh-day Adventists and Jews should have the right to observe their Sabbath and conduct business on a Sunday, President Clark countered, "Suppose you had a group of harlots come in and object to any restrictions you might place on them," and Reuben concluded his rare effort at direct lobbying with a statement of his sense of being a watchman upon the towers of Zion: ". . . it seems to me that in matters affecting, as we think this does, the religious and moral welfare of a community, I am wondering if the minority, where there is no legal right, whether the minority should control."[102] The governor, like many other of President Clark's listeners for nearly three decades, did not accept the warning voice.

Although disappointed at any rejection of his earnest counsel or warnings of impending dangers, Reuben felt that he had fulfilled his responsibility by energetically raising his voice. He was often amused by those who tried to put one kind of label or another upon his efforts. He told the priesthood meeting at April 1935 conference that "in Wall Street I am known as a radical; at home as a sort of man-eating conservative."[103] Fifteen years later he publicly defined himself, since many others had failed to label him accurately.

I am pro-Constitution, pro-Government, as it was established under the Constitution, pro-free institutions, as they have been developed under and through the Constitution, pro-liberty, pro-freedom, pro-full and complete independence and sovereignty, pro-local self-government, and pro-everything else that has made us the free country we had grown to be in the first 130 years of our national existence.

It necessarily follows that I am anti-internationalist, anti-interventionist, anti-meddlesome-busybodiness in our international affairs. In the domestic field, I am anti-socialist, anti-Communist, anti-Welfare State. I am what the kindlier ones of all these latter people with whom I am denying any association or sympathy, would call a rabid reactionary (I am not, in fact, that).[104]

To that list, one must appropriately and necessarily add that J. Reuben Clark was a Watchman upon the Tower of Zion who raised the warning voice to the Latter-day Saints about the dangers he perceived in religious and secular spheres.

"THEY THAT TAKE THE SWORD"

Matthew 26:52

J. Reuben Clark's attitudes toward war, militarism, and pacifism reflected his religious background and the circumstances of the world in which he lived. Prior to his own young manhood, Mormonism traditionally had an ambivalent outlook toward war and peace that could be described as "selective pacifism." Until 1898, Mormons ignored the dictates of secular rulers in matters of warfare and became militarists or remained pacifists according to the instructions of the Church President.[1] Reuben's personal heritage was likewise ambivalent: his paternal grandfather had been a pacifist Dunkard, but Reuben's father served in the Union army during the Civil War; and Reuben's maternal grandfather had been a pacifist Quaker who had converted to Mormonism and had sent his sons to serve in Mormon defensive operations against U.S. troops in 1857–1858.[2] Moreover, Reuben witnessed the actual participation of the United States in the Spanish-American War, World War I, World War II, the Korean War, the Cold War with the USSR, and the early stages of the Vietnam War.

As a young man, Reuben tended to favor militarism and to view pacifism as impractical and dangerous. In the war hysteria and popular clamor that drove the U.S. to war with Spain in 1898, he was kept from volunteering for battle only by the earnest entreaties of his parents and his fiancée. In a letter to his parents he described himself as feeling like a coward for not joining the Utah volunteers and said "the matter has been with me a struggle between love and duty. I should have enlisted at the first call had it not been for the wishes of yourselves and another to whom I feel my consideration is due."[3] Later (in 1912) he accepted the position of director of the American

Peace Society as an extension of his membership in the American Society for Judicial Settlement of International Disputes,[4] but he had little real sympathy for pacifism.

As a succession of unintended events and consequences thrust Europe into the "Great War" of August 1914, Reuben saw the conflict in absolute terms in which England and her allies represented God-given democracy whereas Germany and its Central Power alliance were the "hordes of Satan " representing the monarchies of barbarism. By 1915 he not only expressed earnest wishes for England's victory but wrote legal briefs describing the British naval blockade as simply "extralegal" and argued that the sale of U.S. munitions to England and France did not violate American neutrality in the least. As a Republican loyalist, he had a lifelong dislike for Democratic President Woodrow Wilson, but in April 1917 he wholeheartedly accepted Wilson's message to Congress that U.S. entry into the European war was necessary to make the world safe for democracy. Reuben demonstrated his conviction in 1917 as he had failed to do in the Spanish-American War: he entered the ranks of the military and was commissioned a major in the Judge Advocate General division.[5]

As Europe entered into war in 1914 and the United States followed in 1917, Reuben found pacifism unacceptable. In May 1914, several months before European diplomacy collapsed into war, he informed Theodore Marburg of the American Society for Judicial Settlement of International Disputes of his intention to resign from the American Peace Society directorate because he dissented from the policy and propaganda of the society. In December 1914 he expressed this request directly to the executive director of the American Peace Society because of the society's opposition to the peacetime enlargement of the army and navy, and within two weeks he was condemning his "peace-at-any-price colleagues on the Peace Society Directorate." After resigning from the board of directors of the American Peace Society in 1916, he wrote Marburg on 3 March 1917:

The older I get, the more I see, the more experience I obtain, the more I become convinced that the peace propaganda and the present peace propagandists are both equally impractical and illusory, as also inimical to the interests of this nation. If we get into war, as seems now all but inevitable, we shall have to put some of them in jail, and personally I should like to begin with Mr. Bryan [William Jennings Bryan, former Democratic U.S. Secretary of State].[6]

In one respect, Reuben was as good as his word while he served on special assignment to the U.S. Attorney General's Office during World War I: he supported the imprisonment of thousands of German and Austrian nationals during the war and urged that the legal restrictions on "enemy aliens" in the United States be applied to women as well as men. Nevertheless, Major Clark was appalled at the anti-German hysteria and legal repression of war critics in the United States. "I shall be no party to hounding any man or woman to jail or to the gallows, merely because someone whispers a criminal accusation or levels against him an irresponsible finger of unsupported suspicion."[7]

For twenty years after the armistice of November 1918 ended the world war, Reuben continued to work for sane militarism and to disdain pacifism. He attacked the League of Nations provision of the Treaty of Versailles and the treaty itself in ghostwritten talks for U.S. Senator Knox, and told a crowd of 10,000 people in the Salt Lake Tabernacle in 1919 that the United States should refuse to compromise its sovereignty, reject the League of Nations, and refuse to "waste the strength God has given us" by joining "in petty squabbles over a few rods of miserable European blood-sodden soil."[8] He served as Special Counsel for the State Department in the Washington Arms Conference of 1921–22, and fully supported the conference aims to reduce the possibility of war by treaty provisions that limited naval armaments and thereby reduced the kind of arms race that contributed to the late European war.[9] Moreover, in May 1923 he became Chairman of the New York Committee for the Outlawry of War, but denied that he was either a pacifist or utopian dreamer.

But, as I said in my last letter, ours is not a pacifist movement. We do not proceed toward peace along the path of disarmament; we expect disarmament through the riddance of war, rather than riddance of war through disarmament.

... The main thing, however, is that it will be difficult or impossible to start a war when once we have so re-ordered the world, and international wars have become as unlawful as domestic wars of revolution. These latter cannot be prevented but as they proceed in the teeth of the law, they are rare and are illegal and criminal.[10]

J. Reuben Clark and his brother John W. Clark during World War I.

With such views it is not surprising that he endorsed the Kellogg-Briand Treaty (Pact of Paris) of 1928 which outlawed war.[11] Equally consistent with his position in the two decades after World War I was his refusal to accept election to the board of directors of the American Peace Society in 1930.[12] Thus, by the time J. Reuben Clark entered the First Presidency in April 1933, his attitudes toward militarism, warfare, and pacifism seemed fixed.

During nearly thirty years as an elder statesman in the First Presidency, however, President Clark's pronouncements on war indicated that his views had experienced a transformation varying from subtle shifts of emphasis to complete reversals. Whereas he had previously opposed American alliances and foreign intervention on the basis that they served no vital American interest, President Clark came to oppose any alliance and intervention, even where vital American interests were affected. Although he continued to affirm that wars of one kind or another were inevitable, he no longer believed that there were any "just wars" and was convinced that war was absolutely evil and irredeemably corrupting. Before 1933, Reuben saw scheming militarists only in foreign nations, but during his service in the First Presidency he became concerned about military plotting among the U.S. Joint Chiefs of Staff. In his earlier life Reuben had ridiculed pacifists and had toyed with the idea of jailing conscientious objectors against a U.S. war, but as a member of the First Presidency he became an unmistakable pacifist and gave what encouragement he could to conscientious objectors during wartime. In reversal of his views during World War I, he almost became a Germanophile and Anglophobe during World War II. Although he continued to battle against domestic communism in America, during the post-1945 Cold War President Clark urged that the United States review its efforts to contain international communism and consider diplomatic and military accommodation with the USSR.

Like many Americans and Europeans, Reuben expressed almost immediate queasiness about Hitler's Nazi regime that came to power in 1933. He described Hitler's 1934 purge trials of fellow Nazis as "an assassination tribunal"; and prior to his own first visit to Nazi Germany in 1937, he wrote, "The German authorities have, I am very sure, kept all of the bad of Kaiserism (probably jettisoning much of the good); at any rate, they seem to have kept their criminal methods." After his second visit to Nazi Germany, President Clark told a general priesthood meeting in October 1938 that "there are things about [Nazi Germany] that to me are detestable. . . ." The criticism was compatible with the anti-Nazi evaluations of most contemporaries and historians.[13]

But his reaction to Nazi Germany was complex and in many ways paralleled the views of America's national hero of the 1920s and 1930s, Charles A. Lindbergh. A recent historian has written a description of Lindbergh that almost exactly describes J. Reuben Clark's response to Nazi Germany:

> Despite his world-wide travels, he had never visited Germany before the summer of 1936. Neither he nor his wife spoke or read the German language. He never met Adolf Hitler, and he never embraced Hitler's National Socialism. He disapproved of much that occurred in Nazi Germany. At the same time, however, he admired the German efficiency, spirit, and scientific achievement and technological accomplishments. To a degree he began to "understand" and sympathize with certain German attitudes and actions in the 1930s, even when he did not approve of them.[14]

Although his attitudes were close to Lindbergh's, Reuben saw Nazi Germany through the perspective of his long experience in diplomacy and international law and through his administrative concerns about the Latter-day Saints in foreign countries. Since 1919 he had regarded the Versailles Treaty as a vengeful, unjust punishment of Germany for the mistakes of all of Europe in the Great War of 1914, and he told a U.S. senator in 1935 that he could not blame Hitler for scrapping the treaty.[15] On business for the Foreign Bondholders' Protective Council, President Clark visited Berlin for six days in August 1937 and a couple of days in June 1938, during which times he met with Nazi bank leaders and Church mission leaders. Reuben was favorably impressed with living conditions there, and he took particular note that there was widespread support of Hitler among German Saints when he reported his trip to the First Presidency in July 1938.[16] He later replied to an American critic of Hitler:

> He [Hitler] was to the Germans as a voice crying in the wilderness, and offering to lead them out of the economic and political bondage in which the Treaty of Versailles left them.

. . . .

... I should like you to excuse my warning you against your assuming as truth the most of the criticism you see leveled against Hitler and his regime in Germany. I visited Germany twice within the last half-dozen years, and I saw no more contented and seemingly happy people in Europe—indeed none so much so as in Germany. Hitler is undoubtedly bad from our American point of view, but I think the Germans like him.[17]

The Twelfth Article of Faith expressed an acceptance by the Church of any nation's leaders, and President Clark could see no benefit to German Saints if American Church leaders criticized the German government.

By the time Hitler's revitalized Germany put much of the rest of Europe, particularly Great Britain, on the defensive, Reuben had already come to the conclusions arrived at by many American diplomats, historians, journalists, political scientists, and "average" Americans: Great Britain had exploited U.S. neutrality and trade in such a way from 1914 to 1917 as to virtually force American intervention against Germany in 1917; Great Britain and France were ultimately responsible for the rise of Nazi Germany because of their punishment of the conquered nation in the Versailles Treaty; British propaganda after 1933 was painting a false picture of Nazi Germany in order to justify a war to protect British power against a resurgent Germany; and the British government and Anglophiles in the United States were doing everything possible to obtain another military alliance of Great Britain and the United States in a war against Germany.[18]

As the European situation steadily deteriorated, Reuben saw Americans generally (including the Latter-day Saints) adopting what he considered a lopsided support of Britain, and he felt it imperative as a former diplomat and present member of the First Presidency to argue for true neutrality. A month after the commencement of World War II he drafted a First Presidency statement that condemned all war, and his own conference talks from 1939 to 1941 told the Latter-day Saints to expect "deceit, lying, subterfuge, treachery, and savagery" on the part of both the British and the Nazis, and that the war was an "unholy war" that "began as a war for empire" to determine which of the two nations would dominate Europe.[19] When Latter-day Saints expressed to him the conviction that Britain must be victorious for the benefit of the rest of the world,

Mutual Improvement Association convention in Berlin, Germany, 18 July 1936.

German-American Saints at German War Memorial, Salt Lake City, 1938.

President Clark countered, "The Germans appear to have the idea that they are fighting for their lives. And of course England and France, not Germany, declared this war."[20] Mindful of his role as elder statesman in the First Presidency, he provided government leaders with copies of the 1939 First Presidency statement on the war and on the necessity of American neutrality, as well as copies of his own conference talks on those subjects.[21]

By 1941 President Clark had publicly identified himself among the many prominent Americans who were doing everything they could to oppose the Roosevelt administration's open support of Great Britain. He had warned the October 1940 general conference that "By all the rules and principles by which nations have governed their conduct in the past, the United States has already committed several hostile acts [against Nazi Germany] and we are in fact now at war."[22] He used a 1941 Lincoln Day address at Boise, Idaho, as a vehicle for lashing out against those who urged U.S. intervention to aid Great Britain in order to preserve democracy. He claimed that Britain "is neither a democracy nor a republic," catalogued Britain's offensive conduct toward Americans from the Revolutionary War to the Civil War, and said that in that conflict "We did not ask Britain to help us; we only asked her to be neutral."[23]

Reuben told an associate that his Lincoln Day talk "pretty well stirred up all the Anglophiles in this area," and he received criticism from pro-British Latter-day Saints.[24] The address also caused leaders of the nationally organized America First Committee to ask his support in the effort to stop U.S. aid to Great Britain, but he declined to affiliate with the organization and said that he would restrict his activity to public statements, with the comment: "I think a little reflection will show you why this seems to be wisdom."[25] In August 1941 J. Reuben Clark joined former President Herbert Hoover and fourteen other "Republican leaders" in a national appeal that the "American people should insistently demand that Congress put a stop to step-by-step projections of the United States into undeclared war," which statement also affirmed that World War II was "not a world conflict between tyranny and freedom," and insisted "that American lives should be sacrificed only for American independence or to prevent invasion of the Western Hemisphere." J. Reuben Clark was deep in the mainstream of isolationism.[26]

Most of those who opposed intervention from 1939 to 1941 were supportive of the U.S. entry into World War II after the Pearl Harbor attack by Imperial Japan, an Axis ally of Nazi Germany, but J. Reuben Clark remained implacably opposed to declaration of war against either Japan or Germany. Instead of regarding the Pearl Harbor attack as justification for war, he stated publicly and privately that Franklin D. Roosevelt had goaded both Nazi Germany and Imperial Japan into attacking the United States so that there would be reason to declare war on the side of Great Britain. President Clark therefore regarded U.S. participation in World War II as unnecessary and criminal.[27] Within days after his own son-in-law died at Pearl Harbor, President Clark drafted a proposed message of the First Presidency "To the Fathers and Mothers, Sons and Daughters of the Church Throughout the World" that was in extraordinary contrast to the war fever that had gripped the United States since 7 December 1941:

... we have seen and we shall see these young men go out with commissions to kill their fellow men. Every lofty instinct of their souls and ours has cried out and will still cry out against this mission of destruction. It is not the Master's way. It is the jungle law of the beasts.
. . . .
... For they who die have neither the option nor the power to determine whether their country's cause is true or false.

Instead of using this statement during the impassioned nationalism of December 1941, the First Presidency issued a toned-down "Greeting" on 13 December which urged soldiers throughout the world to avoid "cruelty, hate, and murder."[28]

Part of the reason for not using Reuben's message was the differing viewpoints of the two counselors in the Presidency. As a fervent nationalist and isolationist, Reuben was appalled in 1940 to learn that internationalist David O. McKay "was so pro-ally he is ready to go to war, almost,—probably not so much pro-ally as *anti-Hitler*," and President Clark reported this "division of opinion" to Heber J. Grant, who agreed with his neutral position.[29] In the summer of 1942 Reuben thought that Britain and Russia would soon be forced to capitulate to Nazi Germany, and he drafted a First Presidency message which condemned "hate-driven militarists' and urged a negotiated and immediate end to hostilities. He read it as a statement of the First Presidency at the general conference of 3 October 1942. *Time* magazine reported a "disagreement in the First Presidency itself," when President McKay gave an impassioned sermon on 4 October in which he catalogued the "fiendish" conduct of Nazi Germany and its Axis counterparts and categorically stated "that peace cannot come until the mad gangsters ... are defeated and branded as murderers, and their false aims repudiated...."[30] Reuben downplayed this difference between the counselors, but he made no secret of his pessimistic assessment of World War II.[31] His views were in sufficient currency throughout the United States that two months before the D-Day invasion of Nazi-occupied Europe in 1944, the *New York Sun* reported that he was among the men recommended to form a treaty conference to arrange for "a peace magnanimous and just."[32]

In view of J. Reuben Clark's consistent hostility toward U.S. participation in World War II, it is not surprising that he used his considerable administrative influence to forestall any Church support of the war effort. When asked whether the First Presidency ought to allow Church members to work in munitions plants, President Clark immediately replied "we as Christians should be against war" but acquiesced in allowing the Latter-day Saints their free choice in the matter as "the lesser of the two evils."[33] Then he used every argument he could muster in conversations with Church leaders and in a six-page, single-spaced typed letter to the Secretary of War urging that there be no added munition plants or military installations in Utah.[34] He grudgingly allowed the FBI to have the names of returned missionaries who could furnish information about "towns and cities in Axis countries" during World War II, but he absolutely refused to allow returned missionaries to act as spies in the countries where they had served their missions.[35] In October 1941 President Clark drafted a Presidency letter to the director of the U.S. Defense Bond program stating that "we do not believe that aggression should be carried on in the name and under the false cloak of defense." After the Pearl Harbor attack he refused to cooperate in providing Church payroll deductions for war bonds, and he told a government representative for the war bond drive in 1944 that the Church purchase of bonds had been "liberal," but he stated, "I know we have been criticized ... [but] the Church will not take over the responsibility of financing this war and in this area."[36] He also declined to allow the Salt Lake Tabernacle or its famed choir to be used for what he regarded as wartime propaganda films and victory rallies.[37]

His perceptions about World War II caused him to reverse his views of pacifism. In contrast to previous hostility toward pacifists and pacifist organizations, he accepted membership in the National Advisory Council of the American Peace Society in June 1939, commenting that he would not be able to be very active in the society, "but I am happy to be numbered among you, and to add my bit in sane movements for peace."[38] Although the First Presidency since 1898 had urged Latter-day Saints to follow their governments in matters of military service and war, by 1942 President Clark wished that the Church was pacifist. In June 1942 he told the president of a Quaker college "that your Church is wise in its stand against war."[39] In June 1943 he told the secretary of the Society of Friends of Philadelphia that he was "in deep sympathy" with the Quaker view of war, and he also confided to another Quaker in California that he had repudiated earlier acceptance of defensive war and had become as ardently pacificistic as his Quaker and Dunkard ancestors. He stated that "it is very difficult for me to act in accordance with my ideas on what seems to be wisdom in this terrible situation."[40]

President Clark could not (and did not try to) alter the official position of the Church that approved defensive war in principle and condoned participation of Latter-day Saints in any war of their respective governments. Nevertheless, before the United States had put its enemies under its feet in 1945, he had declared his own repudiation of both defensive and offensive warfare as a matter of public record. In November 1944 he accepted a position as a member of the board of directors of the oldest pacifist organization in the United States, the American Peace Society, whose publication *World Affairs* listed him as one of the directors until his death in 1961.[41]

J. Reuben Clark's status as a nationally recognized elder statesman, high Church officer, and one of the Mountain West's most prominent citizens combined to give his antiwar sentiments after Pearl Harbor a sinister cast in the eyes of some observers. He had been alerted as early as 1940 that the FBI was keeping tabs on Utah

"Hitlerites," and he expressed puzzlement that the informant had singled him out for this disclosure.[42] By 1943 a Mormon had publicly condemned one of Reuben's talks as "near seditious," and an undercover investigator of Fascism in the United States reported in a national best seller that "a nest of pro-Axis Americans was functioning quietly" in Salt Lake City. The author identified by name his pro-Nazi contacts in Utah, all of whom were Latter-day Saints.[43] In the paranoia about loyalty that attends war, it is not surprising that navy intelligence agents made reports about President Clark's public statements on pacifism and against World War II and that FBI interrogations of suspected subversives in Utah during World War II turned up reports that he had given private encouragement to their antiwar views. President Clark was unintimidated by any critic, however, and it is doubtful that he would have altered any of his public pronouncements even had he known about the suspicious interest of government intelligence agencies.[44]

Reuben's attitude toward American participation in World War II and his conversion to unilateral pacifism put him in an awkward position as a member of the First Presidency, whose official stance was to praise the heroism and patriotism of any soldier in service to his country. Despite his powerful prejudices against war, he refused to give specific counsel against participating in it. Less than two weeks after the Pearl Harbor attack and U.S. declaration of war, members of the Church asked whether their sons should enlist or wait to be drafted. President Clark told the anxious parents that the only virtue in enlisting was the ability to choose one's service and added that "there was no dishonor or disgrace" in waiting to be inducted into the armed forces during the war.[45] He was more candid with members of his own family in 1942: he wrote that he "shall feel a little better" if his brother's son stayed out of military service altogether, and he told another nephew that the indifference and "actual opposition" of many Americans to the war was the result of "the fact that there is a considerable portion of our people who do not believe that we should be in this war."[46] When an American member of the Church in Colonia Juarez, Mexico, asked in April 1943 whether he should send his sons (who were technically Mexican citizens) on missions for the Church or let them enter the U.S.

military, President Clark replied that if they were his sons he would send them on missions.[47]

Four months later a young elder in the Church asked Reuben a question that put into sharp focus the difficulty of Latter-day Saints for whom he was the silent mentor of pacifism. "Can I feel that my Church understands and recognizes the validity of my being a conscientious objector," the young man asked, "or am I repudiated, as a matter of Church policy, in my stand?" Perhaps never before had President Clark seen the agonizing personal dimension of the tension between the imperative of the latter-day gospel for pacifism and the acquiescence of Church policy for militarism. He told the young man that the Church had no policy regarding conscientious objection and that it did not censure Latter-day Saints who were conscientious objectors to a war.[48]

Although the First Presidency had stated in March 1942 that it would not assist draft evaders by calling them on proselyting missions, he struggled with government authorities to obtain draft deferments for members of ward bishoprics. He also resisted the suggestion in 1944 that the First Presidency initiate investigations of possible draft evasion by missionaries and members of bishoprics.[49] When the field secretary for the National Service Board for Religious Objectors informed President Clark in May 1944 that the U.S. government had interred several Latter-day Saints in conscientious objector camps for refusing to do military service or alternate service making any real contribution to the conduct of the war, President Clark commented that he himself had adopted the pacifism of his ancestors.[50]

He sympathetically monitored the status of Mormon conscientious objectors to World War II through the representatives of the "peace churches" who were providing financial support to the objectors during their wartime internment. After the war President Clark arranged for the Church to refund to the "peace churches" the costs of maintaining Latter-day Saint conscientious objectors who "were apparently treated to all intents and purposes as were prisoners of war."[51] When a local draft board tried to prevent a Latter-day Saint conscientious objector from serving a full-time mission after his release more than a year after the end of World War II, President Clark did what he could to intercede on the young man's behalf.[52]

Reuben was sympathetic and cautiously supportive of conscientious objectors during World War II but said that the tragedy of those who would not or could not escape the war's horrors "has shaken me to the very roots . . . and grieves me beyond expression."[53] World War II left sixty million dead and 80 percent devastation of most of the cities of continental Europe and of Japan. For its limited number, the Church also suffered heavy human losses: Utah's military deaths (most of whom were Mormon) were above the national average by population and reached 1,450 at war's end; 600 Latter-day Saint civilians in Germany perished in the warfare, and hundreds of soldiers from the rest of the United States, the Pacific, Europe, and the British Empire also died.[54]

President Clark was so convinced of the unrighteousness of World War II and the futility of its losses that he could hardly conceal his bitterness. When one Latter-day Saint sent him the "Roll of Honor" of family members who had served in the U.S. armed forces during the war, he thanked him for the gift, but commented, "I could say something about the real 'Cause' for which they served and for which some died, but I refrain."[55] When everyone else prepared to hail the victorious American soldiers as returning heroes, he sounded a more somber note in his conference address of April 1945:

> These boys out in the field have placed before them constantly, achievements and the value of achievement in the destruction of human life. The thing for which they now receive praise, the things for which they work to get commendation, are unknown to us in our lives of peace.

And President Clark urged the Latter-day Saints to be understanding of the brutalizing influence of the war on the returning soldiers and to give "our best effort and best thought" to helping the returning veterans to make the difficult transition to a world where all life is valued and violence is abhorred.[56]

Nevertheless, the casualty of World War II about which J. Reuben Clark grieved for the rest of his life without consolation was what he saw as America's betrayal of its God, of its moral mission to the world, and of the human race through the saturation bombing of German cities and dropping atomic bombs on the Japanese. He wrote that the United States and England attempted "virtually to destroy the German people, a loss which is not only fiendish in its conception but in its execution. There is no people in the world to replace the German people. . . ."[57] Two days after the atomic bomb devastated Hiroshima and a day before its use on Nagasaki, he wrote an editorial for the *Deseret News* which said that the United States had perverted scientific truth, betrayed God's trust, and used the atom bomb without justification, even though he acknowledged that it might save countless American lives that would be lost in a prolonged war with Japan. Then President Clark expressed this chilling prediction about the atomic bomb as a consequence of its use by the United States against civilians:

> Its use to kill will become the aim and practice of all nations. Sometime our children's children will have it turned against them, that they, too, may be exterminated, annihilated. When that time comes they will have no moral weapon against it, for we, their ancestors, will have cursed humanity by its first use; they may have no physical weapon to combat it. And humanity may be as depraved and Christian virtue as dead then as now. Our posterity must pay the penalty, to the last farthing.[58]

Convinced that a future enemy would drop atomic bombs on the cities of the United States, he warned the Latter-day Saints to prepare themselves for the total disruption such a holocaust would cause in America.[59] Shortly after the atomic bombs fell in Japan in 1945, President Clark also began urging the First Presidency to build underground, bombproof storage areas for the irreplaceable records of the Church, and in 1958 the First Presidency finally agreed to begin work on such a project, the result being the Church's Little Cottonwood Canyon granite vaults, which were constructed to withstand "a hydrogen or atomic bomb."[60]

Even though he acknowledged that several of the General Authorities felt differently about the atom bomb and its use,[61] President Clark continued his unqualified condemnation of the American military, leaders, and people for the use of the atom bomb in 1945 and continued preparations for nuclear war. He gave his most extensive Church address on this topic at the general conference of October 1946. After condemning the American military for killing 250,000 civilians in a two-day bombing of nonmilitarized Dresden, he told the general conference that the United States committed "the crowning savagery of the war" by using the atomic bomb against Japanese "men, women, and children, and cripples." President Clark then expressed his amazement that there was not a general protest in the United States against the use of the atomic bomb, "but that it actually drew from the nation at large a general approval." He said that "God will not forgive us" for celebrating means of such wholesale slaughter and for continuing to research even more efficient weapons of nuclear destruction and concluded his October 1946 talk with an emotional protest:

And, as one American citizen of one hundred thirty millions, as one in one billion population of the world, I protest with all of the energy I possess against this fiendish activity, and as an American citizen, I call upon our government and its agencies to see that these unholy experimentations are stopped, and that somehow we get into the minds of our war-minded general staff and its satellites, and into the general staffs of all the world, a proper respect for human life.[62]

After former President Hoover told him about reading the minutes of the decision to use the atomic bomb despite the imminent collapse of Japan's war effort, President Clark prepared another editorial "Day of Atonement," in September 1950, which condemned the wanton character of the bombings.[63] His total repudiation of the purposes, conduct, and outcome of World War II inevitably determined his reactions to the post-1945 world of American international supremacy and its "Cold War" with the USSR.

The first item on his postwar agenda was a frontal assault on the U.S. military and the proposals to have a peacetime conscription of American youth. After he was informed that the Military Affairs Committee of the Utah House of Representatives had introduced a resolution asking Congress to provide for a standing army of peacetime draftees, President Clark drafted a memorandum on 5 February 1945, which read in part:

1. A great standing army has always led to a destruction of liberties and the establishment of tyranny . . .
2. A great standing army, with its war-minded controls, always looks for opportunities for use of the army, and military influence is always exerted to that end.
3. A great standing army has the effect of making the whole nation war-minded. It makes a nation truculent, overbearing, and imperialistic, all provocative of war.[64]

As local and national support grew in June 1945 for a peacetime draft, "Pres. Clark served notice that he proposed to force the brethren to take a stand for or against the resolution except to repel invasion or imminent national danger. He expressed his opinion that the Church of Jesus Christ could not consistently take any other position," and President Clark confided to his Quaker friends that the First Presidency would soon issue a statement against peacetime military conscription.[65] When the First Presidency did issue such a statement in December 1945, it followed the general outline of President Clark's February memorandum.[66]

Even after the post-1945 hostility between the United States and the Soviet Union resulted in the Cold War and Russia's possession of nuclear weapons, Reuben did not relax his assaults on the military. When President George Albert Smith seemed willing to agree to the military's request that the First Presidency encourage Mormon youth to enter the National Guard, President Clark objected in September 1947 that such an action "would be going back on our position taken on Universal Military Service.[67] Two months later he gave an address to insurance executives in Chicago (subsequently published as a pamphlet by the *Deseret News*) warning:

Furthermore, I regret to say, indeed I am almost ashamed to say, that at the moment, our military branches seem in almost complete control of our own government. They appear to dominate Congress, and under the circumstances, we may assume they are in sufficient control of our foreign relations to be able to set the international scene. . . . We are not justified in doubting, on the facts we have, that we of the United States are, for the first time in our history, under a real threat from our military arm, and if the plans of the militarists carry, we shall become as thoroughly militarized as was Germany at her best, or worst.[68]

In this light it is not surprising that he informed a U.S. senator in December 1947 that the veterans of Utah would go to jail rather than serve in another war, and that he was unperturbed by reports in 1948 that Utah had the lowest rate of national guard training in the nation.[69] Even as the Cold War intensified, President Clark warned his Church associates to be on the vigil against any steps toward "a military dictatorship" in America, and he informed a prospective instructor of the Air Force ROTC program at Brigham Young University "that he, personally, would not like to have on his conscience the destruction of one human life, however justified, to say nothing of the destruction of hundreds of thousands that might be involved in the use of the H-bomb."[70]

In fact, despite his lifelong opposition to Marxism and communism, J. Reuben Clark joined the minority of pre-1941 isolationists who also opposed the Cold War efforts of the United States to stop the spread of international communism.[71] In 1947, for example, he expressed his opposition to sending military aid to Greece, Turkey, and China to assist them in fighting communist insurgents and possible Russian intervention.[72] In 1949 he was also the only former or current U.S. ambassador who refused to endorse the ratification of the North Atlantic Treaty, and a NATO supporter testified before the U.S. Senate Foreign Relations Committee that J. Reuben Clark was among the "well-meaning but impractical pacifists, pseudo-liberals, rabid isolationists, and, of course, the Communist party with its assorted fronts" who opposed NATO.[73]

President Clark undoubtedly felt grim amusement at the irony that super patriots in America had accused him of being a Nazi sympathizer during World War II and now accused him of being a fellow traveler with the communists. In reality, he was consistently a patriotic American who opposed international intervention by the United States against any presumed evil of whatever source or political philosophy. He was typically undeterred by those who aligned him with the communists, and in August 1949 he delivered a major address against NATO in a meeting at Salt Lake City.[74] Moreover, a month after the United States agreed in 1950 to join the United Nations in waging a "police action" against communist North Korea following its invasion of South Korea, President Clark advised his cousin to resign from the U. S. Army Reserve.[75]

President Clark was even more anxious that the United States get out of the United Nations because "all they do is send our boys to Korea."[76] He regarded the philosophy and conduct of the United Nations as identical with the League of Nations, against which he had battled since 1919.[77] Rather than being an instrument of international arbitration, diplomacy, cooperation, and peace, the United Nations in Reuben's eyes eroded U.S. national sovereignty and virtually required U.S. intervention in international conflicts. When the United Nations Charter was announced in 1945, President Clark immediately drafted a sixty-two-page, double-spaced, typed critique of the document which he addressed to the editor of the *Deseret News* with the comment: "Acceding to your request I am submitting to you a few general observations upon some of the more obvious and important factors of the San Francisco Charter. I have not attempted to make anything but a more or less cursory analysis."[78] He told rank-and-file Church members about the document, but by the end of 1945 he had concluded that it might never be published, and he gave the official explanation that "the Church had avoided taking any stand pro or con on the United Nations because our people were on both sides of the question."[79] To like-minded friends, however, President Clark affirmed that "the sooner we get out of the U.N. the better off we will be, but there are an awful lot of people who still are blinded by the brilliant rainbows which the pro-U.N. people can produce."[80]

David O. McKay's ascension to the office of Church President in 1951 greatly diminished President Clark's freedom to express his opposition to the Cold War. President McKay was a lifelong internationalist whose disagreement with President Clark over American participation in World War II was a matter of public comment, and after becoming Church President he affirmed his views of the Cold War by assuring a non-Mormon that "the Church was militantly opposed to the godless atheism of communism and would not hesitate to oppose force with force if it became necessary."[81] Despite his knowledge of President Clark's opposition toward war generally and toward the Cold War specifically, in June 1952 President McKay assigned the counselor to give a talk to the young men of the Church in support of their participation in the Korean War. President Clark began his talk by commenting that "I would not want to spend two years in the service," referred to his sympathy with the pacifist view of his Quaker ancestors, said "I loathe war, and all that goes with it," and then dutifully went on to address the theme, "Two Years in the Service Can Be Profitable."[82]

In deference to President McKay, Reuben gave little publicity to his conviction that the United States enter into a diplomatic and military accommodation with the Soviet Union. In 1947 President Clark had publicly expressed hope that the United States and the Soviet Union would "reach a mutual-live-and-let-live understanding," but throughout the 1950s he expressed only privately his

President Clark presenting BYU correspondence booklet to Latter-day Saint serviceman, in keeping with the philosophy of his talk "Two Years in the Service Can Be Profitable."

condemnation of U.S. policy toward Russia and his hope "to see if something could not be worked out in a friendly way, with the Russians."[83] When asked about what the United States should do concerning the communist menace in Indochina (soon to be partitioned into Laos, Cambodia, and North and South Vietnam), President Clark replied that it was not worth shedding blood over. Expressing himself as being "unalterably opposed to Communism," he nevertheless felt that French colonialism had been "decrepit, deficient, corrupt."[84]

When President Clark visited the State Department in 1958 to inquire about the situation in Asia, he said "first, that they only told us about the things they wanted us to know about; second, that . . . they only told us what they thought we ought to know; and third, that they lied whenever it seemed convenient."[85] By the time Reuben died in 1961, the United States was gradually accelerating its plunge into the Vietnam War.[86]

Throughout his service in the First Presidency, J. Reuben Clark had publicly expressed his conviction about the absolute futility of war and the unrighteousness of American participation in World War II even after the Pearl Harbor attack. It is unlikely that he would have remained silent had he lived to see the full enormity of the Vietnam War on the television screen, in the newspapers and magazines, and in the protests against it by the youth across the United States. But death had stilled the voice of Mormonism's extraordinary twentieth-century peace advocate. The 10 percent of Latter-day Saint youth who protested against the Vietnam War could turn only to President Clark's published statements about war, because there was no comparable spokesman against war among the Church authorities during the Vietnam conflict.[87] For the 90 percent of Mormon youth who had generally supported American participation in the Vietnam War, who had served as soldiers there, and for those who had surrendered their universal love of mankind there,

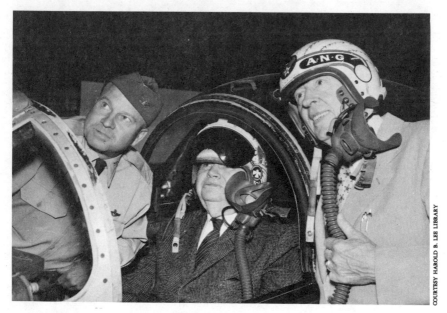

President Clark in cockpit of F-86 Saberjet, accompanied by Colonel Alma G. Winn of the Air National Guard and President Joseph Fielding Smith, 1956.

who had survived Viet Cong and North Vietnamese prisons, who had been horribly wounded there, or who had died there, J. Reuben Clark also had a message of comfort that he expressed to a post commander of the American Legion in 1956:

I honor greatly men who make the last sacrifice for a Cause which they know and in which they believe.—In major part such was the position of those who died that our Government might be born. But I think I honor more those who at the bequest of their Government, in the matter of pure patriotism, give their lives for a Cause which they do not understand and which is not understood by those who called them to the Colors.[88]

"ALL NATIONS, AND KINDREDS, AND PEOPLE, AND TONGUES"

Revelation 7:9

Enormous changes in the attitudes and conduct of Western society, the United States, and the Church toward the races and ethnic peoples of the world occurred during J. Reuben Clark's life span from 1871 to 1961. During his childhood and young manhood, few political leaders, religious teachers, moral philosophers, or ordinary citizens of the Western world questioned the belief in the superiority of the Caucasian race, the inferiority of darker-skinned races and peoples, the necessity of racial separation, the evils of racial intermarriage, or the appropriateness of Western colonialism in Africa, Asia, and the Pacific.[1] Although the United States was a land of immigrants, by the 1880s the native-born Americans who had descended from early north European immigrants had added one further distinction to humanity: the millions of "new" immigrants to the United States after 1870 were "undesirables" because they were primarily some combination of Roman Catholics, Jews, Asiatics, or swarthy east and south Europeans.[2] Throughout two-thirds of Reuben's life these attitudes flourished from the cities to the hamlets of America, but during the years of his service in the First Presidency, such attitudes and the practices they fostered began to crumble.

Although young Reuben had virtually no personal contact with alien races in rural Utah, the youth had the full endowment of racism, nativism, and xenophobia characteristic of late-nineteenth-century America. The University of Utah audience gave a wild ovation when his 1898 valedictory address condemned the New Immigration.[3] Reuben's travels to cosmopolitan New York City did nothing to encourage egalitarianism, for among his associates at

Columbia University and in the State Department were champions of the currently popular theories of Anglo-Saxon racial superiority.[4]

But Reuben's career convinced him of the necessity of justice in the relationships of all races and peoples. In a letter to former President Herbert Hoover in 1942, Reuben said that the British and Americans were primarily responsible for the "color-hate" that was dominant and which had antagonized the colonial peoples of the world, especially the Japanese. Then he added:

> I believe in a pure white race, but I believe in justice to the colored races, a justice they have not heretofore had, and feel that justice to them is indispensable to a peaceful world.[5]

In his mature life President Clark's legal, diplomatic, and religious careers all contributed to a modification of his youthful racial views.

For example, on account of his regard for the law and his personal experiences, Reuben reversed his earlier preconceptions about the Mexican people. Reuben had been enmeshed in the legal and diplomatic aspects of the Mexican Revolution and its manifold atrocities and sufferings from 1910 to 1913 and periodically thereafter.[6] These experiences added to his early cultural indoctrination and resulted in a pronounced dislike for the Mexicans whom he had never met except in formal interchanges with Mexican emissaries to Washington. More than twenty years after he actually went to Mexico, he admitted to a priesthood conference of the Church that "I went with a great prejudice against the Mexican people." But he studied "the history of the people, their oppression—they were downtrodden and had been for 400 years under the heel of despotism," and he associated with the Mexicans, and the result was a melting away of his negative prejudices.[7] Years after he had last been in Mexico, he wistfully spoke of his desire "to visit again that beautiful land and have some association at least with that soft-voiced and generally gentle people."[8] Administratively, President Clark was very interested in the Mexican Latter-day Saints and was concerned that they not be intimidated by non-Mexicans. When the authorities of the Church discussed incorporating the Mexican branches of the American Southwest into the regularly organized stakes of the area, "Pres. Clark felt a bit apprehensive about turning the Mexicans over to these

J. Reuben Clark among the Mexican Saints.

President Clark laying corner stone for Mexican Branch, Salt Lake City, 21 August 1949.

223

cold-blooded Americans."⁹ The Mexicans represented the most complete reversal of his earlier views of peoples and races.

Although not as dramatic as his shift in attitude concerning the Mexicans, Reuben's response to the Japanese people was extraordinary because of the dramatic context in which the Japanese nation affected his own life. He always was uncomfortable with Japanese military power in the Western Pacific where America had vital interests, but there is no evidence that Reuben ever had negative prejudices toward the Japanese. In fact, he represented the Japanese embassy in 1913 against a discriminatory California law and seriously considered accepting the offer of the Japanese imperial government to serve them in Tokyo in an advisory capacity.¹⁰ But the anti-Japanese prejudices of many Americans, particularly Californians, seemed vindicated when the Japanese attacked Pearl Harbor on 7 December 1941. President Clark's son-in-law died as one of the first casualties of the Pearl Harbor attack, and the grief of that loss never completely left the Church leader.

Nevertheless, he neither felt nor manifested any bitterness toward the Japanese. Even though the conversations of most people and the headlines of the *Deseret News* during World War II were sprinkled with the derogatory "Japs," he almost never used the term, even in corresponding or speaking with those who did.¹¹ He also said that "personally I had no antipathy toward the Japanese," when telling a government official of his opposition to the establishment of a relocation center in Utah for both alien and American-born Japanese who were being involuntarily removed from California.¹² Moreover, his cousin Spencer W. Kimball observed that even though President Clark manifested deep and continued grief for the death of his son-in-law in the Pearl Harbor attack, he never heard him utter a word of antagonism toward the Japanese.¹³

Reuben felt no recrimination against the Japanese for the death of a member of his own family but maintained his opposition to intermarriage between Caucasians and Orientals. A young Mormon serviceman in Hawaii wrote that he wanted to marry a Japanese-American girl who had just completed a full-time mission there. Although the two young people shared the gospel in common, President Clark wrote the young man a three and one-half page, typed, single-spaced letter which stated in part:

Presidents McKay and Clark greeting a Japanese city official, 1960.

Your race excells in one line of activity, her race in another, and I am not prepared to say which is the better, though, of course, I do prefer my own race, but that is not because I regard her race as inferior.... So that, personally, I have nothing but kindness for the race and am free from race prejudice....

. . . .

The experience of the human race shows that the mixation of races so different as are the Anglo-Saxon and the Japanese, is frequently not healthy, either biologically, temperamentally, or as a matter of character.[14]

The young man listened to the advice, married within his own race, raised a happy family, and President Clark sent copies of the above-quoted letter to parents whose sons were considering marrying Oriental girls.[15]

Although Mormons have traditionally gotten along very well with the small Jewish population of Utah,[16] Reuben had personal prejudices toward Jews that he expressed to many people, including those of high position such as Herbert Hoover.[17] Reuben's views may have crystallized after he moved to the East Coast, where he confronted a large Jewish population for the first time in his life. In his later law practice in New York City, Jewish businessmen were numbered among both his clients and antagonists in legal cases. Perhaps most important in the personal dimension of his relationship with Jews was his humiliating political defeats for the U.S. Senate nomination in the 1920s at the hands of a Jewish opponent.[18] In any event, he had the habit of making derogatory notations when he met "a typical Jew."[19]

Beyond whatever personal reasons for his anti-Semitism, there was also a political dimension of his attitudes toward the Jews. Some of the most prominent political radicals in Reuben's knowledge were Jews: Karl Marx, author of *Das Kapital* and the *Communist Manifesto*; Emma Goldman, an American anarchist; V. I. Lenin and Leon Trotsky, architects of the Bolshevik revolution in Russia; Rosa Luxemburg, founder of the German Communist party; and Leon Blum, Socialist Premier of France beginning in 1936.[20] In these few, sensational examples of Jewish radicalism, he thought he perceived the basic character of the Jewish people and told ex-President Hoover in 1942 that the Jews "are essentially revolutionary." At the time, 32 percent of surveyed Americans shared his view.[21] Even though there were equally prominent Jews who opposed Marxism and communism and even though anti-Semitism flourished in the Soviet Union,[22] J. Reuben Clark never altered his political assessment of the Jewish people.[23] He was personally intrigued by the Zionist-conspiracy argument of the *Protocols of the Elders of Zion,* and as late as 1958 continued to buy copies of that publication for distribution to his politically oriented friends.[24]

The Democratic New Deal provided Reuben with even more reasons to fear Jewish influence. Just as conservatives were recoiling at the New Deal innovations, they noticed an unprecedented presence of Jews in the Executive Branch. This created a "passing phenomenon" of public opinion against Jewish influence in government.[25] It was no coincidence that Utah's first anti-Semitic pamphlet appeared the year of Roosevelt's reelection effort in 1936, and even though he did not explain it in terms of anti-Roosevelt ideology, a Utah political scientist noted in 1940 that "Anti-Semitism is beginning to raise its ugly head in the historically congenial and cooperative atmosphere of the Utah metropolis."[26] Reuben regarded the politically liberal Jews in the Roosevelt administration as cause for concern.[27]

At the same time that these attitudes were on the rise in the United States, anti-Semitism was entering a violent phase in Nazi Germany, where tens of thousands of native Latter-day Saints and hundreds of American missionaries were struggling to coexist with an increasingly brutal regime. As Hitler intensified his repression of Jewish civil liberties and threatened a continental war of conquest in Europe, many of Europe's Jewish millions tried desperately to escape by emigrating to the United States. These circumstances caught many Americans like Reuben in the dilemma of conflicting values, priorities, and realities: they sympathized with the human suffering of the Nazi oppressed, but how could Depression-wracked America absorb millions of refugees? And those who idealized the Christian Anglo-Saxon race and who already felt that there was a "Jewish problem" in America had still further reasons to resist encouraging Jewish immigration in the late 1930s. When Jewish families appealed to the First Presidency for returned missionaries to sponsor their exit from Nazi dominions, President Clark dictated the reply in January 1939 that "we have so many requests of this sort from various persons, including members of the Church, that we have found it necessary to ask to be excused from making the required guarantee," and recommended that the petitioners contact Jewish organizations for help.[28]

Even when the collapse of the Nazi empire revealed the systematic extermination of millions of Jews, nearly 80 percent of surveyed Americans in 1945 reported that this knowledge did not alter their attitude toward the Jews and Jewish influence in the United States.[29] Apparently, Reuben shared this majority feeling. From 1945 to 1951 he continued to use his personal and administrative abilities against what he perceived as national Jewish influence.[30]

Although he never altered his personal anti-Semitism, President Clark's public allusions to anti-Semitism and his negative influence on administrative decisions involving Jewish questions ended when pro-Jewish and pro-Zionist David O. McKay became Church President in 1951. For example, the Church President obtained the counselor's acquiescence in such actions as the purchase of thousands of dollars worth of bonds issued by the State of Israel, "merely to show *our sympathy with the effort* being made *to establish the Jews in their homeland.*"[31] After 1951 Reuben's allusions to Jewish influence and his administrative voice against Zionism were effectively stilled. In this respect, President McKay's positive attitudes toward the Jews, Zionism, and the State of Israel were more representative of the Latter-day Saints generally than were the anti-Semitic views of President Clark.[32]

Rivalling his preoccupation with the Jews was his personal and administrative interest in people of Negroid ancestry, especially American Blacks. To understand his attitude toward Blacks, it is necessary to recognize that he was heir to a double-edged legacy: first, traditional American attitudes toward Afro-Americans; and second, a policy of the Church to exclude all persons of Negroid ancestry from the priesthood.

Decades, even centuries, before Reuben's birth, Americans had already developed discriminatory attitudes and practices toward Afro-Americans. White American explorers, philosophers, educators, biologists, politicians, and literary authors had defined Negroes as inherently inferior by race in matters of intelligence, social stability, morality, and physical beauty. Moreover, American theologians and clergymen held the virtually universal belief that Negroes were descendants of Adam's son Cain and of Noah's son Ham and as such had been cursed by God.[33] Despite the post-Civil War amendments to the U.S. Constitution that emancipated the Negroes and granted them civil rights, segregation continued in the North in housing, transportation, and public assembly. By the time Reuben graduated from the University of Utah in 1898, the U.S. Supreme Court had declared constitutional the practice of racial segregation in transportation, education, and other areas, giving free reign to the states of the American South in establishing total segregation through enactment of a multitude of "Jim Crow" laws.[34]

Although there is evidence that Joseph Smith had positive attitudes toward the potentials of black Americans,[35] the Mormons of Utah were consistent with the nearly universal white discrimination against Negroes. While three Negro slaves were among the first company of Mormon pioneers to enter the Salt Lake Valley in July 1847, only about thirty slaves and an equal number of free blacks lived in Utah from 1850 to the 1860s. Utahns shared the scientifically defined racial views of the nineteenth century and the nationally implemented legal restrictions of Blacks. Prior to the civil rights amendments to the U.S. Constitution in the 1860s and 1870s, Utah law had prohibited free blacks from voting, jury duty, and holding public office, and from 1888 to 1963 prohibited the marriage of a white with a Negro (including persons only one-eighth Negro).[36] Beyond *de jure* considerations, Utah had a patchwork of *de facto* segregation from the time of Reuben's birth in 1871 until his final year in the First Presidency. There was no legal residential or educational segregation, but 40 percent of Utah's employers refused to hire Negroes at all or discriminated against them in job assignment, promotion, and salary; all bowling alleys excluded Negroes; theaters required Negroes to sit in specially designated seats; the privately owned resorts of Lagoon and Saltair prohibited Blacks from dancing or swimming; 47.6 percent of Utah restaurants refused to serve Negroes; and 72 percent of the hotels refused accommodations to Negroes. In all these respects, Utah and the Mormons were probably representative of the rest of America's white society.[37]

But there was one further dimension of Church relations with Blacks of African descent, and that was the policy in force throughout President Clark's life whereby Blacks were excluded from receiving priesthood ordination and related blessings. Although Joseph Smith allowed the ordination of at least one free black to the Melchizedek Priesthood,[38] explicit and publicly known references to a Church policy of priesthood exclusion were lacking until 1852. Brigham Young reminded members of the Utah Legislature of the general Christian belief that African Negroes were the descendants of Cain and then told the Mormons that "any man having one drop of the blood of Cain in him cannot hold the priesthood."[39] Church leaders occasionally spoke of a time in the distant future when Negroes would receive the priesthood, but throughout J. Reuben Clark's life the emphasis of all Church leaders was on the denial of the priesthood to all persons of African Negro descent.[40]

In his position as a member of the First Presidency, J. Reuben Clark reflected the racial attitudes of the general white population, the fact that segregation had been declared the constitutional law of the land since the 1890s, and the implications of Church teachings about Negroes. In October 1947, he told the other authorities of the Church his attitude toward the slow increase of national favor for racial integration.

President Clark called attention to the sentiment among many people in this country to the point that we should break down all racial lines, as a result of which sentiment negro people have acquired an assertiveness that they never before possessed and in some cases have become impudent.[41]

For his own part, Reuben encouraged residential segregation and was constantly on the lookout to prevent any tendency in the Church that might encourage social integration and racial intermarriage with Negroes.[42]

When the U.S. Supreme Court in May 1954 reversed its prior decisions regarding racial segregation and ruled in *Brown vs. Board of Education of Topeka* that racial segregation was inherently unequal and illegal under the Constitution, the people and institutions of America were suddenly thrust into a new era of race relations.[43] President Clark concluded that the Church could not maintain silence in regard to the new constitutional decision concerning civil rights of Blacks, and he began to prepare a major address on the status of Blacks with regard to the Church. Part of his intended talk at the October 1954 general conference dealt specifically with the question of Black civil rights:

The Latter-day Saints willingly accord to them in civil matters all the rights, privileges, liberties, and protection guaranteed them by the Constitution of the United States and laws in this country, and by equivalent instruments in other countries, in all their social, economic and political activities.[44]

This was a clear reversal of his previous position on what he had referred to as "so-called social equality" for Negroes. Despite his own attitudes toward race relations, J. Reuben Clark had an unyielding reverence for the supremacy of law and a rigid respect for the decisions of the U.S. Supreme Court in interpreting the Constitution.

Despite his determination to align the position of the Church in 1954 with the decision of the Supreme Court on Negro civil rights, he never spoke publicly on the topic. Church President David O. McKay had already expressed his opposition to civil rights legislation with the comment that "no matter what the law says, there is going to be discrimination against the colored people."[45] Thus it was that the Church remained silent concerning Negro civil rights from 1954 to 1963, at which time national fervor for the civil rights movement and concommitant criticism of the Church's attitudes toward Negroes resulted in an endorsement of Negro civil rights being read at general conference by a counselor in the First Presidency who was known to be a political liberal.[46] J. Reuben Clark had judged that such a statement would have received far more credence and positive reception had it been given at the earliest possible date by a member of the First Presidency who was known to be a political and social conservative.

Nevertheless, there were two areas of racial segregation in which he never altered his position—intermarriage and blood transfusions. In one respect, President Clark's views on miscegenation were independent of Negroes, because he consistently opposed intermarriage between any racial and ethnic groups,[47] but the inability of Blacks to receive the priesthood according to Church policy was a further argument against marriage between Caucasians and Negroes. He told the mission presidents in 1960, "Personally, I am· unalterably opposed to the amalgamation of the negroes, both on religious and biological grounds."[48] With regard to blood tranfusions, a nationwide hospital practice of segregating the blood of Negroes from Caucasians had been instituted during World War II when millions of Americans donated blood as part of the war effort, and both the Roman Catholic and Latter-day Saint hospitals in Salt Lake City segregated blood by race in accordance with the national trend.[49] President Clark insisted that Latter-day Saint hospitals continue this policy because he wondered whether Caucasian members of the Church might be disqualified from the priesthood after receiving a transfusion of Negro blood.[50] Nevertheless, he declined to advise Latter-day Saints to refuse blood transfusions from people of Negroid ancestry.[51]

The question of blood transfusions led him to another racial preoccupation—obtaining a medical procedure whereby it would be possible to identify persons with Black ancestry. For more than a decade he conversed and corresponded about this quest with Dr. G. Albin Matson, formerly head of the Blood Grouping Laboratory of the University of Utah and subsequently director of the Minneapolis

War Memorial Blood Bank.[52] President Clark wrote Dr. Matson in 1959, "This question of negro blood is becoming increasingly complicated and for us increasingly difficult."[53]

The joint council of the First Presidency and Quorum of the Twelve Apostles had not had a major discussion and review of the Negro priesthood restriction for thirty years when J. Reuben Clark initiated a total review of the question in 1940.

President Clark explained that this matter has come up at various times in the past, that it is *the question of what should be done with those people who are faithful in the Church who are supposed to have some Negro blood* in their veins.

President Clark said *at his request* the clerk of the council had copied from the old records of the Council discussions that have been had in the past on this subject. He said that he was positive that it was impossible with reference to the Brazilians to tell those who have Negro blood and those who have not, and we are baptizing these people into the Church. The question also arises pertaining to the people in South Africa where we are doing missionary work, and in the Southern States, also in the islands of the Pacific.

President Clark suggested that this matter be referred to the Twelve who might appoint a sub-committee *to go into the matter with great care and make some ruling* or reaffirm whatever ruling has been made on this question in the past as to whether or not one drop of Negro blood deprives a man of the right to receive the priesthood.[54]

Despite his racial views and support of segregation, he was concerned about the policy of attempting to deny the priesthood to persons with "one drop of Negro blood." With a lifelong emphasis upon justice, legalism, and administrative uniformity, he was troubled at the inevitably haphazard manner in which the priesthood blessings were denied to persons who happened to know of their far-distant Negro ancestry, but were likewise given to other persons who undoubtedly had some Black African heritage.

President Clark decided to ask for another reconsideration of the policy on 9 October 1947:

President Clark again repeated what he had previously said on a number of occasions that in South America, and particularly in Brazil, we are entering into a situation in doing missionary work among the people where it is very difficult if not impossible to tell who has negro blood and who has not. He said that if we are baptizing Brazilians, we are almost certainly baptizing people of negro blood, and that if the Priesthood is conferred upon them, which no doubt it is, we are

facing a very serious problem. President Clark said that his heart bleeds for the negroes, that he had had them in his home and some of them were very fine people,
that he felt we should give them every right and blessing to which they are
entitled.[55]

Although he repeatedly asked the First Presidency and Quorum of
the Twelve to recognize the inequities in present procedures of
priesthood restriction and to consider altering the policy toward persons of African Negro ancestry, President Clark continued his practice of not trying to "over-persuade," and he loyally supported the
Church policy on Negroes, while at the same time he sought medical tests to eliminate the capriciousness of denials and conferrals of
priesthood blessings. Nevertheless, he recommended "preparatory"
priesthood quorum organization and training for persons of African
Negro identity because he firmly believed that they would one day
receive the priesthood during this life.[56]

In this anticipation, the year 1954 seemed to President Clark to
herald the near approach of the day when Negroes would receive the
priesthood. Aside from the watershed legal decision of the U.S. Supreme Court in May of that year, President David O. McKay had
made a momentous decision regarding African Negroes and the
priesthood in January. On 17 January 1954 President McKay told
the missionaries in South Africa, "Well, until the Lord gives us another revelation changing this practice established anciently and
adopted in our day we will follow that policy [of excluding the
Blacks from priesthood]. It is true in the days of the Prophet Joseph
one of Negro blood received the Priesthood. Another in the days of
President Brigham Young received it and went through the Temple.
These are authenticated facts but exceptions." Then the Church President announced that members of the Church in South Africa would
no longer have to prove non-Negro ancestry by tracing their genealogy out of the country.[57] When President McKay informed his
counselors and the Quorum of the Twelve Apostles about this unexpected new policy, he extended its application to members of the
Church in Brazil.[58] Although the change liberalized the ordination
of members of the Church in Africa and Brazil, the new policy actually increased the difficulty about which President Clark had been
speaking for nearly fifteen years: ordaining men who were undoubtedly of Negro ancestry but who could not prove it, while denying

the priesthood to millions of people of such ancestry who could not conceal it.⁵⁹

Nevertheless, the constitutional and Church developments of 1954 seemed to J. Reuben Clark as steps toward the eventual circumstances under which the Church would make the priesthood available to all men, regardless of color or race. He intended to announce that fact to the entire Church membership in his remarks to the October 1954 general conference. Although he maintained much of the racial philosophy and terminology of the nineteenth century, his undelivered talk expressed his hopes and anticipations for a new era.

> Furthermore, modern prophets have declared that in the due time of the Lord, the great burden the colored folk now bear will be removed from their shoulders and they will be permitted to enjoy the Priesthood, to the full extent to which they are heirs. But until the Lord again speaks, the situation will remain as it is.
>
> I say again, the Latter-day Saints know that our colored folk will get all the blessings they live for. They know that in the due time of the Lord, the burdens they now carry, and which were placed upon their shoulders by the Lord, not by the Latter-day Saints, will be lifted and they will come out into the sunshine of the glory of the Priesthood, in such measure as has been decreed and as they have earned. Meanwhile, the Latter-day Saints deeply sympathize with them for the burden they carry, for which the Saints are in no way responsible, and the prayerful hope of the Saints is that the colored folk will carry the burden with fortitude, preparing themselves for the day of release.⁶⁰

President Clark foresaw that day of release for all persons of Black ancestry but did not live to see the fulfillment of his expectations in 1978, when his first cousin, Spencer W. Kimball, as President of the Church, announced that a revelation of God authorized that "all worthy male members of the Church may be ordained to the priesthood without regard for race or color."⁶¹

Reuben was preeminently a U.S. nationalist in his attitudes and activities, but he nonetheless proclaimed that the Church of Jesus Christ of Latter-day Saints must have a larger destiny. In October 1937 he told the general conference that "too long have we remained somewhat aloof from the organizations of ours on the other side of the water and in the islands of the sea."⁶² President Clark had traveled relatively little among the nations of the world, but he knew enough of Americans generally and of Mormon missionaries in particular to recognize the temptation to export American and Utah values throughout the world.

Presidents Grant and Clark with Hawaiian Saints, June 1935.

Presidents Clark and Grant unveiling centennial plaque commemorating the first Latter-day Saint baptisms at the River Ribble, near Preston, Lancashire, England, 30 July 1937.

We must give up this idea too many of us have, that our way of life and living is not only the best, but often the only true way of life and living in the world, that we know what everybody else in the world should do and how they should do it. We must come to realize that every race and every people have their own way of doing things, their own standards of life, their own ideals, their own kinds of food and clothing and drink, their own concepts of civil obligation and honor, and their own views as to the kind of government they should have. It is simply ludicrous for us to try to recast all of these into our mold.[63]

He saw his personal mission as limited to America and the welfare of Americans, but he had a clear vision of the international mission of the Church.

Far in advance, President Clark also foresaw that the international mission of the Church must be joined with technology. In November 1953 President Clark told the Chairman of the Federal Communications Commission that he had hoped for several years that the Church could purchase "an international short-wave station," but his hopes were not fulfilled until October 1962, a year following his death.[64] In 1954 he told the general conference priesthood meeting that he could "foresee in no distant future" that the general priesthood meeting would be broadcast live to an audience of 150,000 men and boys gathered together in their own stakes throughout the United States. That was fulfilled at the general conference of April 1969.[65] In 1958 he told the general priesthood meeting of April conference that he could "envision within the reasonable future that we shall broadcast throughout the civilized world" sessions of the general conference translated into the various languages as the conference talks were given. That development in Church conference broadcasts began in April 1967.[66]

J. Reuben Clark was a product of the nineteenth century, and he alternately accepted and resisted the twentieth century's changing status of race. But supreme to him were the majesty of law, the principle of justice for all mankind, and the expansiveness of the gospel. Despite his own acknowledged limitations, he affirmed that the gospel of Christ must be universal. Despite his American national emphasis, he perceived that the gospel was protected in America, not limited to America, and that the Church must extend itself in attitude, in manpower, and in technology to "all nations, and kindreds, and people, and tongues."

First Presidency contemplating the international church, 1958.
J. Reuben Clark, Stephen L Richards, David O. McKay

"PRECIOUS THINGS OF
EVERY KIND AND ART"

Helaman 12:2

J. Reuben Clark never claimed to be a cultural esthete and once characterized his artistic judgment by commenting: "Now I know nothing about art and my opinion about the artistic value of a piece of work is worse than nothing, and, as a matter of fact, is in the red. . . ."[1] Nevertheless, as a member of the First Presidency he inevitably became involved in administrative decisions about artistic endeavors with which the Church was involved. Moreover, long before he became a Church administrator, Reuben had an untrained interest in both poetry and music that continued throughout his life as a member of the First Presidency.

Aside from poetry, Reuben Clark had little interest in literature. Although he collected a massive personal library that he intended to be self-sufficient for his every need, it contained only four novels: Jonathan Swift's satirical allegory *Gulliver's Travels,* James Fenimore Cooper's frontier romances, *The Leatherstocking Saga,* Rudyard Kipling's fantasy *Puck of Pook's Hill,* and Somerset Maugham's historical novel *Then and Now.* Even the literary essay held little appeal—his library had separate imprints of six of Thomas Babington Macaulay's essays, and two volumes of Montesquieu's *The Spirit of Laws.*[2] Lute's personal library, however, contained much of the prose literature her husband's lacked.

On the other hand, Reuben demonstrated an early interest in poetry by composing a six-verse poem when he was thirteen years old.[3] Shakespeare's *Complete Works* was one of the staples of Reuben's early education, and his library contained two editions of the Bard's works, plus two imprints of Christopher Pearse Cranch's translation of Virgil's epic *Aeneid* and two editions of John Milton's complete

239

poems. Aside from two anthologies of English poetry, Reuben also maintained copies of Chaucer's *Canterbury Tales* and Edward Fitzgerald's translation of the *Rubaiyat of Omar Khayyam.*[4]

He was not only selective in the number of poetry volumes in his library, but also in choosing favorite poems. From an extensive anthology of English poetry, Reuben underlined and made marginal notations only on the poems of Milton, Dryden, Pope, Johnson, Goldsmith, and Burns.[5] While in the First Presidency he manifested particular attachment to the *Rubaiyat of Omar Khayyam.* When he composed a poem to some friends on their departure from Salt Lake City, President Clark introduced it "with abject apologies to Omar," and his own copy of the *Rubaiyat* reminded him on its flyleaf to "See Special verses: VII, XI, XVII, XVIII, XIX."[6] The first two of these preferred stanzas from this Moslem poet seem somewhat atypical of

President Clark in his personal library at 80 D Street, Salt Lake City, 1957.

President Clark's own disdain for the sensuousness of life: "Come, fill the Cup, and in the Fire of Spring The Winter Garment of Repentance fling ... Here with a Loaf of Bread beneath the Bough, A Flask of Wine, a Book of Verse–and Thou." However, the last three of his favorite stanzas manifested his somber reflections on the impermanence of power during his years in the First Presidency: "They say the Lion and the Lizard keep The Courts where Jamshyd gloried and drank deep; and Bahram, that great Hunter–the Wild Ass Stamps o'er his Head, and he lies fast asleep." In keeping with the mood of this and the other companion "Special verses" in the *Rubaiyat,* he also marked only the following lines in his 1945 edition of Bartlett's *Familiar Quotations:* "Imperious Caesar, dead and turn'd to clay, Might stop a hole to keep the wind away" (*Hamlet,* V, i, 226).[7]

President Clark composed poetry only infrequently, but during a decade of his service in the First Presidency, members of the Church were able to see public evidence of his creativity. In June 1941 he published his poem "When I Would Pass" in the *Relief Society Magazine,* but used the pen name "Jay Rubark" ("Rubark" had been the cable address for his Washington law firm).[8] In November 1942 he wrote the first draft of a poem titled "A Hymn to the Seed of Ephraim and Manasseh," published it under his own name in the *Church News* in January 1946, and permitted it to be performed with his daughter Luacine's musical score during the 1950 June conference of the youth organizations of the Church.[9] He did not consider himself a poet and did not project that image to his contemporaries, but a common man's feel for poetry characterized J. Reuben Clark from adolescence to old age.

Although he wrote and read little of literature, he had pronounced ideas about the quality of any literary work he happened across. Lute found this out to her chagrin when she asked him to read the manuscript draft of a children's story she hoped to publish. Reuben began his critique by telling Lute that she had the right idea, but then he continued:

As it now stands however it seems to me it might be improved along the lines suggested below:

In the beginning of my observations I may say that as I understand it, it is of *vital* importance in a short story that you have no unnecessary words–space is almost all important and no word, thought, or incident should be allowed in the story which is not absolutely essential. Every thing in the story should be useful, little or nothing should be purely ornamental.—Again your short story should have a motive, a moral, or a purpose. Of course many stories are told for the sake of the story itself, but I take it yours is not of that class. As I surmise it, you wish to show that ghosts do not exist and that the children's fear of them is groundless. Therefore your whole story should turn around this motive and nothing that does not contribute to it, either directly or indirectly should be admitted within the sacred precincts of your tale.

After his maiden voyage as a literary critic of his wife's first effort at creative writing, he added a postscript to the letter: "I have also ordered a book on the Art of Short Story Telling which I shall send you as soon as it comes." Reuben anticipated that his critique would make Lute "angry," and he was probably right, for she neither published the story nor wrote another for several years. Eventually, however, she published a good deal in Church magazines.[10]

Reuben left no specific statement of his views about the graphic arts, but his personal papers give some indication of his preferences. During his visits to Europe on government business, Reuben acquired three etchings: one of a forest, another of a snow scene with an isolated country church, and another of a small street in Zurich. More interesting is Reuben's apparent enjoyment of expressionist caricature that was popular in the early twentieth century. While he was ambassador to Mexico, Reuben allowed a Mexican artist to paint at least three watercolor portraits of him in this style. The fact that these watercolor caricatures were dated from 1930 to 1931 would indicate that Reuben enjoyed this artistic style enough to return to the same artist several times. Perhaps this was a graphic expression of Reuben's famous self-deprecating humor.

Once he was a member of the First Presidency, President Clark often had the responsibility of being artistic critic of Church architecture. His comments about the Celestial Room of the Idaho Falls Temple indicated his usual firmness:

I said it looked to me as if we had too much "art"—too much "decorates"; that one of the chief concerns should be properly to give people the proper inspiration; that we must have more and different furniture in this room. I suggested we must have some relief to the bare walls, and spoke of drapes, describing the wall hangings in Mexico, particularly Elizabeth Cabots, though saying that would not do, but were merely illustrative. I thot we might consider some draperies. I

Watercolor of Ambassador Clark, one of three by a Mexican artist whose style Reuben apparently liked.

also suggested the possibility of introducing some lighting effects in the top of the room—the tower part—a soft radiance that might typify the spirit and its presence. . . . I also suggested the possibility of panelling the walls which would enable us to use a false facing to cover the wall defects.[11]

If he felt discomfort with too much splendor in the special temple construction which was expected to represent the Church's best efforts, it is understandable that he was even less pleased with splendor in local chapels. On a tour of the Oakland Stake Tabernacle in 1945, he gruffly noted that it looked "like an Italian villa."[12]

Because he was untrained in architecture and the arts, President Clark apparently concluded that contemplation would add nothing to his first impressions. Although understandable, such an approach was disconcerting to the Church architects. Architect Georgious Young Cannon described the process by which the First Presidency selected the design of the Los Angeles temple:

President Grant and President Clark and President McKay walked in and almost immediately President Clark stepped in front of President Grant and said, "I don't like this, I don't like this, and I don't like this, I like this, I don't like this," and out they walked. That was all the consideration given to our sketches.[13]

Church architecture was one area where Reuben dispensed with his usual pattern of extensive research and reflection prior to announcing a decision.

Music was one of the arts to which he paid greater attention. As a lawyer and civil servant in Washington and New York City, Reuben displayed little interest in attending concerts or obtaining classical recordings for home listening. While in Mexico City, however, sixty-year-old Ambassador Clark developed a sudden passion for classical music. The turning point apparently occurred on 25 Janaury 1931 when one of the diplomats in Mexico City invited the Clarks to listen to *Aida* one Sunday evening at his home. They stayed at the man's house until midnight, and Reuben obtained a list of

COURTESY HAROLD B. LEE LIBRARY

J. Reuben Clark, seated on the floor in the center, performing music with others in Grantsville, Utah, ca. 1892.

musical recommendations for phonograph records.[14] Three days later, Reuben wrote a letter to his daughter in Washington, D.C., in which he asked her to purchase for him several records of shorter light classics, as well as two operas, Stravinsky's *Fire Bird Suite,* and Dvořák's *New World* and Schubert's *Unfinished* symphonies. The letter indicated Reuben's enthusiasm for the newly discovered world of serious music.

> I would like you to go to the best Victrola store there in Washington and proceed roughly as follows:
> Take one forenoon and hear them play "Aida" in the complete record. That will give you a standard by which to judge.
> Following this experience, hear, as soon as you can, "La Boheme" (in the album described in the attached list), "Rigoletto" (in the album in the attached list), and "La Tosca," which is not in the catalogue which I have seen, but which, I am told, is as good as "Aida." I have heard some doubt cast upon "La Boheme" and also upon "Rigoletto." You might also hear the two symphonies, the one of Schubert and the other of Dvorak.
> Get either or all three of the operas that will compare favorably with "Aida." If the operas are not really good, then of course do not get them.[15]

That was quite an order and an unusual crash course in music criticism, but Louise dutifully followed her father's instructions to the letter. Soon Reuben was writing from Mexico City for recordings of symphonies by Mozart and Beethoven, and he was on his way to creating a personal record library that would give him the music self-sufficiency that his library of books gave him academically.

By the time J. Reuben Clark entered the First Presidency in 1933, he was a passionate aficionado of classical music and grand opera, but the general Mormon public hardly realized the fact. He disliked the jostling and constraints of audience participation, and he almost never attended musical productions of any kind and declined complimentary tickets to the Utah Symphony after its establishment in Salt Lake City.[16] He preferred to hear music in the comfort of his home on radio or phonograph and regarded a local symphony as an unnecessary expense for Utah. President Clark told one of the sponsors of the Utah Symphony that "Personally, I am not at all interested in just having a symphony here," and he opposed state appropriations for the symphony.[17] Moreover, he told the bishops of the Church that he disliked the music of J. S. Bach, and concerning popular music he said, "I do not know how far above the tom-tom of the jungle it is, but it is not too far."[18]

Although the general public might have regarded him as an iconoclast of both classical and modern music, the close associates whom he invited to the inner sanctum of his home at 80 D Street in Salt Lake City knew President Clark as one who loved serious music. Harold B. Lee, Henry D. Moyle, and Marion G. Romney often recorded attendance at the Clark home for dinner, after which they stayed until midnight listening to full-length musical productions such as Donizetti's grand opera *Lucia di Lammermoor* and the Berlioz *Requiem.*[19] President Clark's own musical taste often exceeded the experience and appreciation of his guests: Henry D. Moyle once innocently recorded that he and other guests stayed at the Clark home until 11 P.M. listening to the Verdi opera "Nutacco," when its actual title was *Nabucco.*[20]

With his late-flowering but intense love of music, President Clark could be very generous in his praise. He never explained his dislike for Bach, but (ever the diplomat) Reuben wrote a letter of praise to Leopold Stokowski for the "beautiful" orchestration of two Bach compositions on an NBC radio broadcast.[21] He also commended J. Spencer Cornwall for conducting a "particularly beautiful" performance of the Mormon Tabernacle Choir and commented, "Every once in a while, much to my pleasure I get the rumble of that basso-profundo. He is as good as the Cossacks."[22] To Florence J. Madsen, he wrote, "As I have many times told you, Sister Madsen, I regard you as the ablest [choir] director in the Church."[23]

Nevertheless, Reuben also was an unyielding music critic. After he listened to a "not so good" radio broadcast of the Tabernacle Choir in 1934, he wrote that the "duet, trio and solo work was poor. Asper's pieces were poor, and Richard Evans' announcements were not up to the standard."[24] After hearing a radio broadcast of Brigham Young University's A Capella Choir twenty years later, President Clark wrote the university's president to criticize the inclusion of Bruckner's *O Lord Most Holy,* and asked whether the student singers "are yet sufficiently good to sing a capella."[25] He had an even more intense dislike for contemporary music and did not even listen to the music of Crawford Gates's *Sand in Their Shoes* because "he was afraid that the music was of a modernistic discordant variety."[26]

When another Church musician, Robert Cundick, composed a modernistic quartet in honor of his eighty-ninth birthday, President Clark was publicly complimentary, but one wonders how much he really enjoyed it.[27]

His delayed appreciation of serious music, his aloofness from the concert hall, and his tendency to see Church administration in light of his government experience all left him ill prepared for one of the ongoing necessities of his position in the First Presidency: dealing with the artistic performer. J. Reuben Clark began any administrative contact of this type with an assumption that people "of artistic temperament" did not share his rational view of the world.[28] Rightly or wrongly, he assumed that all artists and performers had succumbed to the temptation of pride, and therefore any artist was already at a disadvantage in administrative relationships with President Clark. Thus, he chided Richard L. Evans for being "enamored" of the microphone during the "Spoken Word" portion of the Tabernacle Choir broadcasts, yet also told him, "I continue to marvel, Richard, at your fertility, unequalled I am sure in the history of the Church, and perhaps in the history of English literature."[29] Likewise, he praised J. Spencer Cornwall's performance as conductor of the Tabernacle Choir, but also criticized him for declining to give the assistant conductor, Richard P. Condie, opportunities to use the baton in performances.[30] But the clearest example of J. Reuben Clark's impatience with the artistic performer lies in his administrative relationship with one of the tabernacle organists, Alexander Schreiner, the only Latter-day Saint artist about whom President Clark recorded frequent and detailed observations.

Alexander Schreiner began playing piano at age five and had been one of several organists at the Salt Lake Tabernacle since 1924 and was described by President Heber J. Grant as "the greatest organist in the Church."[31] Although he had served at the tabernacle less than his fellow organists, Schreiner had been petitioning the First Presidency since 1926 to be given the title of "Chief Organist," because his training and experience "qualify me to fill this place."[32] The First Presidency had declined to make such an appointment out of deference to the greater seniority of the other organists at the tabernacle, but had granted Alexander Schreiner periodic leaves of absence to perform and improve himself professionally in Los Angeles and to perform at the tabernacle only during the summer season.[33] This situation remained unchanged until 1939, when both Alexander Schreiner and the First Presidency indicated interest in his becoming a full-time organist with the Salt Lake Tabernacle.

During the process involved in securing the full-time employment of Schreiner at the Salt Lake Tabernacle, J. Reuben Clark's bias toward all artistic performers distilled itself upon the hapless organist. President Clark had reassured his friend Frank W. Asper, a tabernacle organist with longer continuous tenure than Schreiner, that Schreiner's return would not eclipse the former's work at the tabernacle.[34] A meeting of the First Presidency with Alexander Schreiner to resolve some misunderstandings about his return to the tabernacle became a bit heated. In fact, the meeting had been unexpectedly difficult for both men, but Alexander Schreiner's justifiable estimation of his abilities as an organist had triggered all of Reuben's suspicions about artistic performers.[35] Throughout his service in the Presidency, President Clark continued to monitor activities and attitudes of Church artistic performers.

Until he was past eighty President Clark had never cared for motion pictures, but he was involved administratively in the production of the Hollywood film *Brigham Young* in 1939–40. The First Presidency was very concerned about this movie because it was based upon Vardis Fisher's best-selling novel *Children of God,* which they regarded as an anti-Mormon book. The First Presidency wanted to influence the manner in which the movie was produced, and for their part the Hollywood producers were anxious to have the cooperation of the leaders of the Church.[36] In October 1939 President Clark accompanied President Grant and Elder John A. Widtsoe to the Hollywood studio and listened to a reading of the script for *Brigham Young.*

The First Presidency was dissatisfied with a script version of a prayer Brigham Young was to utter at the time crickets threatened the Mormons' first harvest in the Salt Lake Valley, and President Clark sent a substitute to one of the executives of Twentieth Century Fox. His proposed prayer of 193 words began, "Our Heavenly Father: Hear the cry of Thine afflicted people," and ended, "Help us, in Jesus' name, we ask it, or we starve. Amen."[37] There is no record of the reaction of the movie executives toward Reuben's maiden voyage as Hollywood scriptwriter, but the inclusion of a 193-word prayer was out of the question in a fast-paced movie.[38] Although Heber J. Grant was almost rapturous in his praise for the movie, President Clark merely "said it was OK."[39]

He maintained that indifference toward motion pictures as an art form or entertainment until he became a sudden enthusiast of Hollywood spectaculars in the 1950s. While President Clark was in New York City in 1952, Lowell Thomas gave him complimentary tickets for a showing of the innovative movie process titled "Cinerama," and he expressed "astonished enjoyment" of the movie to Thomas and to Church President David O. McKay, of whom Reuben said "he is most anxious to see it as the result of my enthusiasm, because I am notoriously a non-theater goer that he says he wants to see anything that I praise."[40] The next movie that captured his fancy was the 1955 picture *Martin Luther,* which he saw in a private screening at his home with a few close friends and then watched at home a second time afterwards.[41]

Reuben's excitement about Hollywood productions reached an apex when he viewed Cecil B. DeMille's 1956 production of *The Ten Commandments.* With an effusiveness quite unusual for him, President Clark composed a personal letter to Mr. DeMille:

The performance was, in the over all, stupendous, magnificent, overwhelming. I am not experienced in these matters, but so far as my knowledge goes, it is the greatest historical pictoral drama ever produced. It dwarfs such predecessors as "Martin Luther," without any disparagement to that picture.

. . . .

I marvel at your powers of imagination, your vision, your ability to see and to develop such a story of one of the most important eras in all human history; your dramatic skill and high artistry, your sense of proportion, indeed your great abilities in all the lines that combined went in to make this picture what it is.

. . . .

I tender my homage, Sir, to your true and great genius as a modern dramatic pictoral artist and composer of the highest rank. God bless you.

He had never expressed such unrestrained praise for any other artistic work or artist, or indeed for anyone in any field of endeavor. Perhaps embarrassed by his own fervor, he decided not to send the letter to Mr. DeMille.[42] He continued to be awed by subsequent movie spectaculars like the 1957 *Around the World in Eighty Days,*[43] but

DeMille's epic found no rival. As he approached ninety years, Clark had no energy for his new-found love of Hollywood spectacles, and he limited himself to homebound activities of reading, listening to grand opera on the phonograph, and watching the Lawrence Welk show on television.[44]

J. Reuben Clark was not a common man in the secular world or in the religious world, but he had a common man's appreciation for culture and the arts. He freely acknowledged his limited understanding and appreciation of the artistic value of specific works, yet President Clark was often forced to make administrative decisions about the arts and artists. He did the best he could with the understanding he had. Ultimately, he felt that the Latter-day Saints could absorb very well his own inadequacies as an esthete as well as the invidious comparisons some might make between the culture of Zion and the culture of Babylon:

> You know, I feel, and I have traveled somewhat and lived away from you somewhat—I feel that our cultural standards in this Church will match, if not over-match, the cultural standards of any other people taken as a whole. We do have music, and all the rest, and we get from these ennobling activities in which we engage a spiritual uplift. . . .
>
> But in large measure these are but the condiments, valuable as they are. The real food is the spiritual food which must be obtained in addition to the things which shall make it pleasant to eat.[45]

"THE WELFARE OF THIS PEOPLE"

Alma 60:9

J. Reuben Clark entered the First Presidency when the Church and the nation faced the greatest economic crisis of American history, and he devoted a major portion of his attention to the economic welfare of the Church members. Most often, his efforts in this regard are identified with the Welfare Plan, as indicated by Elder Harold B. Lee's eulogy: "Perhaps there was nothing closer to his heart during 28 years years of his presidency than the Welfare Program."[1] What became known as the Welfare Program loomed large in President Clark's thoughts and activities, but that endeavor was only one element of what he regarded as his sacred trust in managing the resources of the Church to benefit the Latter-day Saints. Aside from the Welfare Program itself, he was preoccupied with the safeguarding of the voluntary tithing donations of the Latter-day Saints, the cautious expenditure of those funds, and the conduct of Church business enterprises. As a General Authority over an unpaid priesthood, Reuben also regarded tightly circumscribed personal finances as part of that sacred trust. His thoughts and activities from 1933 onward must be understood in relation to the previous century of Church teachings and activities concerning the economic responsibilities of the Church.

The ultimate economic goals of the Latter-day Saints were clearly indicated when the Book of Mormon was published a couple of weeks before the organization of the Church in 1830. The ancient message, revealed anew, directly concerned those who were entering the Church through baptism: if they wished to retain a remission of their sins, "ye should impart of your substance to the poor, every man according to that which he hath, such as feeding the hungry,

251

clothing the naked, visiting the sick and administering to their relief, both spiritually and temporally, according to their wants" (Mosiah 4:26). In the new Church, this was amplified through a series of revelations requiring economic equality among the Latter-day Saints: "But it is not given that one man should possess that which is above another, wherefore the world lieth in sin" (D&C 49:20), and "every man [should be] equal according to his family, according to his circumstances and his wants and needs" (D&C 51:13). At the most immediate level, the Church members were to provide for the poor and needy, until the Church achieved the ultimate goal of economic equality, according to circumstances and needs.[2]

The means provided by revelation to achieve these ends were the Law of Consecration and Stewardship and the United Order. Basic to the Law of Consecration is the doctrine that the earth and every material thing on it belong to the Lord—they are His property (D&C 104:14–16). As President Clark later said, "The basic principle of all the revelations on the United Order is that everything we have belongs to the Lord; therefore, the Lord may call upon us for any and all of the property which we have, because it belongs to Him."[3] By extension, mortals may either aggrandize to themselves alleged property, or they may in faith recognize that they are stewards (servants) of the Lord whom He entrusts with the custody of that which is His property, not theirs: "Behold, all these properties are mine, or else your faith is vain.... And if the properties are mine, then ye are stewards, otherwise ye are no stewards" (D&C 104:55–56; also 104:12–13). The revelations provided that the Saints who accepted this economic perspective indicate it by consecrating to the Lord by deed all that they possessed. Then they would receive back by deed sufficient for their needs in consultation with the bishop, and then consecrate each year everything they had earned above their needs (D&C 42:30–37; 51:4–6).

At first the leaders of the Church sought to incorporate stewardship with deeded property by making the deeds to individuals in the form of a legal lease-and-loan agreement. This "effort to draft the Law of Consecration and Stewardship into the language of civil law" ran into legal and practical difficulties, and in 1833 the Prophet instructed that the deeds be restructured to give the steward "his

individual property, his private stewardship," even though in the revelatory context a steward did not really own his Master's property.[4]
Even with the refinements the Prophet made in the administration
of the United Order between 1831 and 1834, the Saints had difficulty living such an exalted economic order which tended to drasti-
cally redistribute wealth. In 1838 a lesser law was implemented
which required an initial total consecration to be followed by annual
tithings of increase. Even this proved too difficult for the Saints to
live, and in 1841 initial consecrations were eliminated but tithing
was retained as the means by which to fulfill the economic goals of
the Lord for the Saints.[5] Aside from the Bishopric (which had been
established in 1831 specifically to administer the consecrated revenues of the Saints on behalf of the needy and to supervise the United
Order), the only other organized body Joseph Smith created to care
for the poor and needy was the Relief Society in 1842.[6]

After the Church was established in Utah, Brigham Young instituted several practices that provided important points of reference
for twentieth-century relief programs in the Church. President
Young said:

> My experience has taught me and it has become a principle with me, that it is
> never any benefit to give, out and out, to man or woman, money, food, clothing,
> or anything else, if they are able-bodied and can work and earn what they need,
> when there is anything on the earth for them to do. . . . To pursue a contrary
> course would ruin any community in the world and make them idlers.

In order to implement this philosophy, he put the unemployed to
work in building the Salt Lake City Council House, Social Hall, Endowment House, Church Historian's Office, Salt Lake Temple, city
wall, and numerous other civic projects. The central tithing office
also soon expanded to a bishop's storehouse in every settlement of
Saints, where tithing primarily in kind (produce, livestock, manufac-
tured items) was stored for the benefit of the poor and for other purposes of the Church. Brigham Young also reminded the Saints of
the ultimate goal of equality in the revelations by having the Saints
consecrate all their properties to the Church in the 1850s (although
not actually involving physical transfers of the properties), inaugurat-
ing a cooperative manufacturing and merchandising program for

every settlement in 1868, and in expanding that to a renewal of the United Order in 1874.[7]

Of the hundreds of united orders established in the Great Basin—most of which failed within a couple of years—the most communal and successful was at Orderville, Utah. All residents subscribed to the principle that "every person is simply a steward and not an owner of property he has in charge, and . . . in living as a patriarchal family, and in common, according to their circumstances fare alike." Dressed alike, eating communal meals at a common dining hall, becoming nearly self-sufficient, and enjoying a higher standard of life than most of the participants had prevously experienced, the Orderville form of the United Order lasted until the General Authorities dissolved it amid the onslaught of the U.S. government's economic and political campaign against the Mormon Church in the mid-1880s. Some Orderville residents moved to Mexico and inaugurated the last Church-sponsored united order, but it also disbanded in 1895.[8]

President Clark preferred the revelatory ideals of the Law of Consecration and Stewardship to the practical attempts to live the United Order from 1831 to 1895, experiments which he publicly called "early deviations . . . from the principles set out in the revelations."[9] Although he disliked the communal character in many of these early Church-sponsored efforts, Reuben acknowledged their historical existence in a letter to a friend in Massachusetts:

> I think you may have some misconception about the setup of the Church, since you speak of our "cooperative" system. We do not have a cooperative system in the Church. In the early days of the Church they set up what was called then the United Order, which was in one sense communal and in another sense wholly individualistic.
>
> Then, after a time, Brigham Young again set up a United Order system in some parts of the West, where it was more of a communal order than that set up by the Prophet Joseph Smith in Missouri and Kirtland. Under the plan set up in the West, the community owned the property and they had a common eating hall, and like matters were held in common, though the family relationship was sacredly guarded. This was later abandoned when the Federal Government confiscated all of the Church's property other than churches.[10]

President Clark's preference was for a system that incorporated the ideals of the revelations on the economic responsibilities of the

Church and the Saints but enshrined individuality and avoided the cooperation he identified with socialism and communism.

By the twentieth century a number of changes had occurred in Mormon society that would provide a significant background to the situation in 1933. Utah's economy, despite efforts at "home industries," was so closely linked with the national economy that the periodic "panics" of small, short-term depressions in the national economy had almost immediate effect in Utah, which recovered more slowly than the national economy.[11] By 1908 nearly all tithing was being paid in cash rather than in kind, and the Church discontinued the Bishop's General Storehouse in Salt Lake City. Local bishops' storehouses, tithing barns, and granaries were either diverted to other purposes, razed, or left to the elements.[12] Beginning in 1899 Church leaders sent out handbooks to local leaders describing their responsibilities and, in 1901, instructed the bishops to give whatever employment possible to persons receiving financial aid. In 1903 the Presiding Bishopric established an employment bureau in Salt Lake City. Under the direction of the Presiding Bishopric, and administered primarily by local bishops, the Church provided direct aid to families and individuals as necessary. For example, in the relatively prosperous year of 1915, the Church gave financial assistance to 19,547 Latter-day Saints. Under the direction of the Presiding Bishopric, the Relief Society conducted its charitable activities in cooperation with both private charities and government agencies, and the 1928 *Handbook of Instructions* specified that the order of responsibility for aiding needy Church members was first their families, second the county relief agencies, and third, as a last resort, the Church. Nevertheless, more than 78 percent of needy Latter-day Saints on the eve of the Great Depression turned to the Church rather than to county agencies.[13]

For a decade before the famous stock market crash of 1929, Utah's mining, manufacturing, and agricultural economy had been either depressed or stagnant. During this period, Utah's annual agricultural production declined 20 percent. After 1929, farm income continued to plummet until the national agricultural income in 1932 was less than half of the pre-1929 level. In a country awash with farm surpluses, Utah farmers would have to triple production to pay pre-1929 debts; the result was that nearly half of Utah farm mortgages were delinquent by 1933.[14] The situation in Utah cities was worse than on the farms or in the nation generally. While the national unemployment rate was 25 percent, more than 63 percent of the breadwinners in Salt Lake City's Grant Stake were unemployed in 1932, and the rest of the metropolis was not much better off.[15]

As the Great Depression decimated the national and local economy, many wondered if any resource was adequate to meet a crisis that was impoverishing tens of millions. Salt Lake County spent $1,750,000 for direct relief in 1933, and Presiding Bishop Sylvester Q. Cannon noted, "If the Church were to undertake to take care of this amount, it would bankrupt us." The entire Church expenditure for relief that year was only one-third of the amount Salt Lake County spent on poor relief.[16] State and Federal revenues were based upon corporate and personal income taxes that were vanishing as businesses closed their doors and millions went unemployed throughout the nation, county revenues were based upon property taxes that were as uncollectible for the newly impoverished majority of people as were mortgage payments, and Church revenues were based upon the tithing of incomes that increasing numbers of Latter-day Saints no longer had. For the nation at large and for many Latter-day Saints in 1932, the solution to this national crisis seemed to lie in the election of Franklin D. Roosevelt, who promised a "New Deal" and implemented it through massive deficit spending by the federal government that pumped billions of dollars into state and local economies through direct relief, farm price support programs, and make-work projects such as the Public Works Administration (PWA), Works Project Administration (WPA), and Civilian Conservation Corps (CCC).

Other Latter-day Saint leaders felt that there was a better way than dependence upon government charity and deficit spending. For a time, the most innovative responses to the Depression were coming from local leaders rather than from Church headquarters. In Cache Valley, ward bishops and Relief Society presidents reestablished storehouses for collection of surplus produce and clothing which was then distributed to the needy Saints. The greatest innovations came in 1932 in the Salt Lake Pioneer Stake, under the direction of its youthful president, Harold B. Lee. With unemployment exceeding 50 percent of the men, the Pioneer Stake conducted its own employment agency and obtained permission to keep its tithing revenues in the stake. The Pioneer Stake used its tithing funds to purchase a farm to be operated for the employment of stake members in exchange for food, to purchase a warehouse to be operated as a stake "Bishop's storehouse," to operate a cannery, and to market excess produce and canned goods to distant points. The stake used its cash profits to purchase and renovate for sale defective products from the Logan Knitting Mills. All these activities provided jobs for Pioneer Stake's unemployed.[17]

But in 1933 both local and general Church responses to the economic plight of Latter-day Saints depended upon acceptance of supplemental government funding, federal and local.[18] This was not a departure from Church policy at the time, but was consistent with the Presiding Bishopric's *Handbook of Instructions* that Church members were to turn to county relief before turning to the Church.[19] Prior to the Depression the majority of Saints had turned to the

Welfare beginnings.

Church rather than to government agencies, but by 1933 the reversed proportion of dependency indicated that Latter-day Saints generally felt that only the resources of the government could cope with the crisis.

President Clark, however, was convinced that the resources of government should not be allowed to displace the responsibilities of the Church and of the individual. He indicated this during his first talk as a General Authority when he affirmed that "no man may rightfully violate [God's] law by living by the sweat from the brow of his brother." But on that occasion he admitted he knew what he opposed better than what to specifically propose as a remedy to the economic tragedy his audience was facing.

The world is moaning in tribulation. I do not know the cure. The questions involved are so nearly infinite in their greatness, that I question whether any human mind can answer them. But it is my faith that if the people shall shun idleness; if they shall cast out from their hearts those twin usurpers, ambition and greed, and then shall re-enthrone brotherly love, and return to the old time virtues—industry, thrift, honesty, self-reliance, independence of spirit, self-discipline, and mutual helpfulness—we shall be far on our way to returned prosperity and worldly happiness.[20]

As he became more aware of the extent to which Utah's state and local governments, business sector, and citizens were accepting federal funds to combat the Depression, Reuben sounded a warning in his talk to the Salt Lake Community Chest on 19 June 1933: "Interference or help from the central government should be availed or permitted as little as possible. We should not permit our selfishness to interfere with our patriotic duties; nor to blind us to the dangers of centralization in government," and he praised the strong social unity of Mexico where the government had not intervened in the economic lives of its people and where "unemployment was not evident and there had been no appreciable increase on the demands on charitable organizations," despite the Depression and the repatriation of nearly 130,000 Mexicans from the United States.[21] Concerning the current policy of allowing government funds to supplement Church relief activities, he expressed his views in a meeting with the presidents of the six Salt Lake City stakes on 8 August to discuss their plan for relief: "My objections to the plan were that it assessed non-Mormons to maintain our churches, and in a reciprocal situation I would object to a scheme which provided money to buy candles for the Roman Catholic altars. . . ."[22]

Typical of his public career in government, Reuben was not content merely to criticize one mode of operation, but he was feverishly working to devise a new approach. He started preparing "a possible press announcement in re care of poor" the day after he received his first orientation from Harold B. Lee concerning the Pioneer Stake relief activities that had been in operation for a year.[23] A week after his Community Chest talk, Reuben personally inspected the "relief set up" of the Pioneer Stake and reported that it was "a very splendid organization doing excellent work."[24] Two days later, 30 June 1933, Reuben decided to expand beyond a simple press release and began the first draft of his "Suggestive Directions for Church Relief Activities." A single sentence from that manuscript indicated the major departure he was hoping to achieve in Church administration and philosophy: "*Church Aid.* It is to this aid that the Church members must and should primarily look in these times of stress."[25] This would constitute a momentous departure from a thirty-year Church policy of cooperation with government relief agencies and of encouraging Latter-day Saints to avail themselves of government funds.

President Clark's desire in 1933 to cut the umbilical cord of supplemental funds that connected Church relief with government relief was the primary focus of discussion between the First Presidency and the Presiding Bishopric for the next several years. Later, he publicly explained that his dissent from the relief policy of the Presiding Bishopric dated from the 1920s when he visited Salt Lake City and heard "one of the Presiding Bishopric exhort the brethren and sisters of the audience to make application and send their needy to the County," because the Church members had paid for county services through taxes. Reuben remarked in one of his oft-repeated tellings of this incident, "I never had a greater shock in my life. He just turned around everything I had been more or less bragging about to my acquaintances in the world." He concluded, "So when we began to reconsider this thing in 1933 it seemed to us that we would better get back to the old way."[26]

But reversing three decades of Church procedure and philosophy was not something that President Clark could achieve in a day. He drafted a proposed letter about Church relief which he circulated to the other members of the Presidency and to the Presiding Bishopric for their comments and revisions. The letter's provision for a survey of Church members regarding their relief needs and employment was probably based on a similar survey taken earlier in the year by the Pioneer Stake. But (in view of the stated goal of Reuben's first draft of "Suggestive Directions") it is significant that this First Presidency letter, issued on 28 August 1933, reaffirmed previous Church policy: "our people may properly look, as heretofore, for relief assistance from governmental and perhaps other sources." The letter also reaffirmed the policy that the Church relief programs would originate at the local level and not at headquarters: "The Church will, so far as possible, co-operate in any wise and effective local plan for furthering relief work."[27] Thus, the first official statement on relief to which Reuben was a participant was a reaffirmation of policies he was proposing be discontinued.

When the First Presidency first discussed his "Suggestive Directions" draft on 20 July 1933, President Grant recorded that "Brother Clark is to talk with the Presiding Bishopric before a final draft is made or an attempt is made to put the suggestions into operation."[28] Three days previous to this meeting, Reuben had struck from his draft the passage that Latter-day Saints should look primarily to the Church for aid and had substituted a revision that softened his proposed reversal of policy:

Church Aid. Reference has already been made to the fact that members of the Church are entitled, because they are tax payers, to receive their fair proportion of all government aid (whether municipal, county, State, or Federal) that may be distributed to needy unemployed. As participants in Community Chest and other relief activities, they are entitled to consideration in the distribution of relief funds by these organizations. *But it is to the Church aid that Church members may rightfully look in these times of stress for a guarantee against hunger and want when other sources fail.*[29]

This was substantially less than the guiding philosophy President Clark wanted for Church relief, and Marion G. Romney later observed that the *Suggestive Directions* "wasn't exactly as he would have liked it. He left some things out of it and put some things in to get it approved by the other Brethren."[30] In 1933 Reuben was willing to downplay ideology in order to implement the administrative innovation that was the heart of his *Suggestive Directions:* centralizing the relief program at Church headquarters, rather than in local wards and stakes, with a committee of which the First Presidency and Presiding Bishop were part and creating regional councils to administer Church relief for various stakes. Therefore the administrative design of Reuben's 1933 Church relief proposals tended to diminish the previously autonomous role of the Presiding Bishopric in relief at the same time as reversing the Bishopric's traditional emphasis upon decentralization and government cooperation.

Predictably, President Clark's suggested relief program found a lack of enthusiasm in the Presiding Bishopric. Sylvester Q. Cannon had promoted the alternative approach to Church relief since his appointment as Presiding Bishop in 1925. In July 1933 he accepted an appointment from Franklin D. Roosevelt to serve as a member of Utah's three-man advisory committee for the Public Works Administration, and in October he began instructing stake presidents that their stake relief work should be supervised by "qualified and experienced social service workers to be selected by the Stake Presidency and approved by the County Relief Committees, their compensation to be paid by the County Relief Committee."[31]

As instructed by the First Presidency in July, Reuben had been trying to accommodate the Presiding Bishopric in his relief proposals, and by the end of the summer he thought a resolution of the viewpoints was imminent. He told the six Salt Lake stake presidents in August "that we were working on a plan to be applied to the whole Church and that I thought in a month or six weeks this might be completed," and in September he told Franklin D. Roosevelt that "the Mormon Church was undertaking to set up an organization for the relief work this winter."[32] At the end of October the Deseret News Press printed Reuben's *Suggestive Directions*,[33] and he was understandably taken back by the Presiding Bishopric's response to a publication he thought he had sufficiently revised.

Sylvester Q. Cannon, despite whatever discussions had occurred since the previous July, disagreed with the general and specific intent of Reuben's *Suggestive Directions*. In a meeting of the Presiding Bishopric with the First Presidency on 30 October, he defended the present administration of Church relief, said that the pamphlet would demoralize those currently working in Church relief, and asked if the

First Presidency was dissatisfied with the relief activities of the Presiding Bishopric.[34] When Bishop Cannon wrote a critique and suggestions for revisions in the pamphlet several days later, President Clark replied at length in a letter of 9 November 1933:

I observe, however, that you are proposing to eliminate the entire substance of the "Suggestive Directions."

. . . .

Your observations and arguments when you met the Presidency shortly before we left, seem based upon the assumption that our existing Church arrangements are operating satisfactorily and adequately. Your suggestions now made seem based upon the same conclusions.

The reports which have come to me regarding the operation of our Church relief organizations indicate without exception the opposite of such a situation. Federal officers with whom I have talked voiced the same conclusion. I am personally convinced from my own observations and the reports which come to me, that our Church relief system is not now working either satisfactorily or adequately. . . . Your proposal seems to contemplate continuing the system as it now exists.

. . . .

I am unalterably opposed to the continuance of the greed, graft, and corruption which has characterized the use of relief funds among us during the last two years. It is destroying our morale as a people and is seriously undermining our moral and spiritual stamina. If continued, it will make professional paupers of very many of us and our spiritual welfare will be equally threatened. . . .

. . . .

. . . Our course during the last two years has given the lie to our talk about taking care of our own, which was one of our most glorious material achievements and principles.

The plan which was handed you had the approval of all three of us, as I suppose you understood. I do not know how President Grant or President Ivins may now feel about it. I shall, of course, be now guided by their wishes, but, subject to their contrary determination, I personally wish that the plan handed to you be put into immediate operation, with such slight modifications as Bishop [John] Wells suggested and such others of a similar character that may be deemed necessary.

. . . .

As already stated, no new Church agencies are set up by the "Suggestive Directions"; all that is contemplated and provided for is a giving of centralized direction to organizations that now operate in a loose, uncoordinated, and largely undirected way. I have not been able to see how any harm could be done by putting such a plan into operation, and on the contrary I think that much good might be accomplished.[35]

Presidents Grant and Ivins, however, accepted the viewpoints of the Presiding Bishop at the next meeting about this matter on 27

November 1933, and the minutes of their meeting conclude, "after considerable discussion it was felt that it was not necessary to issue [JRC's pamphlet] for the reasons that the relief work throughout the Church is being carried out effectively, and the instructions in the pamphlet might cause some confusion and misunderstanding."[36] Instead of issuing Reuben's pamphlet, the Presiding Bishopric in 1934 published *Care for the Poor,* which restated the policy that the priority in seeking aid was first to the families, second to the county relief agencies, and that "the Church, therefore, should render financial assistance only in a supplementary way, and chiefly in emergency cases." Additionally, bishops were to see that dependent poor or widows obtain the pensions provided by the government.[37] For a time, Reuben's alternative plan remained on hold.

Although the Church had not yet launched the program of welfare independence Reuben so earnestly hoped for, he continued to state his personal views forthrightly. In the October 1934 general conference he personally appealed to the Latter-day Saints, "do not soil our hands with the bounteous outpouring of funds which the government was giving to us," and affirmed that "this people would have been better off materially and spiritually, if we had relied on the Lord's plan and had not used one dollar of government funds."[38] Later that month Reuben wrote to his Grantsville neighbors an assessment of government welfare that was the guiding philosophy of the Church Welfare Program he would promote for the balance of his life:

But, in all I am saying to you, I am not thinking so much of today and of ourselves; we may be able somehow to squeeze along now and spend these tremendous sums we are using up and in good part wasting. I am thinking of tomorrow, when your children and grandchildren, and mine, and others, have to shoulder this great burden of debt we are piling up. I am afraid that if the thing goes on, the mere want we have now will become hunger and starvation for them then; I am fearful that our freedom to live and to work and to worship as we wish, those great boons of our free government, may become a cruel tyranny for them with all freedom gone, and with someone telling them where they must live, someone compelling them to work under a whip if necessary—real slavery—, and someone forbidding them to worship except as they direct, just as the Governments are doing in Russia and Germany. This possibility, indeed it may be a probability if we continue along our present course, must make all of us stop and think. We must all of us soberly and firmly resolve that we shall personally do nothing to bring this about and on the other hand that we will do everything possible to prevent it.[39]

This was a somber view of the consequences of government charity, and many fellow Church members did not share his fears of the ultimate destination of the New Deal relief programs. Nevertheless, it is necessary to recognize this dark vision of President Clark in order to appreciate the urgency with which he promoted Church relief and the philosophy which underlay every program of Church welfare he proposed and implemented.

Shortly after he wrote that private statement of his welfare philosophy, tensions began surfacing between government relief agencies and cooperating Church agencies, and one researcher has noted that "the Church was being pushed toward the position of either abandoning its relief system or striking out separately."[40] Encouraged by these Church-state strains in cooperative relief, President Clark urged the First Presidency to announce its own relief program, and he drafted a proposed First Presidency message for April 1935 conference which would state: "It is the determination of the First Presidency to do the utmost to bring this about and to take our people off the Government's back to the fullest possible degree."[41] However, a joint meeting of the First Presidency, Quorum of the Twelve, and Presiding Bishpric decided not to use Reuben's proposed statement at the April 1935 conference.[42] President McKay reported that "President Grant expresses the fear that the people will not sustain it," to which Reuben replied that whether or not the Saints accepted an independent Church program of relief, "I feel now, as I have for the last two years, namely, that this is something we really must attempt to do."[43]

A survey of relief conditions of Church members the following September was the occasion for the First Presidency to prepare the way for a separate Church relief program. The survey revealed that 16.3 percent of the Church population was receiving government relief whereas only 1.6 percent were receiving Church aid.[44] At the special priesthood meeting of 7 October 1935, Presidents Grant and Clark severely criticized Latter-day Saints who were receiving government relief, and President Clark reminded the priesthood leaders that "every comparative table that is issued regarding the distribution of relief in this country shows Utah as one of those States which is receiving the largest per capita amount from the Federal Government for relief."[45] As the First Presidency began preparing correspondence in anticipation of launching relief work, Reuben's secretary wrote him in November 1935, two full years after he had thought his *Suggestive Directions* would be circulated: "At last the Relief project comes forth; I do not know which will overwhelm you more—the fact that it is out at last, or the marvelous changes it has undergone."[46] At the same time, the federal government announced plans (ultimately not carried out) to end direct relief assistance, and this further prepared the way for the First Presidency's announcement on 7 April 1936 that it was launching its own relief program.[47]

From 1936 onward, President Clark affirmed that the Welfare Plan was inspired of God. In 1936 he stated, "It is my testimony to you that President Grant was inspired to begin this work and this Plan."[48] However, at the same time he testified of its inspiration he also affirmed that the Welfare Plan was the product of long administrative deliberations by several Church leaders:

It was not undertaken overnight. It was talked and re-talked, considered and reconsidered, and Brother Grant declined to go forward in it until he had the approval of his Counselors and those about him. He always regarded it as a matter of inspiration, revelation if you wish, and I am sure that the effects, direct and indirect, have more than justified the establishment of this plan.[49]

Although he had formulated much of the original philosophy and organization of the Welfare Plan in collaboration with Harold B. Lee, President Clark saw the inauguration of this program as the result of a long process of revelation which culminated in President Grant's decision to announce it in April 1936.[50]

When the national press headlined the Church's announcement, Reuben wrote the First Presidency: "We are now 'on the spot', and I think we must see to it that the relief program goes over. Personally I am glad that we are 'on the spot', because it is a spur which should increase our speed."[51] Within six weeks of the announcement, more than 200 welfare projects were established in the stakes of the Church, and by the end of 1936 more than 17,000 people had worked on Church welfare projects.[52] Within a year, fast offerings

COURTESY DESERET NEWS

Presidents Clark and Lee with welfare workers of South Summit Stake, Utah.

increased 53 percent, and the Church expenditures for the needy grew by 97 percent.[53] In conjunction with its relief activities, the Church began a "Beautification Program" in 1937, which Reuben said should begin with "the places to be seen by tourists" but should also include private residences and ultimately the entire community. "Paint your meeting houses, your town hall, repair your sidewalks, keep your park or public grounds looking neat, keep up your fences."[54] In the same year he also encouraged the legal entity of the relief program, The Co-operative Security Corporation, to provide two-year college tuition aid to returned missionaries.[55] Although the Church backed away from that proposal as too expensive, the Welfare Program in 1938 incorporated Deseret Industries, after President Clark received briefings from two members of the Church about the California-based Goodwill Industries that refurbished donated goods for resale and provided employment of the unskilled and handi-capped.[56] Construction also began on a massive Bishop's Central Storehouse complex at Seventh West and Seventh South in Salt Lake City, with the labor coming primarily from unemployed Church members. In many respects, the new Church Security program (re-named Welfare Plan in 1938) moved at great speed.

Nevertheless, typical of his entire administrative style, President Clark resisted the proposals for the Church relief program to promise too much social change or economic recovery. A month before the official announcement he expressed hope "that Brother Lee will not try to insist upon a new social set-up in the situation. It seems to me that our problem is very small in its scope, namely, to relieve the present situation. The plans for social reform can wait until we get back on our feet and see things a little more clearly and with a little more perspective."[57] He was particularly careful to insist that the Church not propose to do more than it could achieve, lest the faith of the Saints be injured. He was especially anxious that the new plan not be construed as a step toward living the United Order. A month after the announcement of the Church relief program, President

Welfare Plan expands.

Clark suggested that the First Presidency not allow "certain of our people to expect and to hope that we are going to undertake some sort of new economic order. I feel very strongly that we should confine this statement merely to the work which we now have in hand reduced to its lowest proportions. We can always enlarge our plans. It will be all but impossible to contract it. . . . Let us try to change the emphasis by promising relatively little and doing much."[58]

In only one respect did Reuben allow his economic and political philosophy to proclaim a goal for the Welfare Program that was beyond the resources of the Church. Although he consistently denied that the new program was intended to reestablish the United Order,[59] he proclaimed that it was intended to supplant the New Deal in the economic lives of the Latter-day Saints. In May 1936 the *New York Times* and the Associated Press reported his talk (in New York City) that the Church relief program intended to remove the 88,000 needy Latter-day Saints from government relief rolls and make them self-supporting.[60] At the October 1936 general conference, President Clark proclaimed, "If we should fail in this, and the Lord will not let us fail, great would be our condemnation," and less than a year later the General Church Welfare Committee agreed "to take one county at a time in the State of Utah and to clear this county entirely of the LDS cases now on county relief."[61] Although officially the Church did not oppose government work programs such as the WPA,[62] President Clark maintained that any form of economic relief was the responsibility of churches and charitable organizations, "and not a problem of government." He went on to say that he was convinced that "many of those on WPA were not very active members of the Church . . . [and] were members in name only."[63]

The Church Welfare Program succeeded in many ways, but failed to fulfill President Clark's hope that it would supplant New Deal economic aid among the Latter-day Saints. In 1937–38 the General Welfare Committee ascertained that Utah ranked fifth nationally in reception of direct government relief, and that the percentage of Utah's working force in federal work projects was consistently above the national average: 19.6 percent above for the WPA, 100 percent above for the CCC, 33.3 percent for NYA, and 33.3 percent above for participation in other government agencies. As one member of the committee remarked, "more success could be attained by the

Church Security Program if there was not the excellent competition offered by the Government."[64] The national press made similar observations about Mormons who were on government relief despite the Welfare Program.[65]

President Clark's intention to substitute the Welfare Plan for New Deal relief inevitably undercut his repeated affirmations that the Welfare Plan was not politically motivated, and the result was that anti-New Dealers supported the program and New Dealers opposed it. Politically conservative magazines throughout the nation regarded it as "an anti-New Dealer's dream come true," and the liberal press labeled the Welfare Plan as "an ultra-conservative gesture of withdrawal."[66] Nearly all of the General Authorities shared Reuben's attitudes toward government assistance, and they wholeheartedly supported the philosophy and conduct of the Welfare Plan as he envisioned it. But those authorities who were sympathetic to the New Deal in the 1930s wanted to soften the program's effort to supplant government aid to the needy. President Clark commented on this in a memo to President Grant in 1937.[67] Even the installation of a new Presiding Bishopric the following year did not solve the divergence in attitude toward the relationship of Church welfare and New Deal aid.[68] Nevertheless, the authorities of the Church sought to harmoniously carry out decisions of the First Presidency on these matters.

However, opposition to the Welfare Program was dramatic among local leaders and members of the Church, 70 percent of whom were New Dealers.[69] President Clark told Church welfare workers that "all the critics of the Welfare Program were members of the Church," and that from the beginning these critics thought it was "a scheme of Republican Clark to turn out the Democratic Party."[70] As late as 1944-45 he told general conferences of the Church that bishops and stake presidents were refusing to support the Welfare Program, and that these opponents were proclaiming that it was a failure, "professing to see in it some deep-laid political scheme."[71] After the death of Franklin D. Roosevelt, the New Deal ceased to be such a divisive issue among the Latter-day Saints, and they were better able to appreciate the real achievements of the Welfare Plan in a nonpartisan light.

President Clark himself was able to make such an assessment less than three years after the announcement of the program. In view of criticism by the national press and opposition even by Church members to the Welfare Program at this time, his remarks to the General Welfare Committee in January 1939 deserve close attention:

I don't believe that you have a thorough appreciation of what you have really done. I think the achievements of this Welfare Plan are not only outstanding, but they are so great that we had no right really to expect that they could be what they have been.

I think your achievements can be divided into two headings, and the first and most important item I would call the intangibles. In the first place you have thoroughly mapped the terrain, the whole area, over which you are operating, and that is no small job.... In the second place you have discovered your weak spots.... Then, the third thing you have done is to bring to the people a consciousness of the program and what it is trying to do. That is no small achievement....

. . . .

Your tangibles you fail to appreciate and what you have done in this way. Your central storehouses, your stake storehouses, your industries—you have your projects you have taken on, your coal mine, saw-mills and all of the others. They are all really great achievements not only of themselves but in the fact that you have shown the way.

Then, of course, you have done a marvelous job in the production of foodstuffs, clothing, fuel, shelter. That was in a way, your initial problem, and you have particularly brought the consciousness of the people to this problem. If you have to intensify it at a later time there will be no real difficulty in increasing it. The problem of distribution you have been working on.... Labor is still your greatest problem. How you are going to put these people to work and at what, and to get to them the idea that they should work for what they get. You will not be able to do this fully until a change comes in our national policy. With the government spending billions, compared with our thousands, it isn't possible not to have a reaction against the plan. This will all work out in time.[72]

He spoke these words at the first meeting of the General Welfare Committee in 1939, the year the Church reached its Depression apex of providing assistance to 155,460 Latter-day Saints. As a wartime economy and mobilization ended the national depression that the New Deal was unsuccessful in ending, Church members participated in the general recovery and the numbers receiving Church assistance plummeted.[73] At the Welfare meeting of April 1940 general conference, Reuben was euphoric:

Now, my brothers and sisters, we are over the hump. There have been times when I have been anxious about this work. I wondered, my faith must have been weak, I wondered whether we could compete with all of the free stuff that was being handed out. But, I am over that and this enterprise is undertaking. It is over the hump.[74]

At the same time Reuben was reporting the successful and permanent establishment of the Welfare Program to his co-workers, he was also launching what Marion G. Romney has described as J. Reuben Clark's second most important contribution to the Church—a reorganization of Church finances.[75] The first element of that contribution was the establishment of a general Church budget for each year's expenditures. In Reuben's words:

Living within your income requires the making of a budget, then of course afterwards living within your budget. I may say that I think until 1938 or 1939 the Church had never had really a budget prepared beforehand; there was always a complete accounting for funds expended, but apparently before that time it was never projected what would be needed for this item, that item, and the other item. Since 1939 we have had a budget and we have guided our course by it.[76]

COURTESY DESERET NEWS

President Clark's three closest associates in the Welfare Program, 1948: Elder Harold B. Lee, managing director; Elder Henry D. Moyle, chairman of the general committee; and Elder Marion G. Romney, assistant managing director.

President Clark proposed the introduction of a comprehensive Church budget in 1939 in order to control in advance the kinds of expenditures that had exceeded Church revenues during the previous two years. Welfare activities severely drained Church resources, but he was determined that the Church would not attempt to relieve economic distress through deficit spending.[77]

In his efforts to have the Church live well within its income, President Clark gained a reputation for parsimony. "Some of our own members seem to be thinking that the Church too has a pile of gold," he told the April 1938 general conference. "It has not. All the Church has is the moderate income it receives from investments it has made out of the savings from your past contributions, and the tithing and donations which you faithful members—usually not the critics and fault-finders—make for the support of the work."[78] Publicly and privately he insisted that the Church leaders must protect the sacred trust of donated monies by the most careful expenditure of funds. From 1943 to 1945, for example, he pared down Church expenditures to only 27 percent of annual revenues, holding the balance in reserve for the postwar depression he expected.[79] But he was not satisifed with saving 73 percent of Church income in reserve annually; in 1945 he privately "expressed some anxieties about Church finances."[80] As the end of the war brought continued prosperity and the long-postponed opportunity to build needed chapels, Church expenditures increased. In 1947 Reuben was able to hold only 36 percent of Church income in reserve, and he expressed his anxiety to the general conference of April 1948: "The expenditures of the Church are increasing at what seems to me to be a disturbing rate. . . . I should like to urge the people to cease building cathedrals for ward meetinghouses, and to stop furnishing them as if they were palaces."[81]

Aside from his philosophy of budgets and expenditures, Reuben introduced an administrative reorganization of Church finances. At a First Presidency meeting early in 1941, President Grant referred to the periodic efforts during the previous sixty years to satisfactorily balance the roles of the Presidency and the Presiding Bishopric in the administration of Church funds. Reuben later noted, "I took it therefore upon myself to make a study of the financial operations of the Church from the beginning down through and until after the death of the Prophet." His sources for that understanding were the Doctrine and Covenants and the seven-volume *History of the Church,* and Reuben also spent five months in 1941 consulting with the financial secretaries of the First Presidency in order to ask them questions about Church finances and to compile a "Compendium of Information on Financial and Property Interests of the Church." Having amassed the necessary sources, Reuben then began to study them carefully. But because he did this at his own initiative, his administrative sense of propriety dictated that it had "to be done of course always at nights." It took him two years of evening work in his home library to research these sources, to contemplate the doctrinal, historical, and current financial situation, and to draft a proposal for reorganizing the administration of Church finances. He presented it to the combined meeting of the First Presidency and Quorum of the Twelve Apostles on 8 April 1943.[82]

In a comprehensive presentation, Reuben reviewed the revelations concerning the collection and administration of Church funds and the history of the Church. He noted:

I am impressed with this fact, that while the Prophet in his thinking was frequently ahead of the revelations which he received due to inspiration of course, nevertheless, he did not see the thing from the beginning, and the Lord gave these general instructions, and the brethren more or less floundered about within broad limits as to the details of the situation which they set up.[83]

President Clark then proposed that: (1) the Presiding Bishopric be responsible for receipt of tithing and fast offerings, the Welfare Committee for the proceeds of welfare production, and the First Presidency for all other revenues from all other sources; (2) a Committee on Budget be comprised of the First Presidency, two or three members of the Council of the Twelve, and Presiding Bishopric in order to approve in advance a binding budget of expenses, and that the Committee on Expenditures be likewise comprised for the actual expenditure of budgeted funds; (3) there be subcommittees on expenditures for such areas as building, purchases, missions, and ranches; and (4) administration of fast offerings and welfare production be administered by members of the First Presidency, Presiding Bishopric, and Welfare Committee.[84]

Elder Harold B. Lee described this as "a most historical meeting," and Elder George Albert Smith noted, "I think the proposition now involves this body of men individually as nothing else has in a long time. We will be assuming a responsibility that we have been relieved of for a long time—I speak of the Twelve. The Presidency have carried the burden and the Presiding Bishopric."[85] President Clark was gratified at the enthusiastic response from the Apostles and other members of the First Presidency, but he was stunned after the meeting when the Church historian brought a copy of an unpublished revelation President Joseph F. Smith received on 1 November 1918 which provided for the kind of reorganization in the administration of Church finances that Reuben had just presented. "I had never seen or heard of this 'revelation' till Brother Joseph Fielding Smith mentioned it in Council Meeting on April 8/43. He brought it to me to read at 3:30 p.m. April 8/43, my first view." For President Clark it was an inspiring and humbling evidence that the work he had taken "upon myself" had divine approval.[86]

The outline of responsibilities for the receipt and disbursement of Church funds was only the first part of the financial reorganization President Clark introduced in 1943. At the heart of his two years of work was his detailed "General Principles Underlying Church Finances," which received the unanimous approval of the First Presidency and the Quorum of the Twelve on 29 April 1943. Reuben's opening remarks provided a sufficient summary of the philosophy governing the lengthy document:

We start out with the basic purpose and mission of the Church which may be briefly stated thus: To work out the purposes of God among and for His children upon this earth by saving the living and by saving the dead. Therefore the test of every Church financial operation, both incoming and outgoing, is, Does this help to carry out the purpose and mission of the Church? This principle we have behind us at all times.[87]

Following the approval and implementation of this financial reorganization, President Clark announced its basic outlines to the general conference of October 1943.[88]

In pursuing his philosophy toward the financial mission of the Church, President Clark regarded Church-owned or -controlled businesses as a special challenge. He explained his attitude toward such enterprises in a letter to Elder John A. Widtsoe:

Furthermore, I think there was none of them organized for the mere purpose of making money. They were all organized to help develop this great Intermountain community and to help stabilize the financial and industrial conditions to the direct benefit of all our people in the areas affected. . . .[89]

Because of that view, President Clark actually wanted to discourage Church-owned or -controlled businesses from "making so much money; there is no difficulty in making money, the question is making too much," as he told a meeting of the Quorum of the Twelve.[90] When the president of one Church-owned company said that it was "making too much money, I told him that was the situation of all of our enterprises."[91] J. Reuben Clark was an officer or director of many Church-affiliated businesses, but he displayed a consistent disdain for commercialism. To him, these businesses were part of the sacred trust of the Church rather than the freewheeling enterprise of capitalism.

In his administration of Church finances as a sacred trust, Reuben went to great lengths to avoid both the appearance and substance of profiting from his Church position. He told the general priesthood meeting in April 1935, "There is a general impression, I am told, that I am a man of wealth. My Brethren, I am not." Six years later he was amused to receive an invitation from a New York law firm for him to purchase the New York Yankees baseball team, to which he responded: "Your letter of the thirtieth ultimo constitutes one of the high spots in my life. It is one of the few real compliments I have ever had paid me. . . . I could not buy the boy that carried the water to the team, much less the team itself."[92] President Clark refused to accept payment or honoraria for his many Church publications or for public speaking even at non-Church functions after he entered the First Presidency. If someone still sent him a check in payment for such activities, he either returned it or turned it over to the Primary Children's Hospital.[93] In addition to his tithing and other regular Church donations, Reuben also gave the use of his flour mill in Grantsville to the Welfare Program.[94] In terms of Church compensation, President Clark either declined to receive or accepted only part of the salary he was authorized as an officer of Church-affiliated corporations, and in 1950 he refused to accept the 5 percent increase in compensation authorized by the Church President.[95] Reuben sought in every dimension of his life to safeguard what he regarded as the awesome responsibility he had in the management of and response toward the funds of the Church and the welfare of the people.

During the last decade of his life, the expansion of the Church in membership brought tremendous increases in both the revenues and expenditures of the Church. "A new year in the financial history of the Church began in 1950–51!" stated a new financial secretary to the First Presidency. He reported that tithing revenues paralleled state and national personal income for eleven years. But starting with 1951, Church income commenced to rise independently.[96] With the Presidency of David O. McKay, Church membership grew at a dizzying pace. Corresponding increases in tithing revenues required either increased investment of the Church's reserve income or greatly increased Church expenditures to keep the reserves in control. President McKay chose to do both, and ushered in an era in which the Church's investment portfolio expanded and diversified at the same time the Church spent tens of millions of dollars on expanding Brigham Young University and other educational facilities, on building

President Clark at his Grantsville ranch, April 1959.

new temples and chapels throughout the world, on microfilming genealogical records, on caring for increased welfare needs of a membership that was doubling every twenty years, on developing public relations exhibits and media, and on related expenditures. Although the momentum for this change in Church finances had been developing for years, it seemed to explode at the time of David O. McKay's Presidency. His optimistic, expansive personality was equal to the new financial circumstances that confronted the Church as it accelerated into becoming a world religion.

As counselor in the Presidency, Reuben had supervised finances and welfare through the harrowing Great Depression and the uncertainties of a wartime economy, and it was difficult for him to accept expansively administered Church finance. Concerning the Church's investment portfolio of its reserve fund, he expressed opposition to the "investment of Church funds in governments or in other securities."[97] As Church-affiliated businesses became ever more profitable, he said "that was not, as I had always understood, the prime purpose. I then said it looked as if we were going to take the funds of the Church and try to make money out of them. . . ."[98] By 1960 President Clark wanted to curtail all construction on Church schools in the United States and all buildings in Europe.[99] He had already raised a warning voice about Church expenditures at general conference: ". . . but I do know this, that in the carrying on of human undertakings, wherever you begin to make great expenditures of money there is always some lack of wisdom, sometimes a lack of foresight."[100] This was vintage J. Reuben Clark, who had carefully husbanded Church finances for nearly two decades as his responsibility for the "welfare of the people."

In the last years of his life, President Clark's apprehensions about Church growth and even about the permanence of his contributions to the Welfare Program[101] brought him much unnecessary distress. In the early 1940s he had stated that the growth of the Church would one day bring such large revenues that either spending them or saving them would be problematical, and that the Welfare Program might need to contract as well as expand.[102] When these changes did occur, Reuben felt himself in decline physically and personally and regarded them with suspicion. But it was Reuben's decade-long policy of keeping more than 70 percent of Church revenues in reserve that provided the solid financial basis for the enormous expansion of Church expenditures in the last decade of his life. And the continued vitality of the Welfare Plan and its importance to the Saints is indicated by the growth of the program from 1946 to 1960. In 1946 the scope of the plan became international as the Church sent 85 railroad freightcars of food, clothing, and bedding to war-devastated European Saints. The value of commodities in bishop's storehouses increased from $385,836 in 1946 to $2,420,770 in 1960, total assets of the Welfare Plan increased from $4 million to $44 million, and the number of families assisted increased from eight to twenty-seven thousand.[103] Throughout his service in the First Presidency, J. Reuben Clark's devotion to the cause of the Latter-day Saints was unfailing, and his contribution to their welfare and the financial stability of the Church remain a lasting legacy.

International Church Welfare Plan: the first convoy of sixty tons of foodstuffs en route to the starving German Saints after World War II. These particular foodstuffs were prepared by the Dutch Saints following the visit of Elder Ezra Taft Benson as the Church's first emissary to war-ravaged Europe.

"IN HONORABLE REMEMBRANCE"

Doctrine and Covenants 124:96

Reuben's life was one-third in the nineteenth century and two-thirds in the twentieth, and he reflected both eras. The educated, middle-class, white, Anglo-Saxon Americans of the late-nineteenth century tended to be intensely nationalistic, pessimistic regarding human nature but optimistic toward America's destiny, fearful of foreigners, confident of natural laws and of one's own world view, apprehensive of social change, opposed to government domestic intervention except to preserve civil order, intensely partisan in politics, legalistic, and fervent in the belief that the U.S. Constitution and capitalism were divinely sanctioned.[1] In all these respects, Reuben was a typical nineteenth-century man throughout his life.

But even while relatively young, Reuben also was more typically a twentieth-century Mormon. He did not feel the nineteenth-century Mormon's zeal for the security of life in the tightly knit Zion of the West, nor did he regard the metropolitan East as simply an unpleasant stopover. Like most mid-twentieth-century Mormons, Reuben appreciated the Church society of Zion but was willing to live in religious minority or isolation in order to develop his talents and profession.

The intersection of J. Reuben Clark's civic life and his service to the Church demonstrated the Mormon rejection of the traditional secular-sacred division. "All things to me are spiritual" were the words of an early revelation to Joseph Smith. Theologically, Mormonism rejects the idea that the spiritual and material are distinct, or that the religious and secular are incompatible. Prior to his call to the First Presidency, Reuben unflinchingly demonstrated his Mormonism at the same time he was undeniably very much in the world. He was a secular Saint and maintained his integrity in both the secular and religious spheres of his life. As an elder statesman in the First Presidency, he continued to be a secular Saint and contributed to both spheres of endeavor. His life stands as refutation of the idea that one cannot be both religious and secular.

The unusual circumstances of his call to the First Presidency will probably always distinguish J. Reuben Clark in Church administrative history. The untypical qualities of his background prior to that calling are without parallel: no administrative experience whatever in branch, ward, district, stake, or mission leadership; his entire previous Church experience limited to Sunday School teacher and auxiliary board member; absent most of his adult life (including the years immediately prior to his call) from an organized stake of the Church. Yet he was called as counselor to the Church President, served in that capacity longer than anyone else, and is one of the most recognized names among Latter-day Saints.

Of the many tributes expressed concerning J. Reuben Clark's service to the Church, Spencer W. Kimball's brief statement may be the best: "What leadership you have given to this Church! What power! What vigor! You have been an example to all the people and will be long remembered and quoted."[2]

Quotes from President Clark's talks have found their way into dozens of Church lesson manuals, hundreds of general conference talks, and several anthologies in the years since his death. Quite simply, J. Reuben Clark was an eminently quotable speaker. He was a profound exponent of the topics he treated; he was a master of the English language, and in a nearly unprecedented way he introduced the Latter-day Saints to sermons that were scholarly as well as eloquent. But J. Reuben Clark could have had the halting speech of a Moses and still he would have left a profound legacy through his administrative influence on the Church.

The Church was more than a century old when J. Reuben Clark entered the office of the First Presidency, but he permanently altered the conduct of administrative matters within that office. Nearly twenty years after President Clark's death, D. Arthur Haycock, secretary to the Church President, said, "In the Presidency's office today, most of the procedures and language phrasing we use were developed by J. Reuben Clark."[3] With the perspectives gained as a second-ranking official in the burgeoning federal bureaucracy, J. Reuben Clark anticipated the necessary administrative adjustments that the First Presidency's Office would need as it coped with an international and massive population growth.

Although the Church Presidents he served made final decisions about any recommendations by a counselor, President Clark advocated an impressive list of Church innovations; some of these the Church Presidents authorized him to implement and others were refined and introduced years later by other Church authorities. Among the long-lasting Church contributions which J. Reuben Clark originally proposed were the centrally directed Church Welfare Plan, reorganization of Church finances, establishment of Assistants to the Quorum of the Twelve Apostles, establishment of regional priesthood leadership, closed-circuit media broadcasts of general conferences to outlying Church wards and stakes, simultaneous translation of general conferences into the languages of non-English speakers, and construction of multi-ward buildings. Although resistant to social change, President Clark was in the vanguard of innovation in Church administration.

Equally important was the seeming contradiction that the innovative President Clark was also a bulwark of stability within an often-buffeted First Presidency. Reuben distinguished himself during these years as an articulate, calm, and unyielding exponent of views approved by the Church President but opposed by a large sector of the membership. Even more important, when the Church for the first time faced the administrative challenge of prolonged sickness of the Prophet, Reuben provided complete stability and avoided self-aggrandizement. His life will remain as an extraordinary example of integrity and loyalty.

Although J. Reuben Clark's strongly stated views were not always the universal expression of other General Authorities, he became an advocate for several positions to which members of the Church continue to refer: the importance of refraining from dogmatism about unessential theologies, the dangers of rationalized religion, the evils of government support as a social system, the difficulties of exporting Americanism to non-American converts to the Church, the imperatives of peace compared with the horrors of even just war, the unparalleled threat of philosophical and institutional communism, and the stabilities of the U.S. Constitution.

An obvious manifestation of J. Reuben Clark's administrative heritage lies in the men whom he trained and influenced who continue to lead the Church. In the years since President Clark's death his protégés and close associates have continued to serve in the First Presidency: Church Presidents Joseph Fielding Smith, Harold B. Lee, Spencer W. Kimball, and Counselors Henry D. Moyle, Joseph Fielding Smith, Harold B. Lee, and Marion G. Romney. Literally thousands of other Church leaders, from General Authorities to ward bishops, look to J. Reuben Clark as their spiritual, philosophical, and administrative mentor. The measure of his continuing legacy is that many of these Latter-day Saints who revere J. Reuben Clark were not adults or even born during his service in the First Presidency.

LIST OF ABBREVIATIONS

(To accompany Notes)

Individuals, works, collections, and archives cited numerous times throughout the notes are abbreviated below.

Clark, *Messages of the First Presidency* James R. Clark, ed., *Messages of the First Presidency of the Church of Jesus Christ of Latter-day Saints: Introduction, Notes, and Index,* 6 vols. (Salt Lake City: Bookcraft, 1965–1975)

Dialogue *Dialogue: A Journal of Mormon Thought*

Fox, *JRC* Frank W. Fox, *J. Reuben Clark: The Public Years* (Provo and Salt Lake City: Brigham Young University Press and Deseret Book, 1980)

HBLL Harold B. Lee Library, Brigham Young University, Provo, Utah

HDC Historical Department, Church of Jesus Christ of Latter-day Saints, Salt Lake City

JRC J. Reuben Clark, Jr.

JRCP J. Reuben Clark, Jr. Papers, Harold B. Lee Library, Brigham Young University, Provo, Utah

JWML J. Willard Marriott Library, University of Utah, Salt Lake City

Nibley, *Presidents of the Church* Preston Nibley, *The Presidents of the Church,* rev. ed. (Salt Lake City: Deseret Book, 1971)

PC Private Collection

SFP George A. Smith Family Papers, J. Willard Marriott Library, University of Utah, Salt Lake City

USHS Utah State Historical Society, Salt Lake City

NOTES

THE WASTE PLACES OF ZION

1. The most reliable general histories of the LDS Church and the Mormons are: James B. Allen and Glen M. Leonard, *The Story of the Latter-day Saints* (Salt Lake City: Deseret Book, 1976), and Leonard J. Arrington and Davis Bitton, *The Mormon Experience* (New York: Knopf, 1979).

2. For a detailed presentation of JRC's secular career, see Fox, *JRC.*

3. A useful presentation of JRC's childhood and youth is David H. Yarn Jr., *Young Reuben: The Early Life of J. Reuben Clark, Jr.* (Provo, Utah: Brigham Young University Press, 1973).

4. Andrew Jenson, *Encyclopedic History of the Church of Jesus Christ of Latter-day Saints* (Salt Lake City: Deseret News, 1941), 299.

5. Leonard J. Arrington, *From Quaker to Latter-day Saint: Bishop Edwin D. Woolley* (Salt Lake City: Deseret Book, 1976), 73, 74, 375, 404, 455; William E. Hunter, *Edward Hunter, Faithful Steward* (Salt Lake City: Mrs. William E. Hunter, 1970), 234–50.

6. JRC membership card, Deceased Membership File, HDC.

7. Heber J. Grant Journal, 30 October, 11 November 1900, HDC; Francis M. Gibbons, *Heber J. Grant: Man of Steel, Prophet of God* (Salt Lake City: Deseret Book, 1979), 19–20, 39–40; Arrington, *From Quaker to Latter-day Saint*, 482–83; "Journal of Rachel Emma Woolley Simmons," *Heart Throbs of the West* 11 (1950):197.

8. Heber J. Grant Journal, 7 October 1881, HDC; Gibbons, *Heber J. Grant.*

9. Joshua R. Clark Diary, 22 December 1880, JRCP.

10. Yarn, *Young Reuben,* 24–25.

11. Joshua R. Clark Diary, 9 December 1885, 19 December 1887, JRCP.

12. Ibid., 30 March 1890.

13. JRC to Priesthood Meeting, 8 October 1938, manuscript, Box 151; JRC to Roscoe Grover, 18 April 1934, Folder 3, Box 351; JRCP.

14. JRC Office Diary, 23 October 1959, JRCP.

15. Yarn, *Young Reuben,* 45–54; Fox, *JRC,* 10–12.

16. Yarn, *Young Reuben,* 59.

17. Fox, *JRC,* 15.

18. *Deseret News Church Section,* 23 June 1956, 4.

19. Concerning the intertwined histories of the three institutions, see D. Michael Quinn, "The Brief Career of Young University at Salt Lake City," *Utah Historical Quarterly* 41 (Winter 1973):69–89.

20. JRC Scrapbook, 6 October 1897, JRCP; *Salt Lake Tribune,* 16 June 1898.

21. James E. Talmage Journal, 14 September 1898, HBLL. Talmage was given the sealing power as a temple worker thirteen years before he became an Apostle.

22. Joshua R. Clark Diary, 1 January 1891, JRCP.

23. Ibid., 16 January 1891.

24. John R. Talmage, *The Talmage Story: Life of James E. Talmage–Educator, Scientist, Apostle* (Salt Lake City: Bookcraft, 1972), 154–59. For examples of doctrines that were regularized or rejected altogether, see James E. Talmage Journal, 29 November 1893, 5 January 1894, 13 January 1899, HBLL. See also Thomas G. Alexander, "The Reconstruction of Mormon Doctrine: From Joseph Smith to Progressive Theology," *Sunstone* 5 (July–August 1980):27–31.

25. *Deseret News Church Section,* 23 June 1956, 4.

26. "Two Years in the Service Can Be Profitable," *Improvement Era* 55 (August 1952):611.

27. William James Mortimer, ed., *How Beautiful Upon the Mountains: A Centennial History of Wasatch County* (N.p.: Wasatch County Chapter of the Daughters of Utah Pioneers, 1963), 85.

28. Lute to Ida, 25 January 1899, Box 328, JRCP.

29. Fox, *JRC,* 19.

30. Yarn, *Young Reuben,* 98.

31. Ibid., 102–16; Fox, *JRC,* 19–20.

32. Fox, *JRC,* 21–22.

33. JRC remarks to Missionary Meeting, 4 April 1958, in April 1958 Conference Binder, Box 167, JRCP.

34. JRC to R. W. Madsen, Orval W. Adams, and Herbert A. Snow, 5 September 1951, Folder 2, Box 364, JRCP.

35. JRC to William Cullen Dennis, 30 June 1910, Folder 10, Box 343, JRCP.

36. JRC to Bishops' Meeting, 3 April 1953, Box 151, JRCP.

37. Fox, *JRC,* 27–41.

38. Ibid., 42–215.

39. Ibid., 234–365.

40. JRC talk in men's portion of MIA Conference, 9 June 1934, manuscript, Box 151, JRCP; remarks paraphrased in *Deseret News,* 9 June 1934, 1.

41. Fox, *JRC,* 366–75.

42. Marianne Clark Sharp Oral History, 1977, The James Moyle Oral History Program, 2, 9, HDC.

43. Lute to JRC, 24 April 1923, Folder 1, Box 333; Luacine S. Clark Autobiography; JRCP; Fox, *JRC,* 414.

44. Luacine S. Clark letters to JRC, Boxes 32 and 33, JRCP; "The Prophet's Sailing Orders to Relief Society," *Relief Society Magazine* 36 (December 1949):797.

45. Marianne Clark Sharp Oral History, 18.

46. Fox, *JRC,* 380–81.

47. Marianne Clark Sharp Oral History, 7.

48. Ibid., 14.

49.   Ibid., 5–7; Fox, *JRC,* 377; Joshua R. Clark Diary, 7 January 1886, JRCP; Lute to JRC, 6 January 1923, Folder 3, Box 333, JRCP; Reed Smoot Diary, 14 February, 7 March, 4 July 1909, 16 January, 17 December 1910, HBLL; Gene A. Sessions, *Mormon Democrat: The Religious and Political Memoirs of James Henry Moyle* (Salt Lake City: The Historical Department of The Church of Jesus Christ of Latter-day Saints, 1975), 248–51.

50.   Lute to JRC, 3 October 1906, also 21 September 1906, Box 328, JRCP.

51.   *Proceedings Before the Committee on Privileges and Elections of the United States Senate in the Matter of the Protests Against the Right of Hon. Reed Smoot, a Senator from the State of Utah, to Hold His Seat,* 4 vols. (Washington, D.C.: Government Printing Office, 1904–1907), 3:183, 184, 189, 207; Reed Smoot Diary, 8 May and 27 November 1910, 8 January, 12 February, 13 August, 19 November, 3 December, 17 December 1911, 21 January, 3 March, 21 April, 5 May, 1 December 1912, 13 January, 26 April 1913, HBLL.

52.   Sessions, *Mormon Democrat,* 251; Fox, *JRC,* 432.

53.   JRC 1907 Memorandum Book, Box 2, JRCP.

54.   JRC, "Letter to Pa on my position," in 1907 Notebook, Folder E9, Box 16, JRCP.

55.   JRC Memorandum no. 6, Folder J9, Box 90, JRCP, dated 4 February 1914, but from context of memorandum, it was written on 4 March; JRC Memorandum, "Knowledge and Belief," no. 31, Folder J9, Box 90, JRCP.

56.   JRC talk outlines in Box 90, JRCP.

57.   JRC Diaries, 19 July, 8 November 1914, 3 January, 22 August 1915, 23 April 1922, JRCP.

58.   Lute to JRC, second letter of 12 February 1923, Folder 1, Box 333, JRCP.

59.   Fox, *JRC,* 433; Lute to JRC, 30 October 1906, Box 328; JRC financial records, Box 512; JRCP.

60.   Fox, *JRC,* 432; JRC to James E. Talmage, 24 November 1912, Box 346, JRCP.

61.   Allen and Leonard, *Story of the Latter-day Saints,* 441–44.

62.   Fox, *JRC,* 434–35.

63.   JRC Conversation with Mathonihah Thomas, 2 March 1914, Memorandum no. 6, Folder J9, Box 90, JRCP.

64.   JRC Memorandum, "Knowledge and Belief," no. 31, Folder J9, Box 90, JRCP.

65.   JRC Memorandum, "Are We Not Only Entitled But Expected to Think for Ourselves," Box 90, JRCP.

66.   JRC Memorandum nos. 3 and 20, Folder J9, Box 90, JRCP.

67.   JRC to Cloyd H. Marvin, 1 December 1956, Binder of JRC-Marvin Correspondence, Box 189, JRCP.

68.   Ibid., 9 December 1959.

69.   JRC to Mrs. Harold M. Stephens, 4 November 1960, Folder 13, Box 409; JRC to Cloyd H. Marvin, 1 December 1956, JRC-Marvin Binder, Box 189; JRCP.

70.   *April 1950 Conference Report,* 182, HDC; JRC to Jesse R. S. Budge, 15 October 1953, Folder 3, Box 390, JRCP.

71.   Fox, *JRC,* 415–18.

72.   Lute to JRC, 6 January 1923, Folder 1, Box 333, JRCP.

73.   Ibid., 14 January 1923.

74.   Ibid., 24 April, 25 April, 17 March, 29 April 1923.

75.   Ibid., 9 April 1923, first letter of that date; Fox, *JRC,* 442.

76.   JRC Diary, 21 May 1923, JRCP.

77.   Fox, *JRC,* 360.

78.   Lute to JRC, 17 July, 21 July 1923, Folder 1, Box 333, JRCP.

79. JRC talks, Boxes 114 and 115, JRCP; Washington D.C. Branch Sacrament Meeting Minutes, 1923–1930, HDC.

80. JRC talk to Deseret Sunday School Union on 6 October 1947. "The bulk of the work which I did in the Church until I was called to my present position was as a teacher in the Sunday Schools." He then referred to the pre-Columbia classes he taught, followed by his teaching the adult class in the 1923–25 period. (Manuscript in Box 151; course outlines in Box 115; JRCP.)

81. *Deseret News,* 8 June 1925.

82. JRC talks, Box 115, JRCP.

83. JRC to Fred Morris Dearing, quoted in Fox, *JRC,* 387.

84. Ibid., 451–75.

85. Ibid., 476–502.

86. Ibid., 503–30.

87. Ibid., 531–84; *Register of the Department of State, January 1, 1929* (Washington: Government Printing Office, 1929), 41–67.

88. Fox, *JRC,* 550.

89. JRC Account Book of Embassy, 1932–1933, Folder R46, Box 45a, JRCP.

90. JRC to S. Wayne Clark, 23 August 1943, Folder 1, Box 367, JRCP.

91. Emilio Portes Gil, *The Conflict Between the Civil Power and the Clergy* (Mexico City, 1934); Charles S. Macfarland, *Chaos in Mexico: The conflict of Church and State* (New York: Harper & Brothers, 1935), 246; G. Baez Camargo and Kenneth G. Grubb, *Religion in the Republic of Mexico* (London: World Dominion Press, 1935).

92. Luacine S. Clark Diary, 16 November 1930 to February 1933, JRCP.

93. JRC to J. R. Bost, 22 July 1932, Folder R17, Box 40, JRCP.

94. Luacine S. Clark Diary, 4 January, 1 March, 16 August 1931, JRCP.

95. Ibid., 4 April, 16 August 1931, 12 February 1933.

96. JRC ("Hubpop") to Lute, undated, 1930 Folder, Box 335, JRCP.

97. Heber J. Grant letters to JRC, Folder 3, Box 334, JRCP; JRC to A. W. Ivins, 9 February 1931, Ivins Papers, USHS: Luacine S. Clark Diary, 18 August 1932, 12 February 1933, JRCP.

98. Luacine S. Clark Diary, 15 February 1931, JRCP.

99. Ibid., 15 November 1931.

100. Ibid., 8 February 1931; chapter, "Precious Things of Every Kind and Art," this volume.

101. JRC to J. Reuben Clark III, 23 May 1929, Box 335, JRCP.

102. JRC to Ivor Sharp, undated, in Box 335, JRCP.

103. JRC to John A. Widtsoe, 8 December 1929, Box 27, JRCP.

104. George D. Parkinson, "How A Utah Boy Won His Way," *Improvement Era* 17 (April 1914):557.

105. Lute to JRC, 15 August 1918, Folder 1, Box 332, JRCP.

106. James B. Allen, "Personal Faith and Public Policy: Some Timely Observations on the League of Nations Controversy in Utah," *BYU Studies* 14 (Autumn 1973):83–98; Fox, *JRC,* 293–95.

107. JRC Diary, 18 June, 28 June 1920, JRCP.

108. JRC to Heber J. Grant, 24 May 1922, Box 344, JRCP; and Box 24, CR 1/44, HDC.

109. Heber J. Grant to JRC, 8 June 1922, Box 24, CR 1/44, HDC.

110. JRC Church Document no. 9, Box 114, JRCP.

111. *Salt Lake Tribune,* 10 May 1924, 7.

112. Folder N5, Box 29; JRC to Heber J. Grant and David O. McKay, 18 May 1936, Folder 1, Box 355, JRCP; and JRC Folder, CR 1/48, HDC; Heber J. Grant Journal, 2 February 1926, HDC.

113. *April 1926 Conference Report,* 11, HDC.

114. *October 1930 Conference Report,* 97, HDC.

115. S. J. Quinney to JRC, 19 May 1931, and JRC to S. J. Quinney, 27 May 1931, Folder 13, Box 39, JRCP.

116. N. Eldon Tanner, "The Administration of the Church," *Ensign* (November 1979):44; Heber J. Grant Journal, 21 May 1931, HDC.

117. Heber J. Grant Journal, 29 May, 1 October 1931.

118. Reed Smoot Diary, 28 May 1925, HBLL.

119. Related by Heber J. Grant to his granddaughter's husband, Waldo M. Anderson. Anderson to Rowena J. Miller, 31 January 1961, with comment by JRC to his secretary, Folder 1, Box 410, JRCP.

120. Author's interview with Louise Clark Bennion and Marianne Clark Sharp, 7 November 1977.

121. Heber J. Grant and Anthony W. Ivins to JRC, 19 December 1931, JRC Folder, CR 1/48, HDC. JRC referred to his foreknowledge of the contents of the letter on 4 July 1960, Spencer W. Kimball Journal, PC.

122. Marianne C. Sharp, "Born to Greatness: The Story of President J. Reuben Clark, Jr.," *The Children's Friend* 53 (September 1954):362.

123. JRC to Mrs. Levi Edgar Young, 23 February 1938, attached to JRC letter to Heber J. Grant and David O. McKay, 23 February 1938, JRC Folder, CR 1/48, HDC; JRC to Oscar R. Houston, 4 March 1957, Folder 1, Box 399, JRCP.

124. JRC to Heber J. Grant and Anthony W. Ivins, 19 [*sic*] December 1931, JRC Folder, CR 1/48, HDC.

125. Author's interview with Louise Clark Bennion, Marianne Clark Sharp, and J. Reuben Clark III, 7 November 1977; Joseph Anderson, *Prophets I have Known* (Salt Lake City: Deseret Book, 1973), 90; Marianne Clark Sharp Oral History, 42.

126. JRC to Heber J. Grant and Anthony W. Ivins, 28 December 1931, with folds matching the accompanying letter and memorandum, JRC Folder, CR 1/48, HDC.

127. Anthony W. Ivins Diary, 2 January 1932, USHS; A. W. Ivins to Heber J. Grant, 2 January 1932, JRC Folder, CR 1/48, HDC.

128. JRC to Heber J. Grant, 9 January 1932, JRC Folder, CR 1/48, HDC.

129. Heber J. Grant to JRC, 4 March 1932, and JRC to Heber J. Grant, 11 March 1932, JRC Folder, CR 1/48, HDC; JRC to Anthony W. Ivins, 11 March 1932, Ivins Papers, USHS.

130. Related by JRC in Spencer W. Kimball Journal, 4 July 1960, PC; Heber J. Grant Journal, 9 March 1932, HDC.

131. JRC to Heber J. Grant and A. W. Ivins, 11 March, 20 June 1932, JRC Folder, CR 1/48, HDC.

132. JRC to A. W. Ivins, 28 August 1932, Ivins Collection, USHS.

133. JRC to "Dear Brethren," 16 December 1932, ibid.

134. JRC to Louis S. Cates, 4 May 1932, Folder R17, Box 40, JRCP.

135. *Deseret News,* 29 October 1932; *Salt Lake Telegram,* 3 November 1932.

136. D. C. Davies to JRC, 11 January 1933, and Marianne C. Sharp ("Mem") to JRC, 18 March 1933; Box 336, JRCP.

137. *Austin Statesman,* 16 February 1933; *Salt Lake Telegram,* 18 March 1933.

138. Heber J. Grant Journal, 20 March 1932, HDC; author's interview with Louise Clark Bennion and Marianne Clark Sharp, 7 November 1977.

DIFFERENCES OF ADMINISTRATION

1. JRC to Deseret Sunday School Union, 6 October 1947, Box 151, JRCP.

2. Marion G. Romney Oral History, 1976, 14, HDC; author's interview with Spencer W. Kimball, 2 February 1979.

3. Frank W. Asper to JRC, 5 August 1939, Folder 1, Box 361, JRCP.

4. Lute to JRC, 15 May 1923, Folder 1, Box 333, JRCP.

5. JRC to Frank and Gertrude Clark, 17 November 1953, Folder 5, Box 388, JRCP.

6. JRC to W. Paul Chipman, 8 March 1956, Folder 1, Box 396, JRCP.

7. Examples in JRC Office Diary: 13 February 1935, 5; 24 April 1936, 2; 8 July 1940; 17 July 1940; JRCP.

8. Ibid., 23 November 1949.

9. JRC to Mrs. B. H. Stradling, 27 December 1949, Folder 4, Box 379, JRCP; author's interview with Marion G. Romney, 26 October 1977.

10. JRC Office Diary, 10 July 1939, JRCP.

11. JRC to "Brother and Sister" Reynold Irwin, 2 March 1956, Folder 2, Box 397, JRCP.

12. JRC Office Diary, 2 July 1948, JRCP. David O. McKay also stated this in *Deseret News Church Section,* 11 June 1952, 3. Harold B. Lee quoted JRC as saying, "When we were discussing some subject the President would turn to each of us and say, 'What do you think about this?' or 'What is your opinion?' When he asked me I gave it to him straight from the shoulder, as forthrightly as I knew how, even though my opinion was sometimes contrary to his. Then there was the business of resolving our different points of view. But when the President of the Church finaly declared, 'Brethren, I feel that this should be our decision,' President Clark said, 'That was the Prophet speaking, and I stopped counseling and accepted without question the decision that he thus announced.' " ("Elder Lee Pays Tribute to A Great Leader," *Deseret News Church Section,* 14 October 1961, 14.)

13. JRC to Frank R. Clark, 1 June 1945, Folder 3, Box 371, JRCP.

14. Ernest L. Wilkinson Diary, 17 April 1960, HBLL. Henry D. Moyle made this statement while he and JRC were counselors in the First Presidency.

15. JRC Office Diary, 7 March 1947, JRCP.

16. Ibid., 24 May 1933.

17. Ibid., 19 April 1950.

18. *April 1940 Conference Report,* 14, HDC.

19. JRC to F**** H. J****, 17 August 1943, Folder 2, Box 411, JRCP.

20. Marion G. Romney Diary, 18 November 1952, PC.

21. Ernest L. Wilkinson Diary, 30 March 1956, HBLL.

22. Rowena J. Miller to Mrs. Robert F. Bird, 20 March 1950, Folder 2, Box 381, JRCP.

23. Related by several General Authorities to John K. Edmunds, former president of the Chicago Stake and of the Salt Lake Temple (Edmunds Oral History, 1979–80, typescript, volume 2, 102, HDC).

24. JRC to Richard R. Lyman, 31 October 1933, Box 349, JRCP.

25. JRC to Franklin S. Harris, 5 November 1931, Box 38, JRCP.

26. JRC to Bishop's Meeting, 5 April 1949, manuscript, Box 151, JRCP.

THREE PRESIDING HIGH PRIESTS: HEBER J. GRANT

1. *April 1933 Conference Report,* 102, HDC.
2. JRC Scrapbook; JRC Office Diary; JRC 1933 Memorandum Book; JRCP.
3. JRC Office Diary, 3 May, 22 May, 24 May, 20 July, 28 August, 31 August 1933, JRCP.
4. Heber J. Grant to John A. Widtsoe, 20 March 1936, Box 97, CR 1/44, HDC.
5. JRC to J. C. Grey, 20 October 1941, Folder 1, Box 363, JRCP.
6. JRC to Bryant S. Hinckley, 20 September 1956, Folder 6, Box 395, JRCP; Henry A. Smith, "Pres. Clark Notes 88th Anniversary," *Deseret News,* 1 September 1959.
7. JRC Office Diary, 14 September 1944, JRCP; JRC Folder, Post-Presidential Individual File, Herbert Hoover Presidential Library, West Branch, Iowa; *New York Herald Tribune,* 17 May 1934; *New York Sun,* 4 June 1934; *New York Times,* 7 May 1949, 4.
8. William H. Ryan to JRC, 6 October 1937, Folder 1, Box 357, JRCP.
9. JRC Office Diary, 17 April 1933, JRCP.
10. Ibid., 18 February 1958; *Deseret News,* 18 July 1958; Boxes 433–439, JRCP.
11. JRC Office Diary, 22–25 September 1933, JRCP.
12. *Deseret News,* 4 November 1933; Heber J. Grant Journal, 6 November 1933, HDC.
13. JRC to Samuel O. Bennion, 8 November 1937, Folder 1, Box 356, JRCP.
14. *New York Times,* 21 October 1933, 22; *Salt Lake Tribune,* 27 October 1933.
15. Fox, *JRC,* 594–96; Gene Allred Sessions, "Prophesying Upon the Bones: J. Reuben Clark, the Foreign Bondholders, and the Great Depression" (Ph.D. diss., Florida State University, 1974); Boxes 412–420, JRCP; Dana G. Munro, "Sweetening Sour Bond Issues," *World Affairs* 122 (Fall 1959):81.
16. *Deseret News,* 4 November, 10 November 1933; *Salt Lake Tribune,* 6 November 1933.
17. JRC Office Diary, 9 January 1934, JRCP.
18. Ibid., 14 January, 6 February, 7 February, 11 February, 12 February 1934.
19. Ibid., 6 February 1934; for discussion of JRC activities at the Montevideo conference, see Fox, *JRC,* 590–94; also Boxes 143–147, JRCP.
20. JRC Office Diary, 15–17 February 1934, JRCP
21. Lute to JRC, 23 October 1934, Box 336, JRCP.
22. Folder marked "Speeches, etc. (lists)" in Box 302, JRCP.
23. JRC to Samuel O. Bennion, 8 November 1937, Folder 1, Box 356, JRCP.
24. JRC Office Diary, 29 July 1933, 21 February, 4 March 1934, JRCP.
25. JRC to J. H. Gipson, 11 March 1954, Folder 1, Box 391, JRCP.
26. JRC Office Diary, 5 March 1934, JRCP.
27. Heber J. Grant Journal, 3 April 1934, HDC.
28. Heber J. Grant to JRC, 20 June 1934, JRC Folder, CR 1/48, HDC.
29. Noble Warrum to JRC, 7 May 1934, Folder 1, Box 351, JRCP; Heber J. Grant Journal, 5 May 1934, HDC.
30. *Deseret News,* 7 March 1934; *Salt Lake Tribune,* 4 April 1934.
31. JRC to Noble Warrum, 21 May 1934, Folder 1, Box 351, JRCP.
32. Harry Chandler to Heber J. Grant, 4 June 1934; A. A. Tilney to Heber J. Grant, 5 June 1934; JRC Folder, CR 1/48, HDC.
33. *Salt Lake Telegram,* 12 June 1934.
34. JRC to Heber J. Grant, 17 June 1934, 1:52 A.M., JRC Folder, CR 1/48, HDC; *Salt Lake Tribune,* 18 June 1934; *Deseret News,* 18 June 1934.

35. *Deseret News,* 18 June 1934; *New York Times,* 19 June 1934; Heber J. Grant to Preston D. Richards, 18 June 1934, JRC Folder, CR 1/48, HDC.

36. JRC Memorandum, "The Problem," 18 July 1934, Box 347; Albert E. Bowen to JRC, 13 July 1934, Box 347; JRCP. Emphasis in original memorandum.

37. *Salt Lake Tribune,* 18 June 1934, Harry S. Joseph to JRC, 18 June 1934, Box 347, JRCP and JRC Folder, CR 1/48, HDC.

38. JRC to J. Parley White, 2 July 1934, JRC Folder, CR 1/48, HDC; also White's letter to JRC of 26 June and JRC to Harry S. Joseph, both in Box 347, JRCP and JRC Folder, CR 1/48, HDC.

39. JRC to Heber J. Grant, 4 July 1934, Box 347, JRCP and JRC Folder, CR 1/48, HDC, and also USHS.

40. Heber J. Grant to JRC, 9 July 1934, JRC Folder, CR 1/48; Heber J. Grant Journal, 9–10 July 1934; HDC.

41. JRC to Heber J. Grant, 13 July 1934, Box 347, JRCP; JRC Folder, CR 1/48, HDC.

42. Robert Murray Stewart to JRC, 25 July 1934, Folder 1, Box 351, JRCP. Stewart was son-in-law of Elder George Albert Smith, and also one of JRC's staunchest advocates for the 1934 nomination.

43. JRC Memorandum, "The Problem," 18 July 1934, Box 347, JRCP (parentheses in original).

44. John Gunther's national best-seller, *Inside U.S.A.* (New York: Harper & Brothers, 1947) reported on page 202 an alleged long-distance telephone call between Presidents Ivins and Clark on this matter. His son, H. Grant Ivins, was cited on page 927 as one of Gunther's sources for the chapter in which this story appeared.

45. JRC Memorandum, "The Problem," 18 July 1934, Box 347, JRCP.

46. Transcript of telephone conversation between JRC and Heber J. Grant, 16 July 1934, JRC Folder, CR 1/48; Heber J. Grant Journal, 16 July 1934; JRC to Heber J. Grant, 13 July 1934, with "Received" stamp of 16 July 1934; JRC Folder, CR 1/48; HDC.

47. JRC to Byron D. Anderson, 17 July 1934, quoted in full in concurrent telegram of JRC to Heber J. Grant, 17 July 1934, 12:10 A.M., JRC Folder, CR 1/48, HDC; *Salt Lake Tribune,* 18 July 1934.

48. *Salt Lake Tribune,* 18 July 1934.

49. John A. Widtsoe to JRC, 26 July 1934, Folder 1, Box 351, JRCP.

50. Leonard J. Arrington, Feramorz Y. Fox, and Dean L. May, *Building the City of God: Community and Cooperation Among the Mormons* (Salt Lake City: Deseret Book, 1976), 338–39.

51. For a survey of the New Deal, see William E. Leuchtenburg, *Franklin D. Roosevelt and the New Deal, 1932–1940* (New York: Harper & Row, 1963).

52. Heber J. Grant Journal, 7 August 1940, HDC.

53. Heber J. Grant to Morton J. Theiband, 21 November 1936, Box 96, CR 1/44; Heber J. Grant Journal, 8 November 1938; HDC.

54. JRC Office Diary, 1 September 1933, JRCP.

55. Ibid., 12–13 September 1933.

56. *October 1933 Conference Report,* 64–65, 89, HDC.

57. Heber J. Grant Journal, 2 June 1934, HDC.

58. Heber J. Grant to JRC, 18 October 1940, Folder 7, Box 362, JRCP.

59. Heber J. Grant Journal, 17 June 1940; Franklin J. Murdock Oral History, 1973, 52; HDC; Gene A. Sessions, *Mormon Democrat: The Religious and Political Memoirs of James Henry Moyle* (Salt Lake City: The Historical Department of The Church of Jesus Christ of Latter-day Saints, 1975), 347.

60. Heber J. Grant Journal, 12 December 1941, HDC.

61. Heber J. Grant Journal, 21 September 1933, 4 October, 11 October 1934, HDC.

62. Sessions, *Mormon Democrat,* 340–42.

63. LeGrand Woolley to JRC, 17 April 1935, attached to April 1935 Conference Binder, Box 152, JRCP; *October 1934 Conference Report,* 98; *April 1935 Conference Report,* 95; HDC; Raymond Gram Swing, *Forerunners of American Fascism* (New York: J. Messner, 1935); Lawrence Dennis, *The Coming of American Fascism* (New York: Harper & Brothers, 1936); Edwin W. Green, *The Man Bilbo* (Baton Rouge: Louisiana State University Press, 1963); Harnett T. Kane, *Louisiana Hayride: The American Rehearsal for Dictatorship, 1928–1940* (New York: W. Morrow, 1941); Allan P. Sindler, *Huey Long's Louisiana: State Politics, 1920–1952* (Baltimore: Johns Hopkins University Press, 1956); T. Harry Williams, *Huey Long* (New York: Knopf, 1970); Gaetana Salvemini, *Italian Fascist Activities in the United States* (New York: Center for Migration Studies, 1977); Charles J. Tull, *Father Coughlin and the New Deal* (Syracuse, N.Y.: Syracuse University Press, 1965); Sheldon Marcus, *Father Coughlin: The Tumultuous Life of the Priest of the Little Flower* (Boston: Little, Brown, 1973); David H. Bennett, *Demagogues in the Depression: American Radicals and the Union Party* (New Brunswick, N.J.: Rutgers University Press, 1969); Jules Archer, *The Plot to Seize the White House* (New York: Hawthorne Books, 1973).

64. *Salt Lake Tribune,* 8 June 1935.

65. JRC to Heber J. Grant and David O. McKay, 18 May 1935, Heber J. Grant and David O. McKay to JRC, 21 May 1935, JRC Folder, CR 1/48, HDC; Folder U1, Box 149 and Folder 1, Box 365, JRCP.

66. Lute to JRC, 28 May 1935, Box 336, JRCP.

67. Ibid., 5 November 1935.

68. JRC Scrapbook and Office Diary, 15 June–11 July 1935, JRCP.

69. Louise and Reuben to Hon. and Mrs. J. Reuben Clark, 11 July 1935, Box 336, JRCP. Spelling and punctuation of the telegram have been standardized.

70. JRC to J. Reuben Clark III, 12 July 1935, Box 336, JRCP.

71. Heber J. Grant to Melvin D. Wells, 22 April 1936, quoted in Heber J. Grant Journal of same date, also entry of 18 April, HDC.

72. Heber J. Grant to John Connelly, 15 December 1937, Box 98, CR 1/44; Heber J. Grant Journal, 15 June 1936; HDC.

73. Example from Heber J. Grant Journal, 23 July 1924, HDC.

74. Sessions, *Mormon Democrat,* 341.

75. JRC to David O. McKay, 6 March 1936, Folder 1, Box 355, JRCP.

76. JRC Office Diary, 24 May 1958, JRCP; Donald R. McCoy, *Landon of Kansas* (Lincoln: University of Nebraska Press, 1966), 349, n. 19.

77. JRC to 1936 diary, 7–12 June 1936, JRCP; Heber J. Grant Journal, 15 June, 5 July 1936, HDC; JRC Scrapbook, JRCP.

78. Lute to JRC, 19 August, 20 August, 1936, Box 337, JRCP.

79. Ted Clark to JRC, 1 October 1936, Box 337, JRCP.

80. JRC to Fred S. Purnell, Director of the National Speakers Bureau of the Republican National Committee, 7 October 1936, Box 347, JRCP.

81. JRC 1936 Diary, 25–26 September, 18–22 October, JRCP; *New York Sun,* 22 October 1936.

82. Heber J. Grant Journal, 31 October 1936, JRCP.

83. Ibid.; *Deseret News,* 31 October 1936.

84. Sessions, *Mormon Democrat,* 341.

85. Folder 6, Box 8, CR 1/33, HDC.

86. Frank Herman Jonas, "Utah: Sagebrush Democracy," in *Rocky Mountain Politics,* ed. Thomas C. Connelly (Albuquerque: University of New Mexico Press, 1940), 34; Frank H.

Jonas and Garth N. Jones, "Utah Presidential Elections, 1896–1952," *Utah Historical Quarterly* 24 (October 1956):305.

87. Esther to "Reube, Lute and All," 12 November 1936, Box 337, JRCP.

88. JRC to general priesthood meeting, 5 April 1937, manuscript, Box 151, JRCP.

89. JRC to general priesthood meeting, 2 October 1937, manuscript, Box 151, JRCP.

90. Folder 6, Box 8, CR 1/33, HDC; LeGrand Woolley to JRC, 17 April 1935, attached to April 1935 Conference Binder, Box 152, JRCP; Heber J. Grant to David O. McKay, 16 August 1936, JRC Folder, CR 1/48, HDC; Sessions, *Mormon Democrat,* 343–44.

91. JRC to Fred Morris Dearing, 7 November 1958, Folder 6, Box 402, JRCP.

92. JRC to Daniel J. McRae, 1 September 1938, Folder 2, Box 359, JRCP; JRC to Herbert Hoover, 14 May 1942, 2, Post-Presidential Individual File, Herbert Hoover Presidential Library, West Branch, Iowa; *Deseret News Church Section,* 8 August 1951.

93. *October 1942 Conference Report,* 58, HDC.

94. JRC to N**** J*****, 15 April 1943, attached to April 1943 Conference Binder, Box 175; and Anonymous/Crank folders in Boxes 358, 361, 371, 373, 390, 392, 398, 401, 404, 407, 410, JRCP.

95. JRC to general priesthood meeting, 4 October 1947, manuscript, Box 151, JRCP. For JRC's acceptance of his own unpopularity with Church members, see JRC to Milton R. Merrill, 2 June 1941, Folder 2, Box 363, and JRC Office diary, 26 March 1945, JRCP.

96. JRC to General Welfare Committee, 10 April 1938, CR 255/5, HDC.

97. JRC to Lee B. Valentine, 15 August 1954, Folder 19, Box 391, JRCP.

98. Until 1940 David O. McKay had primary responsibility for governing the Welfare Program. In 1937, for example, JRC met only nine times with the welfare committee, in company with David O. McKay or Heber J. Grant, whereas David O. McKay met alone with the committee in exactly two-thirds of the meetings that year (CR 255/18, HDC). Also see chapter "The Welfare Of This People," this volume.

99. JRC to Heber J. Grant and David O. McKay, 1 December 1936, Folder 1, Box 355, JRCP.

100. Luacine to JRC, 9 February 1937, Box 337, JRCP.

101. Heber J. Grant Journal, 2 March, 7 April 1937, HDC.

102. Heber J. Grant to David O. McKay, 20 April 1937, and David O. McKay to Heber J. Grant, 21 April 1937, Folder 13, Box 101, CR 1/44, HDC.

103. JRC Memorandum, 21 March 1939, Folder 6, Box 112, CR 1/44, HDC; *Deseret News,* 28 December 1937, 1.

104. Heber J. Grant to JRC, 2 June 1937, JRC Folder, CR 1/48, HDC.

105. CR 255/18, HDC; Heber G. Wolsey, "The History of Radio Station KSL from 1922 to Television" (Ph.D. diss., Michigan State University, 1967), 222.

106. Heber J. Grant Journal, 9 December 1938, HDC.

107. JRC to special priesthood meeting, 8 April 1939, manuscript, Box 151, JRCP.

108. JRC to Bishops' Meeting, 4 October 1940, manuscript, Box 151, JRCP.

109. For JRC's response to Nazism and World War II, see chapter "They That Take the Sword," this volume.

110. Gilbert W. Scharffs, *Mormonism in Germany: A History of the Church of Jesus Christ of Latter-day Saints in Germany Between 1840 and 1970* (Salt Lake City: Deseret Book, 1970), 91.

111. JRC Office Diary, 21 July 1939, JRCP.

112. Heber J. Grant Journal, 25 [*sic*] August 1939, HDC; Scharffs, *Mormonism in Germany,* 92; Allen and Leonard, *Story of the Latter-day Saints,* 542.

113. Joseph Fielding Smith Jr. and John J. Stewart, *The Life of Joseph Fielding Smith, Tenth President of the Church of Jesus Christ of Latter-day Saints* (Salt Lake City: Deseret Book, 1972), 275.

114. Ibid., 276–81; Scharffs, *Mormonism in Germany,* 92–99. For a detailed study, see David F. Boone, "The Worldwide Evacuation of Latter-day Saint Missionaries at the Beginning of World War II" (Master's thesis, Brigham Young University, 1981).

115. Examples: *New York Sun,* 18 October, 15 December 1939, 11 September 1940; *New York Times,* 2 August 1937, p. 21, 19 September 1937, Section 2, p. 1, 20 September 1937, p. 44, 17 November 1938, p. 37, 16 December 1939, p. 10, 21 November 1945, p. 31.

116. JRC Memorandum, 6 May 1938, Folder 10, Box 360, JRCP.

117. JRC Office Diary, 4 February 1940, JRCP.

118. JRC to J. H. Gipson, President of Caxton Printers, 22 September 1943, Folder 2, Box 367; JRC to Clarence Cowan, 18 June 1945, Folder 3, Box 371; JRCP.

119. Heber J. Grant Journal, 20 October 1933, 7 November 1939, 19 October 1942, HDC.

120. JRC to Church Welfare Committees, April 1938, manuscript, Box 151, JRCP.

121. David O. McKay Diary, 30 November 1939, HDC; Francis M. Gibbons, *Heber J. Grant: Man of Steel, Prophet of God* (Salt Lake City: Deseret Book, 1979), 214–18; *October 1941 Conference Report,* 6, HDC.

122. Reported retrospectively in Spencer W. Kimball Journal, 30 December 1943, PC.

123. Frank Evans Diary, 15 September 1942, HDC; Gibbons, *Heber J. Grant,* 218–30; Nibley, *Presidents of the Church,* 258–60; Heber J. Grant Journal, 1 January–20 January 1941, 1 July–31 December 1943, HDC; Joseph Fielding Smith Journal, 3 June 1943, 15 February 1945, HDC.

124. JRC Office Diary, 2 March, 4 March 1940, JRCP; David O. McKay Diary, 14 March 1940, 3 December 1943, HDC.

125. David O. McKay Diary, passim, HDC; Nibley, *Presidents of the Church,* 338.

126. JRC to Louise Bennion, 13 December 1940, Box 338, JRCP.

127. Marion G. Romney Diary, 28 August 1942, PC. At this time, Elder Romney was an Assistant to the Quorum of the Twelve Apostles. See also Sessions, *Mormon Democrat,* 346.

128. JRC to Heber J. Grant and David O. McKay, 15 February 1940, JRC File, CR 1/48, and Folder 3, Box 4, David O. McKay Papers, HDC.

129. JRC Office Diary, 15 March 1940, JRCP.

130. Ibid., 22 May 1940, 28 April 1943, 24 October 1944, 16 February, 25 February, 11 March 1945; Heber J. Grant Journal, 24 August 1941, HDC.

131. JRC Office Diary, 26 January 1943, JRCP.

132. Ibid., 4 March, 1 April 1940.

133. Ibid., 3 June 1940.

134. Ibid., 12 January 1943; Heber J. Grant Journal, 27 January 1943, HDC.

135. JRC Office Diary, 22 May 1940, 5 February and 16 February 1945, JRCP.

136. Ibid., 15 October 1943.

137. Heber J. Grant Journal, 29 July, 7 August, 30 September, 1 October, 18 October 1940, HDC.

138. Ibid., 30 October 1940; JRC Office Diary, 13 October 1940, JRCP.

139. *Deseret News,* 31 October, 1 November 1940; JRC editorials, Box 208, JRCP; Jonas and Jones, "Utah Presidential Elections," 304.

140. *Deseret News,* 19 October 1940, 1.

141. JRC Office Diary, 19 February 1941, JRCP; Heber J. Grant Journal, 15 March, 6 April 1941, HDC; Gibbons, *Heber J. Grant,* 226.

142. "Assistants to the 12" Folder, CR 1/48, HDC.

143. Ibid.; JRC Office Diary, 14 March 1941, JRCP; *April 1941 Conference Report,* 1, and Heber J. Grant Journal, 15 May 1941, HDC.

144. JRC Office Diary, 9 March 1941, JRCP; Heber J. Grant Journal, 9 March, 6 April 1941, HDC.

145. Heber J. Grant Journal, 7 June 1941, HDC.

146. JRC to Gordon W. Clark, 30 October 1940, Box 338, JRCP. See chapter "They That Take the Sword," this volume.

147. JRC Office Diary, 7 December, 10 December 1941, JRCP.

148. Harold B. Lee Diary, 13 December 1941, 18 September 1942, PC; JRC to Severo Mallet-Prevost, 2 February 1942, Folder 2, Box 365, JRCP.

149. Heber J. Grant Journal, 6 April, 3 October 1942, HDC.

150. Ibid., 6 February 1943.

151. "Budget Beginnings" Binder, Box 188, JRCP; Heber J. Grant Journal, 28 April 1943, HDC; chapter "The Welfare of This People," this volume.

152. Joseph Fielding Smith Journal, 3 June 1943, HDC.

153. Heber J. Grant Journal, 1 July 1943, and entry for the inclusive period 1 July–31 December 1943, HDC; author's interview on 1 March 1980 with A. Hamer Reiser, former manager of Deseret Book Company, counselor in general Sunday School presidency, and former assistant secretary to the First Presidency who also served as chauffeur for J. Reuben Clark from 1957 to 1961 when President Clark had difficulty in driving and walking.

Based on interviews with twenty-one influential Utahns, Gunther's 1947 *Inside U.S.A.* stated on page 202: "Clark's great days came in the period of Grant's senescence. Ivins died, and from 1934 to 1945 he practically ran the church singlehanded. Not since the days of Brigham Young have the Latter Day Saints [*sic*] known such vigorous rule, I heard it said, and as a consequence Clark became highly unpopular in some circles." Nevertheless, President Clark's unavoidable ascendance in the 1940s must be placed in the context of his conscientious efforts to avoid increasing his power, as discussed in this chapter. President Clark dismissed Gunther's assessment with the comment "that the stuff about his taking over the Church is the purest kind of bunk." (JRC Office Diary, 6 May 1947, JRCP.)

154. *Deseret News,* 13 July, 11 August, 7 October 1943.

155. JRC Office Diary, 10 January, 12 January, 24 February, 26 March, 1 April, 3 April, 2 May 1944, JRCP.

156. Harold B. Lee Diary, 5 July, 11 July, 12 July, 18 July, 31 July, 2 August 1944, PC.

157. JRC Office Diary, 10 August, 8 November 1944, 26 June 1950, JRCP.

158. Ibid., 24 October, 3 November 1944.

159. Ibid., 20–23 January, 2–5 March, 27 September–1 October, 20 November 1944.

160. Harold B. Lee Diary, 1 February 1945, PC; JRC Office Diary, 4 February, 16 February, 25 February, 11 March 1945, JRCP.

161. Marianne Clark Sharp Oral History, 47, 52; Belle S. Spafford Oral History, 1975–76, typescript, 79–80; HDC; JRC Office Diary, 4–5 April 1945, JRCP; *April 1945 Conference Report,* 14, HDC.

162. Marianne C. Sharp to JRC, 10 October 1946, and JRC to Marianne C. Sharp, 11 December 1946, October 1946 Folder, Box 158, JRCP.

163. George F. Richards Journal, 14 May 1945, HDC.

164. Harold B. Lee Diary, 15 May 1945, PC.

165. Spencer W. Kimball Journal, 18 May 1945, PC.

THREE PRESIDING HIGH PRIESTS:
GEORGE ALBERT SMITH

1. George Albert Smith Patriarchal Blessing by Zebedee Coltrin, 16 January 1884, Folder 13, Box 96, SFP; Merlo J. Pusey, *Builders of the Kingdom: George A. Smith, John Henry Smith, George Albert Smith* (Provo, Utah: Brigham Young University Press, 1981), 114, 196, 208.

2. *Deseret News,* 21 May 1945, 1; Harold B. Lee Diary, 21 May 1945, PC; Edward L. Kimball and Andrew E. Kimball Jr., *Spencer W. Kimball, Twelfth President of the Church of Jesus Christ of Latter-day Saints* (Salt Lake City: Bookcraft, 1977), 220–21.

3. C. N. L*** to George Albert Smith, ca. May 1945, Folder 8, Box 68, SFP; author's interview on 21 October 1977 with Eldred G. Smith, Patriarch to the Church from 1947 to 1979.

4. Harold B. Lee Diary, 26 May 1945, PC; JRC to James Grafton Rogers of Foreign Bondholders' Protective Council, 15 June 1945, Folder 11, Box 372, JRCP.

5. George Albert Smith Diary, 27 June 1945.

6. Nibley, *Presidents of the Church,* 276.

7. George Albert Smith Diary, 25 February 1909, SFP; Dr. Heber J. Sears to George Albert Smith, 12 April 1909, Folder 11, Box 27, SFP; Glen R. Stubbs, "A Biography of George Albert Smith, 1870 to 1951" (Ph.D. diss., Brigham Young University, 1974), 101.

8. George Albert Smith Diary, 8 January, 24 January, 25 February, 19 March–23 March, 31 March–21 April, 24 August, 28 August, 3 October, 3 November 1909–8 May 1910, 25 June, 10 July, 1 August, 12 September, 24 October, 28 November 1910, 20 January 1911, 14 May 1912–18 May 1913, SFP; Stubbs, "Biography of George Albert Smith," 101–21; Pusey, *Builders of the Kingdom,* 250–52.

9. Heber J. Grant Journal, 16 August 1930, HDC.

10. George Albert Smith Diary, 14 January, 19 January, 3 March, 7 March 1932, 2 January, 6 January 1933, SFP. Also earlier entries for 12 August–26 October 1930, 23–24 September, 9 October, 27 October 1930, ibid.; and Pusey, *Builders of the Kingdom,* 287, 303.

11. JRC Office Diary, 11 July, 15 September 1950, JRCP. In an earlier conversation with President Smith's brother, JRC said "it was too bad he could not feel to rely upon himself [JRC] and Pres. McKay in the matter of handling the correspondence." (JRC Office Diary, 22 January 1949, JRCP.)

12. Pusey, *Builders of the Kingdom,* 245, 288, 294, 342.

13. Author's interview with Spencer W. Kimball, 2 February 1979. Also, author's interview on 1 March 1980 with A. Hamer Reiser, former manager of Deseret Book Company and former assistant secretary to the First Presidency, who stated that President Smith's dependence on his strong-willed daughter Emily was a well-known undercurrent throughout his entire administration as President.

14. JRC Office Diary, 26 April 1949, JRCP.

15. Ibid., 3 August 1945; summary of JRC daily activities from April 1933 to April 1945 in folder marked "Speeches, etc. (lists)," in Box 302, JRCP.

16. *Deseret News,* 8 November 1947, 30 November 1948; attendance of JRC at respective directors' meetings in Boxes 412–419, 423–439, JRCP.

17. *Deseret News,* 21 November 1945, 14 November 1947; JRC Office Diary, 3 April 1948, Boxes 299, 440–442, JRCP.

18. JRC Office Diary, 21 March 1946; JRC Scrapbook, 4 April 1949; JRCP.

19. *Deseret News Church Section,* 29 September 1945.

20. Ibid.; Albert Zobell, Jr., "Dedication Proceedings," *Improvement Era* 48 (October 1945):565.

21. JRC to Bishops' Meeting, 5 April 1946, manuscript, Box 151, JRCP.

22. See sermon outline notes attached to transcriptions of his conference talks from 1933 to 1960 in JRCP.

23. Harold B. Lee Diary, 2–3 October 1943, PC. Joseph Fielding Smith was equally opposed to the practice: "Prepared speeches made days in advance, perhaps weeks, do not breathe the spirit of the occasion." (Joseph Fielding Smith Journal, 6 April 1945, HDC.)

24. JRC to Bishops' Meeting, 5 April 1946, manuscript, Box 151, JRCP. As late as 1958, President Clark was still privately urging general authorities to stop reading their general conference talks (Marion G. Romney Diary, 8 April 1958, PC).

25. JRC Office Diary, 2 May 1944, JRCP.

26. Harold B. Lee Diary, 12 November 1946, PC. For President Smith's enthusiasm about the activity approach to YMMIA, see Pusey, *Builders of the Kingdom,* 289.

27. James B. Allen and Glen M. Leonard, *Story of the Latter-day Saints* (Salt Lake City: Deseret Book, 1976), 478, 603–4.

28. JRC Office Diary, 7–8 May, 15 September 1947, JRCP.

29. *October 1947 Conference Report,* 155, 160. Also see JRC, *To Them of the Last Wagon* (Salt Lake City: Deseret News Press, 1947).

30. Ibid., 158.

31. Author's interview with Marion G. Romney, 26 October 1977; John J. Shumway to JRC, 8 April 1943 Conference Folder, Box 157, JRCP.

32. Henry D. Moyle Diary, 10 June 1951, HDC; George Albert Smith Diary, 9 April 1950, SFP.

33. *October 1947 Conference Report,* 156–57, HDC.

34. JRC, *On the Way to Immortality and Eternal Life* (Salt Lake City: Deseret Book, 1949), 20–21.

35. Ibid., "Note" on xiii.

36. JRC Office Diary, 25 February, 2 March, 8 March 1948, JRCP; JRC, *On the Way to Immortality and Eternal Life,* 225–444; *The* [Intermountain Catholic] *Register* for 1948–1949; Harold B. Lee Diary, 6 April 1949, PC; *April 1949 Conference Report,* 162, HDC; David O. McKay Diary, 28 August, 12 October 1949, HDC; George Albert Smith Diary, 24 September 1949, SFP.

37. *The Christian Register* 129 (April 1950):2.

38. JRC Office Diary, 12 June 1948, JRCP.

39. Harold B. Lee Diary, 1 July 1948, PC.

40. George Albert Smith Diary, 6 October 1948, 14 January, 8 February–March 1949, SFP; *April 1949 Conference Report,* 1, HDC; Pusey, *Builders of the Kingdom,* 344–46.

41. JRC Office Diary, 22 January 1949; JRC to John C. Traphagen and Hendon Chubb, 11 April 1949, Folder 11, Box 380; JRC to Helen Morgan, 3 May 1949, Folder 4, Box 380; JRCP.

42. George Albert Smith Diary, 5 May 1949, SFP.

43. David O. McKay Diary, 15 July 1949, HDC.

44. JRC to VaLois Chipman, 14 September 1949, Folder 3, Box 379, JRCP.

45. George Albert Smith Diary, 9 October 1949, SFP.

46. JRC Office Diary, 19 October 1949, JRCP.

47. E.g., George Albert Smith Diary, 3 August 1949, SFP.

48. Ibid., 27 December 1949.

49. Ibid., 12 January–27 February, 17 March–27 March, 30 July–29 August 1950; Pusey, *Builders of the Kingdom,* 352–55.

50. JRC to Helen Morgan and Archer Morgan, 23 January 1950, Folder 6, Box 382, JRCP.

51. JRC Office Diary, 18–22 September 1950, JRCP; George Albert Smith Diary, 19 September 1950, SFP; Harold B. Lee Diary, 22 September 1950, PC.

52. JRC to Monte L. Bean, 26 September 1950, Folder 2, Box 381, JRCP.

53. George Albert Smith Diary, 24 October, 18 November 1950, 29 January 1951, SFP; JRC Office Diary for the same period, JRCP; Stubbs, "Biography of George Albert Smith," 428.

54. George Albert Smith Diary, 14 Februry 1951, SFP.

55. Nurses' Notes, 25 February–4 April 1951, Folder 6, Box 96, SFP; George Albert Smith Diary, 25 February–4 April 1951, SFP; JRC Office Diary, 13 March, 30 March 1951, JRCP. George Albert Smith's Diary for this period maintains first-person narrative, but his actual physical and mental condition made it impossible for him to attend to his diary, and the entries for the last several months of his life were provided by others. Pusey, *Builders of the Kingdom,* 357–58.

56. David O. McKay Diary, 2 April 1951, *April 1951 Conference Report,* 157, HDC.

57. David O. McKay Diary, 4 April 1951, HDC; JRC Office Diary, 4 April 1951, JRCP; Pusey, *Builders of the Kingdom,* 359.

58. Spencer W. Kimball Journal, 6 April 1951, PC; *April 1951 Conference Report,* 3, 38, HDC.

THREE PRESIDING HIGH PRIESTS: DAVID O. McKAY

1. Lute ("Wiflets") to JRC, 19 July 1908, Box 328, JRCP.

2. Heber J. Grant Journal, 27 September 1934, HDC.

3. *October 1934 Conference Report,* 90, HDC.

4. Leonard J. Arrington and Davis Bitton, *The Mormon Experience* (New York: Knopf, 1979), 339–40.

5. Jeanette McKay Morrell, *Highlights in the Life of President David O. McKay* (Salt Lake City: Deseret Book Company, 1966), 13–62; chapter "The Waste Places of Zion . . . The Rivers of Babylon," this volume; David O. McKay Card, Deceased Membership File, HDC.

6. David O. McKay was not related by kinship or marriage to any other General Authority, living or dead, at the time of his becoming a General Authority. JRC had only distant in-law relationships with other General Authorities, all but two of whom were dead in 1933. His brother was married to a granddaughter of Robert T. Burton of the Presiding Bishopric; his deceased uncle had been a stepfather of B. H. Roberts of the First Council of Seventy; his uncle had married an aunt of former Elder Matthias F. Cowley; his first cousin married former Elder John W. Taylor; a cousin and an uncle married children of former Elder Erastus Snow; an uncle married a daughter of former Elder Charles C. Rich; and other cousins married descendants of former Elders Orson Hyde and Marriner W. Merrill and of former counselor in the Presiding Bishopric, Orrin P. Miller. See D. Michael Quinn, "Organizational Development and Social Origins of the Mormon Hierarchy, 1832–1932" (Master's thesis, University of Utah, 1973), 162, 225; Preston Woolley Parkinson, *The Utah Woolley Family* (Salt Lake City: By the Author, 1967), 198–200, 219, 232–33, 321, 334, 357, 459, 549, 612.

7. Marion G. Romney Diary, 28 August 1942, PC.

8. Author's interview with Marion G. Romney, 26 October 1977.

9. *Conference Reports,* HDC; Box 151, JRCP; David O. McKay, *Gospel Ideals* (Salt Lake City: The Improvement Era, 1953), index; McKay, *Treasures of Life,* Clare Middlemiss, comp. (Salt Lake City: Deseret Book, 1962), index.

10. Ernest L. Wilkinson Diary, 31 July 1960, HBLL.

11. Clare Middlemiss, comp., *Cherished Experiences from the Writings of David O. McKay* (Salt Lake City: Deseret Book Company, 1955), 14, 16, 18, 67, 73–78, 101–2, 145, 155, 161–63; *April 1949 Conference Report,* 182, HDC; JRC talk "Testimony," 23 September 1928, no. 45, Box 114, JRCP. Cf. Heber J. Grant Journal, 4 October 1942, HDC; JRC to Mrs. Francis Huntington-Wilson, 29 March 1947, Folder 13, Box 378, JRCP; JRC to MIA Conference, 14 June 1953, in *Deseret News Church Section,* 20 June 1953, 4.

12. JRC to Cloyd H. Marvin, 2 August 1957, Binder of JRC-Marvin Correspondence, Box 189, JRCP.

13. JRC Office Diary, 22 August 1939, JRCP. Also Marion G. Romney Oral History, 1976, 14, HDC; author's interview with Spencer W. Kimball, 2 February 1979; author's interview with A. Hamer Reiser, 1 March 1980; Harold B. Lee Diary, 11 August 1944, PC.

14. JRC Office Diary, 6 March 1947, JRCP. Also Ernest L. Wilkinson Diary, 20 August 1957, HBLL.

15. JRC to Milton R. Merrill, 2 June 1941, Folder 2, Box 363; Frank W. Asper to JRC, 5 August 1939, Folder 1, Box 361, JRCP.

16. Ernest L. Wilkinson Diary, 22 July 1954, 25 February 1955, 24 May 1957, 11 June 1960, HBLL. Also, this is implicit in David O. McKay's Office Diary, HDC.

17. Rowena J. Miller to Mrs. Robert F. Bird, 20 March 1950, Folder 2, Box 381, JRCP; Fox, *JRC,* 231.

18. David O. McKay, *True to the Faith,* comp. by Lleweln R. McKay (Salt Lake City: Bookcraft, 1966), 192–93; David O. McKay, *Treasures of Life,* 536; *October 1928 Conference Report,* 37, HDC.

19. Nibley, *Presidents of the Church,* 313–33; *April 1927 Conference Report,* 82, HDC.

20. Joseph A. Geddes, "I Remember the Utah Self-Help Cooperative Board," manuscript, 4, USHS.

21. "Mormon Mixup," *Time,* 19 October 1942. Cf. Clark, *Messages of the First Presidency* 6:170–85; *October 1942 Conference Report,* 15–16, 68, HDC; JRC to Jonathan W. Snow, 9 December 1942, attached to October 1942 Conference Binder, Box 156, JRCP.

22. John Gunther, *Inside U.S.A.* (New York: Harper & Brothers, 1947), 202–3.

23. Lute to JRC, 26 April 1938, Box 337, JRCP.

24. Author's interview with Spencer W. Kimball, 2 February 1979. Two Church administrators during this period, Gordon Burt Affleck (an avowed "Clark man") and A. Hamer Reiser (an avowed "McKay man"), provided to the author in separate interviews their assessments of those General Authorities who gravitated toward the philosophy and administrative style of either JRC or of David O. McKay, in the manner indicated by President Kimball. JRC's closest supporters were Joseph Fielding Smith, John A. Widtsoe, Charles A. Callis, Albert E. Bowen, Harold B. Lee, Spencer W. Kimball, Ezra Taft Benson, Mark E. Petersen, Matthew Cowley, Henry D. Moyle, Marion G. Romney, and LeGrand Richards of the Quorum of the Twelve, and Joseph L. Wirthlin of the Presiding Bishopric. President McKay's closest supporters while JRC was in the First Presidency were Stephen L Richards, Adam S. Bennion, and Hugh B. Brown of the Quorum of the Twelve, and Thomas E. McKay, Alvin R. Dyer, and N. Eldon Tanner of the Assistants to the Twelve, Marion D. Hanks of the First Council of Seventy, and Thorpe B. Isaacson of the Presiding Bishopric. Despite such personal alignments, all the General Authorities were loyal to both Presidents McKay and Clark.

25. Lute to JRC, 11 August 1936, Box 337; JRC Office Diary, 10 September 1946; JRCP; author's interview with Louise Clark Bennion, 7 November 1977.

26. JRC to David O. McKay, Folder 7, Box 26, McKay Papers, HDC.

27. David O. McKay Office Diary, 11 April, 13 May 1938, 20 July 1945, HDC; JRC Office Diary, 2 March 1940, 13 November 1946, 28 April 1950, JRCP.

28. Lute to JRC, 14 January and 10 November 1935, Box 336, JRCP.

29. JRC Office Diary, 2 June 1944, JRCP. Also statement by JRC in Spencer W. Kimball Journal, 4 July 1960, PC.

30. Author's interview with A. Hamer Reiser, former assistant secretary to the First Presidency, 1 March 1980.

31. Spencer W. Kimball Journal, 8 April 1951, PC.

32. Ernest L. Wilkinson Diary, 28 April 1960, HBLL.

33. JRC Office Diary, 8 April 1951, JRCP; author's interview with Louise Clark Bennion, 7 November 1977.

34. *April 1951 Conference Report*, 80, HDC.

35. JRC to Lute, 4 June 1929, Box 335, JRCP.

36. Spencer W. Kimball Journal, 8 April 1951, PC. Quoted in part in Edward L. Kimball and Andrew E. Kimball, Jr., *Spencer W. Kimball, Twelfth President of The Church of Jesus Christ of Latter-day Saints* (Salt Lake City: Bookcraft, 1977), 268. Also, Harold B. Lee Diary, 8 April 1951, PC.

37. Marianne C. Sharp to "Dearest Daddy," 19 April 1951, Folder 7, Box 383, JRCP.

38. *April 1951 Conference Report*, 151, HDC.

39. Ibid., 154.

40. Spencer W. Kimball Journal, 9 April 1951, PC. Order of quotes altered here.

41. Joseph Anderson, *Prophets I Have Known* (Salt Lake City: Deseret Book, 1973), 82.

42. Spencer W. Kimball Journal, 9 April 1951, PC.

43. Tyler Abell, ed., *Drew Pearson Diaries, 1949-1959* (New York: Holt Rinehart and Winston, 1974), 201; JRC Office Diary, 28 May 1951, JRCP. A. Hamer Reiser, later assistant secretary to the First Presidency and an avowed "McKay man," remembered that President McKay's 1951 choice of counselors "was interpreted by some people as a demotion for President Clark, and there was some flurry about it among the people, some gossip developed, and there was some uneasiness. Some people were critical and even vocalized their criticism." (A. Hamer Reiser Oral History, 1974, typescript, volume 3, 17, HDC). John K. Edmunds, then president of the Chicago Stake and later president of the Salt Lake Temple, said: "I heard a lot of brethren talk about that remark. Some of them wondered how President Clark could continue in the Presidency and wondered if he would resign his position in the Church and so on.... People felt that he was being demoted" (John K. Edmunds Oral History, 1979-1980, typescript, volume 2, 103, HDC).

44. Marianne C. Sharp to JRC, 19 April 1951, Folder 7, Box 383, JRCP.

45. JRC Office Diary, 11 April 1951, JRCP.

46. JRC to A. Helen Morgan, 12 May 1951, Folder 1, Box 384, JRCP.

47. Marion G. Romney Diary, 13 April 1951, PC.

48. David O. McKay Diary, 20 April 1951, HDC; *Report of "This is the Place" Monument Commission* (Salt Lake City: n.p., 1947), 5.

49. JRC to Stephen L and Irene Richards, 27 December 1957 and 14 September 1949, Boxes 399 and 380, JRCP.

50. Harold B. Lee Diary, 3 May 1951, PC.

51. *Deseret News Church Section*, 20 June 1951, 4.

52. E. LeRoy Hatch Oral History, 1974, typescript, 43-44, HDC.

53. Harold B. Lee Diary, 7 June 1951, PC.

54. Stephen L Richards Office Diary, 30 August 1951, d 4796, HDC.

55. Author's interview with A. Hamer Reiser, 1 March 1980; also referred to in A. Hamer Reiser Oral History, 1974, typescript, volume 3, 78, HDC. Harold B. Lee Diary, 22 April 1955, PC.

56. Copy in JRC Scrapbook, ca. 19 February 1952, of Drew Pearson Report; JRC Office Diary, 25 February 1952; JRCP.

57. Marion G. Romney Oral History, 1976, 8, HDC; Harold B. Lee Diary, 27 January 1952, 6 October 1955, PC; Ernest L. Wilkinson Diary, 24 February 1960, HBLL.

58. Keith Terry, *David O. McKay: Prophet of Love* (Santa Barbara, Calif.: Butterfly, 1980), 100.

59. Ibid., 183; Ernest L. Wilkinson Diary, 14 September 1960, HBLL; author's interview with A. Hamer Reiser, 1 March 1980.

60. JRC Office Diary, 10–11 May, 18 June 1951, 17 March, 14 July 1953, 2 January 1957, JRCP; Marion G. Romney Diary, 26 March 1957, PC; David O. McKay Diary, 6 December 1956, HDC.

61. *Deseret News,* 27 July 1952.

62. Ernest L. Wilkinson Diary, 19 February 1959, HBLL. For references to the illnesses and hospitalizations of Presidents McKay and Richards during this period, see Wilkinson Diary, 27 March, 2 June, 3 September 1958, HBLL; Harold B. Lee Diary, 3 May, 29 August 1951, 14 May 1958, PC; JRC Office Diary, 3 May 1951, 5 January, 30 January 1953; JRC Farm Diary, 25 August 1951; JRCP; Spencer W. Kimball Journal, 22 February 1953, PC; Marion G. Romney Diary, 29 January, 5 February 1953, 2 September 1958, PC; David O. McKay Diary, 26 June, 7 July 1958, HDC; JRC to Dr. J. LeRoy Kimball, 17 August 1958, Folder 14, Box 402, JRCP.

63. Stephen L Richards Office Diary, 7 December 1953, HDC.

64. Harold B. Lee Diary, 4 May 1956, PC; Ernest L. Wilkinson Diary, 4 May 1956, HBLL.

65. E.g., JRC Memo, 8 May 1959, unnumbered box, JRCP; Ernest L. Wilkinson Diary, 6 February 1959, HBLL; Harold B. Lee Diary, 28 June 1958, PC.

66. Author's interviews with Gordon Burt Affleck.

67. Marion G. Romney Diary, 12 April 1955, PC.

68. JRC Scrapbook, 1 October 1954, JRCP.

69. David O. McKay statement in Ernest L. Wilkinson Diary, 11 June 1960, HBLL. President McKay's secretary, Clare Middlemiss, also stated in 1975 that "no decision he made in all his years as president of the Church caused him so much worry and anxiety." See Jerry C. Roundy, "Ricks College: A Struggle for Survival" (Ph.D. diss., Brigham Young University, 1975), 281, which was published under the same title at Rexburg in 1976 (hereafter referred to as Roundy, *Ricks College*).

70. Roundy, *Ricks College,* 223; Ernest L. Wilkinson Diary, 25 March, 21 April, 21 May 1954, HBLL.

71. Roundy, *Ricks College,* 231–47, 258, 268, 270; Ernest L. Wilkinson Diary, 23 April, 26 April, 1 June, 1 July, 17 July 1957, 21 July, 22 July, 27 September 1957, 30 June, 14–15 October, 3 November 1958, HBLL; David O. McKay Diary, 1 July 1957, 31 October 1958, 6 February 1959, HDC; Ernest L. Wilkinson and Leonard J. Arrington, eds., *Brigham Young University: The First One Hundred Years,* 4 vols. (Provo, Utah: Brigham Young University Press, 1976), 3:156–62.

72. David O. McKay Diary, 20 November 1958, HDC; Marion G. Romney Diary, 15 November 1958, PC.

73. Ernest L. Wilkinson Diary, 17 December 1958, HBLL.

74. Roundy, *Ricks College,* 274–76.

75. David O. McKay Diary, 10 February 1959, pp. 1, 25, 28, HDC.

76. *Deseret News,* 14 February 1959; Roundy, *Ricks College,* 277–78.

77. Roundy, *Ricks College,* 278–81, 286–87.

78. Ernest L. Wilkinson Diary, 3 June 1959, also entries for 11 June and 29 June for references to the outside pressures upon President McKay and his vacillation, HBLL.

79. For the general survey of his activities from 1951 onward, see JRC Scrapbook, JRCP.

80. Harold B. Lee Diary, 11 June 1953, PC; *September–October 1967 Conference Report,* 25–26, HDC.

81. JRC to Fred Morris Dearing, 7 November 1958, Folder 6, Box 402, JRCP.

82. JRC to Mrs. A. Helen Morgan, 25 February, 11 September 1952, Folder 5, Box 386, JRCP.

83. Harold B. Lee Diary, 12 August, 30 August, 1 September 1955, PC; *Deseret News Church Section,* 3 September 1955.

84. JRC to Mrs. A. Helen Morgan, 16 June 1953, Folder 2, Box 389, JRCP.

85. JRC to Ernest L. Wilkinson, 9 September 1957, Folder 8, Box 398, JRCP.

86. JRC to LaRue Sneff, 28 December 1957, Folder 5, Box 399, JRCP.

87. Spencer W. Kimball Journal, 21 May 1959, PC; David O. McKay Diary, 20 May 1959, HDC; Gordon B. Hinckley, "An Appreciation of Stephen L Richards," *Improvement Era* 54 (July 1951):499.

88. Ernest L. Wilkinson Diary, 19 May 1959, HBLL.

89. Harold B. Lee Diary, 12 June 1959, PC.

90. David O. McKay Diary, 12 June 1959, HDC; Ernest L. Wilkinson Diary, 20 July 1954, HBLL; author's interviews with Gordon B. Affleck.

91. JRC to Carl W. Buehner, 11 June 1959, Folder 3, Box 404; JRC to President and Mrs. Arwell L. Pierce, 26 June 1959, Folder 13, Box 406, JRCP; *Deseret New Church Section,* 20 June 1959, 12.

92. Marion G. Romney Diary, 15 January, 25 January, 4 April 1959, PC; JRC Home Diary, 17 February, 3 March 1959, JRCP.

93. JRC to Walter and Ebba Mathesius, 15 April 1960, Folder 6, Box 409; JRC to Dr. Lawrence Foss Woolley, 16 September 1959, Folder 22, Box 406, JRCP; Ernest L. Wilkinson Diary, 3 August 1959, HBLL.

94. Marion G. Romney Diary, 18 November 1959, PC; Harold B. Lee Diary, 21 November 1959, PC; JRC Office Diary, 8 March, 9 March 1960; JRC to Walter and Ebba Mathesius, 15 April 1960, Folder 6, Box 409; JRCP.

95. JRC to Fortunato Anselmo, 30 March 1943, Folder 1, Box 367; JRC to J. Willard Marriott, 19 June 1945, Folder 6, Box 372; JRC to William P. Knecht, 20 August 1946, Folder 14, Box 373; JRC to Lloyd Howard, 13 October 1950, Folder 11, Box 381; JRC to President and Mrs. Henry A. Smith, 9 September 1957, Folder 8, Box 398; JRC to John J. Massey, 4 December 1957, Folder 1, Box 400; JRCP.

96. JRC to Mrs. A. Helen Morgan, 5 June 1957, Folder 1, Box 400, JRCP; Ernest L. Wilkinson Diary, 3 June 1959, HBLL; Marion G. Romney Diary, 18 November 1959, PC.

97. JRC to Frank R. Clark, 9 July 1960, Folder 6, Box 408, JRCP.

98. Spencer W. Kimball Journal, 9 October 1960, PC.

99. *October 1960 Conference Report,* 88, HDC.

100. JRC Office Diary, 15 February 1960, JRCP.

101. David O. McKay Diary, 7 October 1960, HDC; Marion G. Romney Diary, 27 October 1960, PC.

102. Harold B. Lee Diary, 10 November, 7 December, 18 December 1960, PC; Harold B. Lee to Spencer W. Kimball, 1 November 1960, in Spencer W. Kimball Journal, PC; Ernest L. Wilkinson Diary, 6 September 1960, HBLL.

103. JRC remarks, 27 April 1961, Box 264; JRC Office Diary, 15 June 1961; JRCP.

104. Marion G. Romney Diary, 6 November 1959, 15 April 1960, PC; Harold B. Lee Diary, 23 June 1960, PC.

105. Ernest L. Wilkinson Diary, 28 April, 7 September 1960, HBLL.

106. Ibid., 4 February 1960; Marion G. Romney Diary, 16 January 1959, PC; Harold B. Lee Diary, 30 March 1959, 7 January 1960, PC.

107. JRC Office Diary, 13 April 1961, JRCP. In an interview on 2 February 1979, President Spencer W. Kimball said that President Clark was opposed to the "kiddie baptism program" as it existed in England, Scotland, North and South Carolina, and elsewhere from 1959 to 1961, but he was weak in health and influence and was not able to stop it. Also, Ernest L. Wilkinson Diary, 6 September 1960, 25 May 1961, HBLL.

108. Ernest L. Wilkinson Diary, 9 January 1960, 10 October 1961, HBLL.

109. Ibid., 24 January 1958; also JRC to J. H. Gipson, 22 September 1943, Folder 2, Box 367, JRCP.

110. Harold B. Lee to Spencer W. Kimball, 1 November 1960, in Spencer W. Kimball Journal, PC; Ernest L. Wilkinson Diary, 22 May 1961, HBLL.

111. Transcript of Hugh B. Brown Inteview, 30 November 1969, Side 2, 23–24, PC.

112. David O. McKay Diary, 14 June, 22 June 1961, HDC.

113. Ibid., 22 June 1961; Eugene E. Campbell and Richard D. Poll, *Hugh B. Brown: His Life and Thought* (Salt Lake City: Bookcraft, 1975), 239–40; Hugh B. Brown Interview, 30 November 1969, Side 2, 23, PC; Harold B. Lee Diary, 22 June 1961, PC.

114. Marion G. Romney Diary, 5 July, 19 July 1961, PC.

115. Ibid., 19 July, 7 August 1961; Harold B. Lee Diary, 15 August 1961, PC.

116. David O. McKay Diary, 23 September 1961, HDC.

117. *Relief Society Magazine* 28 (June 1941):375; Box 224, JRCP.

118. Marion G. Romney Diary, 6 October 1961, PC.

MINISTERING TO THE SAINTS

1. JRC Office Diary, 11 July 1950, JRCP.

2. JRC to Welfare Meeting, 5 April 1958, manuscript, Box 151, JRCP.

3. *Deseret News,* 6 May 1936, 6.

4. JRC 1936 Diary, 5 September 1936; JRC Office Diary, 9 October 1951, JRCP.

5. JRC to Reeve Schley, 6 May 1941, Folder 3, Box 363, JRCP; *Who's Who In America,* 1940–41 ed. (Chicago: A. N. Marquis, 1940), 2283–84.

6. E.g., JRC to Mrs. Francis M. Huntington-Wilson, 29 March 1947, Folder 13, Box 378; JRC Correspondence with Cloyd H. Marvin, Box 189, JRCP.

7. Marion G. Romney Diary, 29 Ocotber 1943, PC.

8. JRC to A*** H******, 15 September 1948, Folder 10, Box 377, JRCP.

9. JRC Office Diary, 4 October 1947; JRC to Missionary Meeting, 6 April 1956, manuscript, 2, Box 151; JRCP.

10. Related by Mr. and Mrs. Clifford Hunter in JRC Office Diary, 9 April 1956, JRCP.

11. JRC to Mrs. Nephi Probst, 7 November 1958, Folder 7, Box 403, JRCP.

12. Spencer W. Kimball Journal, 20 April, 23 April 1950, PC; Edward L. Kimball and Andrew E. Kimball, Jr., *Spencer W. Kimball, Twelfth President of the Church of Jesus Christ of Latter-day Saints* (Salt Lake City: Bookcraft, 1977), 264.

13. JRC Office Diary, 23 November 1960, JRCP.

14. Ibid., 24 March 1959.

15. *October 1952 Conference Report,* 84, HDC; JRC Office Diary, 3 November 1952, JRCP.

16. JRC to Mrs. M****** G. L*****, 6 May 1949, Folder 1, Box 380, JRCP.

17. JRC to Mrs. Romania Woolley, 16 September 1957, Folder 16, Box 400; JRC to Mr. and Mrs. Arthur Bliss Lane, 25 April 1947, Folder 11, Box 376; JRCP.

18. Harold B. Lee Diary, 25 April 1946, PC; JRC Office Diary, 23 June 1949, 2 August 1951, JRCP; Harold B. Lee Diary, 30 June 1952, PC.

19. W****** C*** to JRC, 9 July, 3 September 1933, in "Cranks 1937" Folder, Box 358, JRCP.

20. Folder 2, Box 398, JRCP.

21. Folder 6, Box 403; JRC Office Diary, 8 July 1949; JRCP.

22. JRC to Spencer W. and Camilla Kimball, 6 September 1958, Folder 7, Box 401, JRCP.

23. G***** W. A.***** to JRC, 30 December 1946, Folder 4, Box 373, JRCP.

24. Transcript of JRC ordination of Samuel W. Clark to office of bishop, 15 February 1941, Folder 1, Box 363, JRCP.

25. JRC to meeting of stake presidencies, ward bishoprics, and other officers, 5 April 1937, manuscript, Box 151, JRCP.

26. JRC to Milton H. Ross, 28 March 1951, Folder 6, Box 384, JRCP.

27. JRC to Bishops' Meeting, 1 October 1948, manuscript, Box 151, JRCP.

28. JRC to Bishops' Meeting, 5 April 1949, manuscript, ibid.

29. E.g., JRC to R** M. R******, 18 March 1953, Folder 8, Box 389, JRCP.

30. JRC Office Diary, 2 June 1943, JRCP.

31. JRC to Bishops' Meeting, 1 October 1948, manuscript, Box 151, JRCP.

32. JRC pencil notes, October 1947 Folder, Box 159, JRCP.

33. "Plain Talk to Girls," *Improvement Era* 49 (August 1946):492.

34. *October 1951 Conference Report,* 171, HDC; JRC to Bishops' Meeting, 7 April 1950, manuscript, Box 151, JRCP.

35. *October 1954 Conference Report,* 79, HDC; "Home, and the Building of Home Life," *Relief Society Magazine* 39 (December 1952):793–94. To place the nature of JRC's counsel regarding sexual conduct into perspective, see Marvin and Ann Rytting, "Exhortations for Chastity: A Content Analysis of Church Literature," *Sunstone* 7 (March–April 1982):15–21.

36. *Deseret News,* 9 June 1941, 1; "Home, and the Building of Home Life," *Relief Society Magazine* 39 (December 1952):791.

37. JRC personal copy of Gibbon's *Decline and Fall of the Roman Empire* 1:406, Clarkana, HBLL.

38. "Home, and the Building of Home Life," *Relief Society Magazine* 39 (December 1952):795.

39. JRC Office Diary, 28 November 1941, 24 August 1948, 11 September 1950; JRC Memo, 12 July 1937, Box 385; JRCP.

40. JRC to Richard R. Lyman, 18 April 1956, Folder 15, Box 396, JRCP. Elder Lyman's situation is described in Kimball and Kimball, *Spencer W. Kimball,* 208–9, 346.

41. JRC to Thaddeus A. Davis, Chief of Probation Department, U.S. District, Los Angeles, 21 June 1938, Folder 1, Box 359, JRCP.

42. JRC Office Diary, 29 November 1945, JRCP.

43. JRC to H. H. W***, 24 April 1953, Folder 14, Box 389, JRCP.

44. JRC to R*** T***** W********, 7 February 1941, Folder 3, Box 363, JRCP.

45. JRC to General Priesthood Meeting, 4 October 1947, manuscript, Box 151, JRCP.

46. JRC to Mutual Improvement Associations, 15 June 1958, manuscript, Box 151, JRCP.

47. JRC to B*** C****, 19 August 1947, Folder 6, Box 399, JRCP.

48. JRC to Bishops' Meeting, 3 October 1947, manuscript, Box 151, JRCP.

49. JRC Office Diary, 17 August 1953, JRCP.

50. JRC to L*** C****, 28 November 1959, Box 405, JRCP.

51. Kirk H. Porter and Donald Bruce Johnson, comps., *National Party Platforms, 1840–1956* (Urbana: University of Illinois Press, 1956), 393, 412, 453.

52. *April 1944 Conference Report,* 115–16, HDC.

53. When the general presidency of the Relief Society offered in 1950 to oppose "the bill for equal rights for women, Pres. Clark suggested they keep out of it; there will be some of the women who will think it is a fine thing." (JRC Office Diary, 25 January 1950, JRCP.)

54. "Home, and the Building of Home Life," *Relief Society Magazine* 39 (December 1952):791.

55. JRC Office Diary, 10 August 1933, JRCP.

56. JRC Memorandum, 8 February 1936, Box 87, CR 1/44, HDC.

57. JRC Office Diary, 12 May 1933, JRCP.

58. Ibid., 28 April 1958.

59. *October 1951 Conference Report,* 58, HDC.

60. JRC to David A. Broadbent, 12 May 1948, Folder 2, Box 377, JRCP.

61. JRC to Bishops' Meeting, 3 October 1947, manuscript, Box 151, JRCP.

BY STUDY AND ALSO BY FAITH

1. Lute to JRC, 23 August 1906, Box 328, JRCP.

2. Reported in Lute to JRC, 14 April 1940, Box 338, JRCP.

3. JRC Dictation, 1 September 1956, Box 225, JRCP. Cf. JRC Private Library, HBLL.

4. JRC to Ernest L. Wilkinson, 8 February 1950, Folder 18, Box 382, JRCP.

5. JRC, *Why The King James Version?* (Salt Lake City: Deseret Book, 1956), vii–viii; JRC Office Diary, 7 July 1955, JRCP.

6. JRC to Sidney B. Sperry, 11 January 1956, Folder 7, Box 397, JRCP.

7. JRC to Nephi Jensen, 13 December 1940, Folder 2, Box 362; Rowena J. Miller to Mrs. Walter H. Durrant, 27 October 1959, Folder 7, Box 405; JRCP.

8. JRC to Thomas I. Parksinson, 11 July 1947, Folder 16, Box 376, JRCP.

9. Richard Hofstadter, *Anti-Intellectualism in American Life* (New York: Knopf, 1963), 27.

10. Leonard J. Arrington, "The Intellectual Tradition of the Latter-day Saints," *Dialogue* 4 (Spring 1969):22, n. 22.

11. See The Waste Places of Zion . . . the Rivers of Babylon, n. 68, this volume.

12. *April 1952 Conference Report,* 95, HDC.

13. *October 1954 Conference Report,* 38, ibid.

14. JRC to Ormand Coulam, 3 September 1938, Folder 1, Box 359, JRCP.

15. Ernest L. Wilkinson, ed., *Brigham Young University: The First One Hundred Years,* 4 vols. (Provo, Utah: Brigham Young University Press, 1975–1976), 2:224.

16. JRC, "The Chartered Course of the Church in Education," *Improvement Era* 41(September 1938):572.

17. JRC Office Diary, 21 April, 27 April 1944, 21 April 1950, JRCP.

18.   Heber J. Grant, JRC, and David O. McKay to Committee on Publications, Joseph Fielding Smith, John A. Widtsoe, Harold B. Lee, and Marion G. Romney, 9 August 1944, HDC.

19.   JRC to Ernest L. Wilkinson, 17 November 1956, Folder 5, Box 15, Ernest L. Wilkinson Presidential Papers, HBLL. Quoted in part in Wilkinson, *Brigham Young University* 2:651.

20.   Ernest L. Wilkinson Diary, passim, HBLL; chapter "The Welfare of This People," this volume.

21.   JRC pencil notes, attached to October 1947 Conference Folder, Box 159, JRCP.

22.   JRC to Frank L. Perris, 29 January 1936, Folder 1, Box 354, JRCP; Ernest L. Wilkinson Diary, 18 July 1956, HBLL.

23.   JRC to N. L. Nelson, 24 June 1941, Folder 2, Box 363, JRCP. JRC was outraged, however, when Nelson used quotes from this letter to advertise his book. JRC to Nelson, 5 February 1942, Folder 2, Box 365, JRCP.

24.   JRC Office Diary, 16 April 1948, JRCP.

25.   JRC pencil notes, attached to October 1947 Conference Folder, Box 159, JRCP.

26.   JRC to J. Reuben Clark III, 23 May 1929, Box 355, JRCP.

27.   JRC to M***** R. R***, 24 September 1953, Folder 8, Box 389, JRCP.

28.   JRC to G***** E. W******, 28 October 1936, Folder 2, Box 354, JRCP. The controversy in the nineteenth century concerning the Adam-God doctrine is discussed in Gary James Bergera, "The Orson Pratt-Brigham Young Controversies: Conflict Within the Quorums, 1853-1868," *Dialogue* 13 (Summer 1980):7-49, and David John Buerger, "The Adam-God Doctrine," *Dialogue* 15 (Spring 1982):14-58.

29.   Rowena J. Miller to L***** R*****, 25 August 1953, Folder 3, Box 389, JRCP.

30.   JRC, *On The Way to Immortality and Eternal Life*, (Salt Lake City: Deseret Book, 1949), 314-35, JRCP.

31.   *New Catholic Encyclopedia*, 15 vols. (New York: McGraw-Hill, 1967) 6:821-22.

32.   JRC to Joseph T. Bentley, 26 September 1956, Folder 2, Box 395, JRCP.

33.   JRC to I*** E. L*******, 20 May 1957, Folder 16, Box 399, JRCP.

34.   JRC to Missionary Meeting, 3 April 1957, manuscript, April 1957 Conference Folder, Box 166, JRCP.

35.   JRC notes for talk, "Evolution," 29 November 1915, Box 90; JRC notes for talk, "Science Truths—Theory vs Fact," 7 September 1924, Box 114; JRCP.

36.   JRC letter, 2 October 1946, in Folder for Relief Society Conference of 3 October 1946, Box 158, JRCP.

37.   JRC to Harvey L. Taylor, 2 January 1957, "Copyrights" Folder, Box 277; JRC Office Diary, 1 June 1948; JRCP. For discussion of the historical nature of doctrinal differences among members of the First Presidency and Quorum of the Twelve Apostles, see Clark, *Messages of the First Presidency* 2:214-23, 229-40; B. H. Roberts, *A Comprehensive History of The Church of Jesus Christ of Latter-day Saints, Century I*, 6 vols. (Salt Lake City: The Church of Jesus Christ of Latter-day Saints, 1930) 4:61, n. 16, 5:269-71; Bergera, "The Orson Pratt-Brigham Young Controversies"; Donald Q. Cannon, "The King Follett Discourse: Joseph Smith's Greatest Sermon in Historical Perspective," *Brigham Young University Studies* 18 (Winter 1978):191-92; and Thomas G. Alexander, "The Reconstruction of Mormon Doctrine: From Joseph Smith to Progressive Theology," *Sunstone* 5 (July-August 1980):27-31.

38.   *Deseret News Church Section*, 31 July 1954, 10-11; JRC, *When Are ...* (Provo, Utah: Department of Seminaries and Institutes, 1966); *Melchizedek Priesthood Course of Study, 1969-70: Immortality and Eternal Life* (Salt Lake City: First Presidency of The Church of Jesus Christ of Latter-day Saints, 1969), 215-25; *Dialogue* 12 (Summer 1979):68-81. Titles of this JRC talk have varied in these publications.

39.   Heber J. Grant, JRC, and David O. McKay to Committee on Publications, Joseph Fielding Smith, John A. Widtsoe, Harold B. Lee, and Marion G. Romney, 9 August 1944, quoted in Clark, *Messages of the First Presidency* 6:208–11.

40.   JRC Office Diary, 26 January 1942, JRCP.

41.   "Dale Morgan" Folder, Box 8, CR 1/19, HDC; JRC Office Diary, 8 and 13 November 1951, JRCP.

42.   JRC Memorandum, 19 October 1957, unnumbered box, JRCP; James R. Clark, "The Kingdom of God, The Council of Fifty and the State of Deseret," *Utah Historical Quarterly* 26 (April 1958):131–48; Clark, *Messages of the First Presidency* 1:viii; D. Michael Quinn, "The Council of Fifty and Its Members, 1844–1945," *BYU Studies* 20(Winter 1980):163–97.

43.   George Albert Smith Diary, 1 July 1949, HDC.

44.   JRC Office Diary, 26 September 1955, JRCP.

45.   JRC, *Why the King James Version?* (Salt Lake City: Deseret Book, 1956), preface.

46.   *April 1949 Conference Report,* 187, HDC.

47.   Ibid., 162.

48.   *April 1952 Conference Report,* 95; *April 1949 Conference Report,* 187; HDC; JRC to general priesthood meeting, October 1956, manuscript, Box 151, JRCP.

49.   *April 1940 Conference Report,* 14; *April 1949 Conference Report,* 186; HDC; *Deseret News Church Section,* 31 July 1954, 11.

A WATCHMAN UNTO THE HOUSE OF ISRAEL

1.   Chapter "By Study And Also By Faith," this volume.

2.   *April 1949 Conference Report,* 162, HDC.

3.   *October 1944 Conference Report,* 117, ibid.

4.   *October 1945 Conference Report,* 166, ibid.

5.   JRC to Bishops' Meeting, 29 September 1950, manuscript, Box 151, JRCP.

6.   *April 1952 Conference Report,* 81, HDC.

7.   Robert M. Grant, *A Short History of the Interpretation of the Bible,* rev. ed. (New York: Macmillan, 1963); *Interpreter's Dictionary of the Bible,* 4 vols. (New York: Abingdon Press, 1962) 1:407–18; and the following publications by Fortress Press of Philadelphia, most of which are of pamphlet size: William A. Beardslee, *Literary Criticism of the New Testament* (1970), Norman C. Hable, *Literary Criticism of the Old Testament* (1971), Ralph W. Klein, *Textual Criticism of the Old Testament: The Septuagint After Qumran* (1974), Edgar Krentz, *The Historical-Critical Method* (1975), Edgar V. McKnight, *What Is Form Criticism?* (1969), Edgar V. McKnight, *Meaning in Texts: The Historical Setting of a Narrative Hermeneutics* (1978), J. Maxwell Miller, *The Old Testament and the Historian* (1976), Daniel Patte, *What Is Structural Exegesis?* (1976), Norman Perrin, *What Is Redaction Criticism?* (1969), Walter E. Rast, *Tradition History and the Old Testament* (1972).

8.   For the reaction against higher criticism, see William Henry Green, *The Hebrew Feasts in Their Relation to Recent Critical Hypotheses* (New York: R. Carter and Brothers, 1885); William Henry Green, *Higher Criticism of the Pentateuch* (New York: Charles Schribner's Sons, 1895); L. W. Munhall, *Anti-Higher Criticism, or, Testimony to the Infallibility of the Bible* (New York: Hunt and Eaton, 1894); William Edward Biederwolf, *The New Paganism and Other Sermons* (Grand Rapids, Mich.: William B. Eerdmans, 1934); Willis B. Glover, *Evangelical Nonconformists and higher criticism in the Nineteenth Century* (London: Independent Press, 1955); Carl E. Hatch, *The Charles A. Briggs Heresy Trial: Prologue to Twentieth Century Liberal Protestantism* (New York: Exposition Press, 1969); Ernest R. Sandeen, *The Roots of Fundamentalism: British and American Millenarianism, 1800–1930* (Chicago:

University of Chicago Press, 1970); Paul A. Carter, *The Spiritual Crisis of the Gilded Age* (DeKalb: Northern Illinois University Press, 1971); James Barr, *Fundamentalism* (London: SCM Press, 1977).

9. John A. Widtsoe, *In Search of Truth* (Salt Lake City: Deseret Book, 1930), 90, 81. Prior to JRC's entry into the First Presidency, counselors Charles W. Penrose and Anthony W. Ivins had encouraged higher criticism, and after 1933 two other General Authorities with doctoral training (Joseph F. Merrill and Levi Edgar Young) continued privately to encourage Latter-day Saint explorations into higher criticism. See Charles W. Penrose to Joseph W. McMurrin, 31 October 1921, in *American History: A Syllabus for Social Science 100* (Provo, Utah: Brigham Young University, 1977), 428–29; Thomas G. Alexander's unpublished manuscript, *People in Transition: The Latter-day Saints and Their Church, 1900–1930*; Richard Sherlock, "Faith and History: The Snell Controversy," *Dialogue* 12 (Spring 1979):31–32.

10. JRC to John A. Widtsoe, 29 June 1930, JRCP.

11. JRC Office Diary, 7 February 1934, JRCP.

12. John A. Widtsoe, "Is the Bible Translated Correctly?" *Improvement Era* 43 (March 1940):161.

13. John A. Widtsoe, *Evidences and Reconciliations: Aids to Faith in a Modern Day* (Salt Lake City: Bookcraft, 1943), 99.

14. JRC to Milton Bennion, 19 April 1943, Folder 1, Box 367, JRCP.

15. Clark, *Messages of the First Presidency* 6:211.

16. JRC, "The World Crisis Today," *Deseret News Church Section,* 16 June 1945, 4, 9, 11–12. He again described the higher critics as "atheistic scholars" in *April 1949 Conference Report,* 163, HDC.

17. *Deseret News Church Section,* 20 June 1953, 4; *April 1954 Conference Report,* 38–47.

18. JRC Office Diary, 27 September 1954, JRCP; Harold B. Lee Diary, 22 January, 25 January 1954, PC; JRC, *Why the King James Version?* (Salt Lake City: Deseret Book, 1956).

19. JRC Office Diary, 26 January 1956, JRCP.

20. JRC to Cloyd H. Marvin, 10 March 1958, Binder of JRC-Marvin Correspondence, Box 189, JRCP.

21. JRC to Heber J. Grant and Anthony W. Ivins, 13 March 1934, JRC Folder, CR 1/48, HDC.

22. JRC, "The Chartered Course of the Church in Education," *Improvement Era* 41 (September 1938):572.

23. JRC Office Diary, 4 March 1946, JRCP.

24. JRC to Irvin Hull, 9 March 1946, Folder 12, Box 373, JRCP. See discussion in chapter "By Study And Also By Faith," this volume.

25. JRC Office Diary, 31 August 1933, 3 November 1940, 18 April 1941, 25 April 1950, and correspondence between JRC and several BYU faculty members and students, JRCP.

26. Marion G. Romney Diary, 16 January 1959, PC; Ernest L. Wilkinson Diary, 24 February 1960, HBLL.

27. For references to the situation of Latter-day Saint intellectuals and academics during the period beginning with JRC's entry into the First Presidency, see Davis Bitton, "Anti-Intellectualism in Mormon History," *Dialogue* 1 (Autumn 1966), esp. 124–28; Claude J. Burtenshaw, "The Student: His University and His Church," *Dialogue* 1 (Spring 1966):89–101; William Mulder, "Problems of the Mormon Intellectual," *Dialogue* 5 (Autumn 1970):121–23; Richard Sherlock, "Faith and History: The Snell Controversy," *Dialogue* 12 (Spring 1979):27–41; "Letters to the Editor," *Dialogue* 1 (Summer 1966):9–10, 2 (Spring 1967):7–8, 2 (Summer 1967):15–16, 3 (Spring 1968):8, 4 (Autumn 1969):7–8; Scott Kenney, "E. E. Ericksen: Loyal Heretic," *Sunstone* 3 (July–August 1978):22–27;

Thomas F. O'Dea, *The Mormons* (Chicago: University of Chicago Press, 1957), 224–40; George T. Boyd, *Views on Man and Religion,* ed. James B. Allen, Dale C. LeCheminant and David J. Whittaker (Provo: Friends of George T. Boyd, 1979), 160–68; T. Edgar Lyon Oral History, 1977, HDC; Sterling M. McMurrin Papers, JWML; *Daily Utah Chronicle,* 6 March 1967, 1, 5; *Deseret News,* 13 April 1967, B-14; Hugh W. Nibley, "Zeal Without Knowledge," in *Nibley On the Timeless and the Timely* (Provo: Religious Studies Center, Brigham Young University, 1978), reprinted in *Dialogue* 11 (Summer 1978):101–12.

28. Clark, *Messages of the First Presidency* 3:198; Kenneth W. Godfrey, "The Coming of the Manifesto," *Dialogue* 5 (Autumn 1970):11–25.

29. Richard D. Poll, "The Twin Relic: A Study of Mormon Polygamy and the Campaign by the Government of the United States for Its Abolition, 1852–1890" (Master's thesis, Texas Christian University, 1939); Richard D. Poll, "The Political Reconstruction of Utah Territory, 1866–1890," *Pacific Historical Review* 27 (May 1958):111–26; Gustive O. Larson, *The "Americanization" of Utah for Statehood* (San Marino, Calif.: The Huntington Library, 1971); Edward Leo Lyman, "The Mormons' Quest for Utah Statehood" (Ph.D. diss., University of California at Riverside, 1980).

30. Victor W. Jorgensen and B. Carmon Hardy, "The Taylor-Cowley Affair and the Watershed of Mormon History," *Utah Historical Quarterly* 48 (Winter 1980):4–36; Jerold A. Hilton, "Polygamy In Utah and Surrounding Area Since the Manifesto of 1890" (Master's thesis, Brigham Young University, 1965); personal research of author; U.S. Senate, *Proceedings Before the Committee on Privileges and Elections of the United States Senate in the Matter of the Protests Against the Right of Hon. Reed Smoot, a Senator from the State of Utah, to Hold His Seat,* 4 vols. (Washington, D.C.: Government Printing Office, 1904–1907) 1:114, 2:397–400; Preston Woolley Parkinson, *The Utah Woolley Family* (Salt Lake City: by the author, n.d.), 251, 340.

31. Jorgensen and Hardy, "The Taylor-Cowley Affair," 18, n. 26; and author's study.

32. JRC 1907 Memorandum Book, Box 2, JRCP.

33. Clark, *Messages of the First Presidency* 4:218.

34. *Deseret News,* 30 March 1914; Joshua R. Clark to JRC, 30 April 1914, Box 330, JRCP; Fox, *JRC,* 440–41.

35. Clark, *Messages of the First Presidency* 4:84–85, 151–52, 217–18, 301, 5:193–97, 242, 292–95.

36. JRC Church Document no. 9, Box 114, JRCP.

37. J. Max Anderson, *The Polygamy Story: Fiction and Fact* (Salt Lake City: Publishers Press, 1979), 146.

38. JRC Office diary, 26 April 1957, JRCP.

39. Ibid., 21 June 1948.

40. Ibid., 25 April 1933.

41. Ibid., 22–24 May 1933; Clark, *Messages of the First Presidency* 5:316–30.

42. JRC to W. C. Dennis, 1 August 1933, Box 349, JRCP.

43. Fox, *JRC,* 166–67.

44. Harold B. Lee Diary, 21 March 1945, PC.

45. Example printed in *Truth* 1 (March 1936):128; blank forms also in First Presidency files, HDC. Scores of Latter-day Saints were excommunicated for several years on the *prima facie* evidence of refusing to sign this statement.

46. Folder marked "First Presidency–Plural Marriage–Investigation of Meetings of 'Fundamentalist' Musser-Darter Groups," in CR 1/48, HDC; JRC Office Diary, 2 May 1939, 15 October 1940, 21 August 1944, JRCP.

47. JRC Office Diary, 2 May 1939, 28 February 1940, JRCP.

48. Ibid., 1 March 1940, 4 May 1944.

49. Joseph W. Musser Journal, 17 July 1938, 8 May 1939, HDC; "An Open Letter to J. Reuben Clark, Jr." *Truth* 5 (August 1939):50.

50. F*** E. H. C***** to First Presidency, Attn: JRC, 25 February, 25 August 1941, in "First Presidency–Plural Marriage–Investigation of Meetings" File, CR 1/48, HDC.

51. Ibid., 4 October 1939; JRC Office Diary, 25 January 1940, 26–27 February, 9 April 1941, 29 January 1943, JRCP.

52. JRC Office Diary, 20 May 1944, JRCP; Frank Evans Diary, 4 May 1944, HDC.

53. JRC Office Diary, 12 January 1948, 1 October 1951, 5 August 1953, 26 October 1954, 7 November 1955; "Statement to be given to Mr. Gordon of the Burns Detective Agency, who is investigating the Short Creek situation," 2 October 1951, Folder 3, Box 383; JRCP; folder titled "First Presidency–Statement on Short Creek Situation (Polygamy) July 27, 1953," in CR 1/45, HDC; *Truth* 19 (September–October 1953):97–160; *Time* 63 (3 August 1953):16.

54. Fox, *JRC,* 306, 412.

55. JRC to Roy Matthews, 11 March 1954, Folder 7, Box 391, JRCP.

56. *October 1942 Conference Report,* 58; also *October 1950 Conference Report,* 172; *April 1957 Conference Report,* 50–51, HDC. Reuben was expressing this view publicly as early as 1919 (see Fox, *JRC,* 294). See Doctrine and Covenants 101:77, 80.

57. *April 1944 Conference Report,* 115, HDC.

58. JRC Memo, 30 November 1951, Box 244, JRCP. His memo suggested the need for such a revision, but did not make specific proposals for revision.

59. JRC Office Diary, 6 December 1950, JRCP.

60. *April 1957 Conference Report,* 44; also *October 1942 Conference Report,* 59; HDC.

61. *October 1942 Conference Report,* 58, HDC; also JRC Office Diary, 8 January 1943, JRCP.

62. JRC to Robert LeFevre, President of The Freedom School, 22 January 1957, Folder 8, Box 396, JRCP.

63. Rowena J. Miller to Leroy A. Wilson, 17 November 1949, Folder 14, Box 380, JRCP. He also stated to a general conference, "The Constitution will never reach its destiny through force. God never planted his Spirit, his truth, in the hearts of men from the point of a bayonet" (*April 1957 Conference Report,* 31, HDC).

64. JRC to Ernest L. Wilkinson, 5 February 1949, Folder 16, Box 380, JRCP.

65. JRC to Lucy Wilson, 12 July 1915, Box 346, JRCP, referred to in Fox, *JRC,* 256.

66. For general reading about these matters, see Karl Marx and Friedrich Engels, *The Communist Manifesto* (in various translations and printings since its publication in 1848); Marx, *Das Kapital* (in various translations and printings since its initial publication in 1867); William Henry Chamberlin, *The Russian Revolution, 1917–1921,* 2 vols. (New York: Macmillan, 1935); Lewis A. Coser and Irving Howe, *The American Communist Party* (Boston: Beacon Press, 1957); Adam B. Ulam, *The Bolsheviks: The Intellectual and Political History of the Triumph of Communism in Russia* (New York: Macmillan, 1965); Ulam, *Expansion and Coexistence: A History of Soviet Foreign Policy, 1917–1967* (New York: Praeger, 1968); Robert Conquest, *The Great Terror: Stalin's Purge of the Thirties* (New York: Macmillan, 1968); Svetlana Allilueva, *Only One Year,* trans. Paul Chavchavadze (New York: Harper and Row, 1969); Aleksandr I. Solzhenitsyn, *The Gulag Archipelago, 1918–1956,* trans. Thomas P. Whitney (New York: Harper and Row, 1973).

67. JRC, *Stand Fast By Our Constitution* (Salt Lake City: Deseret Book, 1962), 84; *October 1941 Conference Report,* 16, HDC.

68. Clark, *Message of the First Presidency,* 6:17, 19. As early as 1934, JRC expressed concern about a Church member "who has been bitten by this modern communistic bug, and as I have repeatedly observed I have never seen any of them get over it after they have been infected" (JRC to David O. McKay, 1 November 1934, Folder 3, Box 351, JRCP).

69. Frank H. Jonas and Garth N. Jones, "Utah Presidential Elections, 1896–1952," *Utah Historical Quarterly* 24 (October 1956):299, 305.

70. JRC to David O. McKay, 22 July 1936, Folder 1, Box 355, JRCP.

71. Reports by Lester Wire, Chief of Salt Lake City Detectives, Subversive Detail, 20 July, 23 July, 30 July, 12 August 1936, reports of Lester Wire forwarded in letter of Jeremiah Stokes to David O. McKay, 16 April 1940, and reply of President McKay to Stokes, 19 April 1940, all documents located in Folder 5, Box 34, McKay Papers, HDC. This forwarding of police reports ended when it was publicized in the *Sugar House Post Sentinel*, Extra, 25 May 1940 (see Clarkana, 320.53, Al, no. 534, HBLL).

72. Clark, *Messages of the First Presidency* 6:18.

73. *October 1942 Conference Report,* 54, HDC; JRC to Bishops' Meeting, 1 October 1943, manuscript, Box 151, JRCP; Clark, *Messages of the First Presidency* 6:200.

74. JRC to Edgar B. Brossard, 2 May 1944, Folder 1, Box 369, JRCP.

75. JRC, *Let Us Have Peace* (Salt Lake City: Deseret News Press, 1947), 15; JRC, *Stand Fast By Our Constitution,* 70.

76. JRC to Frank H. Jonas, 15 February 1943, Folder 2, Box 411, JRCP.

77. JRC Office Diary, 17 October 1949, JRCP.

78. JRC to G. Homer Durham, 6 May 1948, Folder 4, Box 377, JRCP; Ernest L. Wilkinson Diary, 2 March 1960, HBLL.

79. JRC to G. Homer Durham, 6 May 1948, Folder 4, Box 377, JRCP.

80. JRC Office Diary, 16 August 1949, JRCP.

81. JRC to Hugh C. Smith, 6 December 1954, Folder 15, Box 391, JRCP. Also Rowena J. Miller to Richard S. Morrison, 1 April 1952: "Mr. Clark wishes me to acknowledge your letters of February 16th and February 22nd, and to say that the editorials in the Deseret News [critical of Joseph McCarthy's anti-Communist tactics], to which you refer, are no more pleasing to him than they apparently are pleasing to you.

"Mr. Clark does not believe that you will find similar articles appearing hereafter in the News" (Folder 5, Box 386, JRCP).

Interpretations of Joseph McCarthy and the anticommunist crusade of the 1950s continue to be divided, but useful studies are: William F. Buckley, Jr. and L. Brent Bozell, *McCarthy and His Enemies: The Record and Its Meaning* (Chicago: Henry Regnery, 1954); Richard H. Rovere, *Senator Joe McCarthy* (New York: Harcourt, Brace, 1959); Earl Latham, *The Communist Controversy in Washington: From the New Deal to McCarthy* (Cambridge, Mass.: Harvard University Press, 1966); Michael R. Belknap, *Cold War Political Justice: The Smith Act, the Communist Party and American Civil Liberty* (Westport, Conn.: Greenwood Press, 1977); David Caute, *The Great Fear: The Anti-Communist Purge Under Truman and Eisenhower* (New York: Simon and Schuster, 1978); Thomas C. Reeves, *The Life and Times of Joe McCarthy* (Briar Cliff Manor, N.Y.: Stein and Day, 1981); also syndicated newspaper editorials as recently as 1981 by William F. Buckley favorable to the intent of Joseph McCarthy's anticommunism.

82. *New York Times,* 7 May 1949, 4; JRC to Henry C. Dworshak, 16 April 1948, Folder 5, Box 377, JRCP. See also chapter "They That Take the Sword," n. 73, this volume.

83. JRC Office Diary, 23 September 1946, 30 April 1948; JRC to Jeremiah Stokes, 13 February 1945, Folder 13, Box 372; JRC to Hugh C. Smith, 6 December 1954, Folder 15, Box 391; JRCP.

84. JRC correspondence with and memos of conversations with Ezra Taft Benson, JRCP.

85. JRC Office Diary, 3 April 1948, 16 August, 19 August 1949; Foundation for Economic Education Files, Boxes 440–442; JRCP; *The Freeman; National Union Catalog, Pre-1956 Imprints,* s.v. Foundation for Economic Education as author; JRC to W. Cleon Skousen, 20 July 1953, 28 March 1958, Folder 10, Box 389, Folder 12, Box 403, JRCP.

86. Joseph Anderson to David A. Law, 13 November 1959, Folder 6, Box 406, JRCP.

87. The best example of this view is his "Constitution" editorial in *Deseret News,* 31 October 1936; Heber J. Grant Journal, 31 October 1936, HDC.

88. JRC talk outline, Box 210, JRCP.

89. JRC Office Diary, 9 July 1940, JRCP.

90. Ibid., 19 July, 2 August 1939, 26 April, 29 April, 30 April, 24 May, 29 May, 28 June, 5 July, 8 July, 11–12 July, 20 July, 23 July, 29 July, 3 August, 13 August, 9 December 1940, 21 April, 2 May, 22 May, 26–27 May 1944, 28 February, 22 March, 9 August, 24 September, 14 October 1948, 1 November 1949, 31 January, 14 April, 26 May, 8 June 1950, JRCP.

91. Ibid., 12 May 1944.

92. Ibid., 4 February 1939.

93. Ibid., 20 July 1940, 1 November 1949; Henry D. Moyle Diary, 26 July, 3 October, 10 October 1950, 24 February, 26 February, 25 July 1951, 12 August, 1 October 1952, 14 January, 6 March, 10 March, 12 March, 30 October 1953, HDC.

94. JRC Office Diary, 18 April 1952, JRCP.

95. JRC to Drew Pearson, 27 November 1950, Folder 11, Box 382, JRCP.

96. Composite quote from his statements in Harold B. Lee Diary, 9 November 1956, PC, and in JRC to Howard W. Hunter, 14 November 1956, Folder 11, Box 396, JRCP.

97. Dennis L. Lythgoe, "A Special Relationship: J. Bracken Lee and the Mormon Church," *Dialogue* 11 (Winter 1978):76, 79, 80, 84; Lythgoe, *Let 'Em Holler: A Political Biography of J. Bracken Lee* (Salt Lake City: Utah State Historical Society, 1982), 33–34, 91–92, 101–2, 104.

98. JRC Office Diary, 10 April 1956, JRCP.

99. Ibid., 9 August 1948, 14 October 1948, 6 January 1949, 25 July 1951, 23 January, 3 May, 8 May, 25 July, 31 December 1952.

100. Ibid., 31 January 1950.

101. Ibid., 12 June 1951, 2 March 1955.

102. Ibid., 30 January 1953. Lythgoe, "A Special Relationship," 82–83; Lythgoe, *Let 'Em Holler,* 98.

103. JRC to General Priesthood Meeting, 6 April 1935, manuscript, Box 151, JRCP.

104. JRC, *Our Dwindling Sovereignty* (Salt Lake City. Deseret News Press, 1952), 4–5; JRC, *Stand Fast By Our Constitution.*

THEY THAT TAKE THE SWORD

1. D. Michael Quinn, "The Mormon Church and the Spanish-American War: An End to Selective Pacifism," *Pacific Historical Review* 43 (August 1974):342–66.

2. Joshua R. Clark Journal, JRCP; Arrington, *From Quaker to Latter-day Saint: Bishop Edwin D. Woolley* (Salt Lake City: Deseret Book, 1976), 86.

3. JRC to Joshua and Mary Clark, 21 May 1898, Box 328, JRCP.

4. JRC to Theodore Marburg, 24 October 1912, in "American Peace Society" Folder, Box 343, JRCP.

5. JRC to John W. Clark, 25 January 1915, Folder 11a, Box 90, JRCP; Fox, *JRC,* 251–58.

6. JRC to Theodore Marburg, 4 May 1914, 15 April 1916, 3 March 1917, in "American Peace Society" Folder, Box 343, JRCP.

7. Fox, *JRC,* 262–63.

8. *Deseret News,* 6 September 1919; James B. Allen, "J. Reuben Clark, Jr., on American Sovereignty and International Organization," *Brigham Young University Studies* 13 (Spring 1973):347–59.

9. Fox, *JRC*, 299–321; Edwin Brown Firmage and Christoper L. Blakesley, "J. Reuben Clark, Jr., Law and International Order," *Brigham Young University Studies* 13 (Spring 1973):336–42.

10. Salmon O. Levinson to JRC, 9 May 1923, and JRC to J. C. Maxwell Garnett, 11 March 1924, in "American Committee for the Outlawry of War" Folder, Box 345, JRCP.

11. Fox, *JRC*, 513.

12. John J. Esch to JRC, 9 May 1930, and JRC to John J. Esch, 21 July 1930, in Box 30, JRCP.

13. JRC to Salmon O. Levinson, 9 July 1934, Folder 1, Box 351; JRC to David O. McKay, 14 June 1937, Folder 1, Box 358; JRC to General Priesthood Meeting, 8 October 1938, manuscript, Box 151; JRCP. The popular and scholarly studies of Nazi Germany are legion, but one of the most significant is Karl Dietrich Bracher, *The German Dictatorship: The Origins, Structure, and Effects of National Socialism*, trans. Jean Steinberg (New York: Praeger, 1970).

14. Wayne S. Cole, *Charles A. Lindbergh and the Battle Against American Intervention in World War II* (New York: Harcourt Brace Jovanovich, 1974), 31.

15. Fox, *JRC*, 290; JRC to Hiram W. Johnson, 18 March 1935, Folder 4, Box 352, JRCP.

16. Luacine S. Clark Diary, 4 August–9 August 1937; JRC 1937 Diary, 4–9 August; JRC 1938 Diary, 24–27 June; JRC Memorandum, 18 July 1938, Folder 4, Box 215; JRCP. For references to the support of the Nazis among German Latter-day Saints, see Joseph M. Dixon, "Mormons in the Third Reich: 1933–1945," *Dialogue* 7 (No. 1, 1972):71–72, 77; Alan F. Keele and Douglas F. Tobler, "The Fuehrer's New Clothes: Helmuth Heubener and the Mormons in the Third Reich," *Sunstone* 5 (November–December 1980):27.

17. JRC to N. L. Nelson, 24 June 1941, 2, 6, in Folder 2, Box 363, JRCP. Also, upon his return from service as LDS mission president in Berlin, Roy A. Welker stated, "The nazi regime in Germany is characterized by marked orderliness and both the government and the people are strongly opposed to war. . . . Jews are safer in Germany today than in many other parts of the world. . . . Nazi dislike of Jews and hatred of communism are at the root of most propaganda against that nation." (*Salt Lake Tribune*, 8 September 1937.)

18. JRC's views are contained in the sources cited in the footnotes to follow. Similar interpretations also appear in the works of other interpreters and scholars, and these writings have also been the subject of varying degrees of controversy. For World War I, see Harry Elmer Barnes, *The Genesis of the World War: An Introduction to the Problem of War Guilt* (New York: Knopf, 1926); C. Hartley Grattan, *Why We Fought* (New York: Vanguard Press, 1929); Walter Millis, *Road to War: America 1914–1917* (Boston: Houghton Mifflin, 1935); James D. Squires, *British Propaganda at Home and in the United States from 1914 to 1917* (Cambridge, Mass.: Harvard University Press, 1935); Edwin Borchard and William Potter Lage, *Neutrality for the United States* (New Haven, Conn.: Yale University Press, 1937); Charles Callan Tansill, *America Goes to War* (Boston: Little, Brown, 1938); H. C. Peterson, *Propaganda for War: The Campaign Against American Neutrality, 1914–1917* (Norman: University of Oklahoma Press, 1939); Warren I. Cohen, *The American Revisionists: The Lessons of Intervention in World War I* (Chicago: University of Chicago Press, 1967); Colin Simpson, *The Lusitania* (Boston: Little, Brown, 1973). For studies that parallel JRC's views of the origins of World War II, see Harold Nicolson, *Peacemaking, 1919* (Boston: Houghton Mifflin, 1933); Harold Lavine and James Wechsler, *War Propaganda and the United States* (New Haven: Yale University Press, 1940); Thomas A. Bailey, *Woodrow Wilson and the Great Betrayal* (New York: Macmillan, 1945); William L. Langer and S. Everett Gleason, *The Undeclared War, 1940–41* (New York: Harper, 1953); A. J. P. Taylor, *The Origins of the Second World War* (London: Hamilton, 1961); Robert A. Divine, *The Illusion of Neutrality* (Chicago: University of Chicago Press, 1962); David L. Hoggan, *Der erzwungene Krieg: die Ursachen and Urheber des 2. Weltkriegs* [The Forced War: Causes and Originators of the Second World War] (Tuebingen: Verlag der Deutschen Hochschullehrer-Zeitung, 1963); Richard M. Watt, *The Kings Depart, the Tragedy of Germany: Versailles and the*

German Revolution (New York: Simon and Schuster, 1968); Mark Lincoln Chadwin, *The Hawks of World War II* (Chapel Hill: University of North Carolina Press, 1968); Charles Roetter, *The Art of Psychological Warfare, 1914–1945* (New York: Stein and Day, 1974); Anthony Rhodes, *Propaganda, The Art of Persuasion: World War II* (New York: Chelsea House, 1976); Joseph P. Lash, *Roosevelt and Churchill, 1939–1941: The Partnership That Saved the West* (New York: W. W. Norton, 1976); D. J. Goodspeed, *The German Wars, 1914–1945* (Boston: Houghton Mifflin, 1977).

19. Clark, *Messages of the First Presidency* 6:89–92; *October 1939 Conference Report,* 11–14; *April 1941 Conference Report,* 20; HDC; JRC to Orval Adams, 25 April 1941, Folder 1, Box 363, JRCP. Also, Firmage and Blakesley, "JRC, Law and International Order," 305. This was the standard anti-interventionist view of the war. See Cole, *Charles A. Lindbergh,* 79.

20. JRC to Amy Brown Lyman, 15 July 1940, Folder 2, Box 362, JRCP.

21. Clark, *Messages of the First Presidency* 6:89; Box 153, JRCP.

22. *October 1940 Conference Report,* 14, HDC.

23. JRC draft of talk, Box 223, JRCP; also *Deseret News,* 13 February 1941.

24. JRC to John Bassett Moore, 18 February 1941, J*** R. S**** to JRC, 13 February 1941, and Z*** B. S****** to JRC, 14 February 1941, Box 223, JRCP.

25. Afton Lowder, Executive Secretary of the Utah Chapter of the America First Committee, to JRC, 29 May 1941, and JRC to Afton Lowder, 2 June 1941, in Folder 1, Box 364, JRCP. On 13 November 1941, President Clark "was greatly agitated over the criticism that had come to the First Presidency because of them allowing the Tabernacle to be used for an America First Rally where young Senator Holt of Virginia is to speak. He intimated that approval had been given without their consent" (Harold B. Lee Diary, PC). For national background of this organization, see Wayne S. Cole, *America First: The Battle Against Intervention, 1940–1941* (Madison: University of Wisconsin Press, 1953).

26. *New York Times,* 6 August 1941, 6; *Deseret News,* 6 August 1941. See also Manfred Jonas, *Isolationi..: in America, 1935–1941* (Ithaca, N.Y.: Cornell University Press, 1966); Martin B. Hickman and Ray C. Hillam, "J. Reuben Clark, Jr.: Political Isolationism Revisted," *Dialogue* 7 (Spring 1972):37–46.

27. Harold B. Lee Diary, 27 October 1942, PC; JRC Office Diary, 9 July 1940, JRCP; October 1940 Conference Report, 16, HDC; JRC to Gordon W. Clark, 29 October 1940, Box 338; JRC to Philip Marshal Brown, 1 February 1941, Folder 1, Box 363; JRCP; *October 1941 Conference Report,* 16–17, HDC. This interpretation of the origin of American entry into World War II has been publicized in several controversial publicatons by persons unconnected with JRC. See Charles A. Beard, *President Roosevelt and the Coming of the War, 1941* (New Haven: Yale University Press, 1948); William Henry Chamberlain, *America's Second Great Crusade* (Chicago: Henry Regnery, 1950); Frederic R. Sanborn, *Design for War: A Study of Secret Power Politics* (New York: Devin-Adair, 1951); Charles Callan Tansill, *Back Door to War: The Roosevelt Foreign Policy, 1933–1941* (Chicago: Henry Regnery, 1952); Harry Elmer Barnes, ed., *Perpetual War for Perpetual Peace: A Critical Examination of the Foreign Policy of Franklin Delano Roosevelt and Its Aftermath* (Caldwell, Idaho: Caxton Printers, 1953); Robert A. Theobald, *The Final Secret of Pearl Harbor: The Washington Contribution to the Japanese Attack* (New York: Devin-Adair, 1954); Husband E. Kimmell, *Admiral Kimmel's Story* (Chicago: Henry Regnery, 1955); George E. Morgenstern, *Pearl Harbor: The Story of the Secret War* (New York: Devin-Adair, 1957); Bruce M. Russett, *No Clear and Present Danger: A Skeptical View of the U.S. Entry into World War II* (New York: Harper and Row, 1972); John Toland, *Infamy: Pearl Harbor and its Aftermath* (Garden City, N.Y.: Doubleday, 1982).

28. JRC unused editorial, Box 208, JRCP; Clark, *Messages of the First Presidency* 6:139–41. The sentiments of JRC's unused editorial were incorporated more fully in the First Presidency Statement of 6 April 1942 (see Clark, *Messages of the First Presidency,* esp. 6:158–60).

29. JRC Office Diary, 20 May, 14 June 1940, JRCP.

30. JRC to William Cullen Dennis, 8 July 1942, JRCP; Clark, *Messages of the First Presidency* 6:183; *October 1942 Conference Report,* 15–16, 68, HDC; "Mormon Mixup," *Time,* 19 October 1942; JRC to Jonathan W. Snow, 9 December 1942, attached to October 1942 Conference Binder, Box 156, JRCP.

31. JRC to Herbert Hoover, 15 January and 22 April 1943, Box 344; JRC to Stephen Abbot, 30 June 1943, Folder 1, Box 367; JRC to U.S. Representative Henry C. Dworshak, 6 October 1941, Folder 6, Box 364, JRCP.

32. *New York Sun,* 1 April 1944, in JRC Scrapbook, JRCP.

33. Welfare Committee Minutes, 28 November 1941, CR 255/18, HDC.

34. JRC Office Diary, 22 November 1941, JRCP; Marion G. Romney Diary, 14 November 1941, PC; JRC to Henry L. Stimson, 11 February 1942, Folder 5, Box 366, JRCP.

35. JRC Office Diary, 17 February and 19 March 1943; JRC to O. S. McBride, 27 May 1941, Folder 2, Box 363; JRCP.

36. Heber J. Grant, J. Reuben Clark, and David O. McKay to William C. FitzGibbon, Defense Savings Staff, U.S. Treasury Department, 11 October 1941, copy in Marriner S. Eccles Papers, JWML; JRC Office Diary, 7 January 1944, JRCP.

37. JRC Office Diary, 10–11 August, 8 September, 18 September, 29 November 1944, JRCP.

38. JRC to Arthur Deering Call, 26 June 1939, Folder 1, Box 361, JRCP.

39. JRC to William Cullen Dennis, 19 June 1942, Folder 1, Box 365, JRCP.

40. JRC to Edward W. Evans, 14 June 1943; JRC to Joshua L. Bailey Jr., 14 June 1943; Folder for October 1942 Conference; JRCP.

41. JRC to Philip Marshall Brown, President of the American Peace Society, 1 November 1944, Folder 1, Box 369, JRCP; *World Affairs* 124 (Fall 1961), inside back cover.

42. JRC Office Diary, 1 July 1940, JRCP; also see article, "Nazis Infest Utah," in *Sugar House Post Sentinel, Extra,* 25 May 1940, in Clarkana, HBLL.

43. C. N. Lund, *Reply to Clark's Speech* (Salt Lake City: Progressive Opinion, [1943]), broadside in Folder 4, Box 50, David O. McKay Papers, HDC, as well as in various other libraries; John Roy Carlson, pseud. [Arthur Derounian], *Under Cover: My Four Years in the Nazi Underworld of America* (New York: E. P. Dutton, 1943), 367, 373–85. The book went through seventeen printings in its first four months.

44. Counter Intelligence Weekly Report, For Week Ending 27 November 1942, District Intelligence Officer, Ninth Naval District, 6, Naval Investigative Service, Suitland, Maryland; Report of Salt Lake City FBI Office on Internal Security and Custodial Detention Case 100-1487, dated 2 January 1943, in Records Management Division, Federal Bureau of Investigation, Washington, D.C. Army intelligence undoubtedly also maintained files on or pertaining to J. Reuben Clark's antiwar statements during and before World War II, but the army's investigative files on private citizens from the 1940s to the 1970s have allegedly been destroyed.

45. JRC Office Diary, 19 December 1941, JRCP.

46. JRC to Frank R. Clark, 23 March 1942 and JRC to S. Wayne Clark, 13 November 1942, Folder 1, Box 365, JRCP.

47. JRC Office Diary, 6 April 1943, JRCP.

48. JRC to J*** L*** B****, 9 November 1943, Folder 1, Box 367, JRCP. Note the lack of reference to conscientious objection in the First Presidency's statement in 1942 about war and soldiers (Clark, *Messages of the First Presidency* 6:157–59).

49. JRC Office Diary, 1 April, 3 April, 2 May 1944, JRCP.

50. Ibid., 8 May 1944.

51. Ibid., 2 October 1945; "Conscientious Objector" File, Folder 2, Box 3, CR 1/33, HDC. See Mulford Q. Sibley and Philip E. Jacob, *Conscription of Conscience: The American State and the Conscientious Objector, 1940–1947* (Ithaca, N.Y.: Cornell University Press, 1952); Gordon C. Zahn, *Another Part of the War: The Camp Simon Story* (Amherst: University of Massachusetts Press, 1979).

52. JRC Office Diary, 16 January 1947, JRCP.

53. JRC to Philip Marshall Brown, 1 November 1944, Folder 1, Box 369, JRCP.

54. *Deseret News,* 27 June 1946, 1; Gilbert W. Scharffs, *Mormonism in Germany: A History of the Church of Jesus Christ of Latter-day Saints in Germany between 1840 and 1970* (Salt Lake City: Deseret Book, 1970), 116.

55. JRC to Ben L. Rich, 6 August 1946, Folder 6, Box 374, JRCP.

56. *April 1945 Conference Report,* 54, HDC.

57. JRC to Ezra Taft Benson, 20 August 1946, Folder 2, Box 373, JRCP.

58. JRC draft of editorial, 8 August 1945, Box 232, JRCP. President Clark did not publish that prophetic editorial, but at the service of all the churches of Salt Lake City on 4 September 1945, he stated the essential elements of the editorial and toned down the reference to future use of the atom bomb against the United States to read "it *can* be turned against us." (*Deseret News,* 8 September 1945, 12. Emphasis added.)

59. *Deseret News,* 4 October 1952, A-5.

60. JRC Office Diary, 27 August 1958, JRCP; *Salt Lake Tribune,* 23 June 1966, B-14; *Deseret News,* 23 June 1966, A-1, 6; *In A Granite Mountain* (Salt Lake City: Genealogical Society of the Church of Jesus Christ of Latter-day Saints, [1968]); "What Is the Granite Mountain Records Vault?" *Improvement Era* 69 (August 1966):699–701 gives JRC credit for originating and promoting the project, and comments on the resistance of the vault to atomic and hydrogen bombs, but denies that the specific purpose of the facility was to prepare for nuclear war.

61. JRC Office Diary, 2 April 1947, JRCP.

62. *October 1946 Conference Report,* 88–89, HDC. See also David Irving, *The Destruction of Dresden* (London: William Kimber, 1963); Robert C. Batchelder, *The Irreversible Decision, 1939–1950* (Boston: Houghton Mifflin, 1962); Barton J. Bernstein, ed., *The Atomic Bomb: The Critical Issues* (Boston: Little, Brown, 1976); Gordon Thomas and Max Morgan-Willis, *Ruin From the Air: The Atomic Mission to Hiroshima* (London: Hamilton, 1977).

63. JRC Office Diary, 3 August 1950; JRC draft of unused editorial, 22 September 1950, Box 208; JRCP.

64. Mark E. Petersen to JRC, 2 February 1945; JRC Memorandum, 5 February 1945; Folder 7, Box 371, JRCP.

65. Harold B. Lee Diary, 7 June 1945, PC; JRC to Tucker P. Smith, American Friends Service Committee, 15 June 1945, Folder 7, Box 371, JRCP.

66. Clark, *Messages of the First Presidency* 6:239–42.

67. JRC Office Diary, 22 September 1947, JRCP.

68. JRC, *Let Us Have Peace* (Salt Lake City: Deseret News Press, 1947), 15–16; JRC, *Stand Fast By Our Constitution* (Salt Lake City: Deseret Book, 1962), 71.

69. JRC to Arthur Vandenberg, 31 December 1947, Folder 22, Box 376; JRC Office Diary, 2 March 1948; JRCP.

70. Harold B. Lee Diary, 2 January 1951, PC; Rowena J. Miller to David I. Folkman, 16 November 1959, Folder 11, Box 405, JRCP.

71. Without mentioning JRC, Justus D. Doenecker provides the national setting in *Not to the Swift: The Old Isolationists in the Cold War Era* (Lewisburg, Pa.: Bucknell University Press, 1979).

72. James W. Gerard to JRC, 11 April 1947, JRC to James W. Gerard, 15 April 1947; JRC to U.S. Senator Henry C. Dworshak, 30 April 1947, Folder 1, Box 376; James W. Gerard to JRC, 14 October 1947, JRC to James W. Gerard, 14 October 1947, 29 October 1947, Folder 5, Box 376; JRCP.

73. JRC to James W. Gerard, 14 April 1949, Folder 9, Box 379, JRCP; *New York Times,* 7 May 1949, 4. Cf. Footnote 71 and Robert Endicott Osgood, *NATO: The Entangling Alliance* (Chicago: University of Chicago Press, 1962).

74. *Salt Lake Telegram,* 17 August 1949; JRC, *Stand Fast By Our Constitution,* 84–94.

75. JRC Office Diary, 27 June 1950, JRCP.

76. Ibid., 8 September 1950. He publicized his opposition to the Korean War in *Our Dwindling Sovereignty* (Salt Lake City: Deseret News Press, 1952), 32–33, reprinted in *Stand Fast By Our Constitution,* 128–29. For background to the Korean War, see Carl Berger, *The Korean Knot: A Military Political History,* rev. ed. (Philadelphia: Universtiy of Pennsylvania Press, 1964); Glenn D. Paige, *The Korean Decision (June 24–30, 1950)* (New York: The Free Press, 1968); J. Lawton Collins, *War in Peacetime: The History and Lessons of Korea* (Boston: Houghton Mifflin, 1969).

77. JRC Office Diary, 4 October 1948, 8 September 1950, JRCP; chapter "Waste Places of Zion . . . The Rivers of Babylon," this volume, nn. 39, 106; Fox, *JRC.*

78. JRC Memorandum on the United Nations San Francisco Charter, June–July 1945, Box 231, JRCP. For studies of the United Nations see the following: Ernest A. Gross, *The United Nations: Structure for Peace* (New York: Harper, 1962); Julius Stone, *Aggression and World Order: A Critique of United Nations Theories of Aggression* (Berkeley: University of California Press, 1958); William A. Scott and Stephen B. Withey, *United States and United Nations: The Public View, 1945–1955* (New York: Manhattan, 1958); James J. Wadsworth, *The Glass House: The United Nations in Action* (New York: Praeger, 1966).

79. JRC to S/Sgt James S. Arringona, 3 December 1945, Folder 1, Box 371; JRC Office Diary, 15 October, 17 October 1955; JRCP. The reason JRC never published his memorandum on the United Nations was probably because Presidents George Albert Smith and David O. McKay were both favorably disposed towards the UN. JRC did give a comparatively brief analysis of the charter in *Our Dwindling Sovereignty,* 23–24, 26–32, reprinted in *Stand Fast By Our Constitution,* 118–19, 122–28.

80. JRC to Mrs. A. Helen Morgan, 16 June 1953, Folder 2, Box 389, JRCP.

81. David O. McKay Diary, 19 September 1961, HDC.

82. *Improvement Era* 55 (August 1952):568.

83. JRC, *Let Us Have Peace,* 15; JRC, *Stand Fast By Our Constitution,* 70; JRC to William Hard, 3 December 1951, Folder 12, Box 383; Interview of JRC with Ezra Taft Benson, 21 March 1955, Folder 5, Box 392; JRC to Alfred M. Landon, 15 August 1956, Folder 16, Box 396; JRCP. In the October 1959 Church general conference, JRC expressed alarm at Soviet Premier Nikita Khruschev's boast that the USSR would exterminate the United States, and JRC warned against the destruction of America's defenses. But he still emphasized primarily a warning against the Latter-day Saints becoming communists, rather than advocating increased defense spending or militarism. See *October 1959 Conference Report,* 46, HDC.

84. JRC to U.S. Senator Henry Dworshak, 17 May 1954, Folder 15, Box 390, JRCP.

85. JRC to Fred Morris Dearing, 18 August 1958, Folder 6, Box 402, JRCP.

86. *The Pentagon Papers* (New York: Quadrangle Books, 1971), 115; Guenter Lewy, *America in Vietnam* (New York: Oxford University Press, 1978); George C. Herring, *America's Longest War: the United States and Vietnam, 1950–1975* (New York: Wiley, 1979). Wiley, 1979).

87. Questionnaires indicated that between 9 and 13 percent of the student body of Brigham Young University expressed opposition to the participation of the United States in the Vietnam War, as judged by various questions. See Knud S. Larsen and Gary Schwendiman, "The Vietnam War Through the Eyes of a Mormon Subculture," *Dialogue* 3 (Autumn

1968):152–62. An example of Mormon anti-Vietnam writings that used JRC quotes is Gordon C. Thomasson, ed., *War, Conscription, Conscience and Mormonism* (Santa Barbara, Calif.: Mormon Heritage, 1971), esp. 9–12, 29–36, 44–72, 56, 84–85.

88. JRC to Everett De La Mare, 6 March 1956, Folder 1, Box 395, JRCP.

ALL NATIONS, AND KINDREDS, AND PEOPLE, AND TONGUES

1. John S. Halber, *Outcasts from Evolution: Scientific Attitudes of Racial Inferiority, 1859–1900* (Urbana: University of Illinois Press, 1971); Christine Bolt, *Victorian Attitudes to Race* (London: Routledge and K. Paul, 1971); Richard A. Thompson, "The Yellow Peril, 1890–1924" (Ph.D. diss., University of Wisconsin, 1957); C. C. Eldridge, *England's Mission: The Imperial Idea in the Age of Gladstone and Disraeli* (Chapel Hill: University of North Carolina Press, 1973); Richard Faber, *The Vision and the Need: Late Victorian Imperialist Aims* (London: Faber, 1966); Agnes Murphey, *The Ideology of French Imperialism, 1871–1881* (New York: H. Fertig, 1968); Walter LeFeber, *The New Empire: An Interpretation of American Expansion, 1860–1898* (Ithaca, N.Y.: Cornell University Press, 1963); Richard W. Van Alstyne, *The Rising American Empire* (New York: Oxford University Press, 1960).

2. John Higham, *Strangers in the Land: Patterns of American Nativism, 1860–1925* (New Brunswick, N.J.: Rutgers University Press, 1955); Thomas J. Curran, *Xenophobia and Immigration, 1820–1930* (Boston: Twayne, 1975).

3. *Salt Lake Herald*, 16 June 1898, 5, which printed the complete text of JRC's valedictory. Joshua R. Clark's Diary, 15 June 1898, JRCP, quoted only the sentence on immigration and described the audience reaction.

4. Fox, *JRC*, 631–32, n. 2.

5. JRC to Herbert Hoover, 14 May 1942, 7, Post-Presidential Individual File, Herbert Hoover Presidential Library, West Branch, Iowa.

6. Fox, *JRC*, 111–215, 451–583.

7. JRC to Bishops' Meeting, 5 April 1956, manuscript, Box 151, JRCP.

8. JRC to F. W. Smith, 29 November 1941, Folder 3, Box 363, JRCP.

9. JRC Office Diary, 13 July 1950, JRCP.

10. Ibid., 6 June 1951; Fox, *JRC*, 314–16, 346.

11. Cf. nearly every issue of the *Deseret News* during the period, and correspondence of JRC, 1941–1945. Only one JRC reference to "Japs" could be found: JRC Office Diary, 13 March 1942, JRCP.

12. JRC Office Diary, 2 November 1942, JRCP. JRC's opposition to the federal government interring the Japanese-Americans in Utah carried no weight with the federal government. See Leonard J. Arrington, *The Price of Prejudice: The Japanese-American Relocation Center in Utah During World War II* (Logan: Utah State University, 1962).

13. Author's interview with Spencer W. Kimball, 2 February 1979.

14. JRC to G***** C. B******, 3 August 1945, Folder 2, Box 371, JRCP.

15. JRC to H***** R. C*********, 30 October 1952, Folder 5, Box 385, JRCP.

16. Juanita Brooks, *History of the Jews in Utah and Idaho* (Salt Lake City: Western Epics, 1973), 69–70; Rudolf Glanz, *Jew and Mormon: Historic Group Relations and Religious Outlook* (New York: Waldron Press, 1963).

17. JRC to Herbert Hoover, 14 May 1942, 8, Post-Presidential Individual File, Hoover Presidential Library, West Branch, Iowa.

18. Fox, *JRC*, 415–19, 422–27.

19. JRC Office Diary, 17 February 1934, 25 February 1944; JRC to Lute, 7 January 1935, Box 337; JRCP.

20. Joan Comay, *Who's Who in Jewish History after the period of the Old Testament* (New York: David McKay, 1974); Robert S. Wistrich, *Revolutionary Jews from Marx to Trotsky* (London: George C. Harrap, 1976).

21. Note 17; Charles Herbert Stember et al., *Jews in the Mind of America* (New York: Basic Books, 1966), 157.

22. Comay, *Who's Who in Jewish History,* 63, 81, 132; Ronald I. Rubin, ed., *The Unredeemed: Anti-Semitism in the Soviet Union* (Chicago: Quadrangle Books, 1968); William Korey, *The Soviet Cage: Anti-Semitism in Russia* (New York: Viking Press, 1973).

23. JRC Office Diary, 8 January 1943, JRCP.

24. JRC maintained several copies of the *Protocols* in his personal library at all times, as well as a 1921 refutation of the publication by the American Jewish Committee and a 1938 defense of the publicaton by the American Nationalist Press (See Clarkana, HBLL). For correspondence concerning the *Protocols,* see Marilyn R. Allen to JRC, 18 July 1946, with JRC notation, "ask for 6 to my home," and Rowena J. Miller to Marilyn R. Allen, 7 December 1949, in Folder 1, Box 379; JRC to Pyramid Book Shop, 22 September 1958, Folder 7, Box 403; JRC to Ernest L. Wilkinson, 5 February 1949, Folder 16, Box 380; JRC to Ezra Taft Benson, ca. December 1957, Folder 4, Box 398; JRCP. For background on the *Protocols,* see "Protocols of the Learned Elders of Zion," *The New Encyclopaedia Britannica,* 30 vols. (Chicago: Encyclopaedia Britannica, Inc., 1974), 8:253; John S. Curtiss, *An Appraisal of the Protocols of Zion* (New York: Columbia University Press, 1942).

25. Stember, *Jews in the Mind of America,* 126–27.

26. David O. McKay Diary, 16 April 1936, HDC; Frank Herman Jonas, "Utah: Sagebrush Democracy," in *Rocky Mountain Politics,* ed. Thomas C. Donnelly (Albuquerque: University of New Mexico Press, 1940), 19.

27. JRC Office Diary, 8 January 1943, JRCP.

28. JRC and David O. McKay to Richard Siebenschein, 27 January 1939, in reply to his two letters of December 1938, in Folder 5, Box 110, CR 1/44, HDC; also letter of Egon E. Weiss, a Church member of Jewish ancestry, to First Presidency, 23 November 1938, Folder 6, Box 111, CR 1/44, HDC. For related correspondence on this matter, see JRC to Allen Dulles, 11 April 1939, Folder 1, Box 361; JRC to Clarence E. Pickett, 14 April 1939, Folder 2, Box 361; JRCP; and JRC to Green H. Hackworth, 24 April 1939, Box 113, CR 1/44, HDC.

29. Stember et al., *Jews in the Mind of America,* 143.

30. Harold B. Lee Diary, 22 March 1945, PC; "Pres. Clark Warns of Plot to Wreck U.S.," *Deseret News,* 18 September 1946; JRC Office Diary, 28 February, 10 April, 16 April 1948, 14 May 1952, JRCP.

31. David O. McKay Diary, 14 October 1952, HDC, emphasis in original; David O. McKay and JRC to Tracy-Collins Trust Co., 11 February 1953, CR 1/46, HDC.

32. Note 16; Armand L. Mauss, "Mormon Semitism and Anti-Semitism," *Sociological Analysis* (Spring 1968):11–27.

33. Winthrop D. Jordan, *White Over Black: American Attitudes Toward the Negro, 1550–1812* (Chapel Hill: University of North Carolina Press, 1968); George M. Fredrickson, *Black Image in the White Mind: The Debate on Afro-American Character and Destiny, 1817–1914* (New York: Harper & Row, 1971); Gunnar Myrdal, *An American Dilemma: The Negro Problem and Modern Democracy* (New York: Harper & Brothers, 1944), 100; Eugene H. Berwanger, *The Frontier Against Slavery: Western Anti-Negro Prejudice and the Slavery Extension Controversy* (Urbana: University of Illinois Press, 1967); Leon F. Litwack, *North of Slavery: The Negro in the Free States, 1790–1860* (Chicago: University of Chicago Press, 1961).

34.   James M. McPherson, *The Struggle for Equality: Abolitionists and the Negro in the Civil War and Reconstruction* (Princeton, N.J.: Princeton University Press, 1964), 223–37; C. Vann Woodward, *The Strange Career of Jim Crow*, 3d rev. ed. (New York: Oxford University Press, 1974).

35.   Joseph Fielding Smith, *Teachings of the Prophet Joseph Smith* (Salt Lake City: Deseret News Press, 1938), 269–70.

36.   Kate B. Carter, *The Negro Pioneer* (Salt Lake City: Daughters of Utah Pioneers, 1965); Dennis L. Lythgoe, "Negro Slavery in Utah," *Utah Historical Quarterly* 39 (Winter 1971):40–54; Dennis L. Lythgoe, "Negro Slavery in Utah" (Master's thesis, University of Utah, 1966); Ronald Gerald Coleman, "A History of Blacks in Utah, 1852–1910" (Ph.D. diss., University of Utah, 1980); Newell G. Bringhurst, *Saints, Slaves, and Blacks: The Changing Place of Black People within Mormonism* (Westport, Conn.: Greenwood Press, 1981); G[eorge] R[eynolds], "Man and his Varieties," *The Juvenile Instructor* 3 (15 September 1868):141; James E. Talmage Journal, 22 February 1884, HBLL; *Utah Code Annotated* (1953), Replacement Volume 3, Title 30-1-2.2.

37.   James Boyd Christensen, "A Social Survey of the Negro Population of Salt Lake City, Utah" (Master's thesis, University of Utah, 1948), 45–55; Utah, Legislature, Senate, *Report of Senate Committee to Investigate Discrimination Against Minorities in Utah,* 27th Sess., 1947, *Senate Journal,* 66; Wallace R. Bennett, "The Negro in Utah," *Utah Law Review* 3 (Spring 1953):340–48; Elmer R. Smith, *The Status of the Negro in Utah* (Salt Lake City: National Association for the Advancement of Colored People, 1956), 6–7, 12; Margaret Judy Maag, "Discrimination Against the Negro in Utah and Institutional Efforts to Eliminate It" (Master's thesis, University of Utah, 1971), 34.

38.   Andrew Jenson, *Latter-day Saints' Biographical Encyclopedia,* 4 vols. (Salt Lake City: Andrew Jenson Historical Co., 1901–1936) 3:577; Journal History of the Church, 31 May 1879, HDC; William E. Berrett, *The Church and the Negroid People* (Provo, Utah: Bookmark, 1967); "The Book of Abraham," *Times and Seasons* 3 (1 March 1842):705, verses 6–8; "A Short Chapter on a Long Subject," *Times and Seasons* 6 (1 April 1845):857; Lester E. Bush Jr., "Mormonism's Negro Doctrine: An Historical Overview," *Dialogue* 8 (Spring 1973):16–21.

39.   Contained in manuscript versions in Wilford Woodruff Journal, ca. January–February 1852, HDC, Brigham Young discourse, 5 February 1852, Brigham Young Papers, HDC. Published and quoted in the following: Mathhias F. Cowley, *Wilford Woodruff, Fourth President of the Church of Jesus Christ of Latter-day Saints, History of His Life and Labors as Recorded in His Daily Journal* (Salt Lake City: Deseret News Press, 1909), 351; Joseph Fielding Smith, *The Way to Perfection* (Salt Lake City: Genealogical Society of Utah, 1931), 106; Daniel H. Ludlow, *Latter-day Prophets Speak* (Salt Lake City: Bookcraft, 1948, 1951), 204.

40.   *Journal of Discourses,* 26 vols. (Liverpool, England: Latter-day Saints Book Depot, 1854–1886) 7:290–91, 11:272; Brigham Young discourse of 5 February 1852, as discussed in Ronald K. Esplin, "Brigham Young and Priesthood Denial to the Blacks: An Alternative View," *Brigham Young University Studies* 19 (Spring 1979):400-01; First Presidency Statement, 17 August 1949, HDC and published in Berrett, *The Church and the Negroid People,* 16; and historical discussion in Bush, "Mormonism's Negro Doctrine."

41.   Text of JRC Remarks, 9 October 1947, originally in Adam S. Bennion Papers, HBLL.

42.   JRC Office Diary, 30 August 1944, 4 March 1947, 1 May 1950; George Albert Smith Diary, 16 June 1945, SFP; Rowena J. Miller to Mrs. Guy B. Rose, 20 September 1949, Folder 8, Box 380, JRCP; Harold B. Lee Diary, 29 November 1949, PC.

43.   *New York Times,* 10 May 1954, 1, 15, Benjamin Muse, *Ten Years of Prelude: The Story of Integration Since the Supreme Court's 1954 Decision* (New York: Viking Press, 1964).

44.   JRC Draft no. 3 of conference talk, 13 September 1954, 17, Folder 5, Box 210, JRCP.

45. David O. McKay Diary, 25 February 1949, HDC, including comment about Southern segregation.

46. Bush, "Mormonism's Negro Doctrine," 44–45.

47. Notes 5 and 14. Also JRC to T***** J. P******, 8 December 1941: "In the next place, my own observation yields no real exception to the rule that upon an intermarriage, such as is contemplated here, the husband inevitably as time goes on, adopts the standards (above or below his own) of his wife's race. If the situation so worked out with you it would mean that you would become a Brazilian in your habits, your associations, and perhaps in your ideals and concepts.

"I know nothing about the young lady in this case, but I do know that Brazilian standards generally are below our standards in matters of morals and frequently in standards of life generally. Their habits are different; their concepts and ideals are different. They are, in fact, a different race." (Folder 2, Box 365, JRCP.)

48. JRC to Mission Presidents' Meeting, 30 March 1960, manuscript, April 1960 Conference Folder, Box 169, JRCP.

49. James G. Martin and Clyde W. Franklin, *Minority Group Relations* (Columbus, Ohio: Charles E. Merrill, 1973), 75; Wallace R. Bennett, "The Negro in Utah," 347, n. 52.

50. JRC to Dr. G. Albin Mattson, 12 April 1948, Folder 1, Box 378; JRC Office Diary, 10 April 1948, 9 June 1949, 9 July 1951, JRCP.

51. Rowena J. Miller to O. Boyd Matthias, 8 March 1953, Folder 2, Box 389, JRCP.

52. Correspondence between JRC and G. Albin Mattson in Boxes 295, 378, 391 and 406, JRCP.

53. JRC to Dr. G. Albin Matson, 19 January 1959, "Negro" Folder, Box 295, JRCP.

54. Text of JRC Remarks, 25 January 1940, Folder 2, Box 74, SFP. Emphasis added.

55. Text of JRC Remarks, 9 October 1947, originally in Adam S. Bennion Papers, HBLL. Quoted in part in Bush, "Mormonism's Negro Doctrine," 41. For the event that may have occasioned his reopening this matter, see Bush, n. 184.

56. JRC Memorandum, "The Afrikan Branches of the Church of Jesus Christ of Latter-day Saints," undated, Box 207, JRCP.

57. David O. McKay Diary, 17 January 1954, HDC. Farrell Ray Monson, "History of the South African Mission of The Church of Jesus Christ of Latter-day Saints, 1853–1970" (Master's thesis, Brigham Young University, 1971), 45–46; A. Hamer Reiser Oral History, 1974, Volume 2, 165–69, HDC.

58. David O. McKay Diary, 19 January, 25 February 1954, HDC.

59. This is undoubtedly why "Pres. Clark was quite perturbed over the change in policy and predicted we would one day return to the old rule." (Harold B. Lee Diary, 25 February 1954, PC.)

60. JRC Draft no. 3 of Talk, 13 September 1954, 16–17, Folder 5, Box 210, JRCP. See n. 45 for explanation of reason why President Clark did not deliver this conference talk, as he had planned.

61. *Deseret News,* 9 June 1978, 1.

62. *October 1937 Conference Report,* 105, HDC.

63. JRC, *Public Loans to Foreign Countries* (Salt Lake City: Deseret News Press, 1945), 20; quoted in Edwin Brown Firmage and Christopher L. Blakesley, "J. Reuben Clark Jr., Law and International Order," *Brigham Young University Studies* 13 (Spring 1973):301–2.

64. JRC Office Diary, 30 November 1953, JRCP; *Deseret News 1982 Church Almanac,* 63.

65. *October 1954 Conference Report,* 78; *April 1969 Conference Report,* 92, HDC. Cf. *October 1968 Conference Report,* 83, HDC.

66. *April 1958 Conference Report,* 88, HDC; *Deseret News 1982 Church Almanac,* 64.

PRECIOUS THINGS OF EVERY KIND AND ART

1. JRC to Alvin S. Nelson, 19 June 1942, Folder 2, Box 365, JRCP.

2. JRC personal library, Clarkana, HBLL. A presentation copy of a Paul Bailey novel is excluded from consideration here.

3. Joshua R. Clark Diary, 26 December 1884, JRCP.

4. JRC personal library, Clarkana, HBLL.

5. JRC copy of *Hale's Longer English Poems* (London, 1892), in Clarkana, HBLL.

6. JRC copy of Edward Fitzgerald's translation of the *Rubaiyat of Omar Khayyam,* in Clarkana, HBLL.

7. JRC copy of Bartlett's *Familiar Quotations,* in Clarkana, HBLL.

8. Jay Rubark, "When I Would Pass," *Relief Society Magazine* 28 (June 1941):375.

9. *Deseret News Church Section,* 5 January 1946, 4, 25 June 1950, 12.

10. JRC to Lute, 28 August 1913, Box 330, JRCP. Information supplied by family.

11. JRC Office Diary, 18 February 1944, JRCP.

12. Ibid., 27 January 1945.

13. Georgius Young Cannon Oral History, 1973, typescript, 16, HDC.

14. Luacine S. Clark Diary, 25 January 1931, JRCP.

15. JRC to Louise Clark Bennion, 28 January 1931, Box 336, JRCP.

16. E.g., JRC to Thorpe B. Isaacson, 8 November 1950, JRCP.

17. JRC to Adam S. Bennion, 5 November 1946, Folder 2, Box 373, JRCP; Harold B. Lee Diary, 7 February 1949, PC.

18. JRC to Bishop's Meeting, 7 April 1950, manuscript, April 1950 Conference Folder, Box 160, JRCP; "Home, and the Building of Home Life," *Relief Society Magazine* 39 (December 1952):792.

19. Henry D. Moyle Diary, 6 August 1951, HDC; Harold B. Lee Diary, 6 August 1951, PC; Marion G. Romney Diary, 19 December 1954, 2 November 1939, PC.

20. Henry D. Moyle Diary, 31 August 1953, HDC.

21. JRC to Leopold Stokowski, 28 April 1933, Box 349, JRCP.

22. JRC to Richard L. Evans, 18 May 1936, Folder 1, Box 355, JRCP.

23. JRC to Florence Jepperson Madsen and Alberta Huish Christensen, 1 November 1956, Folder 18, Box 396, JRCP.

24. JRC Office Diary, 18 February 1934, JRCP.

25. JRC to Ernest L. Wilkinson, 12 May 1952, Folder 1, Box 16, Brigham Young University Presidential Papers, Ernest L. Wilkinson Administration, HBLL.

26. Ernest L. Wilkinson Diary, 3 June 1959, HBLL.

27. Ibid., 7 September 1960.

28. JRC to Joseph J. Cannon, 28 January 1936, Folder 1, Box 355, JRCP.

29. JRC Office Diary, 3 March 1943; JRC to Richard L. and Alice Evans, 26 December 1955, Folder 6, Box 393, JRCP.

30. JRC Office Diary, 29 November 1944, JRCP.

31. Heber J. Grant Journal, 23 February 1936, HDC.

32. Alexander Schreiner to Heber J. Grant and Counselors, 14 July 1926, Box 43, CR 1/44, HDC; Alexander Schreiner to First Presidency, 14 May 1930, in Alexander Schreiner Folder, CR 1/45, HDC.

33. Alexander Schreiner Folder, CR 1/45, HDC; Heber J. Grant Journal, 11 July, 17 July, 18 July 1933, 23 February 1936, 28 June, 26 August 1938, HDC.

34. JRC Office Diary, 3 February, 3 May 1939, JRCP.

35. Ibid., 22 June 1939.

36. James V. D'Arc, "The Saints on Celluloid: The Making of the Movie *Brigham Young,*" *Sunstone* 1 (Fall 1976):11–28; Heber J. Grant Journal, 11 September 1939, HDC.

37. Heber J. Grant Journal, 27 October 1939, HDC; JRC to Jason S. Joy, 31 October 1939, Folder 5, Box 361, JRCP.

38. Script of *Brigham Young* in Dean Jagger Papers, HBLL.

39. Heber J. Grant Journal, 13 August 1940, HDC; *Deseret News,* 13 August 1940; JRC Office Diary, 14 August 1940, JRCP.

40. JRC to Lowell Thomas, 3 January, 13 January 1953, Folder 12, Box 389, JRCP.

41. JRC Ranch Diary, 16 November 1955; JRC to Robert R. Mullen, 5 December 1955, Folder 16, Box 393; JRCP.

42. JRC to Cecil B. DeMille, 16 August 1956, marked "Not sent," Box 255, JRCP. See also JRC to John Krier, 29 August 1956, Folder 21, Box 396, JRCP.

43. JRC to John O. Denman, 24 August 1957, Folder 15, Box 400, JRCP.

44. JRC Home Diary, 26 April 1958, JRCP.

45. *Deseret News Church Section,* 20 June 1953, 4.

THE WELFARE OF THIS PEOPLE

1. "Elder Lee Pays Tribute to a Great Leader," *Deseret News Church Section,* 14 October 1961, 41.

2. See also Doctrine and Covenants, 1981 ed., s.v. "Consecration" and "Equal" in index; Leonard J. Arrington, Ferrmorz Y. Fox, and Dean L. May, *Building the City of God: Community and Cooperation Among the Mormons* (Salt Lake City: Deseret Book, 1976), 15–19.

3. *October 1942 Conference Report,* 55, HDC.

4. Arrington, Fox, and May, *Building the City of God,* 25–26, 366–71; Joseph Smith, Jr. *History of the Church of Jesus Christ of Latter-day Saints,* 2d ed. rev., ed. B. H. Roberts, 7 vols. (Salt Lake City: Deseret Book, 1960) 1:365–67.

5. Arrington, Fox, and May, *Building the City of God,* 31–38.

6. *History of the Church* 4:567–68; *A Centenary of Relief Society, 1842–1942* (Salt Lake City: General Board of Relief Society, 1942), 40.

7. Arrington, Fox, and May, *Building the City of God,* 59–61.

8. Ibid., 265–93, 309–10; quote from Orderville minutes on 269.

9. *October 1942 Conference Report,* 55, HDC.

10. JRC to Frank W. Wylie, 29 April 1948, Folder 13, Box 378, JRCP.

11. Leonard J. Arrington and Thomas G. Alexander, *A Dependent Commonwealth: Utah's Economy from Statehood to the Great Depression,* ed. Dean May (Provo, Utah: Brigham Young University, 1974), esp. 86; Leonard J. Arrington, "Utah and the Depression of the 1890s," *Utah Historical Quarterly* 29 (January 1961):3–18, esp. 6.

12. James B. Allen and Glen M. Leonard, *Story of the Latter-day Saints* (Salt Lake City: Deseret Book, 1976), 471; Bruce D. Blumell, "Welfare before Welfare: Twentieth Century LDS Church Charity before the Great Depression," *Journal of Mormon History* 6 (1970):90–91.

13. Blumell, "Welfare before Welfare," 91, 93, 104.

14.Arrington and Alexander, *A Dependent Commonwealth,* 57–86; Arrington, Fox, and May, *Building the City of God,* 338.

15. Bruce D. Blumell, " 'Remember the Poor': A History of Welfare in the Church of Jesus Christ of Latter-day Saints, 1830–1980," 83–84, 119, paper in Joseph Fielding Smith Institute of Church History file, Brigham Young University.

16. Ibid., 119.

17. Arrington, Fox, and May, *Building the City of God,* 341–42; Heber J. Grant Journal, 1 June, 16 June 1932, 3 January 1933, HDC.

18. Harold B. Lee, Charles S. Hyde, and Paul C. Child to Heber J. Grant and Counselors, 23 May 1933, Binder 1, Box 196, JRCP; Blumell, "Remember the Poor," 126.

19. Blumell, "Welfare before Welfare," 104.

20. *April 1933 Conference Report,* 103, HDC.

21. JRC Notes for Talk, 19 June 1933, Binder 1, Box 196, JRCP; *Salt Lake Tribune,* 20 June 1933; JRC Office Diary, 19 June 1933, JRCP.

22. JRC Office Diary, 8 August 1933, JRCP.

23. Ibid., 15–16 May 1933.

24. Ibid., 28 June 1933.

25. JRC draft of "Suggestive Directions," 30 June 1933, and his notation on the printed pamphlet in Binder 1, Box 196; JRC Office Diary, 20 June 1933; JRCP.

26. *Deseret News Church Section,* 21 September 1957, 4; JRC remarks to North Utah Welfare Region, 22 June 1944, manuscript, Box 228, JRCP.

27. JRC Office Diary, 9 August, 18 August, 22 August 1933, Pioneer Stake Presidency to First Presidency, 23 May 1933, and draft of First Presidency letter, 26 August 1933, with carbons of actual mailings dated 28 August, all in Binder 1, Box 169, JRCP. Clark, *Messages of the First Presidency* 5:330–36 gives the text of the letter and the instructions for the survey, but incorrectly dates it in July 1933.

28. Heber J. Grant Journal, 20 July 1933, HDC.

29. JRC draft of "Suggestive Outlines," 15 July 1933, with emendation dated 17 July 1933, in Binder 1, Box 196, JRCP. Emphasis added,

30. Marion G. Romney Oral History, 1976, 3, HDC.

31. Sylvester Q. Cannon Journal, annual summary for 31 December 1933, HDC; Sylvester Q. Cannon to Wilford A. Beesley, 4 October 1933, in Binder 1, Box 196, JRCP.

32. JRC Office Diary, 8 August 1933; JRC Memorandum of meeting with Roosevelt, 25 September 1933, Folder 2, Box 350; JRCP.

33. Marion G. Romney Oral History, 1976, 3, HDC, said that the publication occurred on 23 October 1933, but two years after its publication JRC's secretary reported that Deseret News Press records indicated that printing commenced on 27 October 1933. VaLois South to JRC, 18 October 1935, Binder 1, Box 196, JRCP.

34. Blumell, "Remember the Poor," 112.

35. JRC to Sylvester Q. Cannon, 9 November 1933, Binder 1, Box 196, JRCP. Also ibid., JRC to Heber J. Grant, 9 November 1933. See Blumell, "Remember the Poor," 112 for summary of 30 October meeting of Presidency and Presiding Bishopric to which JRC refers in this letter.

36. Blumell, "Remember the Poor," 112.

37. *Care of the Poor* (Salt Lake City: The Presiding Bishopric, 1934), 1, 12.

38. *October 1934 Conference Report,* 97, 99, HDC.

39. JRC to Brother and Sister Richard M. Robinson, 28 October 1934, Folder 1, Box 351, JRCP. The best-known of J. Reuben Clark's published statements of the philosophy of the Welfare Plan were *Church Welfare Plan: A Discussion . . . at Estes Park, Colorado, June*

20, 1939 (Salt Lake City: The General Church Welfare Committee, 1939) and *Fundamentals of the Church Welfare Plan* (Salt Lake City: General Church Welfare Committee, 1944).

40. Blumell, "Remember the Poor," 117.

41. Ibid., JRC to Heber J. Grant, 1 March 1935, CR 1/48, HDC; JRC draft of First Presidency Message, 5 April 1935, Volume 2, Box 196, JRCP.

42. Heber J. Grant Journal, 7 April 1935, HDC.

43. David O. McKay to JRC, 6 May 1935, and JRC to McKay, 11 May 1935, Folder 7, Box 353, JRCP.

44. Clark, *Messages of the First Presidency* 6:10; Leonard J. Arrington and Wayne K. Hinton, "Origin of the Welfare Plan of the Church of Jesus Christ of Latter-day Saints," *Brigham Young University Studies* 5 (Winter 1964):67.

45. Minutes of Special Priesthood Meeting, 7 October 1935, Volume 2, Box 196, JRCP.

46. VaLois South to JRC, 9 November 1935, Volume 2, Box 196, JRCP.

47. Arrington and Hinton, "Origin of the Welfare Plan," 75.

48. JRC remarks to Welfare Meeting, manuscript, 2 October 1936, Box 151, JRCP.

49. JRC to Welfare Agricultural meeting, manuscript, 7, 4 April 1955, Box 151, JRCP.

50. David O. McKay explained this somewhat differently to a reporter for *Time* who asked, "I understand that the Welfare Program started in 1936, and that it came as a revelation to President Heber J. Grant," to which President McKay responded: "I answered: It was not a revelation; it is just a program of the Church" (David O. McKay Diary, 14 July 1947, HDC).

51. JRC to Heber J. Grant and David O. McKay, 5 May 1936, CR 1/48, HDC.

52. Blumell, "Remember the Poor," 141.

53. Arrington, Fox and May, *Building the City of God*, 349.

54. Minutes of Welfare Committee with First Presidency, 12 June 1937, CR 255/18; *April 1940 Conference Report*, 17–18; HDC.

55. Minutes of Welfare Committee with First Presidency, 12 June 1937, CR 255/18, HDC.

56. JRC Office Diary, JRCP; Blumell, "Remember the Poor," 150–51; Welfare Committee Meeting with First Presidency, 3 June and 1 July 1938, CR 255/18, HDC.

57. JRC to David O. McKay, 2 March 1936, Folder 1, Box 355, JRCP.

58. JRC to Heber J. Grant and David O. McKay, 18 May 1936, Folder 1, Box 355, JRCP.

59. JRC's best-known statement on this matter was in 1942: "We have all said that the Welfare Plan is not the United Order and was not intended to be. However, I should like to suggest to you that perhaps, after all, when the Welfare Plan gets thoroughly into operation—it is not so yet—we shall not be so very far from carrying out the great fundamentals of the United Order." (*October 1942 Conference Report*, 57, HDC.)

60. *New York Times,* 25 May 1936, 20; *Salt Lake Tribune*, 25 May 1935, 18.

61. *October 1936 Conference Report*, 114; Minutes of Welfare Committee with First Presidency, 21 May 1937, CR 255/18; HDC.

62. *Deseret News*, 7 April 1936; *LDS Church Welfare Handbook of Instructions* (Salt Lake City: The General Church Welfare Committee of The Church of Jesus Christ of Latter-day Saints, 1944), 62.

63. JRC to Reeve Schley, 28 May 1936, Folder 2, Box 354, JRCP; Welfare Committee Meetings with First Presidency, 21 July 1939, CR 255/18, HDC.

64. Minutes of Welfare Committee with First Presidency, 29 October 1937, CR 255/18; LDS Church Security Program Minutes, 13 April 1938, CR 255/5; HDC.

65. "42,000 Salt Lake Mormons on WPA, Despite 'Dole' Flight," *New York Daily News,* 21 June 1938, 8; "Tithes and Security," *Time,* 1 August 1938.

66. Arrington, Fox, and May, *Building the City of God,* 347–48.

67. JRC Memorandum, "Church Security Plan," 19 October 1937, Folder 1, Box 358, JRCP; Blumell, "Remember the Poor," 148–49; Marion G. Romney Oral History, 1976, 6, HDC.

68. Marion G. Romney Diary, 30 January 1942, PC.

69. Marion G. Romney Oral History, 1972–73, 15–16, HDC.

70. Harold B. Lee Diary, 17 November 1954, PC; *Deseret News Church Section,* 8 August 1951.

71. *April 1944 Conference Report,* 113; *April 1945 Conference Report,* 25; HDC.

72. Welfare Committee Meeting with First Presidency, 6 January 1939, CR 255/18, HDC.

73. Blumell, "Remember the Poor," 158.

74. JRC remarks to Welfare Meeting, 10 April 1940, manuscript, Box 151, JRCP.

75. Author's interview with Marion G. Romney, 26 October 1977.

76. "Budget Beginnings," 26, Binder, Box 188, JRCP.

77. *April 1940 Conference Report,* 14, HDC; JRC Office Diary, 23 January 1939; JRC remarks to Church auxiliary leaders, 1 April 1940 in Folder "Suggestions to Auxiliaries," Box 207; JRCP.

78. *April 1938 Conference Report,* 105–6, HDC.

79. "Financial Report for the Year 1947," 11, CR 1/48, HDC; *Deseret News,* 7 October 1939.

80. Harold B. Lee Diary, 31 August 1945, PC.

81. *April 1948 Conference Report,* 117–18; "Financial Report for the Year 1947," 11.

82. "Budget Beginnings," 9, Binder, Box 188, JRCP; Frank Evans Diary, 5 March, 5 May, 17 July, 4 August 1941, HDC.

83. "Budget Beginnings," 15, Binder, Box 188, JRCP

84. Ibid., 6–8.

85. Ibid., 30; Harold B. Lee Diary, 8 April 1943, PC.

86. JRC Office Diary, 8 April 1943, JRCP; Harold B. Lee Diary, 8 April 1943, PC; "Budget Beginnings," 33–34, Binder, Box 188, JRCP.

87. "Budget Beginnings," 35, Binder, Box 188, JRCP.

88. *October 1943 Conference Report,* 12; *April 1948 Conference Report,* 116–17; HDC.

89. JRC to John A. Widtsoe, 1 May 1946, Folder 2, Box 374, JRCP.

90. "Budget Beginnings," 28, Binder, Box 188, JRCP.

91. JRC Office Diary, 26 May 1943, JRCP.

92. JRC to General Priesthood Meeting, 6 April 1935, manuscript, Box 151; JRC to Henry H. Eyre, 7 February 1941, Folder 1, Box 363; JRCP.

93. JRC Office Diary, 14 February, 24 March 1952; JRC to Beth Moffett, 29 July 1928, Folder 2, Box 359; JRC to Hazel Liston, 14 February 1948, Folder 15, Box 377; JRC to J. H. Gipson, 9 June 1949, Folder 9, Box 379; JRCP.

94. Welfare Committee, 20 July 1936, CR 255/5, HDC.

95. JRC to David O. McKay, 22 May 1951, Folder 19, Box 410, JRC to Rulon H. Tingey, 14 December 1950, Folder 14, Box 382; JRCP.

96. William F. Edwards, "Budget Preparation and Control Report to the First Presidency," 21 October 1955, Stephen L Richards Miscellaneous Files, CR 1/14, HDC.

97.   JRC Memorandum, 21 September 1956, unnumbered box, JRCP; Harold B. Lee Diary, 22 April 1955, PC.

98.   JRC Memorandum of conversation with William F. Edwards, 22 May 1947, unnumbered box; JRC Office Diary, 3 February 1961; JRCP.

99.   JRC Office Diary, 13 February, 19 May 1960, JRCP.

100.   *April 1959 Conference Report,* 45, HDC.

101.   Harold B. Lee Diary, 4 March, 14 May 1952, 31 July 1953, 31 December 1957, PC; Marion G. Romney Diary, 25 March 1947, PC; JRC Ranch Diary, 6 October 1957, JRCP.

102.   Welfare Committee Meeting with First Presidency, 6 January 1939, CR 255/18, HDC; "Budget Beginnings," 28, Binder, Box 188, JRCP.

103.   Arrington, Fox, and May, *Building the City of God,* 353–54.

IN HONORABLE REMEMBRANCE

1.   Ralph Barton Perry, *Characteristically American* (New York: Knopf, 1949); Henry Steele Commager, *The American Mind: An Interpretation of American Thought and Character Since the 1880s* (New Haven: Yale University Press, 1950), esp. 8–10, 29–31, 45–54; David Riesman, "From Morality to Morale," in *The Character of Americans,* ed. Michael McGiffert (Homewood, Ill.: The Dorsey Press, 1964), 256–57; Helene S. Zahler, *The American Paradox* (New York: E. P. Dutton, 1964), esp. 153–234; John Higham, "The Reorientation of American Culture in the 1890s," in *The Origins of Modern Consciousness,* ed. John Weiss (Detroit: Wayne State University, 1965), 34–39; John Morton Blum, *The Promise of America: An Historical Inquiry* (Boston: Houghton Mifflin, 1966), 54–148.

2.   Spencer W. Kimball to JRC, 28 August 1958, Folder 7, Box 401, JRCP.

3.   Author's interview with D. Arthur Haycock, 3 August 1979.

INDEX